AsciiDoc for Beginners

Chinmaya S. Rathore

INDIA • UK • USA

Paperback ISBN: 978-93-6926-240-3
eBook ISBN: 978-93-6926-320-2

First Published on July 2025

Published by Walnut Publication

(an imprint of Vyusta Platforms Private Limited)

www.walnutpublication.com

India

Unit# 909, 9th Floor, Wave Silver Tower, Sector-18, Noida - 201301

UK

71-75 Shelton Street, Covent Garden, London, WC2H 9JQ, UK

Distributed by

For Dad, Mom, Mausi and Pranay

Preface

I have taught and researched in higher educational institutions for close to 4 decades. During this period, working as a Professor, I must have written hundreds of documents — teaching notes, reports of various hues, research papers, technical briefs, software cheatsheets, popular articles and what not. Sadly, most of them were written using a word processing software. And I taught the same to my kids and my students. I also doubled up as the tech support guy for friends and family stuck up with word processing problems. In fact, it is difficult to recall the number of hours spent navigating the tangled web of menus, memorizing keyboard shortcuts and searching for software workarounds when all I really wanted to do was *write !* I suppose it was the momentum of work or the everyday grind or acceptance of workplace norms that prevented me to explore alternative ways to create documents.

So when I discovered *Markdown* and eventually *AsciiDoc*, it was nothing short of *nirvana*. I have been an advocate of free and open source software and an ardent admirer of simple workflows. AsciiDoc fit right into that spot and I got totally hooked on to it. And I haven't looked back. I rarely use a word processing program for my personal writing work these days and enjoy the simplicity and beauty of creating documents in plain text editors using AsciiDoc. This book is a testament to that commitment. It was written entirely in AsciiDoc using a plain text editor on a decade old 32 bit netbook computer running MX Linux.

This book has evolved from my notes that I started creating when I was familiarizing myself with AsciiDoc. As I worked my way through, I started developing workflows that suited me best and finding solutions that were helpful in the creation of large documents. As the notes grew, I thought if I could compile them all together in a book, it might help some others trying to navigate their way across the AsciiDoc landscape. In this book therefore, I have focused more on markup used in everyday writing and have not covered the more complex things — like for example creating man pages — that AsciiDoc can do with great efficiency. I have particularly focused on beginners and switchers providing conceptual explanations and detailed step-by-step instructions and markup examples wherever required.

I have selected topics to provide a comprehensive and practical learning experience with a focus on delivering actionable insights and real-world relevance. Unless something is completely obvious, I have tried my best to show with every example, how raw AsciiDoc markup in the AsciiDoc file will show up in the rendered HTML or PDF document.

In writing this book, I have particularly focussed on trying to make AsciiDoc accessible to non-technical writers and document creators. I feel everyone can use AsciiDoc and its use should become more main stream for everyday writing. This book is a spirited endeavour in that direction.

I hope you enjoy reading this book.

Chinmaya S. Rathore

July 10, 2025

Acknowledgments

It has been wisely said — "Nobody achieves anything alone" ! A book writing project is a difficult undertaking by any standard requiring not only commitment and perseverance from the author, but also unwavering support from friends and family. I have been very fortunate to have received that in abundance.

I would like to express my deep gratitude and thanks to my wife Rajul who has supported this work in all possible ways from start to finish. She has spent hours proof reading the manuscript and has offered many helpful suggestions that have contributed immensely in the creation of this book. This book is as much hers as it is mine.

I am thankful to my wonderful daughters Supriya and Divya for all their encouragement, support and constructive suggestions without which this book would not have been possible.

Over the years, my students have been my most profound teachers. While I stood at the front of the classroom believing I was imparting knowledge, they were quietly and powerfully reshaping my understanding of learning, resilience, curiosity, and human potential. I thank them for their trust and love.

Finally, I warmly acknowledge the work of all contributors to the AsciiDoctor project. In particular, I would like to thank the project leads Dan Allen and Sarah White whose hard work and dedication in creating and supporting this wonderful project has made it possible for so many people around the world to produce beautifully formatted documents.

Thank you.

How to Use this Book

Some Background Information

It is interesting to know the author's thought process when they were writing the book. It gives an insight into the thinking that shaped the work. In creating this book, I had the following predominant ideas and goals in mind:

1. This book is particularly aimed at the beginner. The primary motivation behind creating the book is to help people take their first steps into the beautiful and elegant world of AsciiDoc. In keeping with that purpose, I have tried to stick to simple non-technical language (as far as possible), at times, taking liberty, to replace technically correct terms like the *image macro* with something like *the image tag* or the *image statement*.
2. When I was writing this book, I imagined addressing the content to non-technical users who could use AsciiDoc for their daily writing - people writing articles, students submitting assignments, creating class notes, even writing poems and fiction. The examples that I have chosen to illustrate syntax and other AsciiDoc features therefore have been influenced by that thought and purpose. They are not primarily focussed on computer code or creating technical documentation or man pages. My thinking is that if something is so useful, it should reach everyone.
3. I have written this book on a Linux computer and while this might give a predominantly *linuxy* flavor to the content, I urge the Windows and Mac users not to be put off by that feeling. AsciiDoc works in exactly the same way on Windows and Mac and references in this book for example, to *issue commands from the terminal* should just be read by windows users as issuing commands from the *command prompt*. I have included detailed instructions to install AsciiDoc on Windows and Mac.
4. While writing this book, I had a preferred output format in mind which was PDF or Portable Document Format. PDFs are widely used and most books, reports, assignments, notes etc. that one commonly encounters are shared in the PDF format. Also the stunningly well formatted and polished PDFs created by AsciiDoctor had me enthralled. So the markup that I have included in this book works for PDF in particular but also for HTML and EPUB3. I have tried not to include stuff that in my experience, does not touch the *golden line* that embraces all the three output formats.
5. I have tried not to gloss over any detail assuming that the reader might already be knowing this. As a result, I have chosen the verbose path and tried my best to ensure that no step is missed or assumed.
6. While this book is aimed at the beginner, I believe that it should be a good reference book for everyone using and working with AsciiDoc. Using it as a reference book, you can directly jump to the chapter or section that interests you and move ahead with your writing.
7. I have paid particular attention to explain how to make AsciiDoctor work on very old computers. I

wrote this book almost entirely on a 32 bit decade old computer running Linux. The idea of using (very) old computers as writing laptops has captivated me and with Linux and AsciiDoc, it becomes a workable reality at no cost whatsoever. So if you have an old computer, don't just throw it away. Instead, consider switching to the AsciiDoc workflow and use it as a writing laptop.

Book Conventions

Adding AsciiDoc markup to text and how that markup is displayed when rendered are two distinct processes. I have tried my best to show both of these in almost every example. The following conventions are used in this book to differentiate AsciiDoc markup code, screen output and terminal commands wherever they appear in the text.

AsciiDoc Markup → Markup that you type in your AsciiDoc file

Will be rendered as… → How the markup will appear when rendered by AsciiDoctor.

Terminal Command → Commands that you have to type in a terminal window. Commands in this book are displayed after a $ sign that indicates the Linux terminal prompt. The $ sign is *not* part of the command. So if you copy and paste any commands or type them, please ignore the $ sign.

LaTeX Markup → LaTeX markup (Chapter 10)

In addition to the above, all chapters end with a summary of key learnings. Most chapters also have practice exercises. These sections are denoted using the following icons:

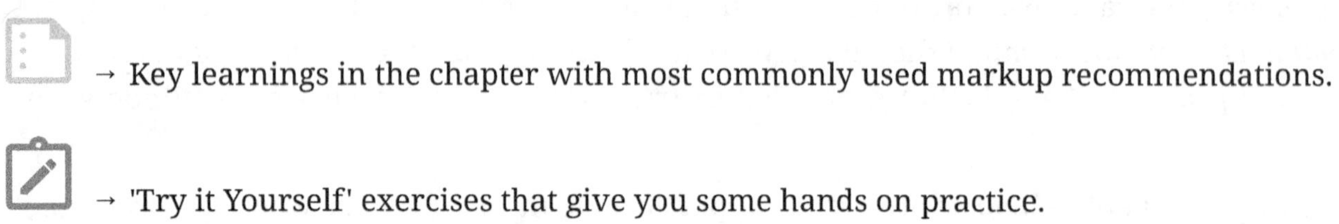

→ Key learnings in the chapter with most commonly used markup recommendations.

→ 'Try it Yourself' exercises that give you some hands on practice.

Download Sample Files from Companion Website

For many chapters, I have included a few 'Try it Yourself' exercises. These exercises should help readers who wish to follow along and engage in hands on work while going through the material in this book. Sample files that I have used in various chapters of this text and referred to in the 'Try it Yourself' exercises, can be downloaded as a single Zip file from the book's companion website:

https://chinmayasrathore.github.io/books/adb/

Any errata that is corrected in subsequent to publication will also be available on this site. I also plan to create some helpful videos in due course to supplement the contents of the book. Links to these videos and other supplemental material added in due course will be posted on the above companion website. So please do keep visiting the site.

Quick Summary of Book Chapters

Following is a quick summary of what is covered in each chapter. If you are reading this book on a computer screen, you can click on the chapter heading to directly reach the chapter for a quick browse.

Chapter 1 - Introduction

This chapter focuses on two key points: (a) How using AsciiDoc can be seen as a new way to create documents when compared to traditional word processors and (b) to conceptually understand the AsciiDoc document creation workflow.

Chapter 2 - Installing the AsciiDoctor Toolchain

This chapter covers installation of AsciiDoctor and AsciiDoctor-PDF on Linux , Windows and Mac. It also covers installing the entire AsciiDoctor Toolchain using the docker AsciiDoctor image container on Linux and running it using Podman. The docker image install of AsciiDoctor is highly recommended for Linux users.

Chapter 3 - The VS Code Workflow: Installing and Using Visual Studio Code to create and Live Preview AsciiDoc Documents

While you can create AsciiDoc files using the simplest of text editors, in this chapter I invite you to try *Visual Studio Code or VS Code* — a hugely popular free code editor. The big advantage of using VS Code to create your AsciiDoc documents is that you can have a *live preview* of AsciiDoc Markup as you type it in your document. There are many other conveniences that VS Code offers that make writing documents easy, efficient and enjoyable. This chapter shows how to install and use VS Code to create documents in AsciiDoc.

Chapter 4 - Essential AsciiDoc Markup Syntax

This chapter is one of the core chapters of this book. This chapter demonstrates core AsciiDoc markup that is used to format text. It covers the most commonly required markup code needed for everyday writing. This chapter can also be used as a reference guide which can be revisited as required.

Chapter 5 - Substitutions and Footnotes

In this chapter we learn how to create user defined attributes which can be very helpful whenever we need to repeat text, links, icons or images etc. in our document. You can set a custom named attribute to refer to a URL or text string and then just use the named attribute to paste the URL or text whenever required. In this chapter, we also learn how to create and work with footnotes.

Chapter 6 - Inserting Audio and Video in HTML Output

This chapter deals with inserting Audio and Video in AsciiDoc documents. It is possible to insert locally hosted or self hosted audio and video files and also videos from YouTube and Vimeo in AsciiDoc documents rendered as HTML.

Chapter 7 - Creating and Using Delimited Blocks

AsciiDoc permits creation of special blocks that essentially help you highlight or visually delineate a block of content from running text matter. You can create many different types of blocks in AsciiDoc, each of which is particularly suited for some specific purpose. This chapter illustrates how to create commonly used blocks and how they can be best used.

Chapter 8 - Conditional Processing

We can use conditional statements in AsciiDoc to include text or images based on attributes being set or unset. We can also test the values of user defined and system defined attributes and include or exclude text based on a conditional test. This is super helpful to customize and re-purpose content. This chapter shows how conditional processing works in AsciiDoc and how to write conditional directives in AsciiDoc documents.

Chapter 9 - Using Icons in Your Document

In this chapter we explore how to use icons to add some sparkle and luster to our documents. AsciiDoc permits the use of icons from different free and open icon libraries to make documents more readable and presentable.

Chapter 10 - Syntax Highlighting for Code

AsciiDoc is particularly suited to accurately and aesthetically present and highlight code blocks in your document. This chapter demonstrates how code written in many different programming languages can be highlighted in color using syntax highlighters.

Chapter 11 - Tables

This chapter demonstrates how to create tables in your documents using AsciiDoc markup. We also explore how to import tables in CSV format created by spreadsheet programs like Excel and Calc.

Chapter 12 - Inserting Citations and Creating Styled Bibliography

Adding citations to text and creating a well styled bibliography is one of the prime requirements of academic writing. In this chapter we explore how to cite references and include a bibliography in documents that conforms to standard styling guides like APA, MLA, Harvard, IEEE and others.

Chapter 13 - Creating a Book Index

If you are writing a book that will be printed, including an Index is really helpful for the readers. AsciiDoc supports marking of index terms in text and creation of a well structured index. This chapter explores AsciiDoc markup used to demarcate primary, secondary and tertiary index terms and generate a well structured index.

Chapter 14 - Math Equations

In this chapter we see how to write nicely formatted math equations in our text using LaTeX Math. This functionality is particularly important for the STEM students , researchers, data scientists and many others who need to frequently write and communicate equations in assignments, lecture notes, books, articles, reports and journal papers.

Chapter 15 - Overriding the Default AsciiDoctor-PDF theme for Some Useful Styling Tweaks

All document styling for the rendered PDF document is done using the default AsciiDoctor theme. However AsciiDoctor permits to extend this default theme making it possible to customize and extend many aspects of the default styling. This chapter demonstrates how to extend the default theme to choose different fonts, create borders, align images and captions and introduce other custom styling changes in your PDF documents.

Chapter 16 - Multi-Page HTML Output

This chapter explores how we can chunk or break the single HTML file generated by AsciiDoctor into multiple files that can be displayed chapter wise or section wise permitting an enjoyable online reading experience. If you are putting up a large document like a book for online viewing, this can be very helpful as readers can easily navigate the document using buttons to move forward or go back and consume content in manageable chunks.

Chapter 17 - Creating a Single Document from Multiple AsciiDoc Files

When working on large projects like books or lengthy reports, it is common to have content spread across many AsciiDoc files — like individual files for every chapter. This chapter demonstrates how we can collate many separate AsciiDoc files and seamlessly render them as one polished HTML, PDF or EPUB document.

Chapter 18 - Generating EPUB 3 Files

AsciiDoc documents can be easily rendered in EPUB 3 format which is highly favored for reading on mobile devices. This is because in EPUB format, content is automatically adjusted to different screen sizes. This chapter demonstrates how to render AsciiDoc documents as EPUB 3 e-books.

Chapter 19 - Converting AsciiDoc Files to MS Word and MS Word files to AsciiDoc

In this chapter, we explore how to convert AsciiDoc files to Microsoft Word format and vice versa. This can be useful if you wish to share documents with non-AsciiDoc users or for people who have documents in MS Word format and who wish to switch over to AsciiDoc.

Chapter 20 - Book Writing in AsciiDoc

In this final chapter, we look at how AsciiDoc can be used to create print ready PDF files that are suitable for black & white book printing. There are many things that need to be taken into account when a book is printed on paper and AsciiDoc provides many features that support this process. If you plan to print your book, this chapter provides many tips that can help you through the process.

Appendices

This book has the following six helpful appendices that supplement chapter contents:

Appendix A — Commands Used in Command Line Install of AsciiDoctor

This appendix provides a more detailed step-by-step guide to install AsciiDoc and AsciiDoctor-PDF using the Linux Command Line. It is aimed to provide helpful explanations for new Linux users.

Appendix B — Shell Script to Start AsciiDoctor Docker Container

Podman or Docker command to start the AsciiDoctor Docker Image is long and tedious to remember and type repeatedly. You can easily forget the command if you don't use AsciiDoc for some time. It is therefore best to create a shell script to run this command. This appendix shows you how.

Appendix C — Installing Podman and AsciiDoctor Docker Image on Windows

This appendix provides a detailed guide on how to install Podman and run the AsciiDoctor Docker container in Windows 11. It provides a step-by-step guide on how to install Podman CLI and Podman Desktop on Windows and pull and run the AsciiDoctor docker image. This is a highly recommended install for Windows users as it gives Windows users access to the entire AsciiDoctor toolchain in one install.

Appendix D — Some Useful Podman Commands

This appendix has some useful Podman commands that can come in handy if you are running the Docker AsciiDoctor Image. These commands are not essential to run the AsciiDoctor image, but knowing them can help you better manage the Docker image and can also help you out of a jam.

Appendix E — Some Useful VS Code Keyboard (and Mouse) Shortcuts

This is a cheat sheet of some super useful VS Code shortcuts if you are using VS Code as your AsciiDoc Editor. If you have just started using VS Code, you can print this sheet and keep it as a handy reference.

Appendix F — AsciiDoctor Online Resources

A compilation of online resources on AsciiDoc and AsciiDoctor to take your learning forward.

Glossary of Key Terms

The book includes a glossary which provides definitions of key technical terms used in various chapters of the book.

The book also has an index that should be helpful for readers who will access the book in its printed form.

Table of Contents

Chapter 1. Introduction

"Simplicity is the ultimate sophistication." ~ Clare Boothe Luce, Stuffed Shirts,1931

Welcome to the beautiful world of AsciiDoc! In this chapter, we will learn about AsciiDoc, its history and how AsciiDoc presents an entirely new paradigm for creation of documents which is quite different from regular word processing software that most people are accustomed to. The documents created using AsciiDoc are of professional quality and quite literally, 'eye-popping'. All software applications used in creation of these documents are free and open source. With AsciiDoc, all you need to create stunning documents is a simple text editor. This chapter provides an overview of the AsciiDoc document creation workflow and lays a foundation for the rest of the book.

1.1. A New Way to Create Documents

If you are new to markup or AsciiDoc, I invite you to take some time out and read this chapter fully. It is not a long read and it will help you get an overview on how the AsciiDoc document creation process works. This understanding will help you a great deal in working through other chapters in this book.

This book that you are reading was created using AsciiDoc Markup. I wrote it entirely in a plain text editor on a decade old 32 bit atom processor *Netbook* running 32 bit MX Linux Xfce — MX Libretto 23.5. If the styling and presentation of this book has impressed you, I would like to clarify upfront that I put in zero effort in formatting or styling it. It was all done quietly behind the scenes by a lightning fast, free and open source AsciiDoc processor software called *AsciiDoctor*. All I did was just pass on my text markup files to it and in a few seconds, it handed me a professionally formatted book that I would have probably taken ages to style in any word processing software. In fact, the impact on seeing the output was so transformative that I *completely* stopped using word processing software altogether — something I had been doing my entire work life. The simplicity of the entire document creation process forced me to recall all the struggles that I had endured over the years, of wading through a jungle of menu options trying to figure out some formatting or styling issue in my word processing software.

As a career educator working in higher education, it was not difficult for me to visualize the positive impact this could have on the productivity of students and researchers if they knew about this alternate way of creating documents early during their education or careers. I felt a deep sense of gratitude towards the creators of AsciiDoctor and appreciated the countless hours of selfless hard work they must have put in to create and support this amazing software. Thanks to their herculean effort, using AsciiDoc has become such a wonderful and fulfilling experience for thousands of users across the world.

These days, I write everything in AsciiDoc. After experiencing this simple, elegant and beautiful way of creating documents, I can say with confidence that I just cannot go back to using word processing software anymore. At least not unless someone forces me to do so for their sake. I am also super thrilled that due to this alternate way of creating documents, I am able to do all my writing on my decade old netbook computer that would have other wise been long buried in some electronic graveyard.

1.2. Moving Beyond Word Processing Software

In word processing programs like MS Word, Google Docs, LibreOffice Writer and others, the content i.e the text you type in and the presentation of that text i.e. all the styling etc. are done by one software. What this effectively means is that when you write an article, you not only need to type in the text for your article but you also need to know various software operations that style and format text. These options include things like choosing fonts, setting up margins, inserting page numbers and many other styling tasks.

In short, the burden of both writing and styling a document is on you. Learning to use these apps and utilizing them to their full potential takes a lot of time and effort. It also practically locks you with that software forever unless you are motivated and courageous enough to learn another software from scratch. Also when you save the document, you cannot simply read that saved file without either the software which created it or some other software that can read that file format. You cannot, for example, open an MS Word file in a simple text editor and read its contents. Figure 1 summarizes some challenges of using word processing software, which for want of better alternatives, is usually accepted by most as an inescapable necessity in modern digital workplaces.

The Steep Learning Curve of Word Processing Software

Many users of popular word processing software have a hard time wrapping their heads around things like styling, section & page breaks, creating table of contents, captioning tables and images, creating a bibliography etc. Almost everyone I know has a nightmare story about getting all tangled up trying to figure out how to do something in their favorite word processing software. Many productive hours are routinely spent browsing the internet for solutions or seeking help from friends and colleagues to sort out how to do this or that. This requirement for software wizardry from users seems quite stressful and out of place when you consider the fact that all people really want to do is to *write*!

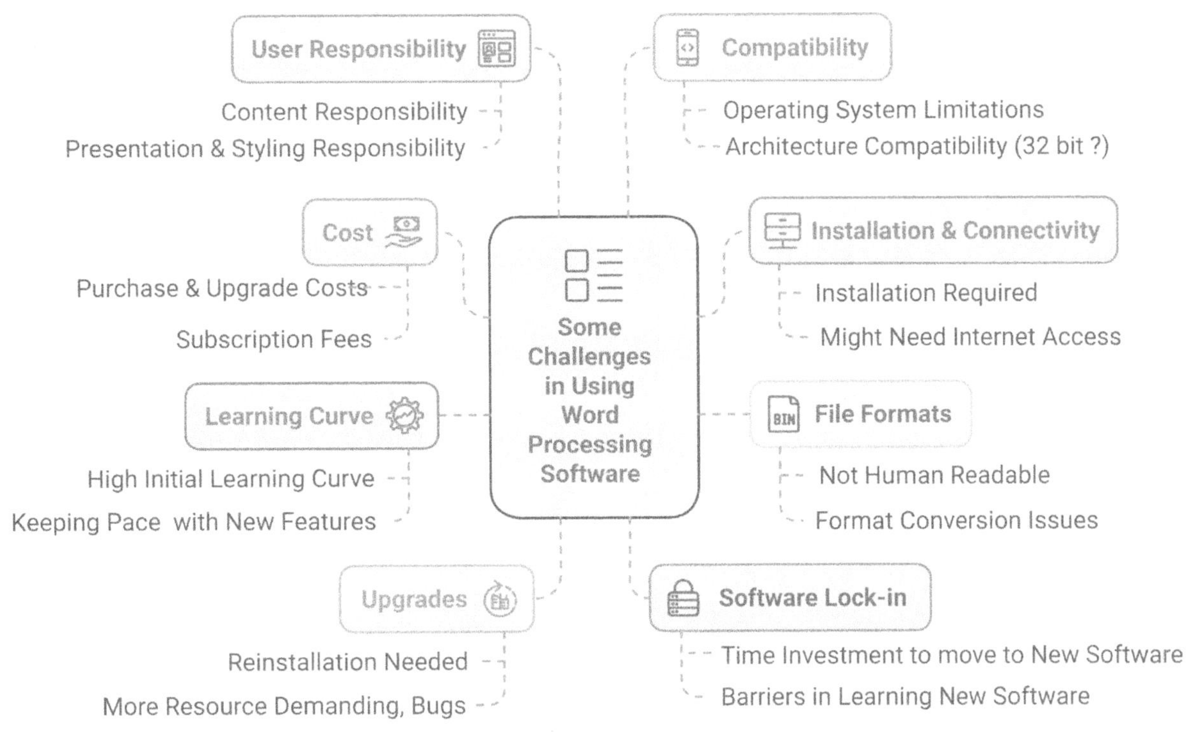

Figure 1. Some challenges of using word processing software

While word processing programs are useful and ubiquitous, one could ask if there was another, simpler way in which documents could be created ? What if we could separate the software that is used to enter text and the software that is used to style the content ? If this were possible, we could then just use a simple text editor which is available on any computer, any operating system and enter our document as plain text adding some simple markup elements to define desired formatting . Such a plain text document could be opened and conveniently read on any other computer. We would then have no need to purchase and install an expensive word processing software or spend countless hours learning its myriad intricacies. To create the final output, we could just pass on the plain text markup file to a software that could pretty it up and create a well styled professional quality document — for free! In such a document creation workflow, we could just concentrate on our writing and leave the presentation or styling part to a specialist software without having the need to learn anything except just a few markup inline elements! Now it is absolutely not my case to argue that word processing programs are not useful and should be abandoned forthwith. All I am suggesting is that there might be a simpler, better and more efficient option — a new document creation paradigm — to produce high quality documents. As it turns out — there exists such an option that redefines document creation and it is called *AsciiDoc* !

1.3. What is AsciiDoc ?

Simply put, AsciiDoc is a lightweight *markup language* that allows users to write documents in plain text, which can then be converted into various output formats such as HTML, PDF , EPUB etc.

AsciiDoctor is the defacto standard for processing text and AsciiDoc markup. The AsciiDoctor software takes in AsciiDoc files and converts them into nicely formatted HTML5, PDF and EPUB3 documents. AsciiDoctor, written in the Ruby programming language, can be seen as a modern implementation of AsciiDoc that enhances its capabilities and performance. AsciiDoctor is open source and completely free. Figure 2 summarizes the history of AsciiDoc and its modern implementation *AsciiDoctor* in a compact comparative schematic.

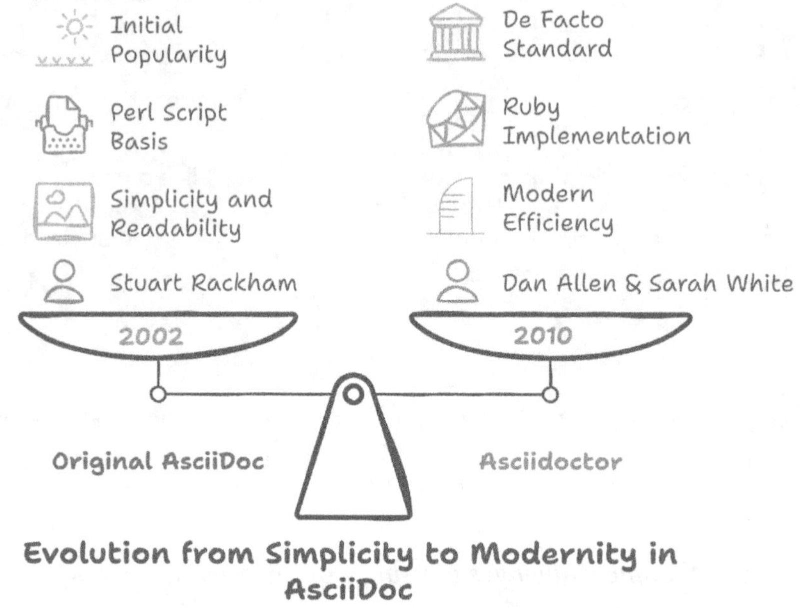

Figure 2. A Brief History and Transition of AsciiDoc

Since the development of AsciiDoctor, AsciiDoc has become extremely popular particularly among technical documentation writers. This is because AsciiDoc makes it extremely easy to highlight code syntax in many popular computer languages and is therefore an ideal choice for creating documentation for software. It also makes creating man pages — documentation for commands in Linux and Unix like operating Systems — a breeze! Having said that, it would be *completely inaccurate* to suggest that AsciiDoc is unsuitable for non-technical everyday writing. In fact in my own experience, I have found that AsciiDoc provides a very rich markup base to support all types of writing when compared to other markup languages. It is therefore as much suitable for writing general articles or even poetry as it is for creating documents explaining intricacies of code. One other standout feature of AsciiDoc is the ease with which books can be compiled and rendered in PDF, EPUB 3 and HTML 5 formats. Above all, AsciiDoc has a well documented *formal syntax* which is very easy to learn and recall.

In summary, AsciiDoc is super easy to learn and once you get the big picture of the AsciiDoc document creation process, you can get going in just a few minutes and start creating beautifully formatted documents in a plain text editor of your choice.

For more information on the need and utility of AsciiDoc, you can read this insightful page [https://AsciiDoctor.org/docs/what-is-AsciiDoc/] on the AsciiDoctor website.

1.4. How does AsciiDoc Document Creation Work ?

Let's now have a quick overview of how the AsciiDoc based document creation process works. Figure 3 presents a summary of the simple three step process involved in document creation using AsciiDoc and AsciiDoctor. As can be seen in Figure 3, the first step is to open your text editor and start typing text inserting AsciiDoc markup elements wherever required. As we will see in the following sections and chapters, AsciiDoc syntax for most commonly used formatting requirements is very easy to learn and recall.

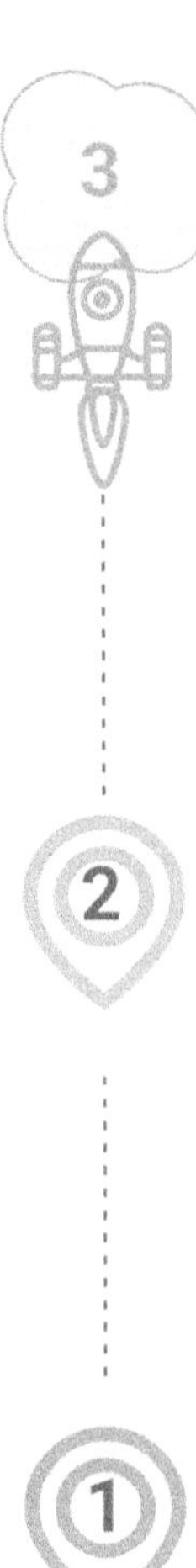

Figure 3. Steps in rendering your AsciiDoc file to HTML, PDF or EPUB3

Once you save this file (file extension *.adoc*), in step 2, you just hand it over to AsciiDoctor which parses (inspects) the file, interprets the AsciiDoc markup, applies the required formatting and renders an output document file in the desired format. Finally, in step 3, the formatted output file is examined by the user to verify if formatting changes, as marked in the original text file (created in Step 1) have been properly applied and if so, publish the file online or share it as needed. Figure 4 presents this sequence graphically. In Figure 4, you can see a small sample of AsciiDoc markup being applied to text. In AsciiDoc markup syntax, any piece of text enclosed inside a pair of asterisks (**) is formatted as bold text while any text enclosed inside an opening and closing underscore character (_) is formatted as *italics*.

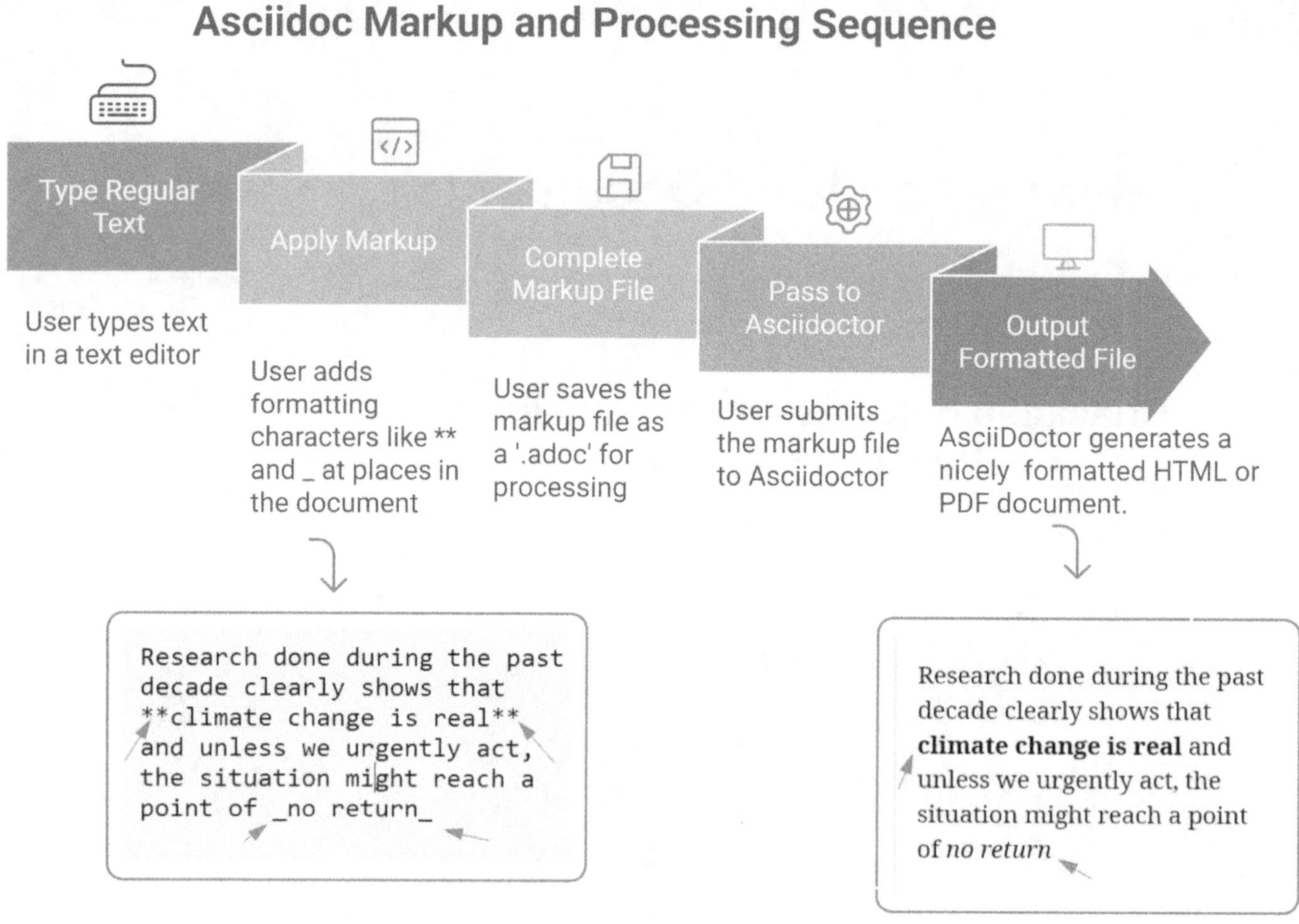

Figure 4. AsciiDoc document creation — conceptual sequence of operations

1.5. How to Get Started

It's actually quite easy. To start, all you need is to install *AsciiDoctor* which creates HTML output from your AsciiDoc file. If you need to convert your AsciiDoc files to a PDF document, then you also need to install *AsciiDoctor-pdf*. We will cover how to install these software in the next chapter, so don't worry about installing anything just yet. Once you have AsciiDoctor installed, you can then start writing your documents in any plain text editor following the typical workflow shown in Figure 5.

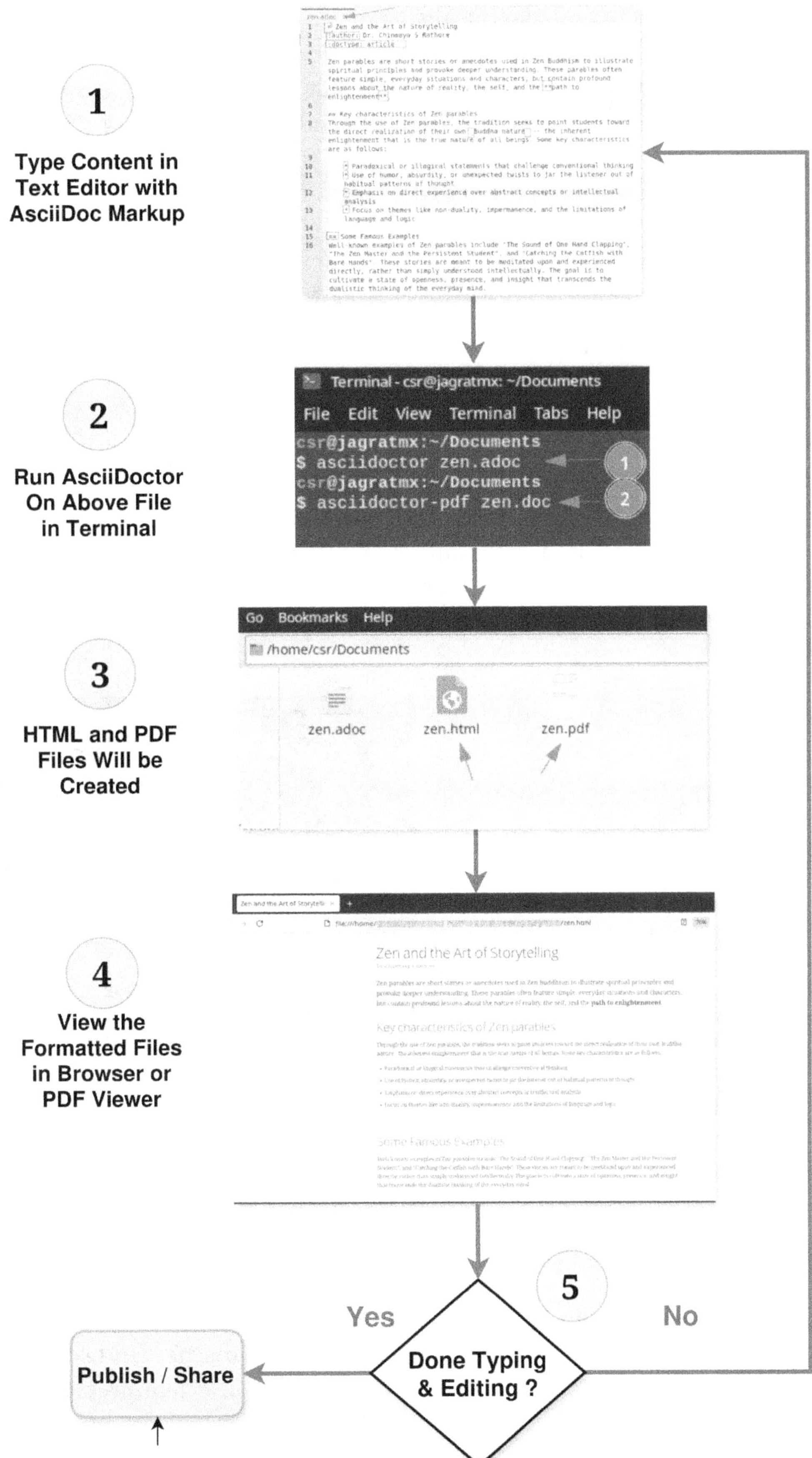

Figure 5. Typical AsciiDoc document creation workflow

As shown in Figure 5, you type in your text in the AsciiDoc file inserting AsciiDoc markup wherever required — highlighted by red rectangles (callout 1). Next, you render the AsciiDoc file using AsciiDoctor (for HTML) or AsciiDoctor-PDF (for PDF) (callout 2). Once you have the rendered file, open and view it in a browser or PDF viewer (callouts 3,4). You then repeat steps 1-4 (callout 5) till you have completed typing your entire content and you are satisfied that the final output which is appearing in the rendered document is as per your expectations. Once done, you can share your document with others.

About Choosing Text Editors

It is best to choose a plain text editor that has a built-in spellchecker otherwise your document might end up having many spelling mistakes which might be difficult to correct later manually. In some plain text editors, you might have to activate spellcheck via settings. So do consult the documentation for your preferred text editor. In Linux, a GUI based plain text editor that has a good spellcheck feature is Geany [https://www.geany.org/]. Some other text editors like Kate [https://kate-editor.org/] or the Linux terminal based text editor *Vim* can highlight AsciiDoc markup embedded inside plain text, in a different color as you type ! (Figure 6). The choice of text editor that you wish to use to create your AsciiDoc files is entirely up to you.

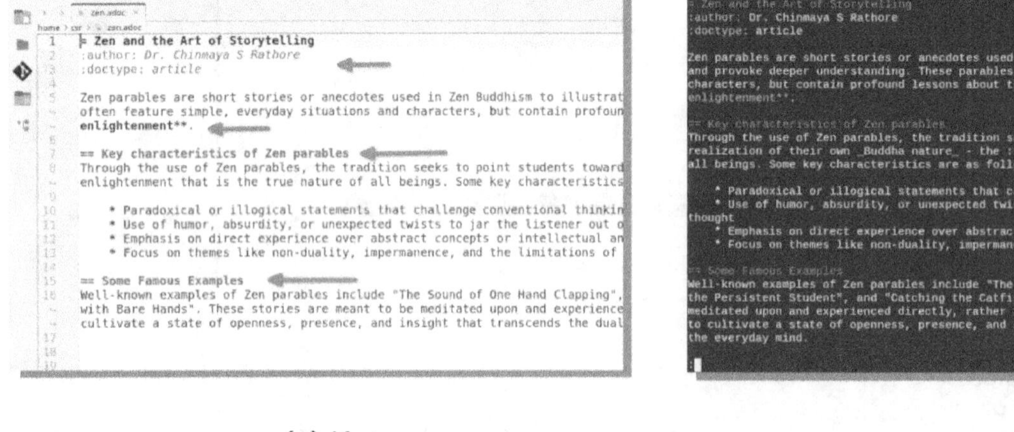

(a) Kate

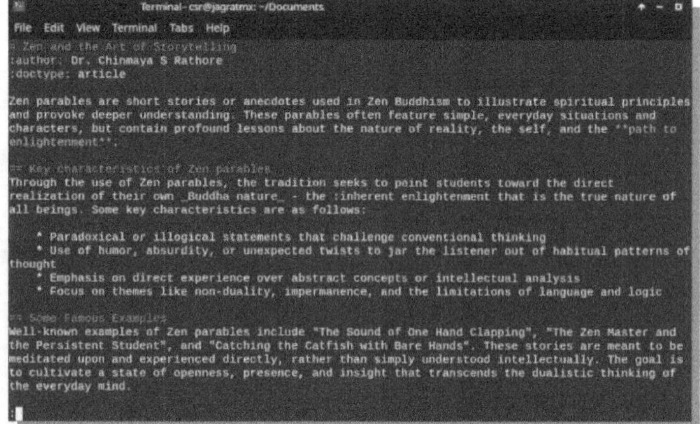

(b) Vim

Figure 6. AsciiDoc syntax highlighting in some popular text editors

1.6. Editing Documents in VS Code

If you are familiar with Visual Studio Code (VS Code) or wish to set up a robust editor for creating AsciiDoc documents , I *highly recommend* that you use VS Code as your default text editor. VS Code not only highlights AsciiDoc syntax in your text, but it also shows you a live preview of your AsciiDoc markup such that you do not need to run AsciiDoctor repeatedly while working on your document as illustrated in the workflow shown in Figure 5. In fact I like creating my AsciiDoc documents in VS Code so much that I have devoted a full chapter to demonstrate how to install and use VS Code for your regular writing. This is a one time install which offers a lifetime of dividends in ease and efficiency. VS Code is open source, very easy to learn and completely free to download and use. Please see Chapter 3 for more details.

1.7. Chapter Summary

Key learnings in this chapter are:

1. In this chapter, we have learnt about AsciiDoc and how it presents an alternative paradigm for document creation. We have also gained an understanding of the typical AsciiDoc workflow for creating professional quality documents.
2. There are essentially two things we need to do to start creating documents in AsciiDoc :
   - Install AsciiDoctor and AsciiDoctor-PDF
   - Learn some commonly used AsciiDoc markup
3. In the next chapter we will see how to install AsciiDoctor and AsciiDoctor-PDF and in subsequent chapters we will learn about the AsciiDoc markup language and how we can use it to create professional grade documents.
4. I would like to conclude this chapter by mentioning *emphatically* that you do not need to memorize all the AsciiDoc markup — nobody can! If you were to do that, it would be a sure way to quickly get overwhelmed!
5. The best approach to get started is to create a small personal cheatsheet of some markup inline elements that you use most frequently in your writing and start creating documents using the AsciiDoc workflow described above. Chapter 4 of this book covers some of the most commonly used markup elements needed for everyday writing.
6. You will find that as you start typing and creating content, you can easily recall these commonly used AsciiDoc markup elements without even the need to refer to your personal cheatsheet. Then if you need something more or if you require to do something that you haven't yet done in AsciiDoc, refer to the other chapters of this book or refer to the AsciiDoctor documentation as and when required.

In my experience, the best way to learn is to take the plunge by writing your next document using AsciiDoc and then take it forward from there. As you churn out beautifully styled documents with supreme ease, you will need no external motivation to move ahead full steam on your AsciiDoc voyage.

1.8. Try it Yourself Exercises

You will find sample files for the following exercises in chapter 1 folder of the exercise packet which you can download from https://chinmayasrathore.github.io/books/adb/.

1. Try to open the MS Word file called *demo.docx* in a text editor available on your computer (NotePad, FeatherPad etc.). Can you find out what is written inside the file ? You will discover that either the text editor refuses to open the file or throws up some funny gibberish. In other words, if you don't have access to MS Word (paid software) or similar word processing software, you can't read what is contained inside this file.
2. Now try opening this file in MS Word or LibreOffice or Google Docs. You will see that you can open it and read it easily. You can also see some formatting and styling applied in the document — heading 1 for title, some text in bold, some in italics and some text, highlighted. I did all this using menu options in the software. If I wish to further improve the visual appeal of my document, I will have to choose a better font, choose appropriate line spacing, set margins among other things, for which, I will have to learn how to do all these things in that software. To be proficient in using this software, I would need to spend considerable time and effort. If I am using Linux, I will normally not have access to MS Word, so I might use LibreOffice to open this document and I might discover to my frustration that the import from MS Word was not hundred percent perfect.
3. Now use the same text editor to open *demo.adoc*. You can immediately read what's inside the file and you can do this on any computer irrespective of what operating system it is running. Sure you will see some text enclosed inside some funny characters like `*text*` or `_text_` or `#text#` and the document title preceded by '=='; all that is AsciiDoc Markup. But if you ignore these markup interludes, you can still read the entire content. You can also add, delete or modify content in your text editor. You have full control over your data which means you don't need any external software beyond a plain text editor to view and edit your text.
4. Take a moment to compare the word processing document creation paradigm with the AsciiDoc markup paradigm. If you think the AsciiDoc document creation process accords the user more freedom to create content, list some of its benefits ? (Revisit Figure 1 for a quick recap)
5. The *demo.html* file in this folder has been generated by AsciiDoctor using *demo.adoc*. Open *demo.html* in your web browser and you can see the finished document created by AsciiDoctor using my raw AsciiDoc markup file. I did practically nothing towards styling the document. The magical transformation of the raw AsciiDoc file into the finished product was handled behind the scenes by AsciiDoctor. You will agree that this document is far more polished and readable than the average MS Word document.
6. Try to get a feel of AsciiDoc online using a simple live editor on the AsciiDoc Website. You can access the online editor by going to the AsciiDoc language homepage [https://asciidoc.org] and then

clicking on `Get Started` as shown on the screenshot below:

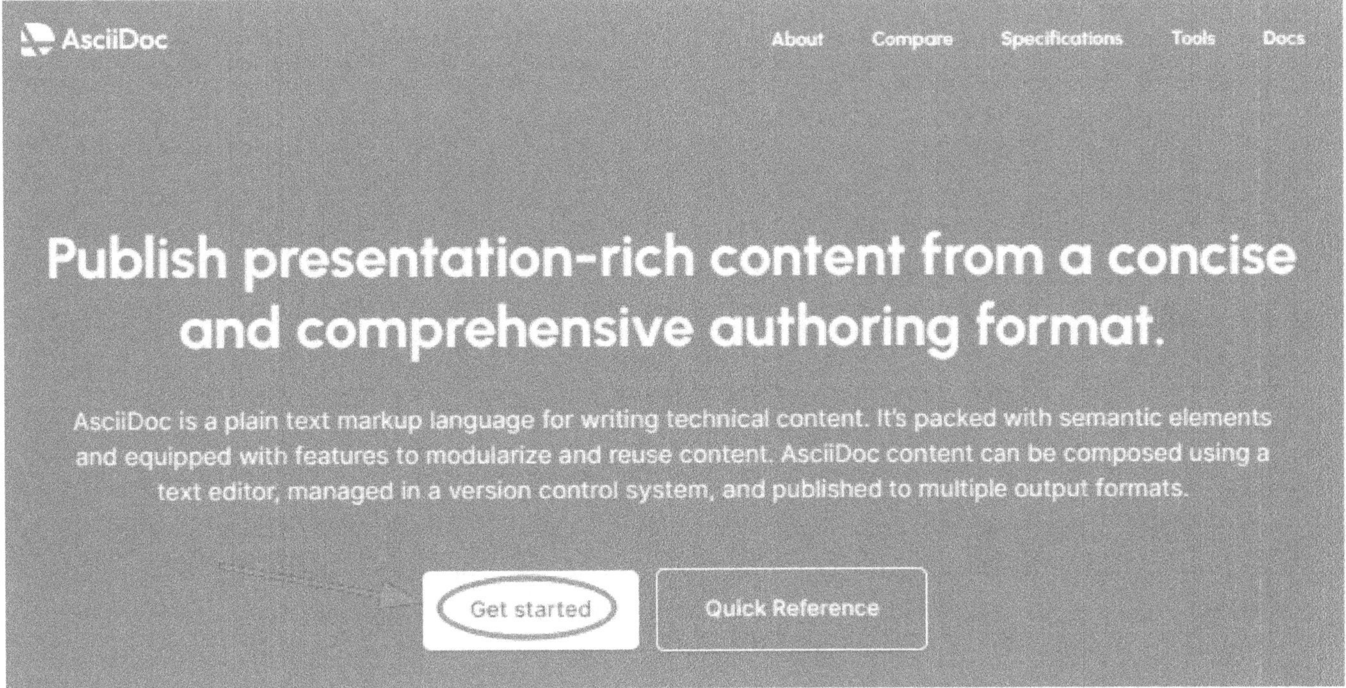

As you reach the live editor page, you will see that in the left pane you have plain text punctuated with AsciiDoc Markup and in the right pane you see what the AsciiDoc markup looks like when rendered by AsciiDoctor.

In the left pane, enclose the words pointed by callout 1 in the following screenshot within a pair of opening and closing 'asterisk' symbols (**) — the AsciiDoc markup for `bold text`.

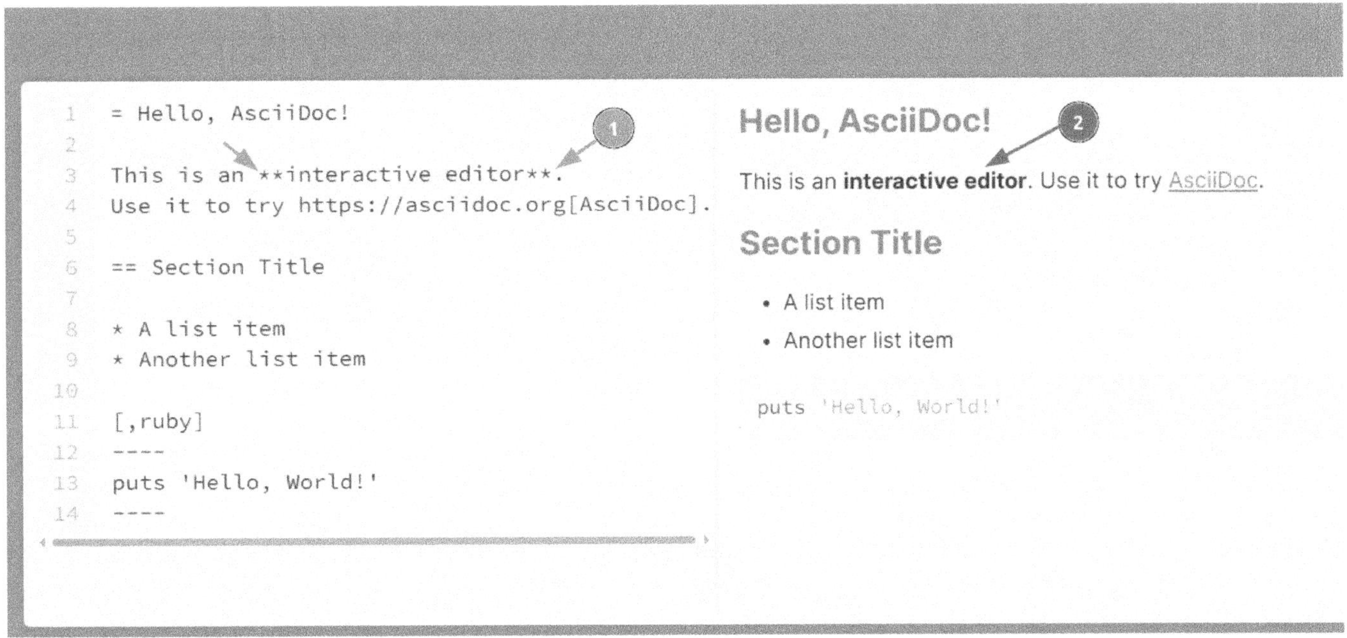

You should see these words becoming bold in the right pane (callout 2).

7. Now *type* (don't paste) the following text after the last line in the left pane:

```
=== How to Use AsciiDoc
You can use _AsciiDoc_ as follows:

. Open Text Editor
. Type Content with AsciiDoc Markup
. Use AsciiDoctor to produce HTML
. View HTML in Web Browser

This is how simple it is to use #AsciiDoc#
```

8. As you type in AsciiDoc Markup in the left pane, you will see it being rendered in the right pane. The three '=' signs preceding the heading 'How to Use AsciDoc' give it distinct styling. Using the '_' markup, you can italicize text. The '.' is the markup for creating a numbered list. Any text inside opening and closing '#', gets highlighted. The AsciiDoc markup for italics and highlighted text can be seen in the screenshot below at callouts 1 and 2 in the left pane and how they appear in the rendered text can be seen in the right pane at callouts 3 and 4 respectively.

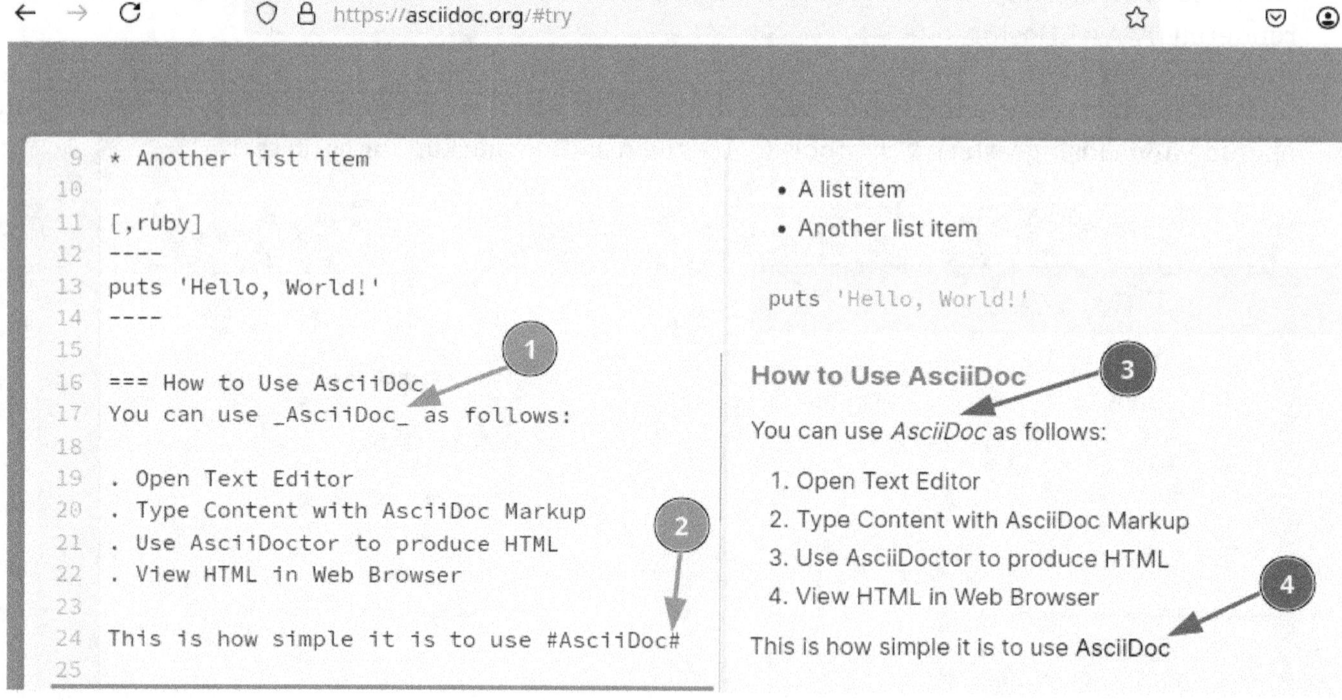

9. Just play around and see how AsciiDoc markup works. Don't worry at all about markup elements as we will learn about them in Chapter 4 and onwards. The right pane is being generated by the AsciiDoctor software. In subsequent chapters, we will see how to install AsciiDoctor on your computer to locally do the work that the right pane is doing on this website and learn how to create documents using AsciiDoc markup. Trust me, it's really easy to learn !

Chapter 2. Installing the AsciiDoctor Toolchain

"For many people my software is something that you install and forget. I like to keep it that way."~ Wietse Venema exit ---

In this chapter, we will see different ways in which we can install AsciiDoctor on Linux, Windows and Mac computers. Installation is simple and you can get started in no time ! You can read the whole chapter or jump directly to the section that describes the installation steps for your operating system. If you are working on Linux though, I do urge you to please read the section on Docker / Podman install which provides access to the full AsciiDoctor toolchain in one single install. The Docker / Podman install is also available to Windows and MacOS users.

Continuing our discussion from Chapter 1, there are two key software packages that we need to install to start using AsciiDoc. These are :

1. AsciiDoctor for rendering AsciiDoc files as HTML.
2. AsciiDoctor-PDF for rendering PDF output.

Some other AsciiDoctor tools are needed if there are special requirements but we will talk about them later. Luckily, AsciiDoctor tools are available for all major Operating Systems (OS) and in this chapter we will see how we can install them.

2.1. Installing AsciiDoctor on Windows 11

2.1.1. Installing Ruby

Step 1

The first thing that we need to do is to install the Ruby Programming Language on our computer. You will recall that AsciiDoctor is written in Ruby. To do that we need to go to the Ruby website, download the Ruby Installer and then run it. The Ruby installer is available from https://rubyinstaller.org/downloads/.

As there are many installers that are shown on the website, it's best to choose the version *recommended* by the Ruby website for your OS and computer. The recommended version can be seen at callout 1 in Figure 7 and we can download this version (appearing at callout 2) from the list of installers.

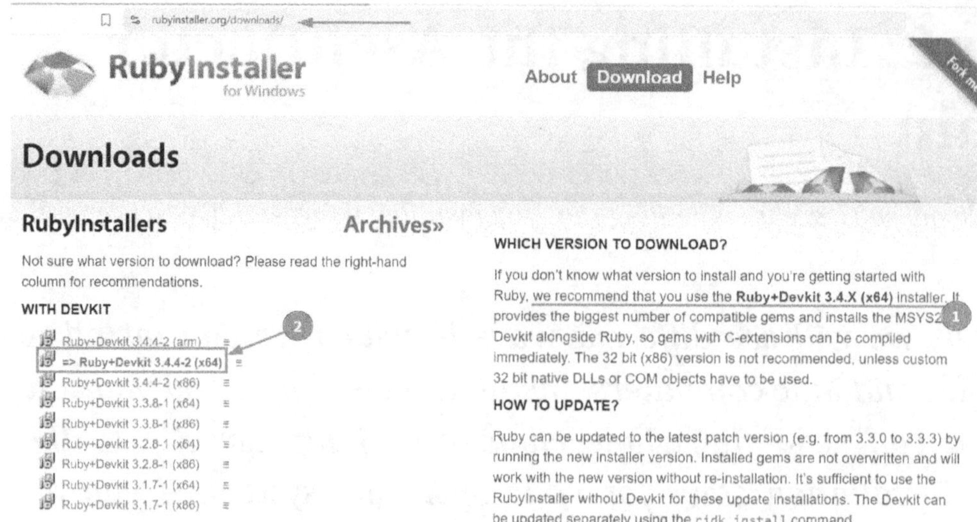

Figure 7. Download Page for the Ruby Installer for Windows

Step 2

Double click on the downloaded installer file which should be named something like `rubyinstaller-devkit-3.4.4-2-x64.exe` (name depends on the current version) and follow the screen instructions to install. At the start and towards the end, you should see screens as shown in Figure 8 and Figure 9 respectively asking you for some input.

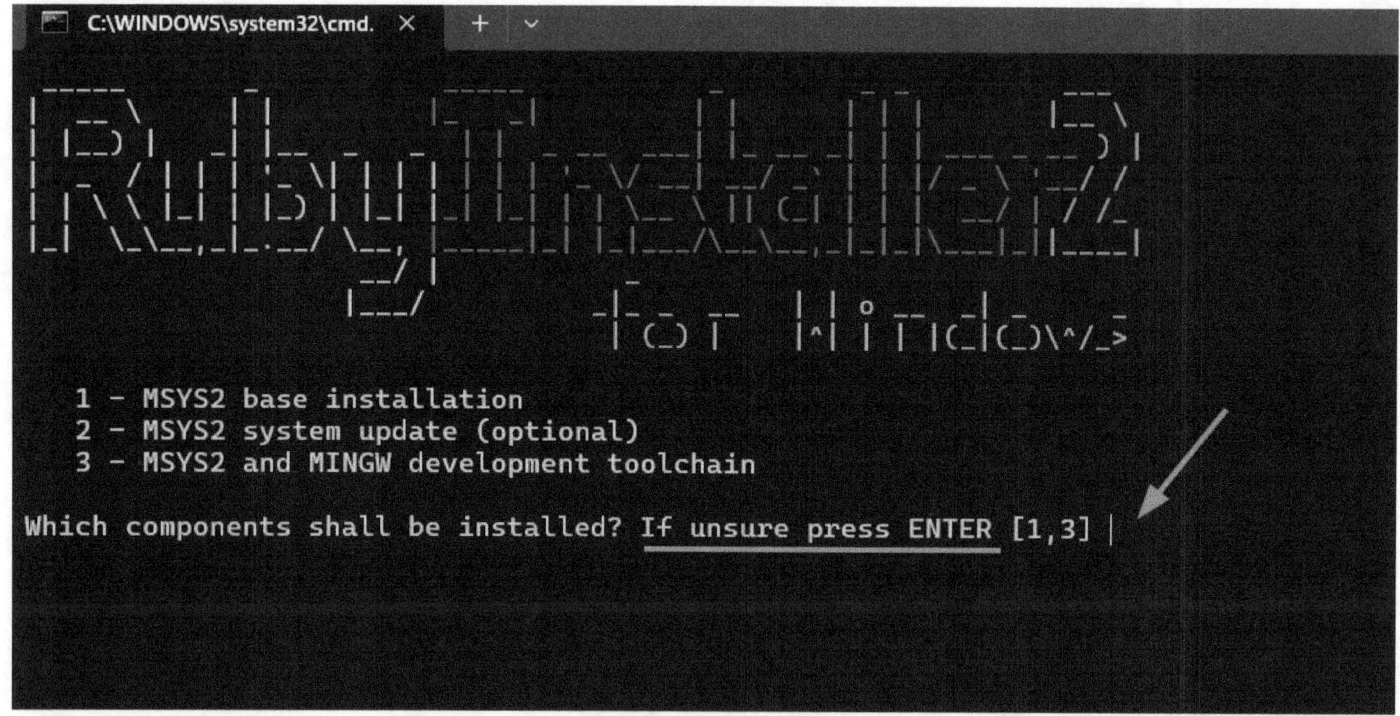

Figure 8. Ruby installer screen seeking confirmation on components to install t the start of installation

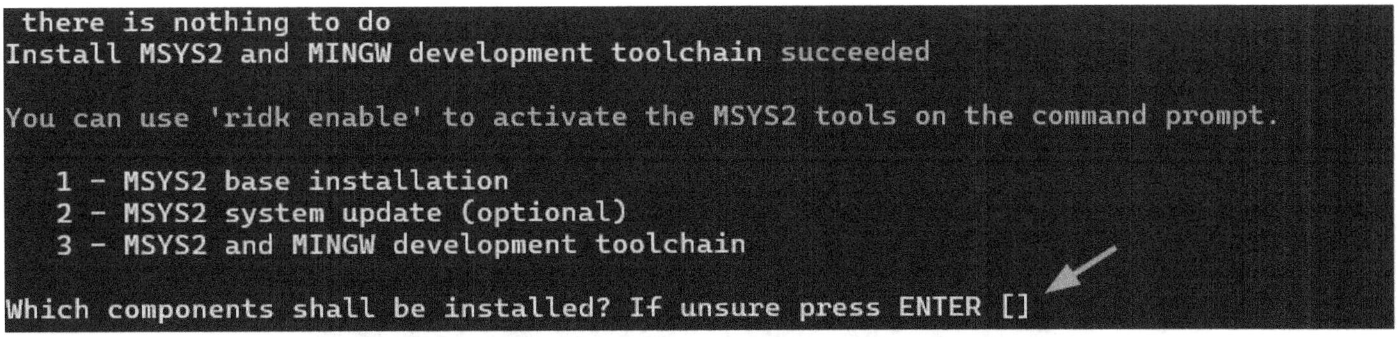

```
 there is nothing to do
Install MSYS2 and MINGW development toolchain succeeded

You can use 'ridk enable' to activate the MSYS2 tools on the command prompt.

   1 - MSYS2 base installation
   2 - MSYS2 system update (optional)
   3 - MSYS2 and MINGW development toolchain

Which components shall be installed? If unsure press ENTER []
```

Figure 9. Ruby installer screen towards the end of installation

Press `Enter` in response to both questions. This should conclude the installation of Ruby on your computer.

To verify a successful installation, you can issue the command shown in Example 1 from the command prompt and you should see the Ruby version as shown in Figure 10.

Example 1. Checking the installed version of Ruby

```
C:\users\me> ruby --version
```

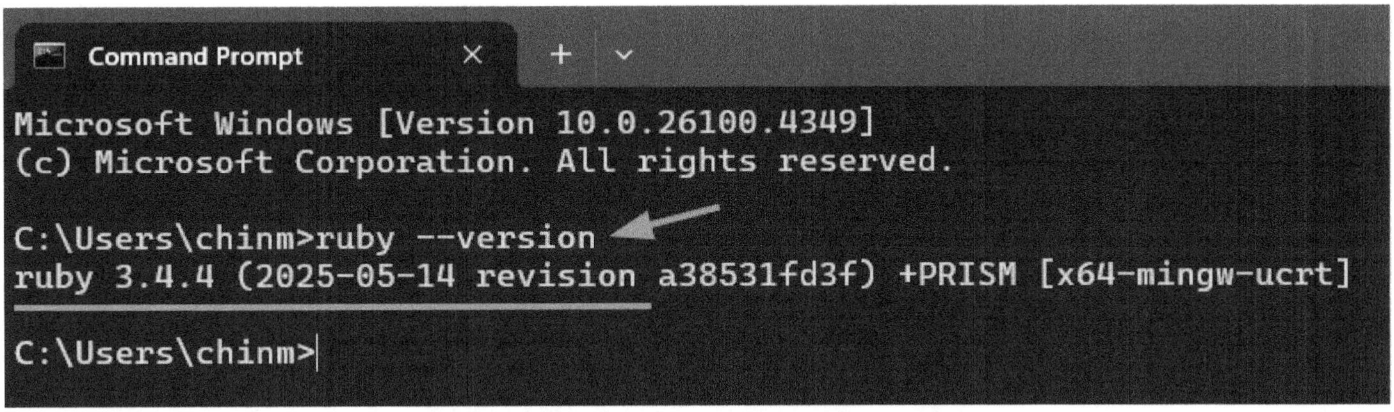

```
Command Prompt
Microsoft Windows [Version 10.0.26100.4349]
(c) Microsoft Corporation. All rights reserved.

C:\Users\chinm>ruby --version
ruby 3.4.4 (2025-05-14 revision a38531fd3f) +PRISM [x64-mingw-ucrt]

C:\Users\chinm>
```

Figure 10. Ruby version check after installation

2.1.2. Installing AsciiDoctor and AsciiDoctor-PDF

Step 3 Search for 'Ruby' in the windows search box and you should see the the option `Start Command Prompt with Ruby` in the left pane ⇒ Click on it to open a command window and type in the command shown in Example 2 to install *asciidoctor* and *asciidoctor-pdf*:

Example 2. Installing the AsciiDoctor Software

```
C:\users\me> gem install asciidoctor
```

Once AsciiDoctor is installed, issue the command shown in Example 3 to install asciidoctor-pdf :

Example 3. Installing the AsciiDoctor Software

```
C:\users\me> gem install asciidoctor-pdf
```

If you issue the command — `gem list` as shown in Figure 11, you should now see both *asciidoctor* and *asciidoctor-pdf* with their versions in the command output indicating a successful install.

```
C:\Users\chinm>gem list
abbrev (default: 0.1.2)
addressable (2.8.7)
afm (0.2.2)
Ascii85 (2.0.1)
asciidoctor (2.0.23)
asciidoctor-pdf (2.3.19)
base64 (default: 0.2.0)
```

Figure 11. Listing of Gem List Command after Installation

That's it ! You are done and the installation is complete. You can now start creating your AsciiDoc documents in a text editor or Visual Studio Code making sure that your files have an `.adoc` extension.

AsciiDoctor Windows Install Documentation Reference

You can also refer to the AsciiDoctor Windows installation page [https://docs.asciidoctor.org/asciidoctor/latest/install/windows/] ('RubyInstaller' Section) for more information on the installation process if required.

2.2. Installing AsciiDoctor on Linux

There are more than one ways to install AsciiDoctor on Linux distros. Typically these are:

1. Installing through the distro's software manager
2. Installing from the command line
3. Installing the AsciiDoctor Docker container Image

Let's go through each installation option in a step-by-step mode.

2.2.1. Install from Repositories via Software or Package Managers

This is by far the easiest way to install AsciiDoctor on Linux. Just use your distro's software installer / software manager / package manager or software centre (whatever it is called) and search for 'AsciiDoctor'. For example, Figure 12 shows the results of a search for *asciidoctor* in the software manager of the popular Linux distro — *Linux Mint*.

Figure 12. AsciiDoctor and AsciiDoctor-pdf install via Linux Mint software manager

The advantage of installing through the software manager is that all dependencies required by AsciiDoctor and AsciiDoctor-PDF are automatically installed which includes installation of the Ruby programming language in which AsciiDoctor is written. The downside is that the versions installed may be older by a bit than the current version of AsciiDoctor. But as we will see, this is not a limiting factor in any way as you can always update AsciiDoctor to the latest version later quite easily.

The installation process via the package manager is straight forward. Just click on the software that you wish to install and choose `Install` . If there are any dependencies, you will see a dialog showing you the extra software that will be installed. You need to just press `Continue` and the software will be installed.

As AsciiDoctor-PDF is dependent on both Ruby and AsciiDoctor (Figure 13), if you start by installing AsciiDoctor-PDF, AsciiDoctor is also installed in the process saving the extra effort to install both independently.

As mentioned above, this install is via the package manager. So the installed software might not be the latest version. To update to the latest version, you can run the following command from the terminal:

Terminal Command

```
$ sudo gem update asciidoctor
```

Once AsciiDoctor is updated, do the same for AsciiDoctor-PDF using the following command:

Terminal Command

```
$ sudo gem update asciidoctor-pdf
```

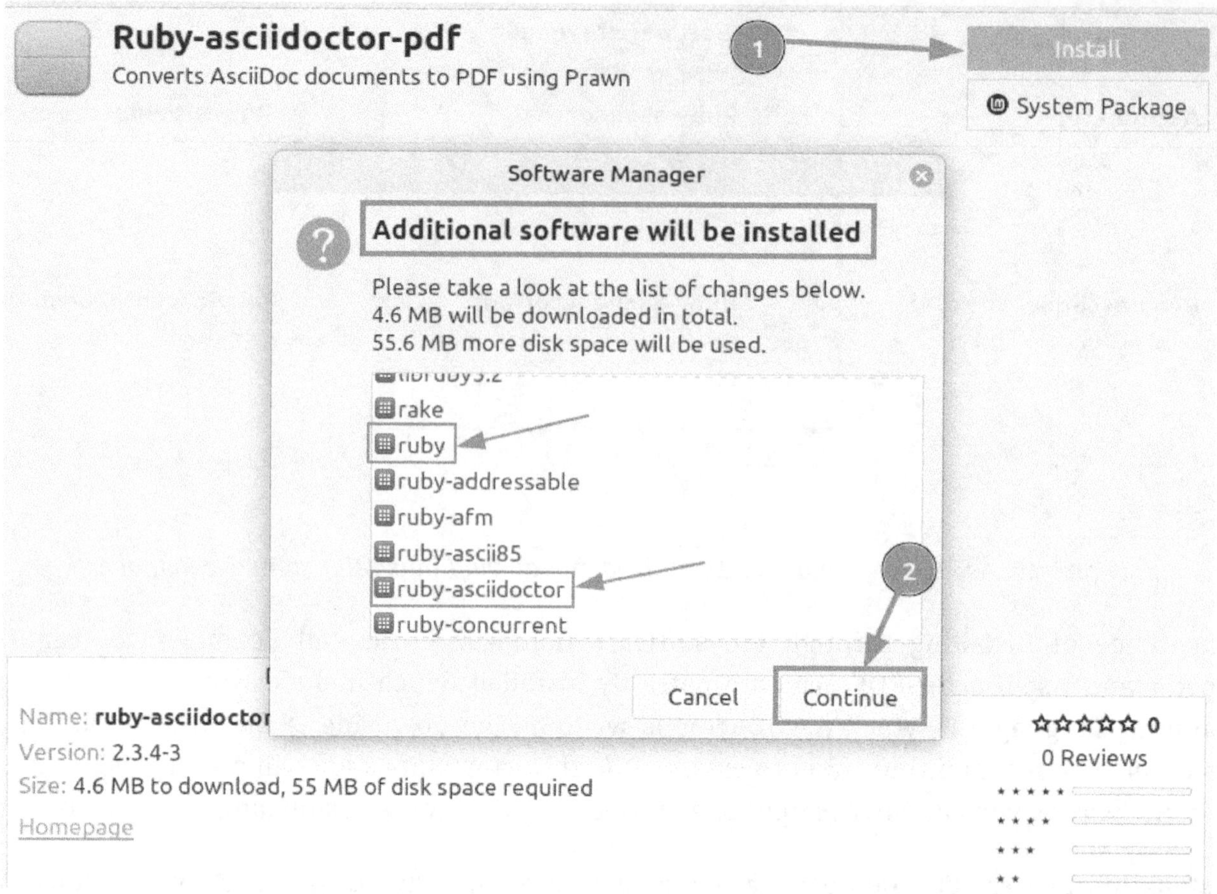

Figure 13. AsciiDoctor-pdf install via Linux Mint software manager installs both Ruby and AsciiDoctor

After updating both *AsciiDoctor* and *AsciiDoctor-PDF* to their latest versions, just close the terminal, start a new terminal and check the versions of the updated software by typing :

Terminal Command

```
$ asciidoctor-pdf --version
```

You will see a response like the one shown in Figure 14 which should show you the installed versions of both software. Done !

```
mint@mint:~$ asciidoctor-pdf --version
Asciidoctor PDF 2.3.19 using Asciidoctor 2.0.23 [https://asciidoctor.org]
Runtime Environment (ruby 3.2.3 (2024-01-18 revision 52bb2ac0a6) [x86_64-linux-g
nu]) (lc:UTF-8 fs:UTF-8 in:UTF-8 ex:UTF-8)
mint@mint:~$
```

Figure 14. AsciiDoctor-pdf and AsciiDoctor version info after install (your version numbers might vary)

2.2.2. Installing AsciiDoctor Tool Chain Using Command Line

This is the second optional route through which you can install *asciidoctor* and *asciidoctor-pdf* on Linux distros.

2.2.2.1. Command Line Install

If you are familiar with Linux and are not uncomfortable with command line installs, you just need to open up a terminal and use the following 3 commands (Ubuntu, Linux Mint , MX Linux and other debian based distros) in sequence (waiting of course for each to finish) and the AsciiDoctor installation will be complete.

Terminal Command

```
$ sudo apt install ruby-full
$ sudo gem install asciidoctor
$ sudo gem install asciidoctor-pdf
```

Done !

If you are interested in a more detailed explanation of the above command line install process, please see Appendix A.

We will see a third optional route to install the *full* AsciiDoctor toolchain on Linux using the AsciiDoctor container image later in Section 2.4.

2.3. Installation on MacOS

There are two easy ways to install AsciiDoctor and AsciiDoctor-PDF on the Mac: (a) Using the Homebrew [https://brew.sh/] package installer and (b) using the MacPorts [https://www.macports.org/] package installer. Both of these have to be installed first — if they are already not installed — before they can be used to install AsciiDoctor. Here I outline steps required for installing AsciiDoctor on Mac using Homebrew. However,if you are more comfortable with a MacPorts install, you can follow the instructions on the AsciiDoctor Documentation Page [https://docs.asciidoctor.org/asciidoctor/latest/install/macos/] to MacPorts install.

2.3.1. Installing Using Homebrew

1. As mentioned above, we will install AsciiDoctor using Homebrew. Very old MacOS versions are not suitable and might result in installation issues. So just make sure that the machine on which you are installing Homebrew is of relatively recent vintage [https://docs.brew.sh/Installation] typically macOS Ventura (13) or higher.

1. The first thing that you want to do is to run a quick check if Homebrew is already installed on your computer. To do this, open a terminal and type the following command:

   Terminal Command

   ```
   $ brew --version
   ```

   If brew is installed , you will get a response mentioning its version number. If not, you will get a `command not found` message. If brew is installed, you can move to step 3 to install AsciiDoctor and AsciiDoctor-PDF.

2. If Homebrew is not installed, the first thing that we want to do is to install XCode — a set of developer tools created by Apple. This is a *recommended* prerequisite for installing Homebrew. We can do this (a) via the Apple app store (search for XCode by Apple and install) or (b) from the command line by typing in the following command from the terminal :

   ```
   xcode-select --install
   ```

3. Once XCode is installed, we can install Homebrew. To do so, just copy and paste the following command in your terminal to install Homebrew:

   Terminal Command

   ```
   /bin/bash -c "$(curl -fsSL
   https://raw.githubusercontent.com/Homebrew/install/HEAD/install.sh)"
   ```

4. This will install Homebrew. The installation may take some time so please be patient.

You can also watch a helpful video by EasyOSX detailing the Homebrew install process.

▶ https://www.youtube.com/watch?v=IWJKRmFLn-g *(YouTube video)*

6. After the installation is complete, you can check for successful installation by once again typing the brew version command (`brew --version`) as mentioned in 2 above.

7. Now we can install *asciidoctor* by issuing the following command:

   ```
   brew install asciidoctor
   ```

8. After AsciiDoctor has been installed using Homebrew, AsciiDoctor-PDF can be installed using the following command:

   Terminal Command

   ```
   gem install asciidoctor-pdf
   ```

That should do it !

In case you run into any issues, please visit this AsciiDoctor Documentation Page [https://docs.asciidoctor.org/asciidoctor/latest/install/macos/] which provides more information on both Homebrew and MacPort installs (not covered in this text).

Just in case, if for some reason you wish to start over and want to uninstall the above, you can execute the following commands in the sequence they appear:
`brew uninstall asciidoctor`
`gem uninstall asciidoctor-pdf` To uninstall Homebrew, copy and paste the following command in your terminal:

```
bin/bash -c "$(curl -fsSL
https://raw.githubusercontent.com/Homebrew/install/HEAD/uninstall.sh)"
```

More details on uninstalling Homebrew and removing any remanent files can be found at https://mac.install.guide/homebrew/5

2.4. AsciiDoctor Podman/ Docker Container Install On Linux

2.4.1. What is Docker / Podman ?

Docker is a platform to create, deploy and run containerized applications. Containers are lightweight, stand alone executable packages that *contain* everything required for a software to run — the code, all required libraries, the run time environment and tools — all in one single unit. Once a software container is created, it can be deployed rapidly in any computing environment. While docker ruled the world of containerized applications for a long time and continues to do so still,*Podman* is a drop in replacement for Docker. It is considered more secure and user friendly. Docker and Podman are both open source and free !

If you haven't yet heard of containerized applications and the above description sounds a bit perplexing, a quick analogy might help to conceptually visualize the idea. Let's say if you were going hiking and you wanted to cover for first aid in case of an accident or illness, what would you do? You would, undoubtedly create a first aid box or container and put everything required to provide first aid - antiseptics, bandages, tape, slings, medicines for allergies, fever, pain relief and whatever else you can think of. You could then deploy this first aid container not only on hiking trips but also on picnics, fishing trips, road trips, overseas trips — in fact you can deploy your first aid container anywhere and anytime. Containerized software applications are somewhat similar in concept. Application software and all dependencies are put in one container image that can be instantly deployed. The bottom line for the user is that they don't need to go through the struggle and hassle of installing a software and its dependencies on their machine. If a container *image* has been created by the software developer, we can use Docker or Podman to download that image and start using that software on our computer in just a few seconds! One other thing about containers is that being lightweight, they are blazingly fast.

While containers are essentially a Linux thing, they can also be run in Windows and on Mac. So how does this *container* thing work in a nutshell ? In short, software developers create a container image for their software and upload it on a container registry like docker hub [https://hub.docker.com/] from where they are available to users. The user installs Podman or Docker on their computer and downloads the required image from the Docker hub and starts using that container on their machine. Hundreds of such containerized applications are available online.

In summary, while this sounds a bit nerdy (and it actually is!), if you are willing to venture out in the deep end of the pool, containers are the fastest and by far the easiest way to run and use software.

2.4.2. AsciiDoc Docker Image [Highly Recommended for Linux Users]

Now that we know what containers do, a good question is what's all this got to do with AsciiDoc? Do we have a container image for AsciiDoc and AsciiDoctor? The answer is a resounding *yes* and it is *magical* ! In fact in my opinion, there can be no better example than the AsciiDoc docker image to see the immense utility and convenience of containerized applications. As we will discover later in the text (or by now you already know this), we need *AsciiDoctor* to convert AsciiDoc files to HTML, we need *Asciidoctor-PDF* to convert AsciiDoc files to PDF, we need *AsciiDoctor-EPUB3* to convert raw AsciiDoc files to EPUB, we need *Coderay*, *Rouge* or *Pygments* for syntax highlighting, *Asciidoctor-Mathematical* for inserting equations and mathematical formulae and some other applications [https://github.com/asciidoctor/docker-asciidoctor] (see the environment section) as well if we need to do some other things with AsciiDoctor. All this runs in Ruby so of course we need Ruby too with all its dependencies. In a typical installation scenario as described in Section 2.2.1 and Section 2.2.2 above, all these have to be independently installed. So while this is all okay and it can be done without much fuss as we have seen above, the thing is that it *has to be done !* Now it so happens that the good folks at AsciiDoctor have created a Docker container for AsciiDoctor and have put all the AsciiDoctor software tools and everything else connected to AsciiDoctor (some things not covered in this book) in one container image [https://hub.docker.com/r/asciidoctor/docker-asciidoctor] and uploaded it on the docker image hub. And for good measure, they keep updating it from time to time when new versions of AsciiDoctor software are released. So if we are comfortable with Docker or Podman, all we need to do is to install Docker or

Podman and then simply *pull* the AsciiDoctor container image on our computer and start using AsciiDoctor without installing any thing ! **How cool is that !** So if you are up to it, keep reading and I will show you how to run AsciiDoctor as a containerized application. The following discussion is focussed on installing Podman and running the AsciiDoctor Docker container in Linux.

2.4.3. Install Podman

The first thing that we want to do is to install Podman [https://podman.io/]. Repositories of all major Linux distributions have Podman and while the latest version might not be available via the repos, I strongly recommend that Podman (or docker if you prefer it over Podman) be installed via the software manager. Just start your software manager and search for *podman*. I demonstrate below, the installation on Linux Mint 22 Cinnamon but the general idea is applicable to all distros. Figure 15 shows the results of the search for 'podman' in the Linux Mint Software Manager.

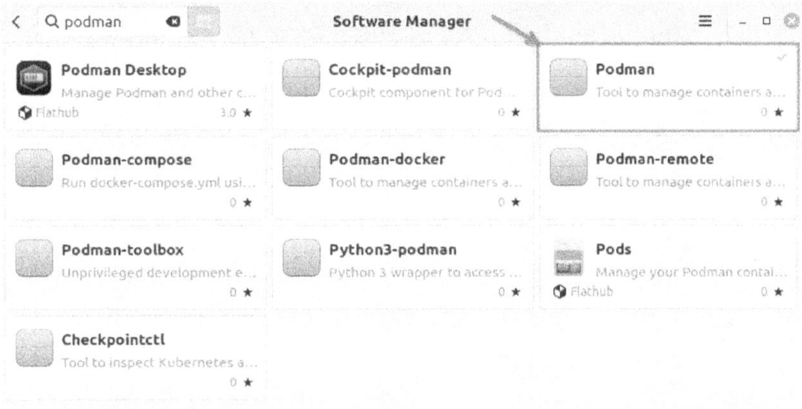

Figure 15. Search results for Podman in the Linux Mint software manager

From the search results , choose Podman (we are interested in just one software — Podman) and press the `install` button on the top right. In the `Additional software will be installed` window that follows, choose the `continue` button (Figure 16). Podman will now be installed on your computer.

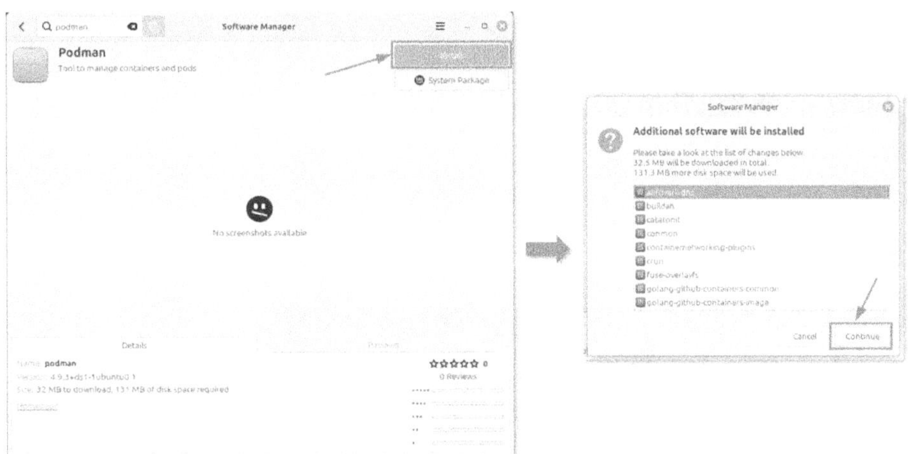

Figure 16. Podman install screens in Linux Mint

The installation may take some time, so please be patient till you get a successful installation message from the software manager. Different repos might have different versions of Podman but most have Podman 4.x and this is perfectly fine for the needs to run the AsciiDoctor container. You can skip Section 2.4.4 and jump straight to Section 2.4.5 if you have installed Podman from the software manager.

2.4.4. Installing Podman Via the Command Line

While I recommend Podman installation via software manager method, you can optionally also install Podman from the command line by opening a terminal and typing in the commands (Debian Based — Mint, Ubuntu, MX-Linux etc.) shown in Example 4.

Terminal Command

Example 4. Installing Podman from the terminal

```
$ sudo apt-get update
$ sudo apt-get -y install podman
```

For command line installation instructions for other Linuxes, please visit the podman installation instructions page [https://podman.io/docs/installation].

2.4.5. Testing Podman Installation

After installing Podman, you can easily test if the installation has been successful by typing in the following command in the terminal:

Terminal Command

```
$ podman --version
```

You should see a response like the one shown in Figure 17 (your version might be different).

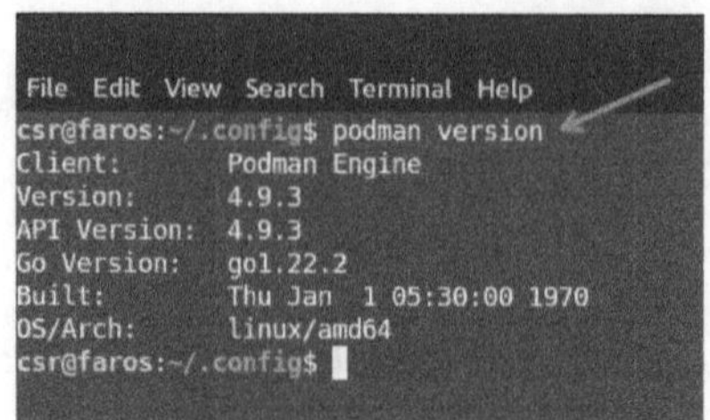

Figure 17. Output of the Podman version command after installation

A response like the one above (without any warnings) indicates that Podman has been successfully installed. You can also use `podman --version` for a shorter output.

2.4.6. Pulling the AsciiDoc Image and Running the AsciiDoc container

With the installation of Podman complete, we can now proceed to *pull* the asciidoctor container image and run the asciidoctor container. To do this, we need to issue the command shown in Example 5 from the terminal prompt (one line command):

Terminal Command

Example 5. Running the AsciiDoctor Container Image using Podman

```
$ podman run -it -v $(pwd):/documents/ docker.io/asciidoctor/docker-asciidoctor
```

The above command will set into motion, the downloading or *pulling* of the docker-asciidoctor container image from the docker hub [https://hub.docker.com/r/asciidoctor/docker-asciidoctor] and then run the container.

The part of the above command that says `$(pwd):/documents/` actually maps your current directory (where your AsciiDoc files are residing) as the default documents folder for the AsciiDoctor container.

About Folder Names

The path to the folder that has your AsciiDoc files **must not** have folder names that have **blank spaces**. Such paths lead to an Error from Podman. For example if your files are in a folder called *my book* in your home directory making the path something like `/home/csr/Documents/my book/` and you issue the podman run command from your terminal, this will end up in the following error: `Error: invalid reference format`. So please make sure that any folder name in the path *does not contain any spaces*. In the above example we could rename our folder as my_book making the path '/home/csr/Documents/my_book/' and the Podman run command will execute without any issues.

You will now see various components of the container image being downloaded with progress bars indicating the download status (Figure 18).

```
csr@faros: ~/Documents/adoc
File Edit View Search Terminal Help
csr@faros:~/Documents/adoc$ podman run -it -v $(pwd):/documents/ docker.io/asciidoctor/docker-asciidoctor
Trying to pull docker.io/asciidoctor/docker-asciidoctor:latest...
WARN[0025] Failed, retrying in 1s ... (1/3). Error: initializing source docker://asciidoctor/docker-asciidoctor:l
tps://registry-1.docker.io/v2/asciidoctor/docker-asciidoctor/manifests/latest": net/http: TLS handshake timeout
Getting image source signatures
Copying blob c9d5c7916cf9 [====>-----------------------------] 12.7MiB / 96.6MiB | 37.1 KiB/s
Copying blob 1f3e46996e29 done   |
Copying blob ce66aa970a50 [=>--------------------------------] 20.6MiB / 354.8MiB | 77.4 KiB/s
Copying blob 1a5a6457f1a2 done   |
Copying blob 3fac26e4d9d6 done   |
Copying blob 1fbf50064507 [=====>----------------------------] 24.2MiB / 144.0MiB | 398.7 KiB/s
Copying blob 6f19dfcef644 done   |
Copying blob 960f67892372 done   |
Copying blob 540ef79f58d0 done   |
Copying blob 0d79aec3c840 done   |
```

Figure 18. Pulling the AsciiDoctor Container Image

As this is a big download, please be *super patient* and let is take its time. The amount of time that it will take to finish depends on the speed of your Internet connection among other things.

Once the download is successfully completed, podman will start the AsciiDoctor container and you should see the following screen with a # prompt as seen in Figure 19 below :

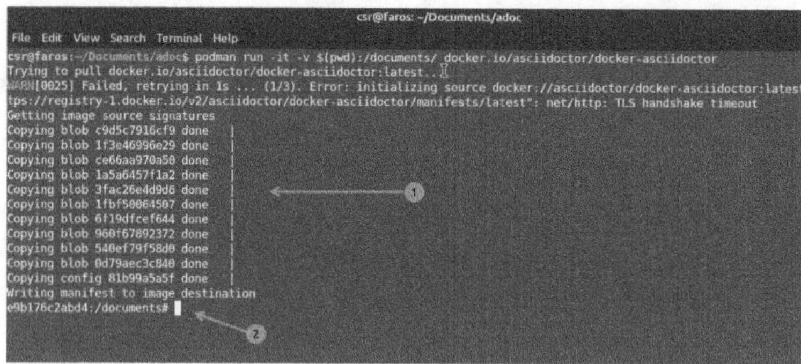

Figure 19. Install finished and Container Running

As can be seen, all components have been downloaded (1) and the # prompt (2) shows that the container is now running and you can issue *AsciiDoctor* commands or exit the container.

2.4.7. Exiting and Restarting the Container

To exit the container type the following command at the # prompt :

```
e9b176c2abd4:/documents# exit
```

The above command stops the container and you will get your terminal $ prompt back (callout 3 in Figure 20).

```
csr@faros:~/Documents/adoc$ podman run -it -v $(pwd):/documents/ docker.io/asciidoctor/docker-asciidoctor   (1)
b0c60ea87cc0:/documents# exit   (2)
exit
csr@faros:~/Documents/adoc$   (3)
```

Figure 20. Restarting (1) and exiting (2) the AsciiDoctor container

To restart the container, first move to the folder that has your AsciiDoc files, issue the command shown in Example 5 and you should get your # prompt almost immediately (as the image is already on your computer) from where you can start using AsciiDoctor.

Running the AsciiDoctor Docker Image Using Docker

While I have described installation and use of Podman for new users, if you are already a Docker user and have Docker installed, you need to navigate to the folder where you have your AsciiDoc files and run the AsciiDoctor Docker image using the following command:

$ docker run -it -u $(id -u):$(id -g) -v $(pwd):/documents/ asciidoctor/docker-asciidoctor

If you are thinking that the Podman command shown in Example 5 to start an AsciiDoctor image is quite long and will be difficult to remember, you are absolutely right! As we need to use this command regularly, the best solution is to create a shellscript and use the script to start the container. To know how to create a shellscript to run the AsciiDoctor container, please see Appendix B. If you are using Docker instead of Podman, just replace the Podman command in the script file with the command in the tip box above.

☞ *If one reviews the above installation, it is not hard to see that after the installation of Podman (one command install), all you need is just one more command to get access to every tool that AsciiDoctor has to offer. It doesn't get easier than that now, does it?*

❗ Some Podman commands that can be useful in managing containers can be found in Appendix D.

2.4.8. Using the AsciiDoctor Container

To use the container image on a regular basis, follow this sequence:

1. First move to the folder that has your AsciiDoc files that you wish to render to HTML or PDF.
2. Issue the Podman command shown in Example 5 (or use the shell script if you have one) and you should see an # prompt.
3. Once your Docker-AsciiDoctor container is up and running i.e. you have your # prompt, you can issue AsciiDoctor commands as described in Chapter 4 and other chapters in this book from the # prompt just like you would do in a regular install. This is shown in the Figure 21.
4. Type `exit` on the # prompt to exit the container.

In Figure 21 at callout 1, we convert an AsciiDoc file called *zen.adoc* to HTML. When this command is run, you will see a *zen.html* file appear in your folder. At callout 2, we use Asciidoctor-PDF to convert *zen.adoc* to PDF. At callout 3, we use AsciiDoctor-EPUB3 to convert *zen.adoc* to EPUB3 file. You can also use AsciiDoctor-Mathematical as described in Chapter 14. Don't worry, we will learn about all this in Chapter 4.

```
csr@faros: ~/Documents/adoc
File  Edit  View  Search  Terminal  Help
a002c4d1dfb8:/documents# asciidoctor zen.adoc          (1)
a002c4d1dfb8:/documents# asciidoctor-pdf zen.adoc      (2)
a002c4d1dfb8:/documents# asciidoctor-epub3 zen.adoc    (3)
a002c4d1dfb8:/documents#
```

Figure 21. Issuing AsciiDoctor commands from the container prompt

Tip

If you are typing your AsciiDoc documents in VSCode with live preview, you do not need to start and use the AsciiDoctor container very often. In fact you need to start the container and use the AsciiDoctor commands only when you need to convert to HTML, PDF or EPUB3 or run AsciiDoctor with some typical flags. In Chapter 3 we discuss how to install and use VS Code to write AsciiDoc documents.

2.5. AsciiDoctor Podman / Docker Container Install On Windows 11

You can also install the full AsciiDoctor toolchain via the AsciiDoctor Docker container by installing Podman on Windows. This single install will give full access to all AsciiDoctor tools just like you have for Linux. I highly recommend this. Appendix C provides a full and very detailed step-by-step guide on how to install Podman CLI and Podman Desktop on Window 11 and how to run the AsciiDoctor Docker container on Windows. The whole install takes about 5 minutes and once done, you have access to the full AsciiDoctor toolchain. As customized information about installing Podman and running the AsciiDoctor container on Windows is not easily available, Appendix C should serve as a valuable resource for anyone looking to install Podman and run AsciiDoctor as a containerized application on Windows.

2.6. AsciiDoctor Podman / Docker Container Install On MacOS

The installation on MacOS is on very similar lines where we install Podman first and then use the Podman run command to get the AsciiDoctor Docker image as described for Linux.

Step 1 - Install Podman This is simple install with Homebrew. You can watch the following helpful video by AutomationOnTheGo that provides step-by-step guidance to install Podman on Mac OS.

▶ https://www.youtube.com/watch?v=8J1Wb7VfS6w *(YouTube video)*

You can also read installation instructions for MacOS on the Podman site at https://podman.io/docs/installation#macos.

Step 2 - Pull and Run the AsciiDoctor Docker Image on Podman

Again the same command shown in Example 5 can be entered from the terminal to download the container image and run the AsciiDoctor container.

You can also consider installing Podman Desktop for Mac OS as explained for Windows in and use it as explained in Appendix C. You can also pull down the AsciiDoctor container from inside Podman Desktop if you experience any issues in doing so using the Podman run command mentioned above.

Once the above installation is done, you can use AsciiDoctor as described for Linux or accessing it through the Podman Desktop as described for Windows in Appendix C.

As you can see, running AsciiDoctor as a containerized image via Podman gives you access to *all* AsciiDoctor tools without having to directly install any of them! You run the container with blazing speed, use the required AsciiDoctor tool and exit the container without suffering any installation anxiety!

In conclusion, which ever way you install AsciiDoctor — software manager, command line or docker container — once you have AsciiDoctor and AsciiDoctor-PDF installed, you are ready to start creating AsciiDoc documents and embark on your AsciiDoc journey. Chapter 4 onwards, we start doing just!

2.7. Chapter Summary

1. In this chapter, we have seen how to install AsciiDoctor and AsciiDoctor-PDF on Linux, Windows and Mac in the conventional way.
2. We have also seen how to install Podman and run AsciiDoctor via a Docker image on a Linux computer.
3. Either ways, it’s a one time setup and once AsciiDoctor and once AsciiDoctor-PDF are available on your machine, you can convert your AsciiDoc documents to HTML or PDF with ease.
4. Installations can be a bit overwhelming for some, but following the steps presented in this chapter, you can install AsciiDoctor easily on your computer and operating system.

1. Podman and Docker can be installed on Mac and Windows too. If you wish to install Podman on windows or Mac, please revisit Section 2.5 and Section 2.6.
2. If you are Linux, Window or Mac OS user and if you are okay with some geeky stuff, I highly recommend using the AsciiDoctor Docker container image via Podman. This one install gives you access to everything and you don't have to install anything further.

Chapter 3. The Visual Studio Code Workflow: Live Preview AsciiDoc Documents

" I started using VS Code for writing my novel and it's the best thing ever!" ~ Craig Russell, Creative Writing in VS Code

---

This chapter is optional . If you have installed AsciiDoctor on your computer, you can start creating AsciiDoc documents using a plain text editor of your choice following the manual workflow described in Chapter 1. However using VS Code as your editor for creating AsciiDoc files is super convenient and if you set it up, you will have the benefit of live preview which will show you how your document will be rendered as you type your AsciiDoc markup. You can also activate CoPilot in VS Code. This is a one time setup and makes writing documents in AsciiDoc very efficient and enjoyable. I personally use VS Code and ***highly recommend it****. In fact I prefer writing AsciiDoc in VS Code (or VSCodium) so much that I thought it fit to devote a full chapter in this book to convince you to follow suit. After all, creating documents with AsciiDoc, is in a way, creating documents with code!*

3.1. What is VS Code ?

In a nutshell, VS Code is arguably *the* most popular code editor that software developers use to create software. It is free, it is open source and it has been created by Microsoft. It supports many programming, scripting and markup languages. Writing code in code editors like VS Code is super convenient for programmers due to many in-built features that considerably ease software development. It can also be used to manage software projects. It is highly customizable and has a huge library of *extensions* that further enhance its capabilities. It is actively used for web development, mobile app development, server side programming and in data science & machine learning to name a just a few use cases. You can get more information about VS Code from it's official website [https://code.visualstudio.com].

3.2. VS Code and AsciiDoc Document Creation

Now that we know something about VS Code, it is legitimate to ask what has VS Code got to do with writing documents in AsciiDoc ? Well VS Code supports AsciiDoc Markup and highlights its syntax as you write your document. So when you look at your AsciiDoc file, you can see all the AsciiDoc Markup that you put inside your document, highlighted in color. But the real magic that VS Code conjures up is through its AsciiDoc extension which permits a *live preview* of the AsciiDoc document that you create. Figure 22 shows how we can set up VS Code to type in our raw AsciiDoc document in the left half of the screen and get a live preview of how it will appear after processing on the right side of the screen. This really cuts many steps that we usually need to repeat if we were using a plain text editor.

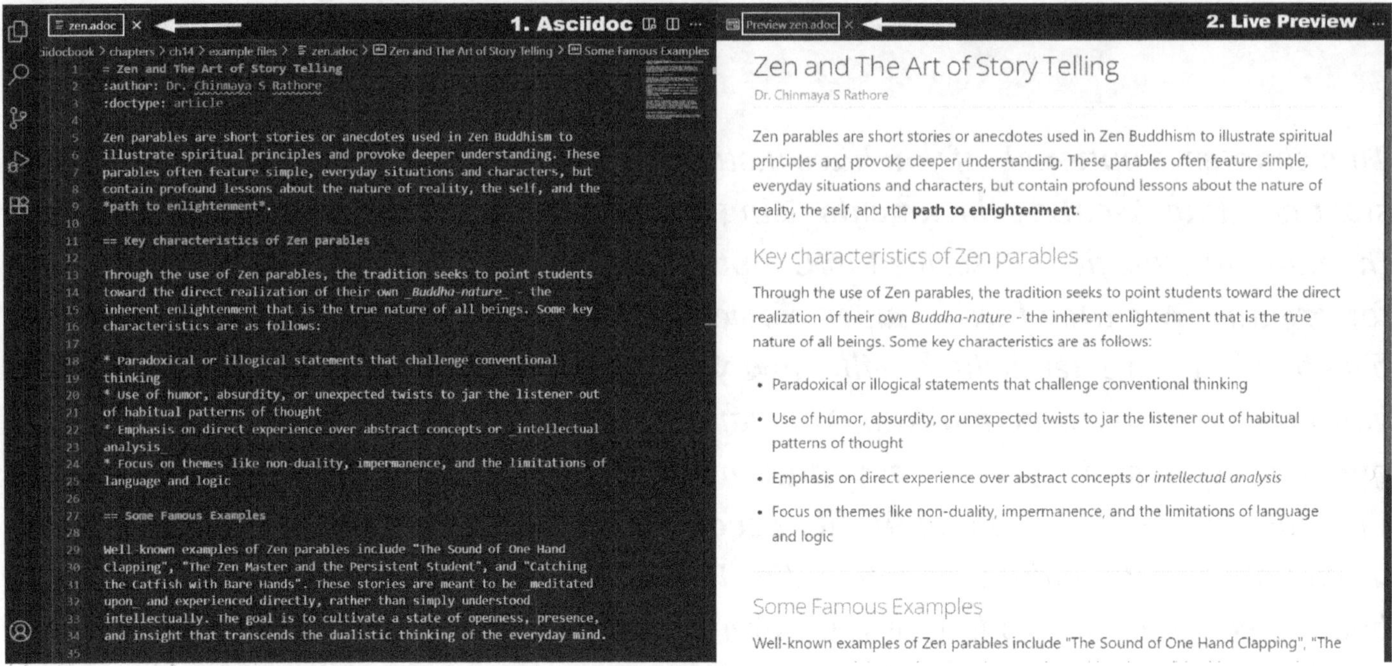

Figure 22. VS Code setup showing (1) AsciiDoc document creation in the left pane and (2) live preview in the right pane

Referring to Figure 22, in the left half of the screen (a) you can see raw AsciiDoc markup being written for a sample file called *zen.adoc*. All AsciiDoc markup syntax is highlighted in color (orange and blue in this document) clearly differentiating text from markup which is very helpful for the document creator. On the right half of the screen (b), you can see the live preview of this file — i.e. how this file will be rendered by AsciiDoctor after processing. This is such a convenience for creating documents because you don't need to run AsciiDoctor in your terminal on your AsciiDoc file every now and then to see how it will be rendered in HTML. You get immediate and live feedback for any AsciiDoc markup that you add in the left pane. This really speeds up document creation. The goodies that VS Code has to offer to streamline document creation in AsciiDoc do not end there. In fact, if you have installed AsciiDoctor and AsciiDoctor-PDF on your computer (i.e. you are not running them via a docker container), whenever you wish to render your AsciiDoc file to HTML or PDF, you don't have to open the terminal to run AsciiDoctor or AsciiDoctor-PDF. You can run it from inside VS Code itself without typing any command! So if you do a lot of writing and plan to use AsciiDoc on a regular basis, I highly recommend doing it using VS Code.

There is another free and open source VS Code-like code editor called *VSCodium*. The VSCodium code editor is a replacement for VS Code and the project is community driven. Visit the VSCodium official website [https://vscodium.com/] for more information.

3.3. Installing VS Code

VS Code is available for all platforms and the easiest way to install the latest version of VS Code is to download the installer package for your operating system — Windows 11, Linux , Mac — from the official VS Code Download Page [https://code.visualstudio.com/Download]. Since April 2023, VS Code (and VSCodium) are available only for 64 bit OSes.The screenshots that you see in subsequent sections of this text are from VS Code version: 1.96.4 Linux X-64 dated 2025-01-16 for Linux x64 6.8.0-51-generic.

If you are using Linux Mint or MX Linux or any other Debian based Linux, you can just download the deb package and double click on it for the software installer to proceed with the install. You can also search for VS Code in your software center or software manager. Many Linux distros include VS Code in their software centers but as you might have guessed, it is usually not the latest version.

3.3.1. Installing the AsciiDoc Extension

Once you have VS Code installed on your computer, start it and click on the extensions button in the left pane, pointed by the arrow in Figure 23.

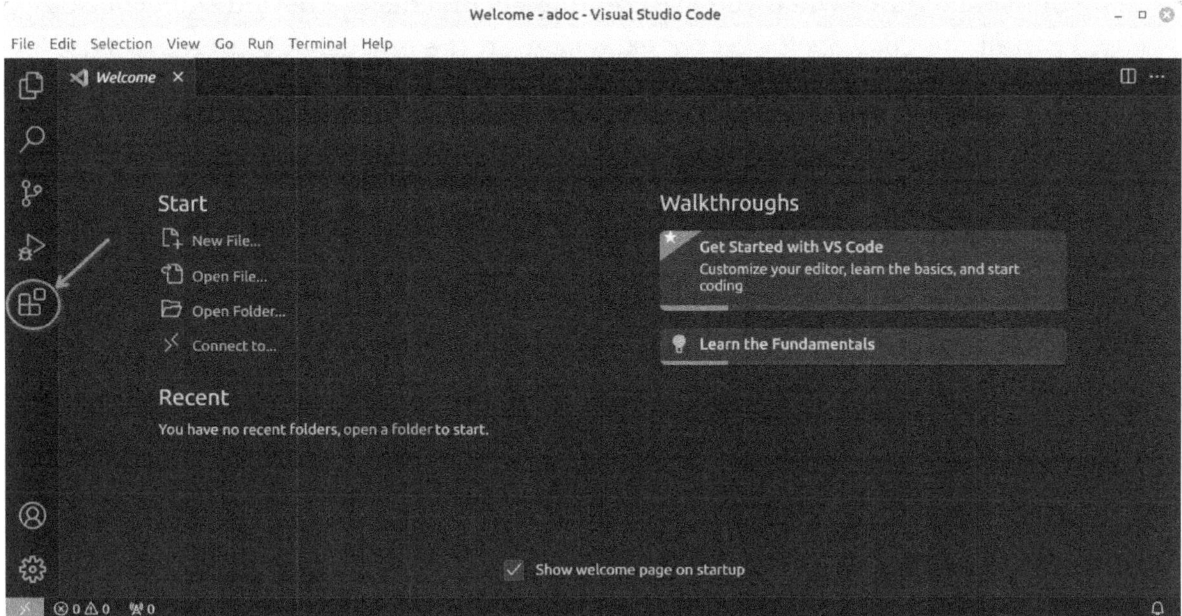

Figure 23. VS Code Welcome Screen showing the Extension Button

This opens up the extensions page. As shown in Figure 24, search for the *asciidoc* extension in the search box (1), choose the extension and press the `install` button (2 or 3) to install the extension. This takes just a few seconds to install.

Figure 24. Installing the AsciiDoc extension in VS Code

3.3.2. Installing the Code Spell Checker Extension

Before we leave the extensions page, we will install one more useful extension. One important capability that you want to have when you are creating documents is a decent spell check as you type. For this we will install the *Code Spell Checker* extension. In the extension search box type 'Code Spell Checker' (1), choose the extension and click on the `Install` button (2,3) to install the Code Spell Checker extension as shown in Figure 25 .

Figure 25. Installing the code spell checker extension - - (1) search for the extension , install extension (2 or 3)

That's it ! We are done. We can now start creating AsciiDoc documents in VS Code.

3.4. A Quick Guide to Creating AsciiDoc Documents in VS Code

While it is not the objective of this text to provide a tutorial on using Visual Studio Code, it might be helpful to those who have not used VS Code before to have enough pointers to start creating documents in AsciiDoc. So far , we have installed two extensions in VS Code that we will be needing. Now that we have everything setup and assuming that we already have *AsciiDoctor* and *AsciiDoctor-PDF* installed, let's quickly see how we can start using VS Code to create AsciiDoc files and view their processed output in real time through live preview. When you start VS Code for the first time, you will see a welcome screen as shown in Figure 26 which has been annotated to show some useful options. Spend a minute to familiarize yourself with the VS Code welcome screen.

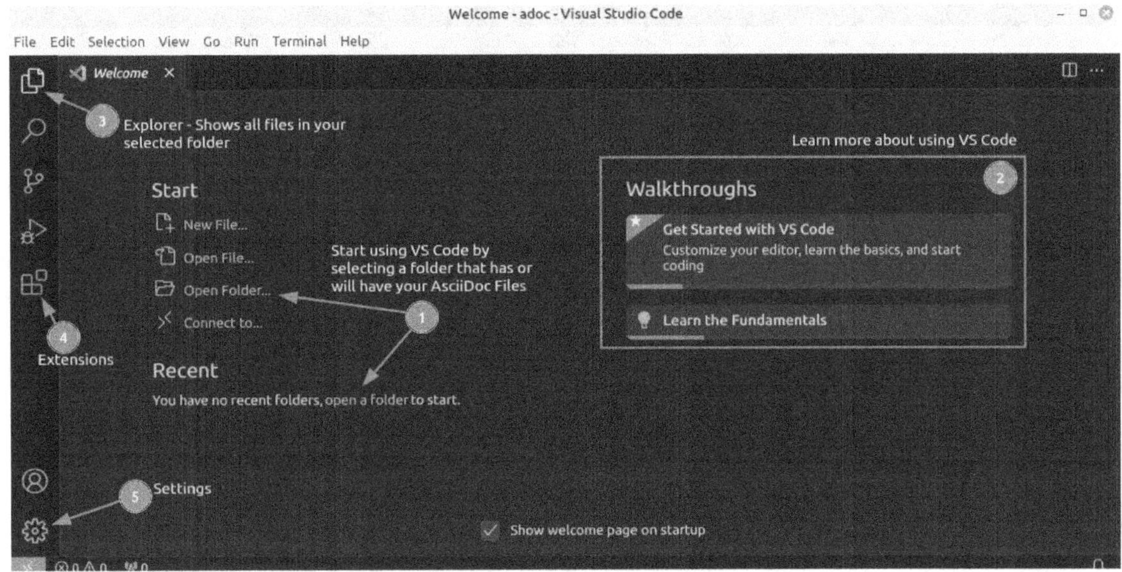

Figure 26. VS Code welcome screen

To start creating documents, choose a folder where these documents will be located using the option shown at callout 1 in Figure 26. You will be asked if you *trust the authors* — say `Yes` (saying no would essentially mean you don't trust yourself!). This will take you to the screen shown in Figure 27 . You can now start a new file. Click on the new file (button 2 in Figure 27) and name it making sure that you end it with an *.adoc* extension like *zen.adoc* .

You can also start a new file from the menu using **File** ⇒ **New File**. From the file menu, you can also open a folder using **File** ⇒ **Open folder** or directly reach a file or folder using **File** ⇒ **Open Recent**. Another useful option available from the File menu is **File** ⇒ **Auto Save** which automatically saves every word that you type ensuring that you never loose a second of work. Auto Save is a toggle option and you can click on it to switch it on or off as per your requirement.

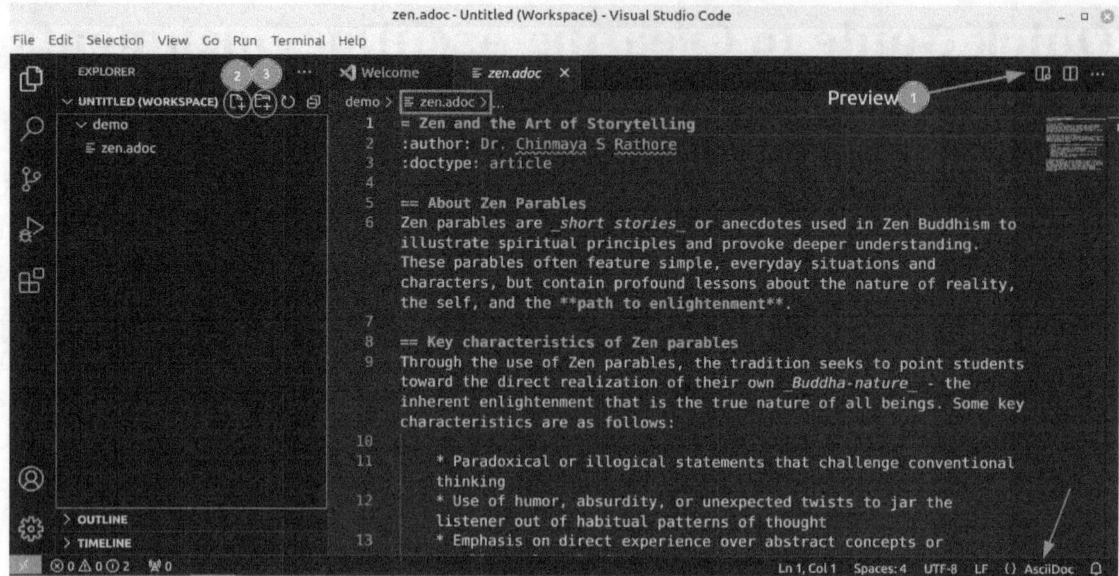

Figure 27. AsciiDoc File Opened in VS Code

To also see a live preview, click on the *preview icon* at callout (1) in Figure 27.

To dismiss the left side pane and have the full screen in two parts, click on the explorer button once. The explorer button is located in the top of the left pane. This is a toggle button that you can press to access your folder structure whenever you want to.

Now as you type, in the left pane, you will see the live preview in the right pane (see Figure 22). Press `CTRL` + `S` to save. This way you can create as many AsciiDoc documents as you like.

There is a very helpful thing that VS Code does whenever you are inserting an attribute in your AsciiDoc document like say `:imagesdir:` (we will discuss this later). As you type in a few letters after the :, VS code tries to guess what you might possibly be wanting to type as shown in Figure 28 and all that you have to do is to choose the option and press `enter` to use that term. This is super helpful as you might not remember the exact syntax of that attribute and the help provided by VS Code can save you a ton of time consulting the documentation.

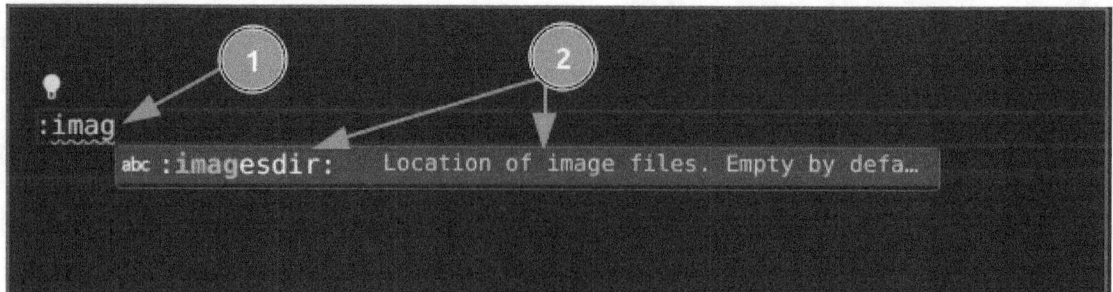

Figure 28. VS Code suggesting AsciiDoc Attribute Syntax (1) you type initial letters (b) VS Code tries to guess the full term which you can choose by pressing enter or a mouse click

The same useful help is also available when you try to insert an image in your document as shown in Figure 29. As you start typing your markup for inserting an image — `image::` — VS Code shows you all the images available in the current or `:imagesdir:` folder and you can choose to insert the one that you want without having to recall and type its name or extension.

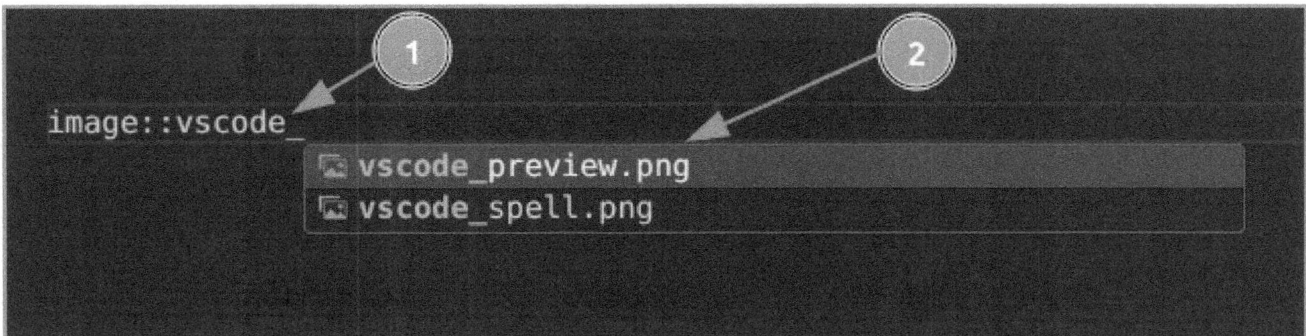

Figure 29. Drop-down for images macro showing available images in the imagesdir that can be inserted

Don't worry if the above does not make sense at this stage. We will talk about how to use AsciiDoc markup and its syntax in the next chapter. I am essentially pointing out here is that using VS Code for typing your text has many benefits that really speed up your writing!

3.4.1. Spell Check

Recall that we had installed the Code Spell Checker extension earlier. We will now see how we can correct spelling mistakes referring to Figure 30. Whenever you make a spelling mistake, you will see misspelled words underlined with a squiggly blue line (1) and when you click on that word you will see a yellow light bulb (2) appear close by. Clicking the bulb or using the keyboard shortcut `CTRL` + `.` will show spelling suggestions (3) and you can choose the correct spelling which will then replace the misspelled word. Please see Appendix E for more spell checking options.

Adding Custom Words to Workspace Dictionary

You can also add custom words to your workspace dictionary by right clicking on the misspelled word and choosing **Spelling** ⇒ **Add Words to Workspace Settings** from the menu.

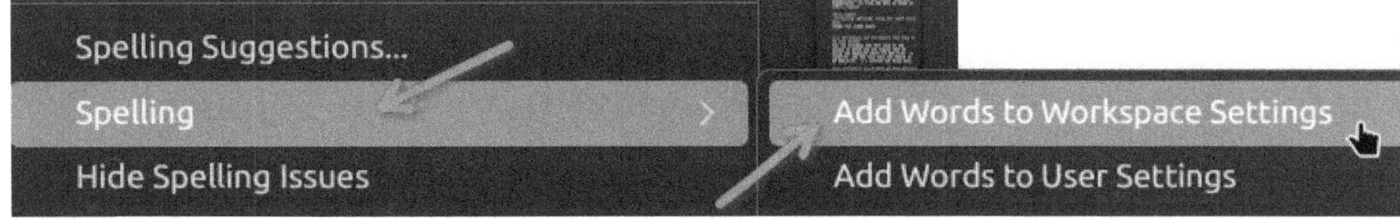

This is useful if you are using a lot of technical terms that are not in the dictionary.

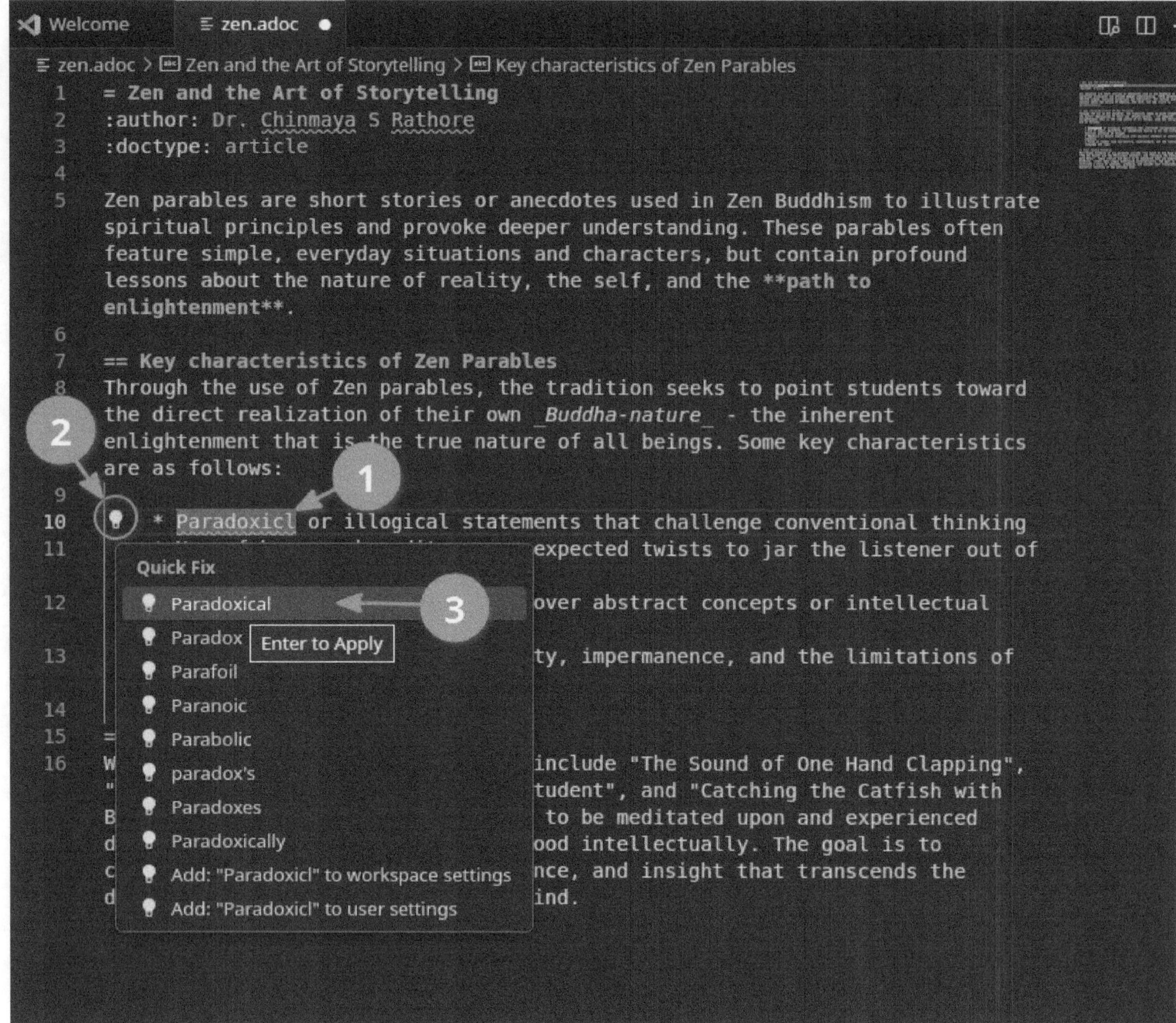

Figure 30. Correcting spellings as you type

Alternatively you can right click on the misspelled word (1) and choose `Spelling Suggestions` (2) from the menu as shown in Figure 31 and choose the correct word from the list of suggestions offered.

3.4.2. Increasing and Decreasing Font Size in VS Code Window

You can increase the font size of the window (zoom) in which you are typing text by using the keyboard short cut `CTRL+` (Control and the Plus key) and reduce it by `CTRL -` (Control and Minus key).

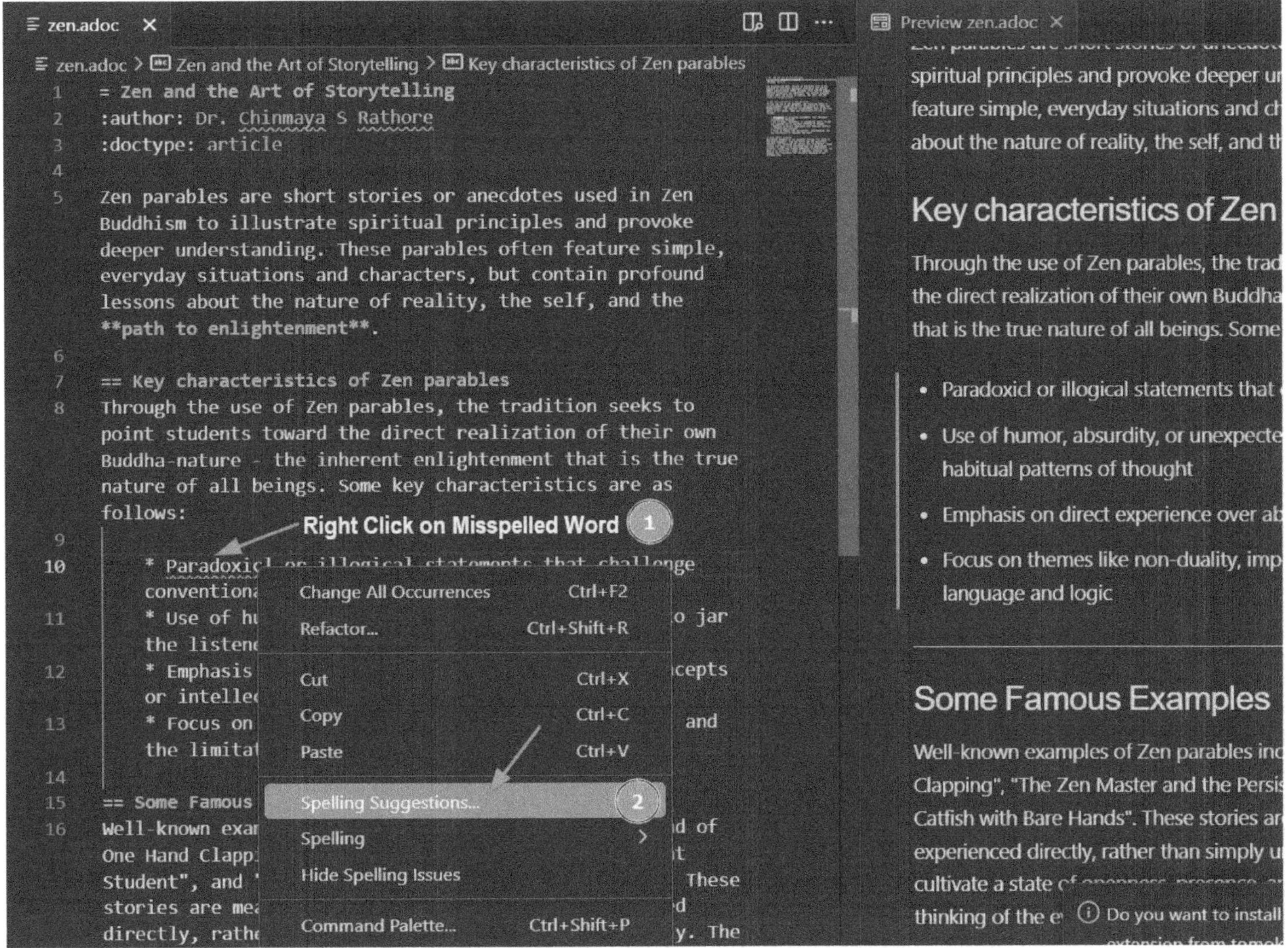

Figure 31. Correcting spellings using the right click menu

3.4.3. Collapsing all Folders in File Explorer

If you have your AsciiDoc and other files in many folders that you are viewing in the VS Code explorer (left most pane, top most icon), you can collapse all of them in one go by first clicking on any folder an then pressing `CTRL` + `Left Arrow Key` keyboard shortcut or the collapse folder icon on the top right of the AsciiDoc window. There is no opposite 'expand all' shortcut, so don't search for one!

3.5. Generating HTML and PDF Output

Whenever you wish to generate HTML or PDF output to view in a browser or PDF Viewer application, just press `CTRL` + `SHIFT` + `P` from inside VS Code and you will see the command palette box open up on the top of the screen. Search for `AsciiDoc:Save Document as HTML` or `AsciiDoc:Export Document as PDF` (as required) and click on it and you will have an HTML or PDF file processed through *AsciiDoctor* or *AsciiDoctor-PDF* in your folder without moving out of the VS Code environment. You can always issue these commands from the terminal which we will discuss in subsequent chapters.

Useful Tip - Switching on Word Wrapping & Navigating

1. When you type AsciiDoc in the left window, you might discover that by default, VS Code does not perform word wrapping in this window. This results in long lines that get out of view even though they appear okay in the preview window on the right. Obviously this is a big annoyance when you are creating a document. Word wrapping is definitely needed in your AsciiDoc window. To start word wrapping, just click once in the left window — the one in which you are writing AsciiDoc markup and press `ALT` + `Z` keys on the keyboard and VS Code will start word wrapping in the left window. You can also do this from the menu by choosing **View** → **Word Wrap** (last option). This is a toggle thing so if you press the same keys again, you will revert to the non-wrapped mode.
2. To reach a particular line number in your AsciiDoc file, press `CTRL` + `G`, type the line number in the box on top and you will be taken to that line in the AsciiDoc File. This can also be accessed from the menu by choosing Go ⇒ Goto Line / Column (Scroll down in the menu to get to this option). You can always *Go Back* to the line from where you started using the menu by choosing `Go` > `Back` or by using the `CTRL` + `ALT` + `-` keyboard shortcut.
3. You can go to the start of the document by pressing `CTRL` + `HOME` and to the end of the document by pressing `CTRL` + `END`
4. Moving text around can be easily accomplished just by selecting that piece of text with your mouse and then dragging and dropping it at the new location.
5. You can use `CTRL` + `F` to find the occurrence of a word or phrase in your document. Likewise, you can use `CTRL` + `H` to find and replace a term.
6. If you wish to change all occurrences of a word in your document, just select the word, *right click* on it and choose 'Change All Occurrences' > Type in the new word > click anywhere else in the text and all instances of the word will be replaced with what you typed in. Use this with care to avoid unintended consequences.

There is another very useful tip shared below that you might find handy since we want to type without any code editing annoyances that might disrupt the flow of writing.

3.6. Switching Off VS Code 'Quick Suggestions'

You will notice that as you type, certain words invoke VS Code to present a drop-box with some syntax that — in the context of writing AsciiDoc documents — is super annoying (super helpful for software developers). This is the 'Quick Suggestions' feature of VS Code and its behavior is demonstrated in Figure 32 as I try to type the word 'Master'!

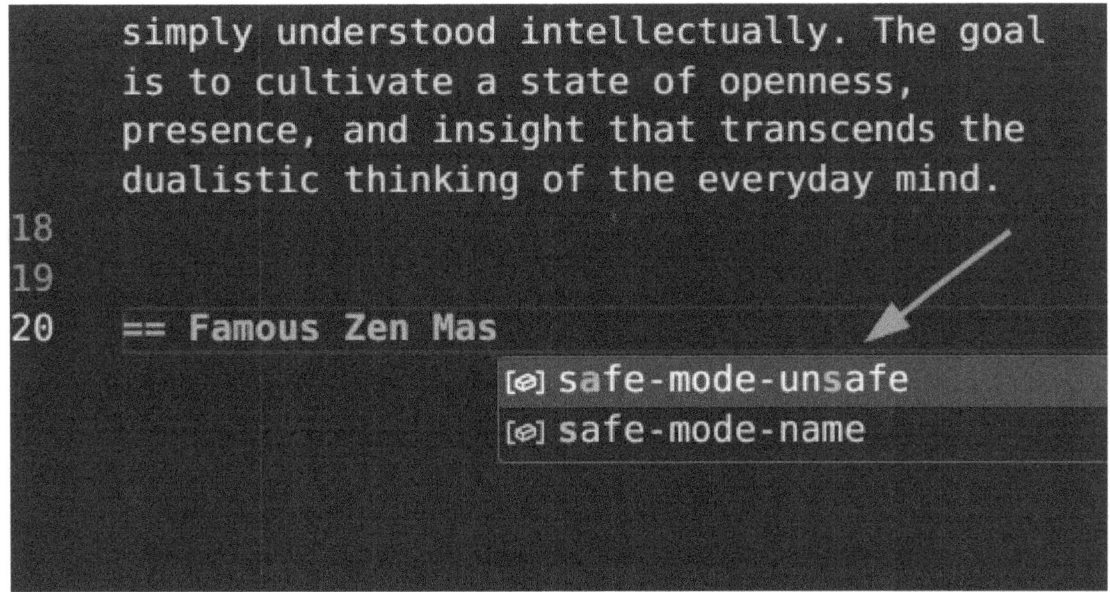

Figure 32. VS Code quick suggestions feature is a distraction in writing

This is quite annoying (at least for me!) as it disrupts your flow and engages you in a completely unconnected battle. If you are writing AsciiDoc, this feature is best muted. To switch this off, click on the gear icon at the bottom left of the VS Code screen (the *Manage* icon), then choose *Settings* and in the settings search box type `Editor:Quick Suggestions` as shown in Figure 33. Once you have it located, *double click* on `other` to reveal the value box , choose `off` (at callout 1 in Figure 33) from the drop-down and then press the blue `OK` button in front of it (2) making all three options on the screen set to `off`.

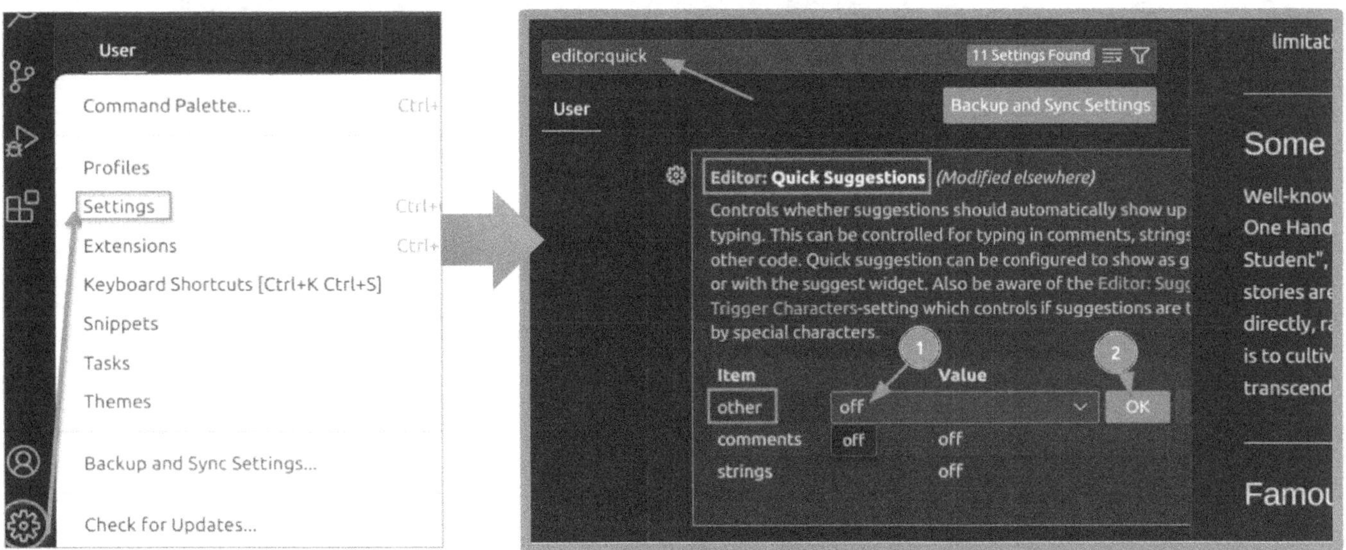

Figure 33. Switching off Quick Suggestions via VS Code Settings

The quick suggestions genie will now leave you in peace and you can type away to your hearts content without being distracted by unsolicited suggestions.

Once you set up VS Code for typing AsciiDoc documents, you will be able to really enjoy document creation using this excellent software.

If you are using the Docker install and running AsciiDoctor in a container, the `CTRL` + `SHIFT` + `P` shortcut to render AsciiDoc documents to HTML, PDF will not work from inside VS Code as it uses the installed versions of AsciiDoctor and AsciiDoctor-PDF. You will have to start the container and run AsciiDoctor and AsciiDoctor PDF from the container command prompt # to render your documents in HTML or PDF.

3.7. Live Preview Style in VS Code

You can view the live preview in the VS Code style (dark theme) or the original AsciiDoctor style which has a white background exactly like it is in the rendered HTML output (Figure 22). To change the live preview style, follow the sequence shown in Figure 34 and Figure 35 below:

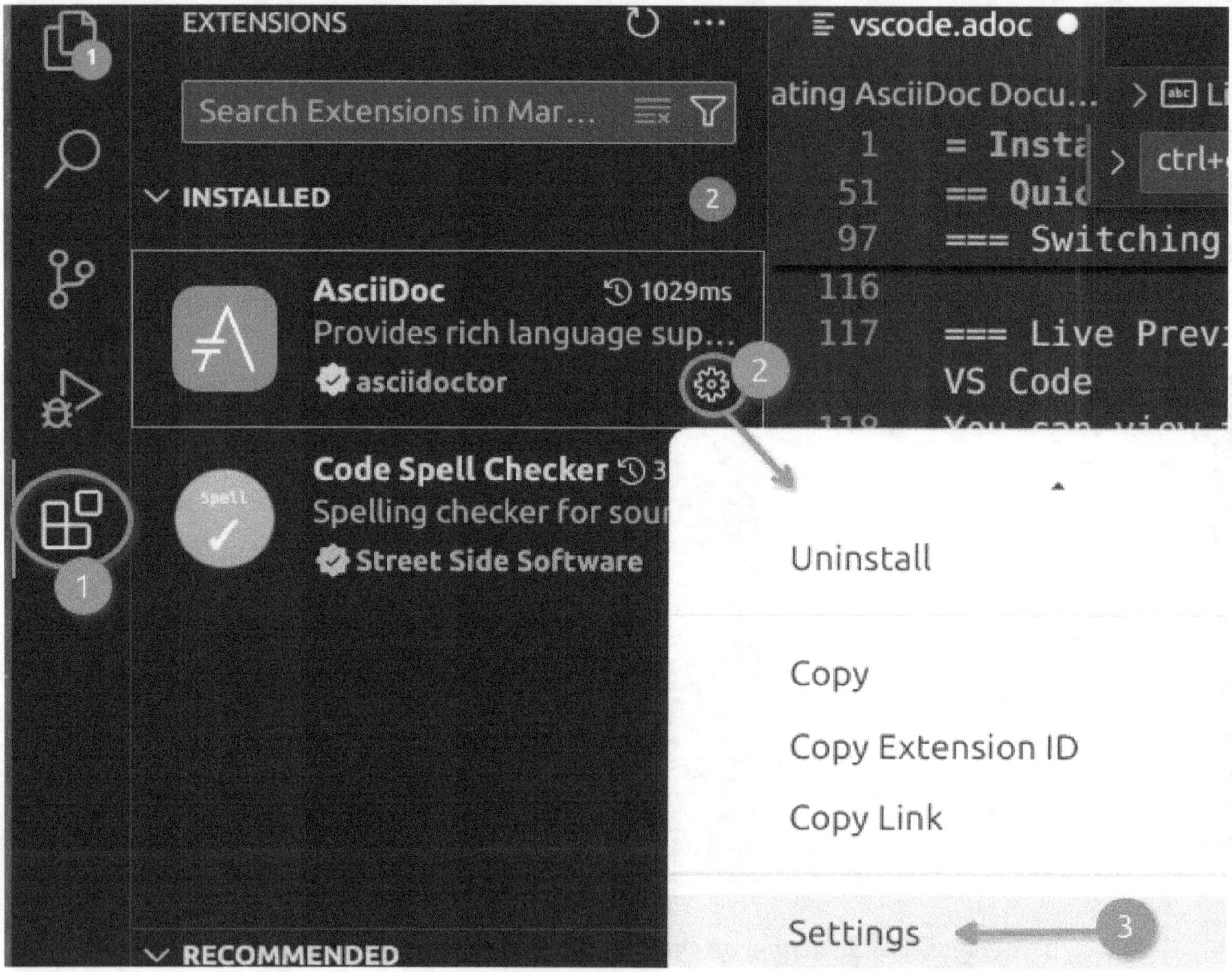

Figure 34. Setting the preview style in the AsciiDoc extension

Sequence: Click on Extension Icon(1) ⇒ AsciiDoc Gear Icon (2) ⇒ Setting (scroll down in the menu to get to this option)

In the settings dialog, clear the search box and type 'use editor' ⇒ Uncheck the 'AsciiDoc>Preview: Use Editor Style' check box (2) as shown in Figure 35. Settings are *saved automatically* and this way you can see the preview in a light or dark background in the preview window.

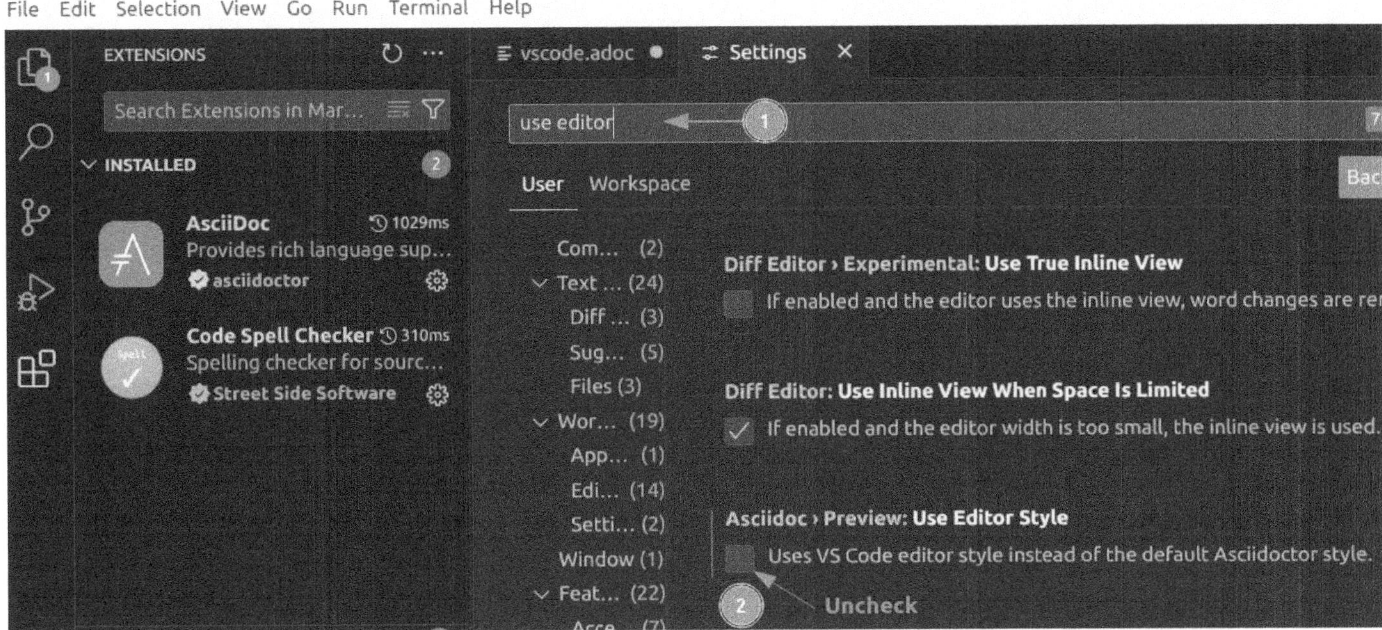

Figure 35. Checking or Unchecking the 'Use Editor Style' setting in AsciiDoc extension

3.8. VS Code Install and Setup on 32 bit MX-Linux Libretto

In February 2019, the last 32 bit version of VS Code — Version 1.32 — was released. After this and till date (2025), only 64 bit versions of VS Code have been released. However, it is possible to set up the VS Code workflow on your old 32 bit computer by installing the old 32 bit version of VS Code and make it work like a charm.

As mentioned in Chapter 1, I wrote this book in AsciiDoc on a two decade old netbook computer which has a 32 bit Atom Processor running MX-Linux 23.5 Libretto Xfce. I could — after a little bit of hit and trial — successfully set up the VS Code environment on this old machine exactly as described above. I am sharing what worked for me in a hope that someone in a similar situation could make use of their old computer (affectionately referred to as a *Potato PC* by the Linux community) to write documents in AsciiDoc and render them in professional quality.

Step 1: Install VS Code
Install VS Code Version 1.32 which is available from the official VS Code website [https://code.visualstudio.com/updates/v1_32] by downloading the deb (or rpm) package as shown in Figure 36.You can also get this 32 bit version for windows or Mac.

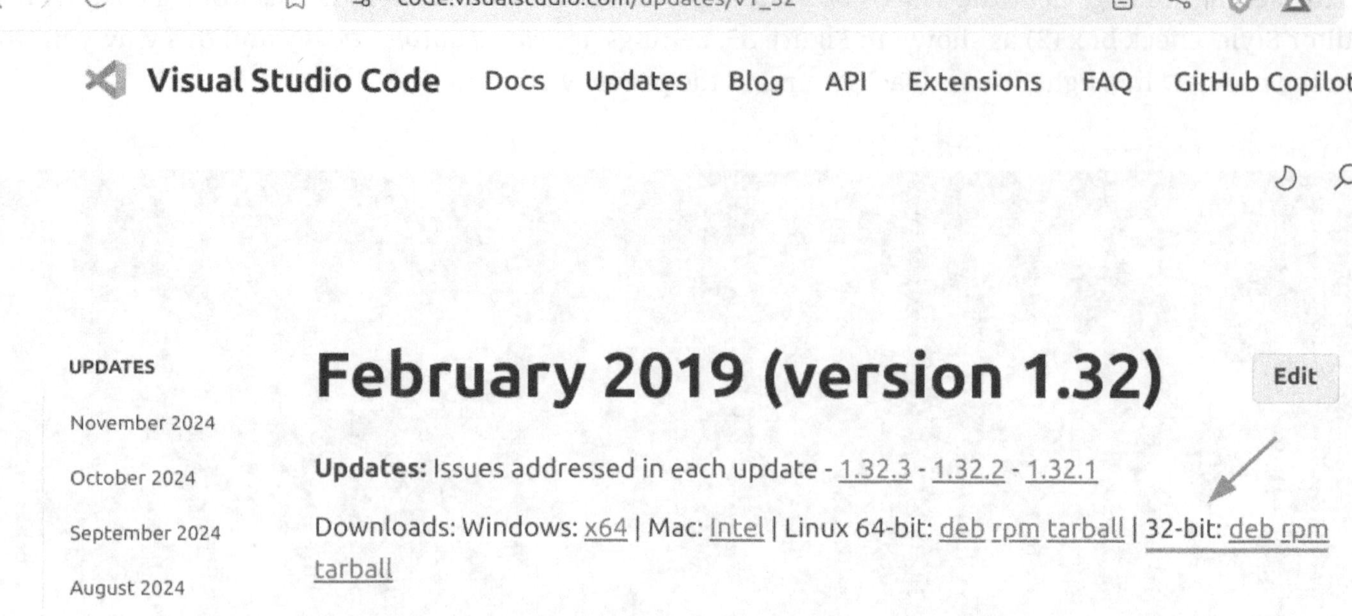

Figure 36. VS Code Version 1.32 — 32 bit deb and rpm Packages

Step 2: Install AsciiDoc and Code Spell Checker Extensions
Start VS Code, click on the Extensions Icon — the last icon in the left panel (or use `CTRL` + `SHIFT` + `X`), search and install *AsciiDoc* extension (last 32 bit version was 2.9.5) and *code spell checker* extension as described earlier in Section 3.3.1 and Section 3.3.2.

Step 3: Verify if Live Preview is Working
Open an AsciiDoc file and click on the preview button (top right) to see if live preview is visible. If yes, you are all set.

If not then you need to install an earlier version of AsciiDoc Extension as explained in step 4 below.

Step 4: Fixing No Live Preview Situation
The version that worked for me was 2.8.8 but before it can be installed, we need to turn auto-update OFF otherwise even after installing version 2.8.8, the moment you reload or restart VS Code again, you are automatically upgraded back to version 2.9.5. To switch off auto update, follow the sequence shown in Figure 37 — (1) Click on the Gear Icon ⇒ (2) Click on Settings ⇒ (3) Type 'autoupdate' in the search box and ⇒ (4) Uncheck Extensions: Auto Update (settings are automatically saved)

Step 5: Install AsciiDoctor Extension 2.8.8 With auto update of extensions set to OFF, we can now install an earlier version of the AsciiDoctor extension. Figure 38 shows the installation sequence. Click on the Extensions Button (1) ⇒ then the Gear Icon in front of the AsciiDoc Extension (2) ⇒ and then choose 'Install Another Version' (3) ⇒ and from the ensuing list, choose version 2.8.8 (or any other version that works for you).

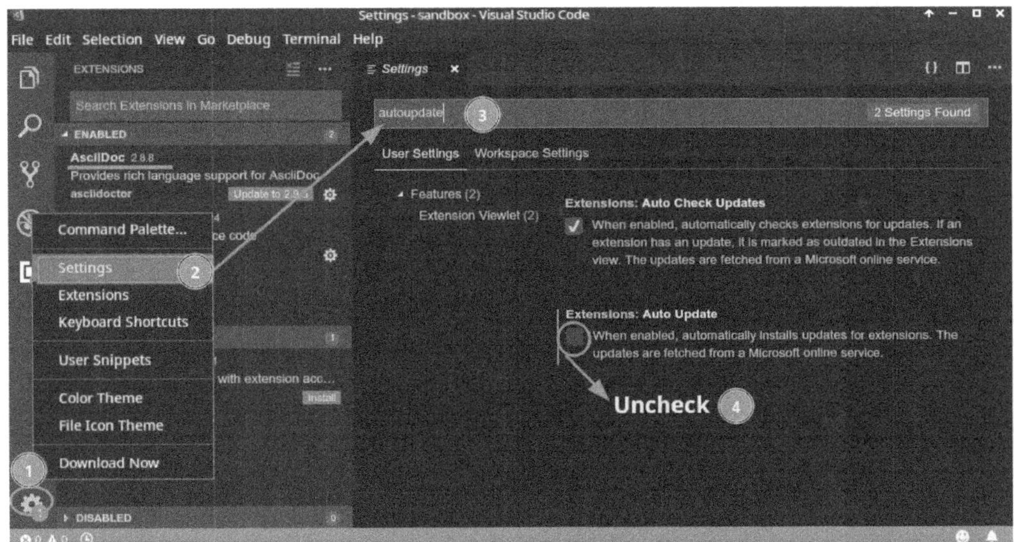

Figure 37. Turn off auto update of extensions

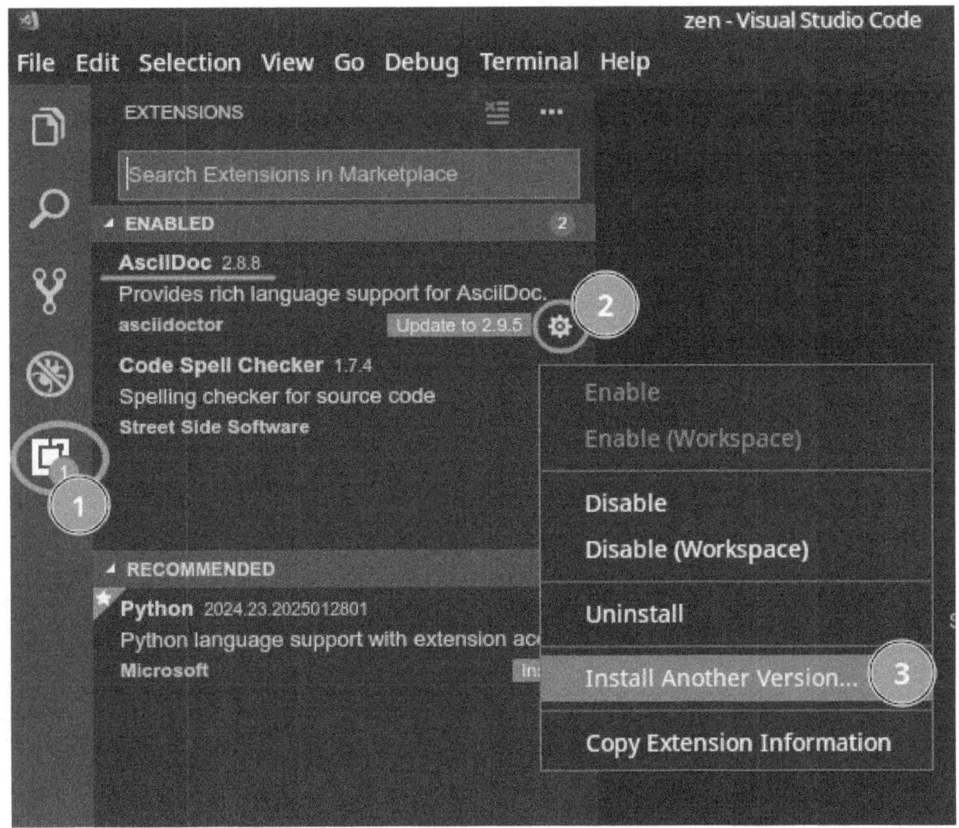

Figure 38. AsciiDoctor extension installation sequence

The chosen version will be installed and you can click on the blue 'Reload' button to restart VS Code.You should now see live preview active as shown in Figure 39 .

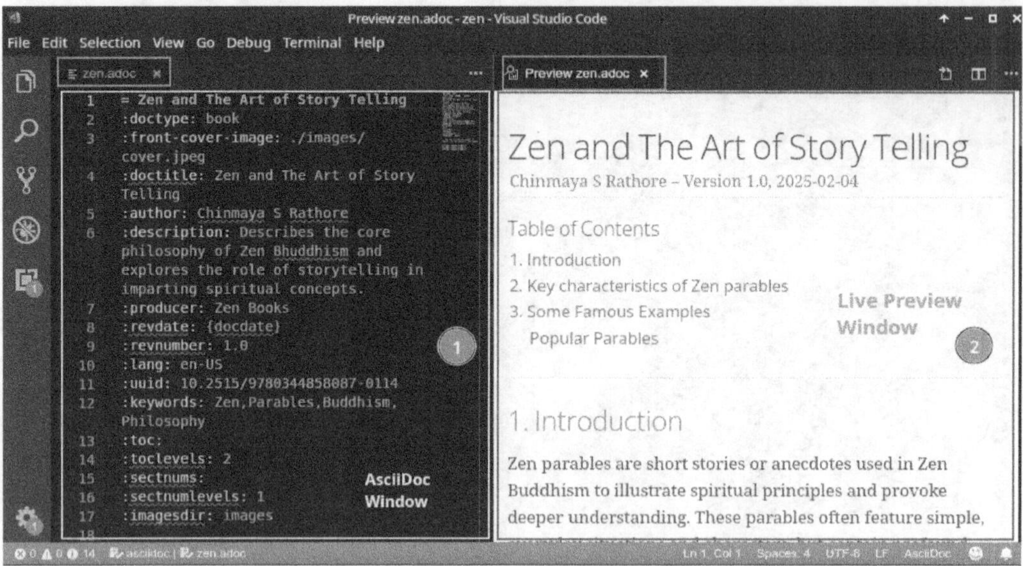

Figure 39. VS Code AsciiDoc and live preview windows on a 32 bit machine

Step 6: Optional Step to See Live Preview in AsciiDoctor Style

If your live preview is in dark mode i.e. VS Code style and you wish to see it in the original AsciiDoctor style as it will be when rendered by AsciiDoctor, you can uncheck the following setting as illustrated in Figure 40 (Gear Icon (1) ⇒ Settings (2) ⇒ Extensions (3) ⇒ click on AsciiDoc ⇒ Scroll to Locate AsciiDoc>Preview: Use Editor Style ⇒ Uncheck) :

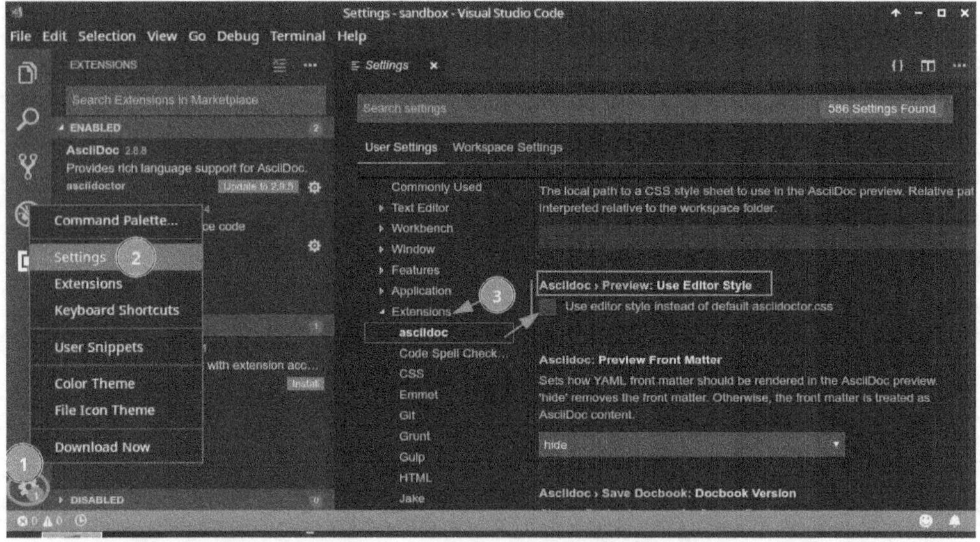

Figure 40. AsciiDoc preview setting

Done! Settings are automatically saved. You can always come back and check it ON if you prefer to see the preview in the dark mode.

3.9. Installing the Bookmark Extension

One useful extension that is quite helpful in navigating a document is the *bookmark extension*. With this extension installed, you can put one or more bookmarks at any place in your document and quickly reach that location within your document. I find this extension very useful to avoid a lot of back and forth while trying to look for figures and code examples that I included in my document earlier. Just click on the extensions button in the left pane as done for AsciiDoc and Code Spell Check extensions and search for `Bookmarks`. There are quite a few extensions that appear in the search results. The one that I use and recommend is written by *Alessandro Fragnani*. Locate this extension and press the `Install` button to install.

Once installed you can use the keyboard shortcut keys in Table 1 to create, remove and navigate to bookmarks.

Table 1. VS Code bookmarks extension keyboard shortcuts

Shortcut	Purpose
`CTRL` + `ALT` + `K`	To Add or Remove a Bookmark(Toggle)
`CTRL` + `ALT` + `J`	Jump to Next bookmark
`CTRL` + `ALT` + `L`	Jump to Previous bookmark
`SHIFT` + `ALT` + `L`	Select from current position to the next bookmark
`SHIFT` + `ALT` + `J`	Select from current position to the previous bookmark

Apart from the above you can also open the VS Code command pallette by pressing `CTRL` + `SHIFT` + `P` and type in `bookmarks:` to access many more more options. You can also click on the bookmark icon in the bottom left pane to reach or delete a bookmark as shown in Figure 41.

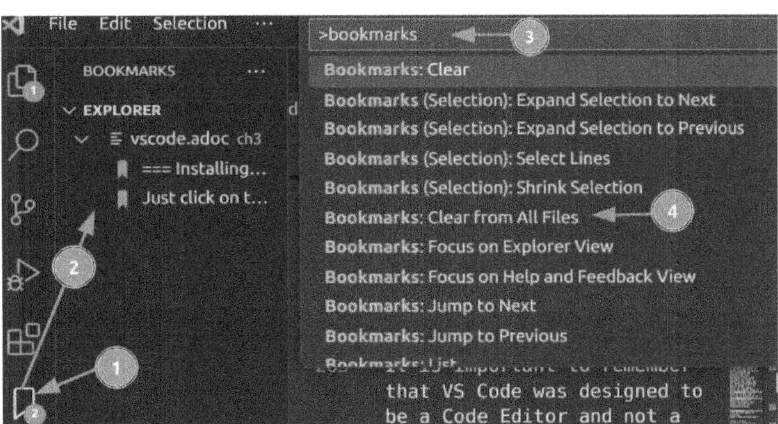

Figure 41. VS Code Bookmark options from the bookmark icon (callouts 1 and 2) and the command pallette (callouts 3 and 4)

For more VS Code keyboard and mouse shortcuts, please see Appendix E.

3.10. Activating GitHub Copilot in VS Code

If you are a copilot fan, you are in luck! One other great advantage of using VS Code is that you can activate GitHub Copilot — the AI-powered code completion tool. You can use it for free (with some limitations) if you have a GitHub account. Copilot is a great tool to help you write code and text faster and with fewer errors.

3.10.1. Install GitHub Copilot Extension

To install the GitHub Copilot extension in VS Code, follow these steps:

1. Open VS Code and go to the Extensions view by clicking on the Extensions icon in the left pane or by pressing `CTRL` + `SHIFT` + `X`.
2. Search for the "GitHub Copilot" extension by GitHub and install it by pressing *install*.
3. Sign in with your GitHub account when prompted.
4. Once enabled, you will see a Copilot icon on the top right corner of the VS Code window. Click on it to open the Copilot sidebar as shown in Figure 42. You can choose to copy suggestions or insert them directly into your document where the cursor is located.
5. Copilot will also start suggesting code or text completions as you type and you can press the `TAB` key to accept suggestions or press `ESC` key to ignore them.
6. You can also see the Copilot status in the status bar at the bottom of the window that tells you about monthly allowance usage and other useful data.

Copilot supports several models, including:

- Copilot for code (based on OpenAI Codex)
- Copilot Chat (powered by GPT, Claude Sonnet, Gemini).
- Copilot for Docs (for documentation and writing help)

You can use Copilot to improve your writing by getting real-time suggestions for sentences or paragraphs, rewriting or rephrasing text for clarity and generating summaries or expanding on ideas. Needless to say, you can also use it to generate code snippets, functions, classes and even entire programs.

It is important to note that the free account usage of GitHub copilot is currently restricted to *2,000 code completions and 50 chat messages per month*. To see details of your free account usage, click on the Copilot icon in the status bar at the bottom of the VS Code window.

To know more about Copilot, please see the official documentation [https://docs.github.com/en/copilot/getting-started-with-github-copilot].

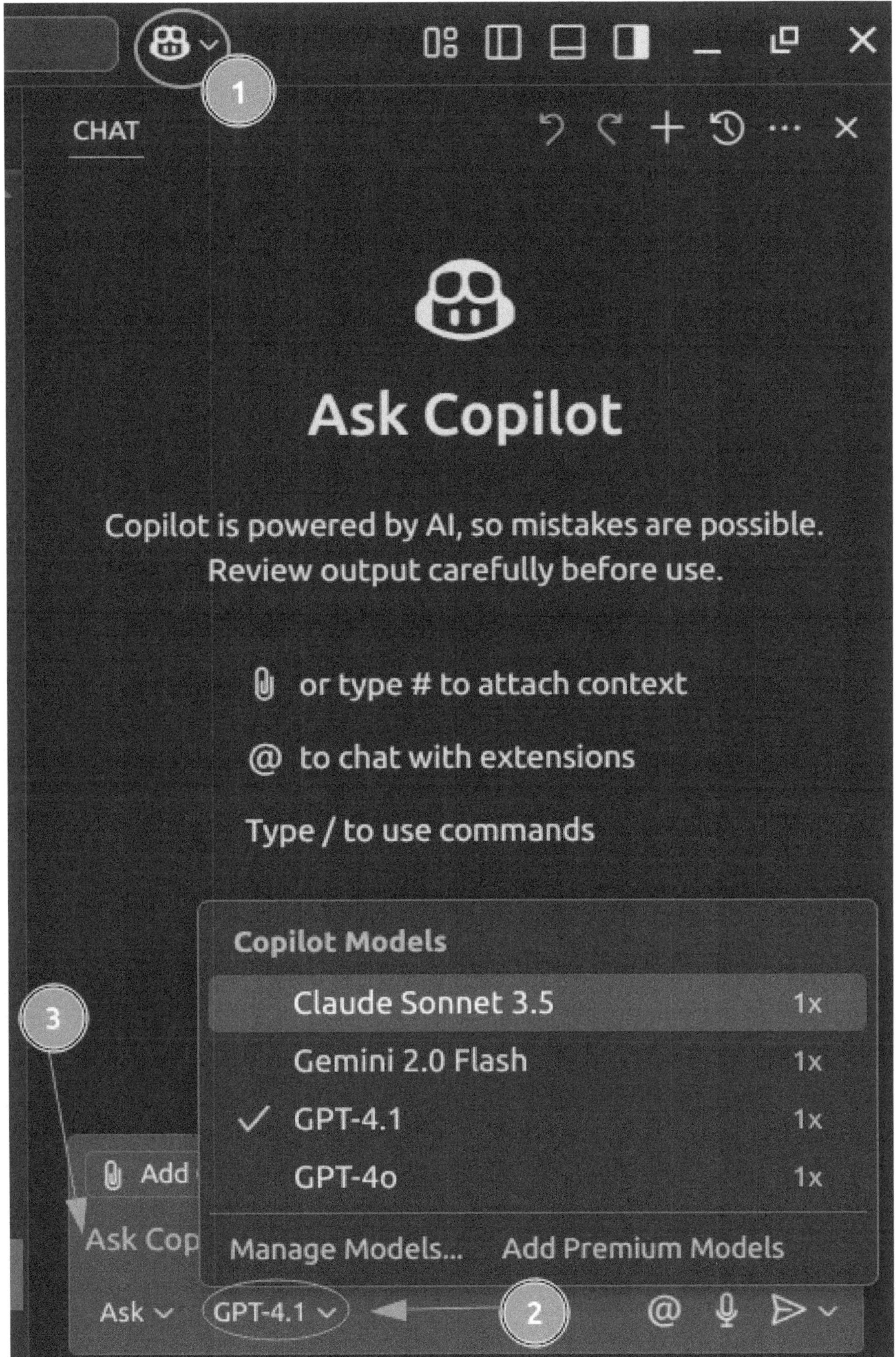

Figure 42. VS Code Copilot Sidebar (1) Click on the Copilot icon to open the sidebar (2) Open drop-down to choose the model and (3) Type in your query or prompt

Please always remember that Copilot is a tool to assist you in writing and it is not a replacement for your own creativity and judgment. It is always a good idea to *rigorously review* the suggestions made by Copilot or other AI assistants for language and factual accuracy before accepting them.

3.11. VS Code is Primarily a Code Editor

It is important to keep in mind that VS Code has been designed to be a code editor and not a word processor. When we are using it to create AsciiDoc documents, we are just rigging it up for document creation and it would be grossly unfair to expect it to behave like a word processor. The setup that I have described above is plenty to create any kind of document using AsciiDoc Markup. In fact once you get the hang of it, document creation in VS Code is so efficient and enjoyable that you will not miss a word processor at all !

3.12. Chapter Summary

Key learnings in this chapter are:

- In this chapter we have explored how to install and use VS Code for creating AsciiDoc documents.
- VS Code is open source & free and is by far, the leading code editor used by developers across the world.
- While you need just a plain text editor to create AsciiDoc documents, installing and creating AsciiDoc documents in VS Code offers many advantages that lead to significant savings in document creation time and prevent many errors.
- After installing VS Code, you can install the AsciiDoc extension which apart from other things, provides you a live preview which prevents you from generating AsciiDoc output via AsciiDoctor or AsciiDoctor-PDF frequently. Please see Section 3.3.1 for a quick recap.
- You can install the Code Spell Checker extension to check spellings as you type. Revisit section Section 3.3.2 for a quick recap.
- You can also install the Bookmarks extension to quickly navigate to any part of your current document or other documents. See Section 3.9 and Appendix E for more.
- VS Code also supports Copilot integration. You can install the GitHub Copilot extension to get AI-powered suggestions for writing code and text. See Section 3.10 for details.

Chapter 4. Essential AsciiDoc Markup Syntax

"Nouns and verbs hold the power but syntax casts the spell." ~ Janet Peery

---

In this chapter we will explore some core elements of the AsciiDoc markup language needed for everyday writing. Learning anything new takes time and patience. So the ideal approach to learning AsciiDoc is to start with simple markup inserts, see how AsciiDoctor and AsciiDoctor-PDF process them to render polished documents and then revert back and continue adding text and markup to your document. If you can't initially remember AsciiDoc Markup syntax, don't worry. This is completely normal. Nobody can remember everything. You will find that as you become more familiar, you can naturally and effortlessly recollect the required markup syntax. If you are transitioning from a word precessing software to AsciiDoc, be extra kind to yourself. It might take some time to adjust to this different way of creating documents. Give yourself that time. As you start creating text documents punctuated with AsciiDoc markup, you will find the process extremely enjoyable and efficient because you can effortlessly concentrate on creating content without distractions. This chapter is also meant to serve as a reference guide which you can revisit multiple times. Whenever you forget syntax or require to lookup something, visit this chapter, choose what you need from the list of topics and jump straight to it.

4.1. The AsciiDoc Document

While an AsciiDoc document can have just text punctuated with AsciiDoc Markup, typically an Asciidoc document has two parts — (a) the document *header* and (b) the document *body* where all the document text goes in. These two parts are separated by a blank line. The document starts with the header part which typically has the document title, followed by some ancillary information such as the author etc. and then some attributes chosen by the document creator that govern the styling of different elements within the document. Figure 43 shows these two parts in a sample document.

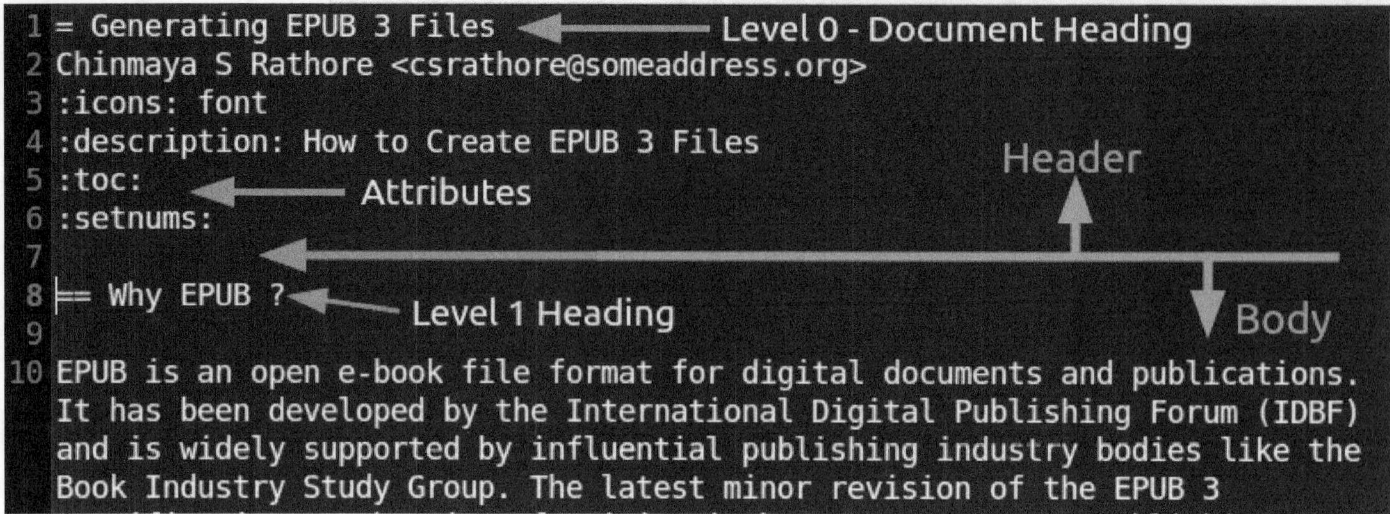

Figure 43. The Structure of an AsciiDoc Document

In Figure 43, the gray line (empty line 7) schematically shows the demarcation of a boundary (imaginary) between the header part and the body part. The header part starts with the Document title , followed by the name of the author. This is then followed by a sample set of attributes that each govern some type of document styling behavior when set of unset. This provides users immense control on how the document is finally rendered. We will talk about many such attributes later in this chapter. The header section ends with a blank line and then the document body starts with a document or chapter heading (in the figure above, a Level 1 chapter heading). Asciidoc files are typically created in plain text editors and saved with an *.adoc* extension.

All AsciiDoc Markup for text formatting that we will explore in the following sections is applied to the text in the body part of the document. As for the header part, it is *not* mandatory for you to include attributes in your document. You could just as well start a document with your text. However, more often than not, to harness the power of AsciiDoc, you will need to add attributes to the header section. I would also like to point out that it is not mandatory that attributes appear only in the header part of the document. They can appear in the body part as well but if you change the value of an attribute that was set earlier in the header, that attribute will then start working with the new value until that value is reset again. We will talk about this later.

4.2. Basic Text Formatting Markup

All you need to write AsciiDoc markup files is a simple text editor. Type or paste a couple of paragraphs of text in your text editor, save the file as *myfirst.adoc* (example file) and then run it through AsciiDoctor issuing the following command from a terminal:

Terminal Command

```
$ asciidoctor myfirst.adoc
```

and

```
$ asciidoctor-pdf myfirst.adoc
```

You will now see *myfirst.html* and *myfirst.pdf* appear in your folder. Click to open these files and see how AsciiDoctor processed them. Now start adding some markup presented in the following sections and keep repeating the above commands from time to time to see how that markup shows up in the processed document.

Note for VS Code Users

If you are using VS Code to write (which I highly recommend), you can see changes as you add markup instantly in the live preview window and you don't have to run the *AsciiDoctor command* repeatedly as mentioned above. If you wish to create a PDF from your AsciiDoc file, just press `CTRL` + `SHIFT` + `P` and in the command palette box, start typing the word—*asciidoc*. As you type, you will see the command palette box suggest some choices. Choose `AsciiDoc: Export Document as PDF` to generate a PDF document and / or choose `AsciiDoc: Save HTML Document` if you wish to generate an HTML document. You don't have leave the VS Code environment at all.

4.2.1. Paragraph Text, Bold, Italics

There is no special markup tag for creating a paragraph. Just start typing. Press `Enter` to start the next paragraph.

Most text editors *enter* and *exit* full screen when you press the `F11` key (toggle key to enter and exit full screen). This gives you a bigger screen area to type in if you prefer this arrangement.

For marking text in Bold, we need to enclose the text `between two * symbols`. For italics, we need to enclose text `between two _ (underscore)` symbols. We can also use a combination of these two symbols to create bold and italicized text. Example 6 shows how to add bold formatting to text. Example 7 shows how toitalicize text.

AsciiDoc Markup

Example 6. Bold Text

```
//Enclose text which has to appear bold between two * symbols.

*This text will appear in bold* while this will not.
```

Will be rendered as...

This text will appear in bold while this will not.

AsciiDoc Markup

Example 7. Italics, Bold and Italics

```
_This text will appear in italics_ while this will not.
*_This text will appear in bold and italics_* while this will not (we can combine
markup).
```

Will be rendered as...

This text will appear in italics while this will not.

This text will appear in bold and italics while this will not.

You can also make text appear bigger or smaller than normal default font size by prefixing a selection of text (`#text#`) with `[big]` and `[small]` as shown in Example 8.

AsciiDoc Markup

Example 8. Using the big and small styling elements

```
This is normal text size!

Beyond normal, you can set any selection to [big]#big text size# or otherwise you can
set it to [small]#small text size#. The opening and closing # marks indicates the
selection to which [big]#big# and [small]#small# apply  !
```

Will be rendered as...

This is normal text size!

Beyond normal, you can set any selection to big text size or otherwise you can set it to small text size. The opening and closing # marks indicates the selection to which big and small apply !

4.2.2. Monospaced Text

You can display any text as monospaced text by enclosing it between two `` (back tics). Mono spaced text can be combined with bold and or italics (HTML). This is useful to distinguish terminal commands or any other term that you wish to highlight in running text. A sample demonstrating all three variants is shown in Example 9.

AsciiDoc Markup

Example 9. AsciiDoc Markup for Monospaced Text

```
To start a python file in the vim editor type `vim helloWorld.py` in the terminal and
press enter. The vim editor is a `*highly configurable*` text editor that many find
quite confusing at first due to switching between `*_normal,insert and command line
modes_*`.
```

Will be rendered as...

To start a python file in the vim editor type `vim helloWorld.py` in the terminal and press enter. The vim editor is a **`highly configurable`** text editor that many find quite confusing at first due to switching between ***`normal,insert and command line modes`***.

4.2.3. Highlight Text

To highlight text, just enclose it within a pair of # symbols as shown in Example 10.

AsciiDoc Markup

Example 10. Highlighting Text

```
Enclose the text to be highlighted in color within two # symbols
#This text will appear highlighted# while this will not.
```

Will be rendered as...

This text will appear highlighted while this will not.

Although the default highlight color is yellow, we can change the highlight color for HTML output. The markup in Example 11 changes the highlight color to lime or green. Two other common highlighter colors are aqua (cyan) and fuchsia (magenta) which can be used in place of lime below. For a full list of highlighter color names that you can use, please visit this web page [https://interglacial.com/~sburke/stuff/16colors.html].

AsciiDoc Markup

Example 11. Highlight text color (visible in HTML output)

```
[.lime-background]#This text will appear highlighted in green# while this will not.
```

Will be rendered as...

This text will appear highlighted in green while this will not.

Visibility of Highlight Color

If you are reading this book in print or PDF, you will not be able to see the highlight color change as the PDF and print output does not support this feature. You can however see this in the HTML output of the book.

4.2.4. Underline Text

You can underline selected text using the markup sequence shown in Example 12.

AsciiDoc Markup

Example 12. Underline Text

```
Feeding wild animals while on the safari is [underline]#strictly prohibited#.
```

Will be rendered as…

Feeding wild animals while on the safari is strictly prohibited.

4.2.5. Strikethrough Text

Similarly you can also create strike-through text — text that displays as if it has been cancelled by a pen stroke — using the markup shown in Example 13.

AsciiDoc Markup

Example 13. Strikethrough Text

```
This theme has now been [line-through]#discontinued# depreciated.
```

Will be rendered as…

This theme has now been ~~discontinued~~ depreciated.

4.2.6. Change Text Color (HTML Only)

You can change text color if you want for some text in the document as shown in Example 14.

AsciiDoc Markup

Example 14. Change Text Color

```
[.red]#It's not a bug#. It's a feature! ①
```

① Words between two # marks will appear in red color

Will be rendered as…

It’s not a bug. It’s a feature!

The color name must be in small case and must be one of *these 16 named HTML colors* [https://interglacial.com/~sburke/stuff/16colors.html].

4.2.7. Embedding Markup in Running Text Without Interpretation

There are times when we wish to show some command or some sequence in running text which if left unconstrained, will end up being interpreted as AsciiDoc. To prevent that from happening, we can fence that bit of text inside `` `+Some Text+` `` as demonstrated in Example 15.

AsciiDoc Markup

Example 15. Embedding markup that will not be interpreted by AsciiDoctor

```
In AsciiDoc markup `+*this will not be printed in bold*+` ①
because we have made sure that it will not be interpreted
by enclosing it within a back tick and a plus sign while in the same sentence,
we can see that *this will appear in bold*.
```

① Words between the ` and + symbols (back tick and plus) will not be interpreted as markup. It will be printed as literal text.

Will be rendered as...

In AsciiDoc markup `*this will not be printed in bold*` because we have made sure that it will not be interpreted by enclosing it within a back tick and a plus sign while in the same sentence,we can see that **this will appear in bold**.

The above is particularly useful if you wish to show AsciiDoc markup code in running text.

4.2.8. Forcing a Line Break

Sometimes you might require text to break at a particular point. Just breaking the paragraph by pressing `enter` will not insert a line break in the rendered text. To do this, you need to press `enter` at that point to move text to the next line and then add a + symbol between the two lines. Let's see this with an example. Say we have the following quote from Mark Twain which under normal circumstances would appears as shown below:

```
In the first place, God made idiots. That was for practice. Then he made school boards.
```

In the above text, if we wanted to bring the sentence — *Then he made school boards* — on the next line without breaking the paragraph, we can add a + sign between the two lines as shown in Example 16.

AsciiDoc Markup

Example 16. Introducing a Line Break

```
In the first place, God made idiots. That was for practice. +
Then he made school boards.
```

Will be rendered as...

In the first place, God made idiots. That was for practice.
Then he made school boards.

4.2.9. Aligning Text

By default, text is left aligned. If you wish to center align a block of text, add the styling markup shown in Example 17 on top of the text block.

AsciiDoc Markup

Example 17. Center Align Text

```
[.text-center]
In the first place, God made idiots. That was for practice. +
Then he made school boards
```

Will be rendered as...

In the first place, God made idiots. That was for practice.
Then he made school boards.

If you wish to align a block of text to the right, use the styling syntax shown in Example 18.

AsciiDoc Markup

Example 18. Right Align Text

```
[.text-right]
In the first place, God made idiots. That was for practice. +
Then he made school boards
```

Will be rendered as...

> In the first place, God made idiots. That was for practice.
> Then he made school boards.

4.2.10. Unordered and Ordered Lists

4.2.10.1. Unordered Lists

To create an unordered or bullet list, use * (single star symbol) followed *by space* and then followed by text. For more levels (multi-level list), indent from the containing or top level list and use ** (two star symbols) for list items at level 2 and *** (three star symbols) for list items at level 3. Make sure to leave a space after * i.e. * and the text in front of it must be separated by a space. This is shown in Example 19.

AsciiDoc Markup

Example 19. Unnumbered Lists

```
* Climate Change
* Biodiversity Loss
* Deforestation
    ** Forest Fires
    ** Agriculture
         *** Slash and Burn
    ** Logging
* Pollution
```

Will be rendered as...

- Climate Change
- Biodiversity Loss
- Deforestation
    - Forest Fires
    - Agriculture
        - Slash and Burn
    - Logging
- Pollution

4.2.10.2. Ordered or Numbered Lists

To create an ordered list item, use . (period) followed by space followed by list item text. For more levels, indent from the containing list level and use .. (Level 2) ... (Level 3). Make sure to leave a space after . i.e. the . and the text in front of it must be separated by a space. Example 20 shows how to create a multi-level ordered list.

AsciiDoc Markup

Example 20. Creating a Numbered List

```
. Download and Install Python
. Setup and IDE
    .. Many IDEs to choose from
    .. Many Open Source Projects
        ... VS Code
        ... VS Codium
        ... Jupyter Lab
 . Start Writing Code
```

Will be rendered as...

1. Download and Install Python
2. Setup an IDE
    a. Many IDEs to choose from
    b. Many Open Source Projects
        i. VS Code
        ii. VSCodium
        iii. Jupyter Lab
3. Start Writing Code

If a list item has non-contiguous text (and/or image), put a + sign on separate lines to connect the disjointed parts. They will then be treated as one bullet point.

4.2.11. Creating Checklists

Checklists can be created easily using the markup demonstrated in Example 21.

AsciiDoc Markup

Example 21. Creating Checklists

```
* [*] Install AsciiDoctor ①
* [ ] Write Markup
* [ ] Process Markup
```

① The * inside the brackets like [*] makes that item checked

Will be rendered as...

- [x] Install AsciiDoctor
- [ ] Write Markup
- [ ] Process Markup

4.2.12. Superscript and Subscript

You can add super and sub scripts in running text using the following AsciiDoc markup tags:

4.2.12.1. Superscript

Use enclose the text to be displayed as superscript by enclosing it within two *caret* symbols (^) as shown in Example 22.

AsciiDoc Markup

Example 22. Use ^ for Superscript

```
The name of the organization is *W^3^ Schools*
```

Will be rendered as...

The name of the organization is **W^{3} Schools**

4.2.12.2. Subscript

Use a pair of tilde symbols ~ to display text as subscript as demonstrated in Example 23.

AsciiDoc Markup

Example 23. Use ~ for Subscript

```
The rise in the amount of CO~2~ in the atmosphere is phenomenal.
```

Will be rendered as...

The rise in the amount of CO_2 in the atmosphere is phenomenal.

4.2.13. The Em Dash

The Em dash is very frequently required in English writing. Use -- (two consecutive dashes) to create an Em dash in your running text. Make sure there is a blank space before and after the pair of dashes as shown in Example 24.

AsciiDoc Markup

Example 24. Use -- for Em Dash

```
"I'm reading a book on anti-gravity -- it's impossible to put down."
```

Will be rendered as...

"I'm reading a book on anti-gravity — it's impossible to put down."

4.2.14. Inserting Blank or Empty Lines in Text

Many times we need to insert blank lines in text. Pressing `enter` to insert blank lines in your AsciiDoc file does not help as AsciiDoctor ignores such blank lines in the document (not treated as hard line breaks when HTML is rendered by AsciiDoctor). However you can easily insert blank lines by using the `{empty}` + substitution markup shown in Example 25.

AsciiDoc Markup

Example 25. Inserting Empty Lines

```
This is my first line
{empty} +
{empty} +
This is my second line
```

Will be rendered as...

This is my first line

This is my second line

4.3.Table of Contents

You can automatically add a Table of Contents or TOC to your document just by adding the following attribute in the header section of your AsciiDoc document:

AsciiDoc Markup

```
:toc:
```

Yes that's it! Figure 44 shows a well formatted 'Table of Contents' (pointed by the arrow) appear in the text as a result of adding just the `:toc:` attribute to the document header.

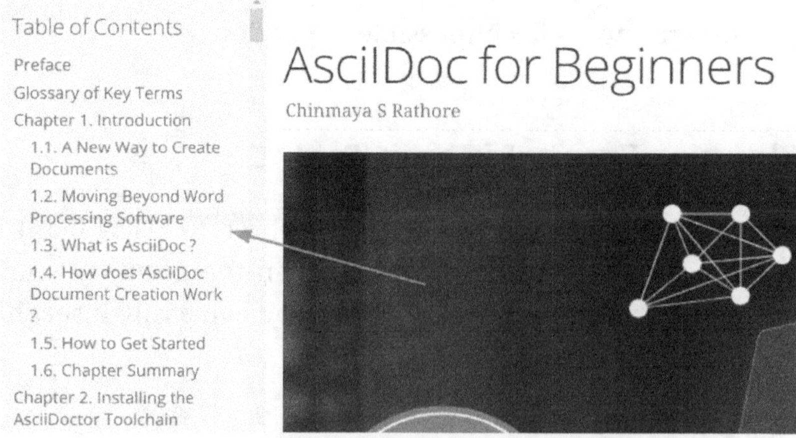

Figure 44. A well formatted TOC added to the document using the toc attribute

You can position this TOC in the left (default) or right pane on your browser page (HTML) by using the following values to the `:toc:` attribute:

AsciiDoc Markup

```
:toc: left  (default)
OR
:toc: right
```

How deep you want the TOC to be can be controlled by the following attribute:

AsciiDoc Markup

```
:toclevels: <number>
```

So say you want the TOC to reflect up to 3 levels of headings, you can declare the `:toclevels:` attribute as:

AsciiDoc Markup

```
:toclevels: 3
```

We will discuss precise placement of TOC within your document when we cover *include statements* in Chapter 17.

4.4. Section Numbers

You can introduce section numbers in your document text for various heading levels by adding the following attribute:

AsciiDoc Markup

```
:sectnums:
```

You will now start seeing various heading levels in your document numbered as shown in Figure 45.

Chapter 2. Installing the AsciiDoctor Toolchain

"For many people my software is something that you install and forget. I like to keep it that way."~ Wietse Venema

In this chapter, we will see different ways in which we can install AsciiDoctor on Linux, Windows and Mac computers. Installation is simple and you can get started in no time ! You can jump directly to the section for your operating system. I do urge you though to please read the section on Docker / Podman install.

Emanating from our discussion in Chapter 1, there are two key software packages that we need to install to start using AsciiDoc. These are : (a) AsciiDoctor for HTML output and (b) AsciiDoctor-PDF for PDF output. Some other AsciiDoctor tools are needed if there are special requirements but we will talk about them later. Luckily, AsciiDoctor tools are available for all major Operating Systems and in this chapter we will see how we can install them.

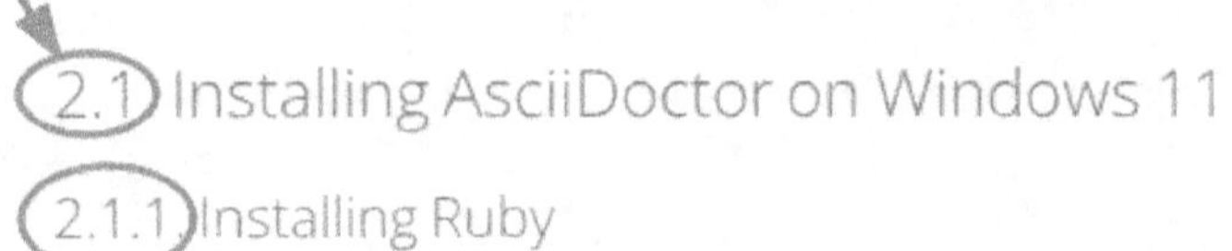

Figure 45. Displaying section numbers using the sectnum attribute

To control the depth of numbering, you can use the following attribute in the header:

AsciiDoc Markup

```
:sectnumlevels: <number>
```

So for example, if you want to have section numbers up to the third hierarchical level, you can assign a value of 3 to the `:sectnumlevels:` attribute as shown below:

AsciiDoc Markup

```
:sectnumlevels: 3
```

4.5. Links

It is common these days to include links to online resources in your documents. Let's see how we can create external and internal links or *hyperlinks*.

4.5.1. External Links

You can create external links in AsciiDoc just by pasting your link in running text. Alternatively, if you wish to *mask* the link itself and show a linked piece of text, you can do that quite easily by placing the link next to the text to be hyperlinked and enclosing the text to be linked inside square brackets.

You can see both these types of external links in Example 26.

AsciiDoc Markup

Example 26. Insert URLs

```
https://www.ipcc.ch/
or
https://www.ipcc.ch/[Intergovernmental Panel on Climate Change]     ①
```

① The link text between [] cannot contain a ',' or an '=' sign. If the text has these, enclose the text in "" quotation marks like ["Intergovernmental Panel on Climate Change,IPCC"].

Will be rendered as...

https://www.ipcc.ch/

Intergovernmental Panel on Climate Change [https://www.ipcc.ch/]

4.5.1.1. Open External Links in a Blank Window

If you wish to open external links in a new browser tab, you can add the ^ (caret symbol) at the end of the link text as shown in Example 27.

AsciiDoc Markup

Example 27. Opening a link in a new browser tab

```
This link to https://www.ipcc.ch/[Intergovernmental Panel on Climate Change^] ①
when clicked, will open in a new tab in your browser.
```

① Adding a ^ symbol in the link text opens the link in a new browser tab.

Will be rendered as...

This link to Intergovernmental Panel on Climate Change [https://www.ipcc.ch/] when clicked, will open in a new tab in your browser.

4.5.2. Internal Links

Like external links, you can also create internal links to any section or place in the document. This is done in two parts — (1) mark a place in the document by creating a unique id and (2) create a link using angled brackets to jump to this point or id from any place in the document. Let's see the markup to do this using some sample text taken from Wikipedia in Example 28.

Example 28. Cross References or Internal Links

```
Wildfires [[wild_fires]] ①
A wildfire, forest fire, or a bush fire is an unplanned, uncontrolled and
unpredictable fire in an area of combustible vegetation. Depending on the type of
vegetation present, a wildfire may be more specifically identified as a bush fire (in
Australia), desert fire, grass fire, hill fire, peat fire, prairie fire, vegetation
fire, or veld fire.

Forest clearance for agriculture is a primary cause of forest fires. The effects of
climate change are another cause via the increased risk of  <<wild_fires,wild
fires>>. ②

_Text Source: Wildfire,Wikipedia_
```

① Creation of an unique ID at a location in the document. You can put such an ID anywhere in the document even inline at any point in the running text.

② Creating an internal link to reach ID created in 1 using two angled brackets. In the markup <<wild_fires,wild fires>>. The first part (before the comma) is the id while the second part after the comma is the text that will appear as a linked text on the page. You can use this multiple times in a document.

Will be rendered as...

Wildfires

A wildfire, forest fire, or a bush fire is an unplanned, uncontrolled and unpredictable fire in an area of combustible vegetation.Depending on the type of vegetation present, a wildfire may be more specifically identified as a bush fire (in Australia), desert fire, grass fire, hill fire, peat fire, prairie fire, vegetation fire, or veld fire.

Forest clearance for agriculture is a primary cause of forest fires. The effects of climate change are another cause via the increased risk of wild fires.

Text Source: Wildfires, Wikipedia

So when you click on the wild fires link above (HTML and PDF viewed on-screen), you will be taken to the wild_fires id location (positioned on top of the screen). Pressing the back button on your browser will take you back to the place in the document from where you clicked the link. You can create a unique ID for sections , examples , code blocks, figures etc. and refer to them from anywhere.

4.5.3. Mail-to Links (for HTML and PDF)

We can also create `mailto:` links which when clicked, open up the default mail program on your computer with a preset receiver address. The markup to do this is as follows:

```
Write to mailto:yoda@dagobah.universe[Yoda] if you are stuck!
```

Will be rendered as…

Write to Yoda [mailto:yoda@dagobah.universe] if you are stuck!

4.6. Quotes

Very frequently we need to include quotes in our documents. AsciiDoc provides a simple way to do this. You can create a beautiful quotation block using the markup shown in Example 29.

AsciiDoc Markup

Example 29. AsciiDoc markup to create a quotation

```
[quote,Terry Pratchett, Wyrd Sisters]
This book was written using 100% recycled words.
```

Will be rendered as…

> "This book was written using 100% recycled words."
>
> — Terry Pratchett, Wyrd Sisters

Please note that there should <u>*not*</u> be a blank line between the *quote statement inside the square brackets* and the quote text itself as can be seen in Example 29.

4.7. Admonitions

Admonitions are like alerts that can be used to draw the attention of the reader to something that needs to be specially highlighted. AsciiDoc provides five admonitions that cover a common range of scenarios. To create an admonition, use one of the five admonition keywords which must be in *upper case* immediately followed by a colon, then a space and then the text that you would like to share in that admonition. Each admonition serves a purpose so be sure to use the right one befitting the requirement. An example of the markup for each admonition is shown in Example 30.

AsciiDoc Markup

Example 30. Admonition Markup

```
WARNING: Never put a metal pot inside a microwave oven.

TIP: In Linux, you can use the CTRL+ALT+T keyboard shortcut to open a terminal!

NOTE: The North Atlantic right whale is one of the world's most endangered large
whale species. Two other species of right whales exist: the North Pacific right whale
and the Southern right whale.

CAUTION: You should never open links or QR Codes sent to you from unknown sources.

IMPORTANT: Please ensure that you keep your OS updated with the latest patches and
fixes.
```

Will be rendered as...

Never put a metal pot inside a microwave oven.

In Linux, you can use the CTRL+ALT+T keyboard shortcut to open a terminal window !

The North Atlantic right whale is one of the world's most endangered large whale species. Two other species of right whales exist: the North Pacific right whale and the Southern right whale.

You should never open links or QR Codes sent to you from unknown sources.

Please ensure that you keep your OS updated with the latest patches and fixes.

4.7.1. Admonition Icons

The icons that you see on the left side of these admonitions appear because of the inclusion of the `:icons: font` attribute in the header of the document. If you do not include the `:icons:font` attribute, you will see these labeled with words like *WARNING*, *TIP*, *NOTE*, *CAUTION* and *IMPORTANT*.

4.8. Images

4.8.1. Inline Images

You can easily insert inline images (an image in running text) in your document using AsciiDoc Markup. Example 31 shows how to insert an inline image .

AsciiDoc Markup

Example 31. Inserting an inline image in running text

```
I just image:heart.png[] creating documents with AsciiDoc!
```

Will be rendered as...

I just ♥ creating documents with AsciiDoc!

4.8.2. Inserting Block Images

Block images are images that are not in-line with the text. They appear as a separate block in the document. These are regular larger sized images that usually appear as figures or exhibits in the running text. In this book, all the figures that you have come across so far have been inserted as block images. One of the great things about block images is that they are automatically numbered in sequence by AsciiDoctor if they have a title. AsciiDoc block images provide a core functionality in document creation and are therefore one of the most important elements in creating visually appealing and engaging documents.

We can insert a block image by using the `image::` macro that can not only insert images but can also alter their size and position them on either side of the page. Example 32 shows how to insert a full sized block image in the document.

AsciiDoc Markup

Example 32. Inserting a regular image in the document

```
image::iceberg.jpg[A Melting Iceberg]
```

Will be rendered as...

Notice that the image macro in Example 32 has double colons (`image::`) and is ending with the text — `[A Melting Iceberg]` inside square brackets (text is not mandatory). At first sight, this might appear like a caption. However, this text is not a caption but what is known as 'Alt Text'. This text does not show up when the document is rendered. However, in case someone who is visually impaired uses a screen reader to read this page, this 'Alt Text' would inform them what the picture is about. The presence of 'Alt Text' therefore makes documents more accessible.

4.8.3. Altering the Width and Height of Images

You can also change the width and height of images using the `width=` and `height=` attributes extending the image macro as shown in Example 33.

AsciiDoc Markup

Example 33. Altering the Width and Height of Images

```
.Melting Iceberg picture with altered width and height
image::iceberg.jpg[A Melting Iceberg, width=250, height=166]
```

Will be rendered as...

The markup shown in Example 33 can also be abbreviated as shown in Example 34. This is useful when you want to quickly change the width and height of an image without having to type the full markup as shown in Example 33. If you want to show the image in its original size, you can use: `image::iceberg.jpg[]` with nothing inside the square brackets.

AsciiDoc Markup

Example 34. Altering the width and height of images (Abbreviated)

```
image::iceberg.jpg[A Melting Iceberg,300,200]
```

The Alt text i.e. the text — A Melting Iceberg — placed before the first comma is optional and if you wish, you can directly use the width and height values like `image::iceberg.jpg[300,200]` to alter the display size of the image. However as explained earlier, it is a good practice to include Alt text.

> *Image Dimensions and Scaling*
>
> The width and height attributes seen in Example 34 are second and third positional attributes qualifying the image macro. The values assigned to width and height must be *integers* without units. The AsciiDoctor documentation also mentions that the default AsciiDoctor style sheet implements *responsive images* which means that if the size of the image is bigger than the content area, it is automatically scaled down to fit the content area preserving the original aspect ratio of the image.

4.8.4. Numbering Images or Figures

If you wanted to give a caption or title and have an automatic figure number for an inserted image that will keep incrementing when more images are added, insert a line just above the image statement starting with a '.' and then immediately follow it up — without any space, with the title text. This is shown in Example 35 and the rendered result of this markup can be seen in Figure 46.

AsciiDoc Markup

Example 35. Adding a Caption and Automatic Numbering to Figures

```
.A Melting Iceberg
image::iceberg.jpg[A Melting Iceberg]
```

Will be rendered as...

Figure 46. A Melting Iceberg

4.8.5. Creating a Border around images in HTML Output

If you want to have a border around your images when you render your AsciiDoc file as HTML (this does not work for PDF output), you can do this via a little hack without adding additional styling as shown in Example 36.

AsciiDoc Markup

Example 36. Creating a Border around Images

```
.A Melting Iceberg
[.thumb]
image::images/iceberg.jpg[A Melting Iceberg]
```

By putting `[.thumb]` (for thumbnail which really does not create a thumbnail!) directly above the image macro as shown in Example 36, your image will show a light gray border as seen in Figure 47.

Figure 47. Image with a border created using 'thumb' styling

Please note that the above `[.thumb]` tag *does not* create a border when you render your AsciiDoc file to PDF. To create similar borders around images in PDF output, please see Chapter 15 in which we discuss how to extend default CSS styling for AsciiDoctor-PDF.

4.8.6. Positioning Images on the Page in HTML Output

It is possible to float or position images to the left or right of the page by adding a positioning *role* to the image macro. When we do this, text automatically wraps around the image leaving an appropriate gap between the text and the image. Both inline and block images can be positioned. Let's first see the result and then we can examine the markup that created it. Figure 48 shows a section of a rendered document where two images float to the right with text neatly wrapping around them to the left.

Planet in Peril

The planet is currently experiencing substantial difficulties due to climate change. Specifically, the rapid removal of forests through logging or forest fires is occurring at an alarming rate.

Figure 1. Deforestation

Deforestation not only ravages the environment but also has a profound impact on the delicate balance of our ecosystem. The consequences of widespread forest clearance are far-reaching.

The devastating impact of forest fires on global climate is not only due to release of carbon in the atmosphere as a result of burning, it is also due to decreased sequestration of atmospheric carbon dioxide due to loss of standing biomass.

Figure 2. Forest fires

Uncontrolled forest fires are a significant contributor to deforestation, causing widespread destruction and loss of biodiversity. These fires not only consume trees and vegetation but also have a devastating impact on the soil, water, and air quality.

Image source: pixabay.com

Figure 48. Text wrapping around images floated to the right

The above result has been achieved through the AsciiDoc markup shown in Example 37.

Example 37. Images floated right with text warped around them

```
== Planet in Peril

The planet is currently experiencing substantial difficulties due to climate change.
Specifically, the rapid removal of forests through logging or forest fires is
occurring at an alarming rate.

.Deforestation
image::deforestation.jpg[200,200,role=right]    ①

Deforestation not only ravages the environment but also has a profound impact on the
delicate balance of our ecosystem. The consequences of widespread forest clearance
are far-reaching.
```

```
The devastating impact of forest fires on global climate is not only due to release
of carbon in the atmosphere as a result of burning, it is also due to decreased
sequestration of atmospheric carbon dioxide due to loss of standing biomass.

.Forest fires
image::forest-fire1.jpg[200,200,role=right]    ②

Uncontrolled forest fires are a significant contributor to deforestation, causing
widespread destruction and loss of biodiversity. These fires not only consume trees
and vegetation but also have a devastating impact on the soil, water, and air
quality.
```

① The first image is floated right using *role=right* (you can also use float="right" but using role=right is recommended for HTML)

② The second image again floated right using *role=right*. Notice we are also simultaneously manipulating the width and height of the image

You can also float an image *left* by simply using `role=left` in place of right. Figure 49 shows the second image floated left and text automatically wrapping around it to the right.

Planet in Peril

The planet is currently experiencing substantial difficulties due to climate change. Specifically, the rapid removal of forests through logging or forest fires is occurring at an alarming rate.

Figure 1. Deforestation

Deforestation not only ravages the environment but also has a profound impact on the delicate balance of our ecosystem. The consequences of widespread forest clearance are far-reaching.

Figure 2. Forest fires

Uncontrolled forest fires are a significant contributor to deforestation, causing widespread destruction and loss of biodiversity. These fires not only consume trees and vegetation but also have a devastating impact on the soil, water, and air quality.

Image source: pixabay.com

Figure 49. Images floated right and left

There may arise a situation when images appearing one after the other in the document do not align exactly on the right or left margin. This may be because the size of the image block above overlaps the image below it. Resolve this by adding some text between them.

If you want a light gray boundary around your image, just extend the *role* attribute in Example 37 as follows (border can be seen in Figure 50):

```
role=thumb right
```

4.8.6.1. Aligning the Image Within the Image Block

You may, at sometime, encounter a potentially frustrating situation while *floating* images. The floated image that is being displayed is actually an *image block* and not just the image. The image block includes the image and the caption. If for example, the caption exceeds the width of the image, the block will become larger and then you may have to align the image *within* the block using the *align* attribute. Let's understand this with an example. In Example 38, the only change that I have made in the markup of Example 37 is a longer caption for the image. The result of this change can be seen in Figure 50 with the image block visible in gray boundary (callout 1) and the image getting aligned by default to the left edge of the block (callout 2).

Example 38. Demonstrating an image block

```
.Deforestation is a global problem
image::deforestation.jpg[200,200, role=thumb right]
```

Will be rendered as...

Figure 50. Image block displayed by the gray border (1) and the image left aligned within the block (2)

To deal with this, just add the *align* attribute to the image macro and assign it one of the following three alignment options: *left, center or right*. This is shown in Example 39 and the result of adding the *align* attribute can be seen in Figure 51.

Example 39. Demonstrating an image block

```
.Deforestation is a global problem
image::deforestation.jpg[200,200, role=thumb right, align=right]
```

Will be rendered as...

Figure 51. Image right aligned inside the image block

Images can also be grouped. You can refer to the AsciiDoctor documentation [https://docs.asciidoctor.org/asciidoc/latest/macros/image-position/] on how to group images and for more options on positioning images and text.

4.8.7. Positioning Images in PDF Output

While the discussion in Section 4.8.6 largely centers around HTML output, images can also be similarly *floated* in PDF output by using `float=right` (or left) in place of `role=right` as was demonstrated in Example 37. However the float image support as per AsciiDoctor-PDF documentation is *basic* with text wrapping on the opposite site of the floated image. In practice, results may vary and some degree of experimentation might be required to position your image as desired. Altering the size of the image and keeping your captions small can be helpful to get an acceptable float.

4.8.8. Hyperlinking your Image in HTML Output

If you need to hyperlink an image i.e. clicking on the image opens a link, you need to extend the image macro with the `link="URL"` attribute as shown in Example 40. When rendered to HTML or PDF, the hyperlinked image displays as shown in Figure 52.

Example 40. Hyperlinking an Image

```
image::albedo.png[Albedo,300,300,link="https://mynasadata.larc.nasa.gov/mini-
lessonactivity/what-albedo"]
```

Will be rendered as...

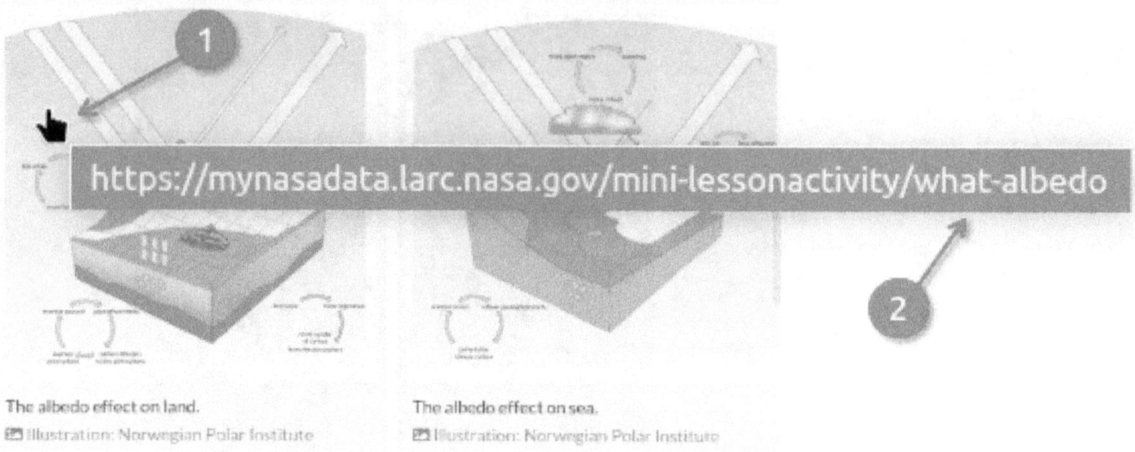

Figure 52. Hyperlinked image which shows (1) a hand-finger cursor icon on mouseover (2) which points to an external URL — (Image source: Norwegian Polar Institute)

Hyperlinked images are operational in both HTML and PDF outputs for on-screen viewing but are obviously not relevant if the PDF is printed in hard copy.

4.8.9. Organizing and Placing Images in a Separate Folder

If you are working on a big project, it might be best to put all images inside an image folder. You can then prefix the folder name in front of the image file name like *images/tree.png* indicating that relative to the document in which the image reference is being made, the image resides inside a folder called *images*. This way the project folder or directory will be more organized and less cluttered. However, you would have to prefix 'images/' to every image that you include in your document which can be somewhat annoying and potentially error prone. To overcome this, all you have to do is to declare the relative path of your image directory only once in the header of the document and then just use the image name subsequently. To declare your image directory using a relative path — the folder where your AsciiDoc markup files are located, use the +`:imagesdir:` + attribute and point it to the images folder as shown in Example 41.

AsciiDoc Markup

Example 41. The imagesdir attribute

```
:imagesdir: images
```

The above attribute assignment is stating that the images that are included in the document are located in a folder called *images* which is inside my current folder (if say *mybook* is your current folder, *images* is a folder inside *mybook*). Note that in Example 41, there is a *blank space* between the attribute and the folder name. You can also provide a full path, if required, to your image directory as shown in Example 42. This approach of providing an absolute path however, is not advisable if you plan to render your document as HTML which will be shared online via a webserver. Using the relative path is the better option.

AsciiDoc Markup

Example 42. The imagesdir attribute

```
:imagesdir: /home/csr/Documents/mybook/images/
```

Subsequent to this *imagesdir* declaration in the header of the document, you can just provide the image name as we were doing in the earlier examples and the image will be automatically picked up from the images folder by AsciiDoctor while rendering the document.

4.9. Chapter Summary

Key learnings in this chapter are:

We have learnt about the most commonly used AsciiDoc markup while creating documents. We have covered a lot of ground in this chapter and you can quickly review markup for some most frequently required text styling operations using the links below:

- Bold, Italics text — (Section 4.2.1)
- Display monospaced text — (Section 4.2.2)

- Highlight Text — (Section 4.2.3)
- Underline Text — (Section 4.2.4)
- Strikethrough Text — (Section 4.2.5)
- Change Text Color — (Section 4.2.6)
- Force a Line Break — (Section 4.2.8)
- Embedding Markup in Text — (Section 4.2.7)
- Unordered List — (Section 4.2.10.1)
- Create an Numbered List — (Section 4.2.10.2)
- Create a Checklist — (Section 4.2.11)
- Superscript and Subscript — (Section 4.2.12)
- Quotations — (Section 4.6)
- Admonitions — (Section 4.7)
- Insert Inline Images — (Section 4.8.1)
- Insert Block Images — (Section 4.8.2)
- Float Images to Right or Left — (Section 4.8.6)
- Hyperlinking Images — (Section 4.8.8)
- Putting Images in a Separate Folder — (Section 4.8.9)

4.10. Try it Yourself

1. Using *adsyntax.adoc* from the exercises folder for this chapter, follow the topics cited in the *Chapter Summary* and insert AsciiDoc syntax as mentioned in the comments inside the *adsyntax.adoc* file.
2. Try putting all the images in an image folder as demonstrated in Section 4.8.9 and use the `:imagesdir:` attribute in the header to declare the images folder. Can you see the images in your HTML output without specifying the path of the image in the AsciiDoc file?
3. Download one image each on deforestation and forest fires, insert them as indicated in *impos.adoc* file which is available in the exercise folder of this chapter and position them as shown in Section 4.8.6. You can get these images form https://pixabay.com/ or https://unsplash.com/.
4. Hyperlink any image as demonstrated in Section 4.8.8.

Chapter 5. Substitutions and Footnotes

"I plan someday to write a scholarly article consisting of a single sentence and a twenty-page footnote."
~ Jeffrey L. Staley

In this chapter we will explore how we can define custom attributes for links, text, icons and images that we need to use multiple times in our text. Using such custom attributes, we need not type reusable content again and again in our text. We can just insert the attribute to paste its value wherever required. This is called substitution. We will also explore how to create and use footnotes in AsciiDoc.

5.1. Substitutions

5.1.1. User Defined

If you use a piece of text or say a link very often in your text, AsciiDoc permits you to assign that text or link to a *user defined attribute*. This can also be, for the sake of understanding, visualized as a user defined *variable* of sorts. I use an example to illustrate this. Let's say I am writing a report on climate change and I need to frequently refer to some pages on the IPCC website in my report. So rather than type the IPCC landing page link `https://www.ipcc.ch` every time, I assign it to an attribute — say *IPCC* — and add it in the header of the document as shown in Example 43.

AsciiDoc Markup

Example 43. Defining the Attribute

```
:ipcc: https://www.ipcc.ch
```

Note that we are free to choose any name for the attribute except for names reserved by AsciiDoctor for system defined attributes. The attribute name must be flanked in the beginning and end by ':' (colons) followed by a space and then the text, emoji or link URL etc. as shown above in Example 43.

Once this attribute has been defined in the header, whenever you need to use that URL, put the attribute inside a pair of braces at that place in the document. In our example, to display the URL of the IPCC website, we will use `{ipcc}` rather than type the URL. AsciiDoctor, while rendering this document, replaces `{ipcc}` with its set value which in this case is https://www.ipcc.ch . This is how *substitution* works.

Example 44 shows a sample paragraph where I have used the `:ipcc:` attribute multiple times. In this example you will also notice that I have used the base link and then extended it to refer to another page on this site.

AsciiDoc Markup

Example 44. Using User Defined Attribute for Substituting a Value

```
Please refer to the IPCC website -- {ipcc} for current and authentic information on
various climate change issues. You can have a look at recent reports at the IPCC
reports page -- {ipcc}/reports. You can also see recent activities of the IPCC at
{ipcc}/activities.
```

Will be rendered as…

Please refer to the IPCC website — https://www.ipcc.ch for current and authentic information on various climate change issues. You can have a look at recent reports at the IPCC reports page — https://www.ipcc.ch/reports. You can also see recent activities of the IPCC at https://www.ipcc.ch/activities.

5.1.2. Substituting Icons and Images

Substitutions, as described above, also work for icons and images. For example, if we were creating a document on sustainable living and wanted to provide some tips on promoting a sustainable lifestyle at various places within the document, we could repeat an icon with a title whenever we wanted to add a sustainability tip. We can do this easily by adding in the document header, a user defined attribute called `:leaf:` and set its value to the leaf icon and a custom title as shown in Example 45.

AsciiDoc Markup

Example 45. A User Defined Attribute with an Icon

```
// Define the following attribute in the document header

:leaf: icon:leaf[] Sustainability Tip   ①
```

① After assigning the attribute in the header, just type `{leaf}` anywhere in the document to insert the leaf icon and the title.

Once our user defined attribute has been declared in the AsciiDoc document header, whenever we want to provide a sustainability tip in our text, instead of typing markup for the leaf icon and the title text, we can just insert the title via the attribute `{leaf}` followed by some tip text as shown in Example 46.

AsciiDoc Markup

Example 46. Inserting the Sustainability tip title via a user defined attribute

```
Sustainable living helps protect the planet by ensuring that we meet our present
needs without compromising the ability of future generations to meet their own.

{leaf}

_Use reusable bags for shopping and opt for wax paper or reusable sandwich bags
instead of plastic bags_.

By practicing sustainable living, communities can improve environmental quality,
reduce their carbon footprint, and decrease air pollution, which is essential for a
healthy community

{leaf}

_Shopping locally helps lower carbon emissions from transporting foods and supports
the local community_.
```

Will be rendered as...

Sustainable living helps protect the planet by ensuring that we meet our present needs without compromising the ability of future generations to meet their own.

Sustainability Tip

Use reusable bags for shopping and opt for wax paper or reusable sandwich bags instead of plastic bags.

By practicing sustainable living, communities can improve environmental quality, reduce their carbon footprint, and decrease air pollution, which is essential for a healthy community.

Sustainability Tip

Shopping locally helps lower carbon emissions from transporting foods and supports the local community.

If the icon placement syntax for the user defined attribute `:leaf:` as shown in Example 45 appears confusing at this stage, don't worry, we cover it in detail in [chapter-6-icons] where we discuss icons.

Changes Are So Easy With Substitution!

One of the great advantages of substitution is that if you wish to make a correction, you need to make it once in the header and it will be reflected wherever that attribute has been substituted. For example, let's assume I have 20 sustainability tips like the ones shown in Example 46. Now after typing all these 20 tips, I decide to change the title of each tip from *Sustainability Tip* to *Sustainable Lifestyle Idea*. So what do I do? Well all I need to do is to make that change at one place in the header by changing the title in my *leaf* attribute to read — `:leaf: icon:leaf[] _Sustainable Lifestyle Idea_` — and voilà, the changed title immediately appears in all 20 tips!

Like icons, you can also use the image macro to insert images in a user defined attribute. Say we have an image called *notes.svg* (can be png or jpg) in our images folder. Like icons as demonstrated above, we can create a user defined attribute — `:usernotes:` which combines image and text as can be seen in Example 47.

AsciiDoc Markup

Example 47. Creating a User Defined Attribute with an Image

```
// Define the attribute in Header using the following

:usernotes: image:notes.svg[] Reader Notes    ①

// To substitute assigned value anywhere in text use the following :

{usernotes}    ②
```

① Create a user defined attribute and assign an image and a title to it.

② Just insert this attribute wherever you need to get this image and title.

Will be rendered as...

Reader Notes

The image insert used in Example 47 is an inline *SVG* image. You can get many such free SVG images from the Google Fonts icon page at https://fonts.google.com/icons . SVG images do not pixelate when zoomed and are therefore ideal for such use.

5.2. System Defined Attributes

While users can define attributes as per their requirement as demonstrated above, some useful attributes are defined by AsciiDoctor itself and they can be very helpful. For example if you wish to write '35 Degrees Celsius' and are fretting over how to get that degree symbol (°), you can just substitute a *system defined attribute* called `` `{deg}` `` as shown in Example 48.

AsciiDoc Markup

Example 48. System Defined Attribute for Degrees

```
The temperature outside is 35{deg}C. It feels like an oven!
```

Will be rendered as...

The temperature outside is 35°C. It feels like an oven!

Likewise if you are looking for smart double quotes (curly quotes), you can use `{ldquo}` for left double quotes and `{rdquo}` for right double quotes as shown in Example 49.

AsciiDoc Markup

Example 49. System defined attribute for left and right quotes

```
On being asked by a user about a feature that was not working, the developer said --
{ldquo}It works fine on my machine!{rdquo}.
```

Will be rendered as...

On being asked by a user about a feature that was not working, the developer said — “It works fine on my machine!”.

For smart single quotes, replace `{ldquo}` with `{lsquo}` and `{rdquo}` with `{rsquo}`-- the 's' denoting *single* quote.

We can create a blank line between two lines of text, by using the system defined attribute `{empty}` as shown in Example 50 (*introduced earlier in Chapter 4 — It was substitution*!).

AsciiDoc Markup

Example 50. Inserting a blank line

```
"Think of a number between 1 and 10. Multiply it by 9 and subtract 1. Now close your
eyes. It's dark isn't it?"

{empty} +          ①

"Dear Math, please grow up and solve your own problems, I'm tired of solving them for
you".
```

① This is where the empty line will be visible in the rendered output

Will be rendered as...

"Think of a number between 1 and 10. Multiply it by 9 and subtract 1. Now close your eyes. It's dark isn't it?"

"Dear Math, please grow up and solve your own problems, I'm tired of solving them for you."

You can explore more system defined attributes that can be used in a similar way from the AsciiDoctor Replacement Attributes Reference Table [https://docs.asciidoctor.org/asciidoc/latest/attributes/character-replacement-ref] by placing the keyword appearing under the **attribute names** column inside braces as demonstrated above.

5.3. Footnotes

To create a footnote, we can use the *footnote* macro. The markup syntax for creating a footnote in AsciiDoc uses the general form shown in Example 51.

AsciiDoc Markup

Example 51. General syntax for inserting a footnote

```
footnote:id[footnote text]
```

Footnote numbering is automatic. It is important to note that footnotes in AsciiDoc — unlike MS Word or LibreOffice Writer — do not appear page wise but at the end of the last HTML page. What this means is that if your document has 5 pages of text and you create a footnote on each page, in your HTML output, the five footnotes will appear as endnotes after all 5 pages of text have been displayed i.e. after the *last* line of the *last* HTML page. As far as footnotes are concerned, the HTML output is continuous even if the content has been organized into distinct chapters using a Level 1 heading (==). However in the case of books or documents having *chapters*, the PDF output generated by *AsciiDoctor-PDF* displays footnotes as endnotes but places them at the bottom of the last page of *each book chapter* rather than at the end of the document. So all footnotes created in a chapter are again not displayed page wise in the PDF but are placed at the end of the chapter in which they have been created. There is no separate provisioning for endnotes in AsciiDoc like you have in MS Word or LibreOffice. With reference to the above footnote markup, what appears in a footnote at the bottom of the page is provided inside the square brackets. The 'id' can be any name and is optional but is useful if we want to refer this footnote again, later on in the text. Let's now see how we can easily create footnotes using AsciiDoc markup with some sample text as shown in Example 52.

AsciiDoc Markup

Example 52. Inserting Simple Footnotes in Text

```
As consumers demand more environmentally friendly products, companies have engaged
actively in greenwashingfootnote:[an attempt to make people believe that a company is
doing more to protect the environment than it is.] ①
In order to sound environmentally responsible, one can see a lot of
'sustainababble'footnote:sbabble[increased frequency of the word □sustainable□;also a
popular podcast] ②
in all company brochures and annual reports.Upon closer examination, many such claims
turn out to be nothing more than 'Green Sheen'.footnote:sbabble[] ③
```

① Footnote starts without any leading space i.e. is joined with the word where the footnote has to appear and after a : has footnote text inside brackets.

② Footnote 2 is same in structure as 1 but after : has an id — sbabble — and has footnote text inside brackets.

③ Footnote 3 starts with a . (dot) and after : refers to the id of footnote 2 and has nothing inside brackets → it is just referring to footnote 2 again. This way you can refer to a footnote multiple times in your text.

If the footnote superscript is making the term unreadable, you can introduce a space between the word and footnote: like `greenwashing footnote:[footnote text]`. Notice that there is a space between *greenwashing* and *footnote*. This moves the footnote superscript one space forward making the term on which the footnote is placed, clearly visible.

Will be rendered as...

As consumers demand more environmentally friendly products, companies have engaged actively in greenwashing[1]. In order to sound environmentally responsible, one can see a lot of 'sustainababble'[2];also a popular podcast in all company brochures and annual reports.Upon closer examination, many such claims turn out to be nothing more than 'Green Sheen'.[2].

Repeat of Footnote 2

1. an attempt to make people believe that a company is doing more to protect the environment than it is
2. increased frequency of the word 'sustainable'

Footnote Text

Figure 53. Footnotes appearing at the end of the page

As can be seen in Figure 53, footnotes appear at the end of the page. If your HTML page is very long, the footnotes might be quite a distance away from where they appear in the text and might actually appear to the reader more like endnotes. The footnote links though are 'clickable' *in both directions* and you can click on a footnote link in text to reach and read a footnote and click on the number link on the footnote to navigate back to the point in text from where the footnote was clicked. This makes footnotes quite functional in AsciiDoc documents.

Please find below, a live reproduction of the footnote example presented in the above example and Figure (which is a screen shot). As footnotes appear at the end of the document, you will see them here after the chapter summary section below. The live demonstration below provides live footnote links that you can click to reach a footnote and clickable footnote number links which bring you back to the point in text from where you clicked the footnote.

You can click on the footnote links in Example 53 only if you are reading an electronic copy of this book. If you are reading the print copy, you can paste the text in Example 53 in an AsciiDoc file, render it as HTML using AsciiDoctor and view this demo on your computer.

Example 53. Footnotes Live Demo

As consumers demand more environmentally friendly products, companies have engaged actively in greenwashing [1]. In order to sound environmentally responsible, one can see a lot of 'sustainababble'[2] in all company brochures and annual reports. Upon closer examination, many such claims turn out to be nothing more than 'Green Sheen'.[2].

Click on the footnote links above to reach that footnote. When you reach a footnote, click on the footnote number link to come back. You can also mouseover the footnote number in the list of footnotes (the one that appears at the end of the document) to see how they are internally set up by AsciiDoc to point to each other in the document. Notice that these footnotes appear at the end of the current HTML page after the chapter summary section where text ends.

5.4. Inserting Footnotes Using Substitution

If you plan to repeatedly refer to a footnote, we can also use attribute substitution to insert a footnote. Let's say I am writing a note on Paris Agreement on climate change and would require to refer to the agreement text at many places as a footnote. I can set the attribute in the header as shown in Example 54:

Example 54. Inserting Footnotes Using Substitution

```
:fn-paris: footnote:pa[Paris Agreement,
https://en.wikisource.org/wiki/Paris_Agreement]
```

Now whenever I want to refer to the paris agreement in my running text, I could just insert the footnote as a substitution as shown in Example 54. The footnote substitution renders as follows:

> It is incumbent on parties as per Article 5 of the agreement to conserve sinks of greenhouse gases[3]. In accordance with Article 9, developed countries will provide financial resources to developing countries for climate change mitigation and adaptation[3].

In Example 54, *pa* is the id of this footnote and irrespective of how many times we use the `{fn-paris}` substitution, it will always refer to the same footnote — *pa* and will have only one entry in the final footnote list. In Example 54, notice that both footnotes have the same footnote number — 3.

Following are some other examples of repeatable footnotes where we can insert footnotes using attribute substitution :

```
:fn-prc: footnote:prc[Personal communication]
:fn-umr: footnote:umr[Unverified media reports]
:fn-cfl: footnote:cfl[Community folklore]
:fn-orh: footnote:orh[Oral history]
:fn-uoe: footnote:uoe[Unofficial estimate]
```

The AsciiDoc documentation mentions that footnotes are currently not officially supported in headings (chapter or section headings). While this situation may change in the future, it is best not to place footnotes on headings. I found that doing so displays the footnote link on the heading but messes up the footnote numbering in the final footnote list.

5.5. Chapter Summary

Key learnings in this chapter are:

- In this chapter, we have discussed how to work with substitutions by creating user defined attributes. With user defined attributes, we can assign text, URL, icon or image to an attribute name and use that attribute name inside braces to insert its set value as many number of times as we want. This saves repetitive typing, accords consistency and prevents mistakes particularly when you are working with URLs.
- If you have to make changes like a change in icon or text, you need to alter the attribute value at just one place in the header and changes will be immediately reflected all through the document.
- Using system defined attribute replacements, you can have access to many commonly used symbols like degrees, copyright, curly quotes, trademark etc.
- We have also seen how to create footnotes in AsciiDoc. In conventional documents, footnotes appear at the end of the page on which they were created. This is not the case in AsciiDoc where footnotes appear at the end of the document almost resembling endnotes. However this should not be an issue in electronic documents as when you click on a footnote link, you are taken to that footnote and when you click on the footnote number, you are transported back to that point in the document from where you clicked the footnote.
- If there are footnotes that are recurring i.e. they can be repeated more than once in the running text, we can use substitution to insert such footnotes.
- Footnotes on chapter or section headings are currently not officially supported. While they may appear to work, they actually mess up with footnote numbering and display of other footnotes.

5.6. Try it Yourself

1. Try to create some footnotes using some sample text as demonstrated in Example 52.
2. Try to create some footnotes using substitution as demonstrated in Section 5.4.
3. The footnotes that appear below were created in the text in Example 53.

[1] An attempt to make people believe that a company is doing more to protect the environment than it is

[2] Increased frequency of the word 'sustainable'

[3] Paris Agreement, https://en.wikisource.org/wiki/Paris_Agreement

Chapter 6. Inserting Audio and Video in HTML Output

> *"If a picture is worth a thousand words, then a video is worth a million." ~ Troy Olson & Jeff Loquist*

In this chapter we will explore how to insert audio and video in our AsciiDoc Documents. With the phenomenal growth in creation and consumption of audio-visual content, it is becoming increasingly common in written documents to include online tutorial videos, films, podcasts, music clips and other audio-visual content. AsciiDoc provides a super easy way to do this using just one line of markup code. It is worthwhile to point out that audio and video markup presented in this chapter largely applies to HTML rendering of AsciiDoc documents.

6.1. Inserting Audio and Video in HTML Output

AsciiDoc permits you to easily insert audio and video in your HTML documents. The audio and video to be included in the document can be self hosted or hosted locally or can be hosted on the Internet by streaming services. Let's see how we can insert both audio and video clips in our AsciiDoc documents considering both these hosting scenarios.

6.1.1. Inserting Audio

6.1.1.1. Locally Available Audio Files

You can use the `audio::` macro to insert audio files in documents. To illustrate this, we will use an audio clip (*king_injustice.mp3*) which has a famous quote from Dr. Martin Luther King, Jr. — *"Injustice anywhere is a threat to justice everywhere"* in his own voice. We can use the markup shown in Example 55 to insert this audio clip in our AsciiDoc document.

AsciiDoc Markup

Example 55. Inserting an audio clip using the audio macro

```
audio::king_injustice.mp3[]  ①
```

① If you have defined an `:imagesdir:` folder in the document header, this file must be inside that folder. Otherwise it must be in the same folder as your AsciiDoc file.

The audio file can be in the same folder as your AsciiDoc file or as mentioned above, you must ensure that the audio file is in the `:imagesdir:` folder if you have defined one. If not, you can create a folder, put your audio files inside that folder and use the `:imagesdir:` attribute in the header to declare that folder as the *images directory* folder. This keeps everything organized and avoids long path names.

After you have inserted the above markup in your document, render the AsciiDoc file to HTML as shown below to see the result (*myfile.adoc* is used here as an example).

Terminal Command

```
$ asciidoctor myfile.adoc
```

Will be rendered as...

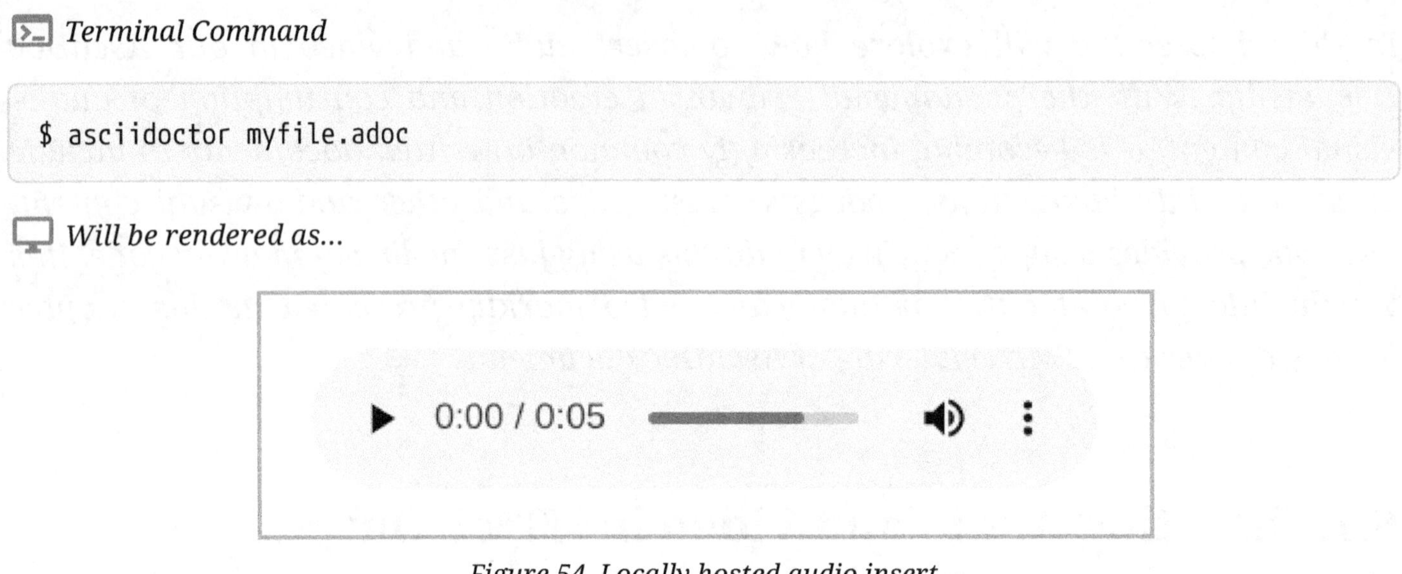

Figure 54. Locally hosted audio insert

▶ ch42/images/king_injustice.mp3 *(audio)*

Audio Credit: WavSource.com [https://www.wavsource.com/people/famous.htm]

As can be seen in Figure 54, the audio clips becomes available on the rendered page via an audio player. While the file used in the above example is an MP3 file, other popular audio formats like *.wav* (Wave) and *.ogg* (Vorbis) are also supported.

You can also start the audio clip from a particular timestamp or end at a particular timestamp by extending the `audio::` marco with *start* and *end* values (in seconds) as shown in Example 56.

AsciiDoc Markup

Example 56. Audio clip with start and end times in seconds

```
audio::king_injustice.mp3[start=3,end=5]
```

Will be rendered as...

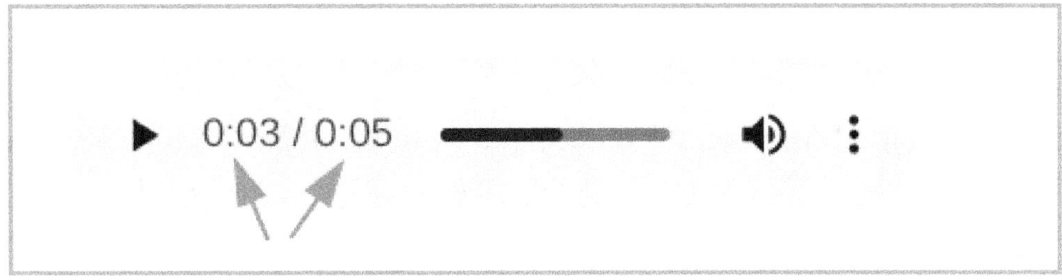

Figure 55. Locally hosted audio insert with start and end times

As can be seen in Figure 55, the clip will start playing at 3 seconds and stop at 5 seconds in the audio timeline. The *start* or *end* tags can also be used independently if you wish to only start or end at some point in the timeline.

6.1.1.2. Audio Hosted Online

For audio hosted online — like podcasts, music tracks, animal vocalizations etc — the URL of the audio needs to be pasted in the `audio::` macro as shown in Example 57.

AsciiDoc Markup

Example 57. Playing an audio hosted on the Internet

```
.Voice of Dr. Martin Luther King
audio::https://www.wavsource.com/snds_2020-10-
01_3728627494378403/people/famous/king_injustice.wav[]
```

Notice in the above example that we have given a title to the audio clip by putting a `.Title` just above the audio macro. The markup in Example 57 is rendered in HTML as seen in Figure 56.

Will be rendered as...

Figure 56. Audio insert with title

You can also use the start and end tags inside the square brackets above as demonstrated earlier.

6.2. Inserting Videos

We can easily insert both self hosted or streaming videos from platforms like YouTube and Vimeo in our documents using the `video::` macro. Let's see how we can do this in our HTML documents.

6.2.1. Inserting Locally Available or Self Hosted Videos

To insert a locally available video in an AsciiDoc file, all you need to do is to enter a single line of markup having the `video::` macro in your document pointing to the video file as shown in Example 58.

AsciiDoc Markup

Example 58. Inserting a video clip using the video macro

```
video::corals.mp4[]
```

Render the AsciiDoc file with the above `video::` insert to HTML and you will see the video inserted in your HTML document as shown in Figure 57.

Will be rendered as...

Figure 57. Locally hosted video insert

Video credit: Jun Ho Lee, Pexels [https://www.pexels.com/video/vibrant-clownfish-on-coral-reef-underwater-31443959/]

The video must be available in the same folder as the AsciiDoc file or in the images folder if the

`:imagesdir:` attribute has been defined in the header. As locally hosted videos are not optimized for streaming in web browsers, you may experience buffering delays while playing the video depending on its size. In view of the above, the option for using locally hosted videos should be avoided or considered mostly for small sized videos.

6.2.1.1. Starting and Ending Videos at Specific Times

Similar to audio files, you can also choose to *start* the video at a specific timestamp (in seconds) and *end* the video at a specific timestamp (in seconds) by extending the video macro with the `start` and `end` values as shown Example 59.

AsciiDoc Markup

Example 59. Inserting a video clip with start and end times

```
.Corals Reef Supporting Diverse Marine Life
video::corals.mp4[start=5,end=10]
```

The above video will start at 5 seconds in the video timeline and end at 15 seconds. Similar to audio, we can give a title to the video by putting a `.Title` right above the video macro as seen in Example 59 (you mouseover pointer over the video to see the start and end time f you reading this book on-screen).

Once you render the AsciiDoc file to HTML, you will start seeing the video player in the document as shown in Figure 58.

Will be rendered as...

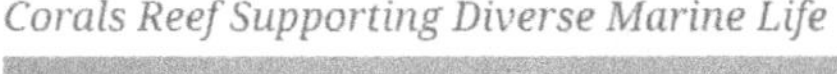

Figure 58. Locally hosted video showing start and end time

Video credit: Jun Ho Lee, Pexels [https://www.pexels.com/video/vibrant-clownfish-on-coral-reef-underwater-31443959/]

6.2.1.2. Altering Viewport Display Size

You can also alter the height and width of the video using the `width=x` and `height=y` attributes of the `video::` macro as shown in Example 60.

AsciiDoc Markup

Example 60. Controlling the video viewport width and height

```
.Corals Reef Supporting Diverse Marine Life
video::corals.mp4[width=240,height=200]
```

When you render to HTML, you will see the resized video viewport as seen in Figure 59.

Will be rendered as…

Figure 59. Video insert with altered viewport size

Video credit: Jun Ho Lee, Pexels [https://www.pexels.com/video/vibrant-clownfish-on-coral-reef-underwater-31443959/]

With reference to attributes mentioned above, you can use them independently i.e just use one or both together separated by commas as shown in Example 61.

Example 61. Using multiple attributes with the video macro

```
video::corals.mp4[start=5,end=15,width=240,height=200]
```

6.2.2. Inserting Youtube Videos

AsciiDoctor permits you to insert videos from YouTube and Vimeo. This is the *recommended way* to insert videos in documents as per the AsciiDoctor documentation. As these video services *stream* video content optimized for browser viewing, videos play smoothly in the user's browser given a stable Internet connection.

You can use the markup shown in Example 62 to insert videos from YouTube in your AsciiDoc documents:

AsciiDoc Markup

Example 62. Inserting a YouTube Video in your Document

```
What is Climate Change ?

If you want to get a quick overview about  the climate crisis facing our planet,
watch this video:

video::QlQ-MEZgRGY[youtube]
```

The YouTube *video id* that you see in the `video::` macro in Example 62 is what you see in the video's URL after the 'v=' as shown in Figure 60.

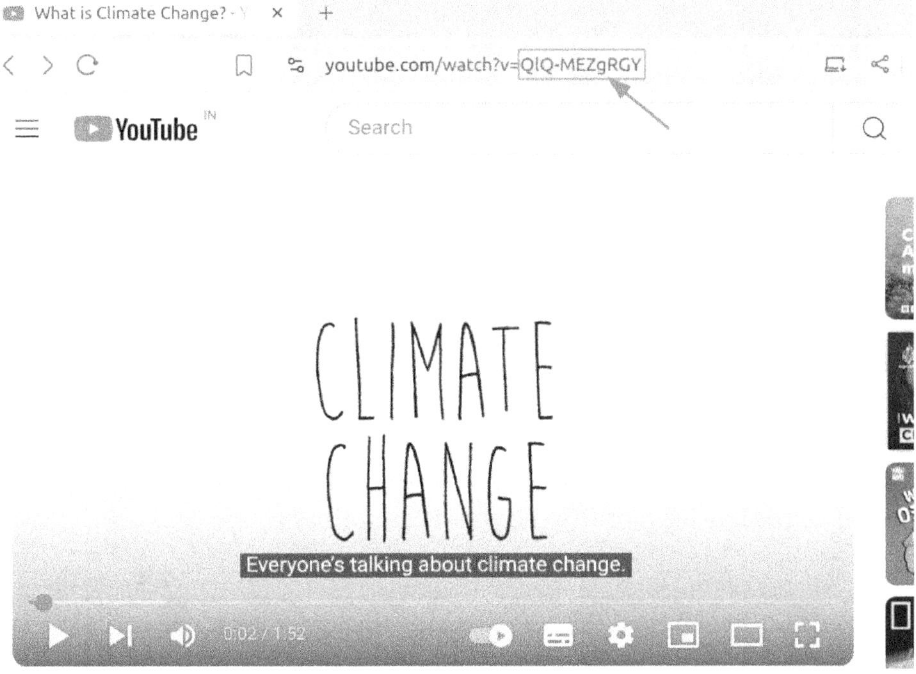

Figure 60. YouTube Video ID

After you render this AsciiDoc file, you will see the video in your HTML as shown below:

Will be rendered as...

What is Climate Change ?

If you want to get a quick overview about the climate crisis facing our planet, watch this video:

You can also extend the above command by starting and stopping at a particular time in the video as shown in Example 63.

AsciiDoc Markup

Example 63. Playing YouTube Video with start and end time values

```
video::QlQ-MEZgRGY[youtube,start=10,end=30]
```

This will start the video at timestamp 10 seconds and end it at timestamp 30 seconds. This is super useful if you wish to play only a certain section of the video. To start at a specific time and play till the end, just remove the *end* part from the markup in Example 63 and to play from the start but end somewhere in between, just remove the *start* part from the markup in Example 63.

You can also use the width and height elements to control the size of the YouTube viewport as shown in Example 60.

6.2.2.1. Insert a Youtube Video Playlist

If you are displaying a YouTube video that is part of a playlist and wish to link the playlist as well, you can do this quite easily. Let's see this with a playlist that I created on using Zotero — an open source reference manager software. The URL of the playlist is as follows:

```
https://www.youtube.com/watch?v=jU3Qspe0JFk&list=PLKR_CvN6SDJgb0ZzYUfKB39lE2AHvVhcJ
```

You will notice that there are two distinct parts in the above URL — (1) the id of the first video in the playlist just after `v=` but *not including* `&` i.e. `jU3Qspe0JFk` and (2) the id of the playlist after `list=` i.e.

PLKR_CvN6SDJgb0ZzYUfKB39lE2AHvVhcJ . We use both these in the video macro using the following generic template:
video::<video-id>[youtube,list=<playlist-id>] replacing <video-id> and <playlist-id> with actual ids. This is shown in Example 64 for my Zotero playlist.

AsciiDoc Markup

Example 64. Including a YouTube Playlist

```
video::jU3Qspe0JFk[youtube,list=PLKR_CvN6SDJgb0ZzYUfKB39lE2AHvVhcJ]
```

Render the AsciiDoc file to HTML and you will see the linked playlist as shown in Figure 61 and Figure 62.

Will be rendered as...

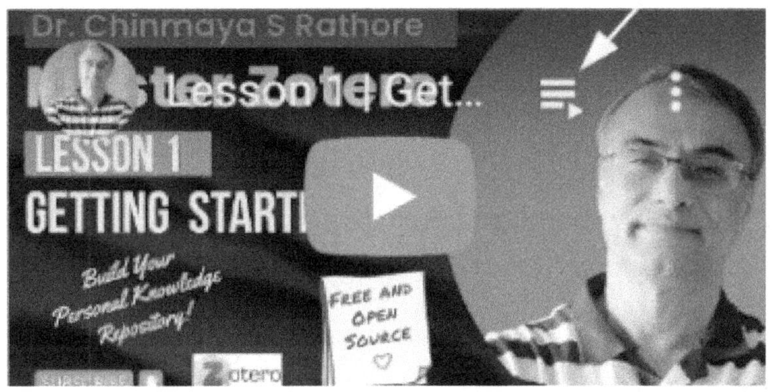

Figure 61. Including a YouTube playlist

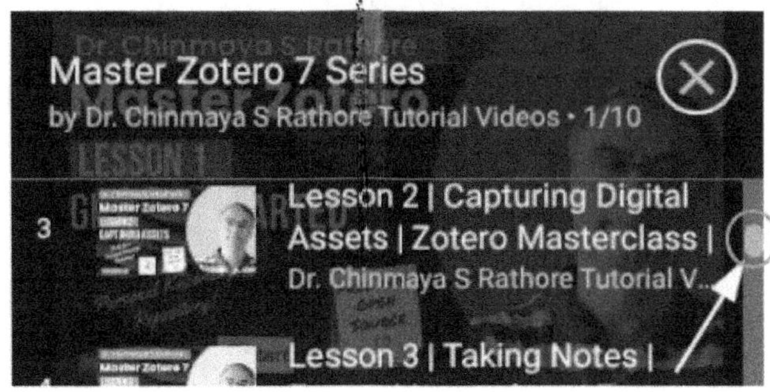

Figure 62. YouTube playlist display (a) clicking on this icon opens up (b) the playlist

The change that you see is small but important. Figure 62 (a) shows how the video playlist appears in the HTML output. Clicking on the 'hamburger' icon (encircled) displays the playlist that is shown in Figure 62 (b) which you can scroll through using the slider bar (encircled and pointed by arrow) and exit using the X icon (encircled top right).

6.2.3. Inserting a Vimeo Video

To insert a Vimeo video, you can use the markup shown in Example 65.

AsciiDoc Markup

Example 65. Inserting a Vimeo Video

```
The following video provides a very good introduction to the Climate Change problem:

video::112042837[vimeo]
```

The numerical video id in the markup snippet shown in Example 65 is taken from the Vimeo video URL as shown in Figure 63 .

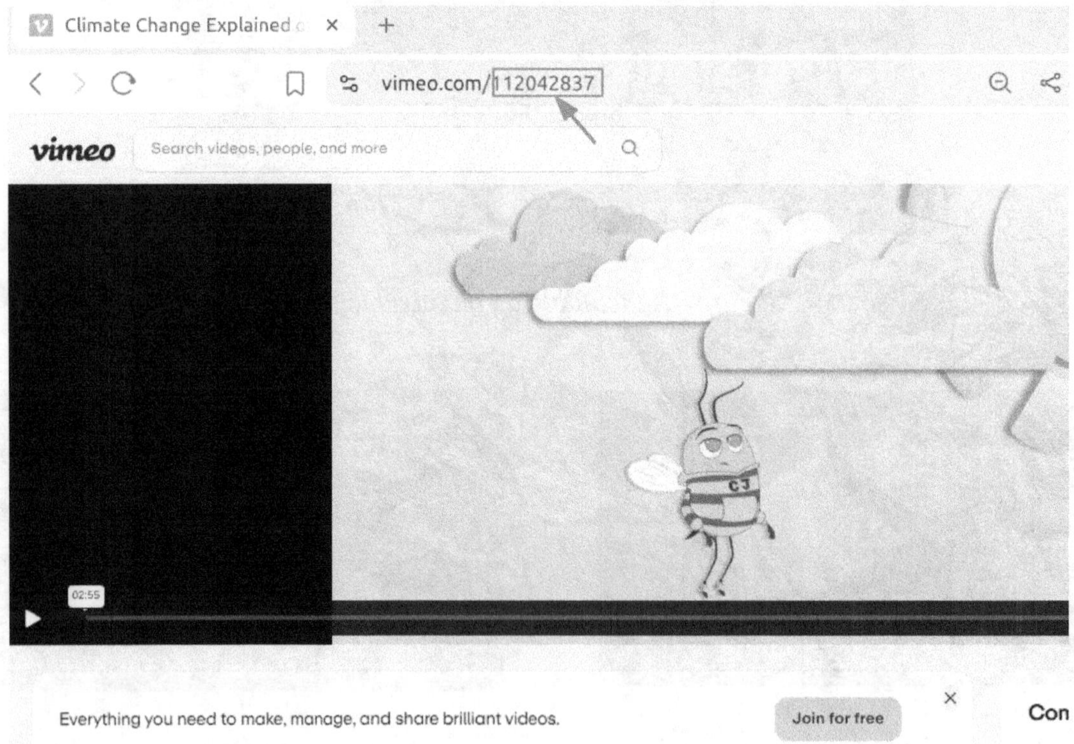

Figure 63. Getting the Vimeo video ID

When you render the AsciiDoc file to HTML using AsciiDoctor, the Vimeo video will be inserted in the document as seen in Figure 64.

Will be rendered as...

Figure 64. Vimeo video after rendering to HTML

VS Code Preview Does Not Show YouTube or Vimeo Video Markup

If you are using VS Code to create and live preview your documents, there is an important point to mention about video and audio inserts. At the time of writing, VS Code does not show a live preview of YouTube and Vimeo videos. What you see is blank space where you expect a video window to appear. There is nothing wrong with the markup and this is just an AsciiDoctor Extension or VS Code quirk. To see the video, you must render your AsciiDoc file to HTML. This can be done from inside VS Code also by pressing `CTRL` + `SHIFT` + `P` and choosing `AsciiDoc: Save HTML Document` from the command pallette. You can then view the rendered HTML in your web browser and the videos will be visible. This behavior may change in future versions of the AsciiDoctor extension and VS Code.

6.3. Controlling the Video Display with More Attributes

There are many more attributes that can be used with the `video::` macro that have not been covered in this introductory text. These attributes provide more control on how the video is displayed on the page and how it behaves. For example we can autoplay a video, loop the video, align the video frame left, right or center, start the video muted, chose between light and dark themes and choose the language of the video frame among others. You can visit the AsciiDoctor documentation page for video and audio [https://docs.asciidoctor.org/asciidoc/latest/macros/audio-and-video/] which has many useful tips.

6.4. Audio and Video Inserts in PDF and EPUB Files

The audio and video markup described in the above sections works well for HTML output of AsciiDoc documents. However, it does not translate the same when you render AsciiDoc documents as PDF (*AsciiDoctor-PDF*) or EPUB3 (*AsciiDoctor-EPUB3*). Some of the notable differences are as follows:

PDF Rendering of Audio and Video

- YouTube video inserts using the `video::` macro appear as *plain links* to the video.
- As the `video::` macro is ignored, attributes like height, width, start and end have no effect.
- Self-hosted video and audio i.e. video and audio files available locally, appear as internal links that show the *local* path of the file. Video and audio files are *not embedded inside the PDF.* So it is best to either move such content to services like YouTube / SoundCloud and use the Youtube link or host them in a publicly shared online folder.
- However if you wish to distribute audio and video content locally, generate the PDF using *AsciiDoctor-PDF*, put the PDF inside a new folder, create an *images* folder inside that folder (where the PDF is located) and put audio and video files in the *images folder* and distribute the PDF with the images folder as a ZIP download. This way when someone clicks on an audio and video link inside the PDF, the audio and video will play using the native players installed on their computer.
- You can include video / audio thumbnail pictures using the `image::` macro above the link for PDF outputs.
- It might be best to work on a copy of your project and tweak it specifically for PDF rendering.

Let's now look at some issues concerning audio and video macro inserts in documents rendered as EPUB3.

EPUB3 Rendering of Audio and Video

- Local self hosted video and audio work well in EPUB3 documents generated using *AsciiDoctor-EPUB3*. Please remember that adding audio and video files increases the size of the EPUB document quite substantially. So if you absolutely need to do this, you must make sure that the file size of audio and video is optimized.
- YouTube and Vimeo videos, at the time of writing, are not embedded or linked in EPUB3 files using the above described `video::` macro markup. You get the following error:

- A good solution is to replace video markup with URL links to YouTube and Vimeo videos or links to podcasts. You can also include thumbnail images if you like for such videos.
- It is always a good practice to work on a copy of your project and tweak it specifically for EPUB rendering.

In conclusion, for HTML output, AsciiDoctor provides a very easy way to insert audio and video content in your documents. You can visit the AsciiDoctor audio-video documentation page [https://docs.asciidoctor.org/asciidoc/latest/macros/audio-and-video/] for details about other attributes of the `video::` macro.

6.5. Chapter Summary

Key learnings in this chapter are:

- We can include audio and video content in AsciiDoc documents using the `video::` macro when generating HTML output.
- Video and Audio files inserted in the AsciiDoc document can be self hosted i.e. provided by the document creator and uploaded with other HTML files. Please see Section 6.1.1 for inserting audio and Section 6.2 for including self hosted videos.
- Videos from YouTube and Vimeo can also be included. For a quick recap, see Section 6.2.2 (YouTube) and Section 6.2.3 (Vimeo).
- Many attributes of the displayed video like start time, end time, width, height etc. can be easily controlled via extending the `video::` macro with attributes. Please see Section 6.2.1.1 and Section 6.2.1.2 for attribute syntax to control video output.
- YouTube playlists can also be included. Refer to Section 6.2.2.1 for a quick recap on how to include playlists.
- Document creators need to be aware that video and audio inserts using the `video::` macro work for HTML output but do not work in a similar manner for PDF or EPUB output. It may be quite challenging (or not possible or required) to embed or insert video and audio in these documents. Please see Section 6.4 for a quick recap on how these issues might manifest in PDF and EPUB files.

6.6. Try it Yourself

Download any audio and video file of your choice from the Internet or use some from your personal collection. Some free audio clips of famous people are available in the *.wav* format (which is supported by AsciiDoc) from the WavSource [https://www.wavsource.com/people/famous.htm] website. Free video and music audio files (MP3) are also available form Pixabay [https://pixabay.com/videos/search/]. The corals video used in Example 58 of this chapter can be downloaded from the Pexels website [https://www.pexels.com/video/vibrant-clownfish-on-coral-reef-underwater-31443959/]. Once you have a video and audio file, you can try working on the following tasks:

See the chapter summary for help on individual tasks below.

1. Create an AsciiDoc file and put some sample text in it. Create a folder called *images* inside the folder where your AsciiDoc file is located and in the header section of your AsciiDoc file, enter the attribute — `:imagesdir: images`. Move your audio and video files inside the *images* folder.
2. Insert a local audio file in your AsciiDoc document using the `audio::<filename>[]` macro. Use AsciiDoctor to render your AsciiDoc file as HTML ($ asciidoctor yourfile.adoc). Open the rendered HTML file in your web browser and verify that you can play the audio file in your browser.
3. Can you play the same audio clip using its online URL https://www.wavsource.com/snds_2020-10-01_3728627494378403/people/famous/king_injustice.wav rather than the locally available version as was done in the previous example ? You can revisit Section 6.1.1.2 for help.
4. Insert a local video in your AsciiDoc file using the `video::<filename>[]` macro. Use AsciiDoctor to render it to HTML. Open the rendered HTML file in your web browser and verify that you can play the video in your browser.
5. The following is the URL to the YouTube video 'Pale Blue Dot' narrated by the famous astronomer Carl Sagan — https://www.youtube.com/watch?v=wupToqz1e2g

   Add the above YouTube video in your AsciiDoc document, render the document as HTML using AsciiDoctor and verify that the video plays.
6. While I recommend that you do watch this *iconic video — Pale Blue Dot* in full (for some great insights!), can you use the *start* and *end* attributes of the `video::` macro to start the video @24 seconds and end it @80 seconds in the video timeline ?
7. Insert the following Vimeo video in your AsciiDoc Document — https://vimeo.com/1005393864

   Render your document as HTML using AsciiDoctor and verify that the Vimeo video plays when you open the rendered HTML in your web browser.

Chapter 7. Creating and Using Delimited Blocks

"Your words are building blocks of which you construct your life and future."
~Charles Capps

In this chapter, we will explore how to create and use blocks. Blocks are basically used to highlight a chunk of text or code in some special manner from the running text matter. AsciiDoc supports the creation of many different types of blocks geared up for specific use cases. The ability to create blocks of many different kinds with simplicity and ease is in my view, one of AsciiDoc's most notable features.

7.1. About Delimited Blocks

Simply put, delimited blocks in AsciiDoc are chunks of content that break the normal flow of text in a document to make it standout in a special way. Delimited blocks can be used to highlight console output, code snippets, create information sidebars, example boxes, display mathematical equations and more. Figure 65 illustrates the concept of delimited blocks.

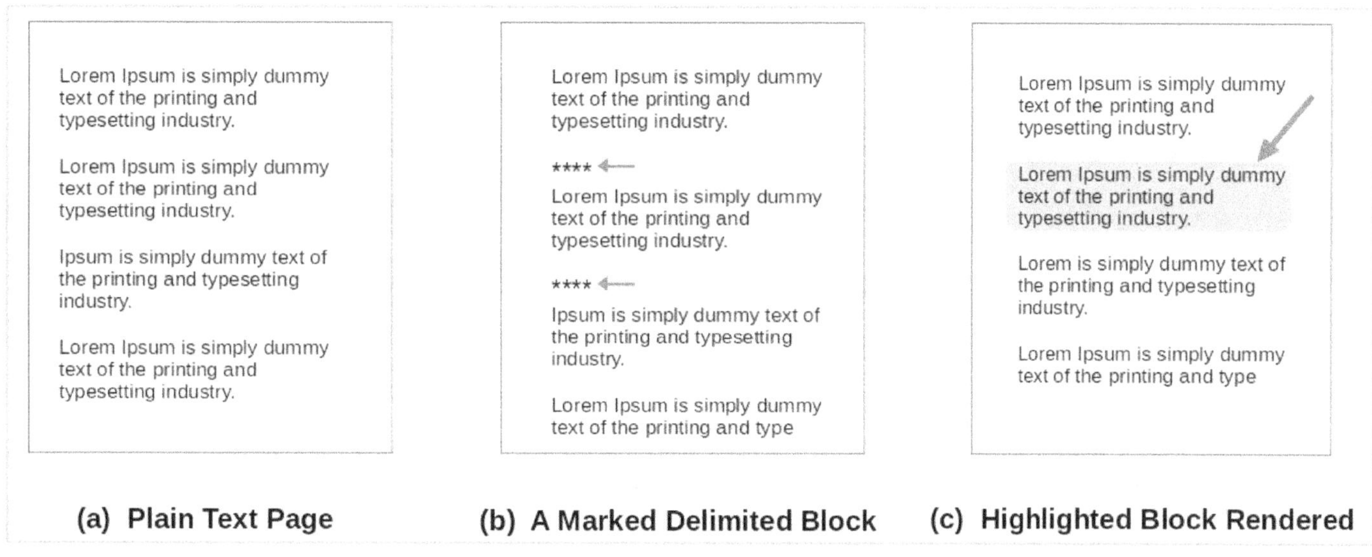

Figure 65. Schematic showing how easy it is to create blocks in AsciiDoc

With reference to the Figure 65 — (a) you have a few plain paragraphs of text. Let's say we decide that we want the paragraph in the center to stand out. So in (b) we fence or delineate that paragraph with a starting line of **** (four asterisks) and then a closing line of **** (four asterisks) — Figure 65 (c) shows the result of this block markup with the delineated paragraph highlighted in a light gray background. This is actually a *sidebar block* in AsciiDoc and we will discuss this later in a subsequent section of this chapter. The **** (four asterisks) are called *delimiters* — that kind of act like a *fence* delineating a text block — and hence the block is called a *delimited block*. There are quite a few different blocks that you can create in AsciiDoc, each having a different purpose and different properties. Some of the commonly used blocks are listed below :

1. Comment Block
2. Listing Block
3. Literal Block
4. Example Block
5. Sidebar Block
6. Source Block or Code Block
7. Verse Block.
8. Pass Through Block

Let's have a look at how each of these blocks are created and when they are typically used.

7.2. Comment Block

We have already seen earlier that if you want to annotate your AsciiDoc files with your comments, you can create a single line comment using *two forward slashes* — // . Everything following the two forward slashes is ignored and not rendered by AsciiDoctor. If however you wish to write multiple lines of comment, you can do so by creating a comment block with an opening and closing series of *four forward slashes* — //// and everything inside the block will not be interpreted and ignored by AsciiDoctor while rendering. Example 66 shows AsciiDoc markup for a comment block.

AsciiDoc Markup

Example 66. Comment block markup using four forward slashes

```
////
You can create bold text by enclosing text inside two * symbols like *text*
You can create italics text by enclosing text inside two underscore characters _text_
////

Learning how to write AsciiDoc markup is super fun  !
```

Will be rendered as...

Learning how to write AsciiDoc markup is super fun !

In Example 66, you will notice that all the text that was inside the comment block does not show up when the file is rendered in HTML or PDF by AsciiDoctor. It's just there inside the AsciiDoc file for us or others reading our AsciiDoc markup to understand what is happening inside the document. Put in another way, comments inside a comment block can also be seen as *notes to self.*

If you are creating a comment block using opening and closing ////, please make sure that the opening and closing //// are on their own independent line exactly as shown in Example 66 i.e. just the //// with no text in front or before the ////.

You can also mark any block of text as a comment block by using the *comment* styling directive as shown in Example 67.

AsciiDoc Markup

Example 67. Comment Block via Comment Styling

```
[comment]
You can create bold text by enclosing text inside two * symbols like *text*
You can create italics text by enclosing text inside two underscore characters _text_
            ①
Learning how to write AsciiDoc markup is super fun  !
```

① Blank line. The contiguous text block above this blank line is treated as a comment block. The line below the blank line — *Learning how to* .... is not part of the comment block.

Will be rendered as...

Learning how to write AsciiDoc markup is super fun !

Notice how the commented part above the blank line in Example 67 does not appear in the rendered output. If you are using the `[comment]` styling shown in Example 67 to mark a comment block, make sure that the comment text is contiguous to the `[comment]` directive i.e. there is no blank line between them.

In summary, notations shown in Example 66 and Example 67 for declaring comment blocks are exactly the same and you can choose whichever suits you best.

7.3. A Listing Block

A listing block is used primarily for including and highlighting any content that you wish to reproduce as it is i.e. *verbatim*. The content inside a listing block is not processed by AsciiDoctor i.e. it appears in the rendered output as you have typed it. The listing block is rendered in a light gray background. The classic use of the listing block is in syntax highlighting of code in different programming or markup languages — a topic that we discuss in detail in Chapter 10. The listing block is also used to display AsciiDoc markup itself verbatim so that readers can see how the markup looks like in the source file. All AsciiDoc markup that you see in this book has actually been created using listing blocks.

Markup and CSS Styling

Please note that things like backgrounds, colors, font type, size etc. that you see rendered on HTML pages are not part of the AsciiDoc markup language but implemented through the default CSS based styling theme which we will discuss in Chapter 15.

To create a listing block, you need to enclose the text that you wish to display in the listing block, with an opening and closing set of ---- i.e. four dashes as shown in Example 68.

AsciiDoc Markup

Example 68. AsciiDoc markup for a listing block

```
----    ①

All your content
in
multiple lines
contiguous or

non-contiguous
----    ②
```

① Listing block starts here

② Listing block ends here

Let's try out a simple example. Suppose that we checked the version of *asciidoctor-pdf* in our terminal and would like to show the output of that version command verbatim inside our document. We could use a listing block to show this output without it being interpreted as markup i.e. to be displayed exactly as it appeared in the terminal. This is shown in Example 69.

AsciiDoc Markup

Example 69. Listing block markup

```
----
$ asciidoctor-pdf --version
Asciidoctor PDF 2.3.19 using Asciidoctor 2.0.23 [https://asciidoctor.org]
Runtime Environment (ruby 3.1.2p20 (2022-04-12 revision 4491bb740a) [i386-linux-gnu])
(lc:UTF-8 fs:UTF-8 in:UTF-8 ex:UTF-8)
----
```

Will be rendered as...

```
$ asciidoctor-pdf --version
Asciidoctor PDF 2.3.19 using Asciidoctor 2.0.23 [https://asciidoctor.org]
Runtime Environment (ruby 3.1.2p20 (2022-04-12 revision 4491bb740a) [i386-linux-gnu])
(lc:UTF-8 fs:UTF-8 in:UTF-8 ex:UTF-8)
```

As can be seen, the listing block ensures that the rendered output appears exactly the same as generated by the AsciiDoctor version command in the terminal.

7.3.1. Annotating a Listing Block with Callouts

One of great things you can do with a listing block is annotate it with *callouts*. This is super useful when you want to highlight specific parts of the block content or provide additional context and explanation.

Callout annotations are very frequently used in AsciiDoc for the following:

1. Annotating computer source code
2. Annotating AsciiDoc markup
3. Annotating console output

Annotations in many examples in this book have been created using *callouts*. Let's explore how we can annotate a listing block using *callouts*.

Example 68 shows a simple example of how to annotate a listing block. You can see that two annotations have been added to the listing block in Example 68. The first one — callout ① , points to the start of the listing block. The second is callout ②, which points to the end of the listing block. At the bottom of the block, you can see both annotations appearing in sequence with their corresponding numbers enclosed within angled brackets followed by their respective descriptions.

Example 70 illustrates how to place callouts in a listing block.

AsciiDoc Markup

Example 70. Placing callouts to annotate a listing block

```
----    <1>
All your content
in
multiple lines
contiguous or

non-contiguous
----    <2>
<1> Listing block starts here
<2> Listing block ends here
```

Please see Example 68 for how the above markup will be rendered.

Example 70 shows how Example 68 was annotated using callouts. To insert a callout in the block, place it at the appropriate location inside a pair of angled brackets like — <1>. For the next callout, use the next number inside a pair of angled brackets like — <2> and so on. Once you are done inserting all callouts *inside* your listing block, you now have to place a *description or annotation* for each callout immediately after the closing delimiter of the block (the bottom `----` where the block ends) as shown in Example 70. For a callout to be complete, it must therefore *appear twice* — once *inside* the listing block to mark the location of the callout, and once *outside* the listing block to provide a description for the callout. If you fail to provide a description for a callout marked inside the listing block, that callout *will not appear* in the block when the file is rendered to HTML or PDF. So always remember — callouts work in *mark-describe* pairs.

You can also place callouts in a similar way in *literal blocks* (to annotate console output) and *source code blocks* (to annotate code). We discuss these block types later in the chapter in Section 7.5 and Section 7.9 respectively.

7.3.2. Styles in Listing Block

AsciiDoc permits listing blocks to be further styled for more specialized situations. For example, the listing block is generally used for highlighting verbatim output and prevents AsciiDoc to process or interpret whatever is contained inside it. However the listing block styling can be further customized to meet specialized requirements. For example, it can be styled as a *source code block* which permits computer code in different programming languages to be highlighted by a syntax highlighter software.

Another example of specialized styling of the listing block is the *verse block* which permits breaks between lines of text to be retained. In the following sections, we will see how these styles are implemented in the *verse block* and *source code block*, both of which can be seen as special cases of the listing block.

7.4. A Verse Block

As mentioned above, a verse block is a specially styled case of a listing block. Let's see how we can create a styled listing block called the *verse* block. When you type text inside a regular AsciiDoc file, if lines of text appear on separate lines i.e. they are contiguous without a blank line in between but on separate lines, the AsciiDoc markup *does not* treat them to be on separate lines. When you render this AsciiDoc file, you will find that all the text is displayed on one line. To avoid this happening, we use the *verse styling or verse block.*

Let's see this in action in Example 71. The following lines of text show how someone typed this profound verse from the Sufi mystic Rumi inside an AsciiDoc file.

Example 71. Text Typed Inside a Raw AsciiDoc File

```
 I am so close,
 I may look distant.
 So completely mixed with you,
 I may look separate.
 So out in the open,
 I appear hidden.
 So Silent,
 Because I am constantly talking to you!
~Rumi
```

Clearly whoever typed these lines would want these nine lines of text to appear exactly as they have been typed — each on a separate line like a poem — when this AsciiDoc file is rendered by AsciiDoctor. But observe what happens when the file is rendered by AsciiDoctor in HTML or PDF:

Will be rendered as...

I am so close, I may look distant. So completely mixed with you, I may look separate. So out in the open, I appear hidden. So Silent, Because I am constantly talking to you! ~Rumi

As you can see, unless every line of text is clearly separated from the line above and below by a blank line, text appearing inside the AsciiDoc file on separate lines is all bunched up together as unbroken paragraph text when it is rendered. This is where the *verse* block comes in. The verse block simply respects how you place text on separate lines and when rendered, shows text exactly as you typed it inside the AsciiDoc file.

To create a verse block, you start by typing in `[verse]` and then entering your text from the very next line. You need to make sure that there is no blank line between `[verse]` and the text block as shown in Example 72. As can be seen in the rendered output, the text block is reproduced exactly as it was typed with line breaks nicely preserved.

AsciiDoc Markup

Example 72. A Verse block

```
.I Am Always with You  ①
[verse]
I am so close,
I may look distant.
So completely mixed with you,
I may look separate.
So out in the open,
I appear hidden.
So Silent,
Because I am constantly talking to you!
~Rumi
```

① If you wish to add a title to the block, just use '.Title Text' *directly* above the [verse] or any other block. There should be no space between the '.' and the title text otherwise the title will appear as a numbered list item !

Will be rendered as...

I Am Always with You

> I am so close,
> I may look distant.
> So completely mixed with you,
> I may look separate.
> So out in the open,
> I appear hidden.
> So Silent,
> Because I am constantly talking to you!

Notice that the font size in the verse block is larger making the verse stand out.

You can also extend the *verse* block styling — `[verse]` in Example 72 to include the author and the source of the verse in the format — `[verse, Rumi,The Masnavi]` — which would not require you to separately write the name of the author and the source of the work at the end as can be seen in Example 73.

Example 73. Extending the Verse Block Styling

> I am so close,
> I may look distant.
> So completely mixed with you,
> I may look separate.
> So out in the open,
> I appear hidden.
> So Silent,
> Because I am constantly talking to you!
>
> — Rumi, The Masnavi

As mentioned earlier, the *verse* block respects line breaks in regular text as long as the text under `[verse]` is **contiguous** i.e. there are no blank lines in the text that follows. If however the text in the verse block is non-contiguous and is separated by a blank line or lines, the verse block operates only on the contiguous part and not on the text which follows the blank line. So while using verse, be sure that the text is contiguous.

7.5. Literal Block

We can create a literal block by starting and ending the block with `....` i.e. four dots as shown in Example 74. From a beginners perspective, a literal block appears quite similar to a listing block. It however preserves formatting such as fixed-width font and endlines, and only replaces special characters and callouts. Unlike a listing block, it does not permit any interpretation or processing of text contained within it — *not even for code highlighting*. It is typically used to display console output exactly as it is appears in the terminal.

Example 74. A literal block

```
....
csr@faros:~$ podman --version
....
```

A case in point is Example 70 that shows markup for a listing block in which I wanted to display to the readers, the `----` markup that starts and ends a listing block. I cannot do that by enclosing it inside another listing block (to force AsciiDoc not to interpret it) and so I did this by *nesting* the whole listing block—with the starting and ending listing block delimiters (`----`)—inside a *literal block* which started with `....` and ended with `....` sequence. We will talk more about *nesting* blocks inside each other later when we discuss sidebar blocks in Section 7.7.

You can also create a literal block just by indenting the first line. Instead of starting from the first position (leftmost) on a line, push tab once or just push the space bar a couple of times and start typing and you have created a literal block which will be displayed in light gray background as seen in Example 75.

Example 75. Creating a literal block using indentation

```
This is a literal block that has been created just by indenting the first line. When
you see the left margin of this text, you will notice that it is a couple of spaces
to the right of other text on this page. Below is another literal block as there is
an empty line but the text on the line after the empty line is also indented creating
a second literal block.
```

```
$ ruby --version
  ruby 3.1.2p20 (2022-04-12 revision 4491bb740a)
```

☞ The literal block ends when I start typing again from the leftmost position on a new line.

7.6. Example Block

An example block is another great way of visually highlighting content. It can be of use if you are illustrating a concept or the results of an operation. You the writer are the best judge of what you think is an conceptual explanation in context of whatever you are writing. The default styling theme that AsciiDoctor uses (at the time of writing this text) distinguishes an example block by showing it in a light yellow background (HTML) with a lightly shadowed brighter gray border that gives a slight halo effect. One other great thing about example blocks is that they are automatically numbered (like Example 1, Example 2 etc.) by AsciiDoctor when you give them a title. What this means is that whenever you create an example block, it gets automatically numbered in sequence if you put a title just above it starting with a '.' and *immediately* followed by the title text.

To create an example block, you can just delineate text that you wish to include inside the block with a starting and closing line of ==== i.e. four equal to signs. Example 76 uses some sample text to show how we can create an example block and how it looks in the rendered document.

AsciiDoc Markup

Example 76. The Example Block

```
.The Albedo Effect        ①
====                      ②
Albedo is an expression of the ability of surfaces to reflect sunlight (heat from the
sun). Light-coloured surfaces return a large part of the sunrays back to the
atmosphere (high albedo). Dark surfaces absorb the rays from the sun (low albedo).

image::albedo.png[]                                                          ③

Decrease in dark surfaces leads to higher uptake of energy and, hence, warming.

[small]#_Diagram and Text Source: Norwegian Polar Institute, Norway_#

====   ④
```

① Example Title

② Start example block (4 '=' symbols)

③ Example block content

④ End example block (4 '=' symbols)

Will be rendered as...

Example 77. The Albedo Effect

Albedo is an expression of the ability of surfaces to reflect sunlight (heat from the sun). Light-coloured surfaces return a large part of the sunrays back to the atmosphere (high albedo). Dark surfaces absorb the rays from the sun (low albedo).

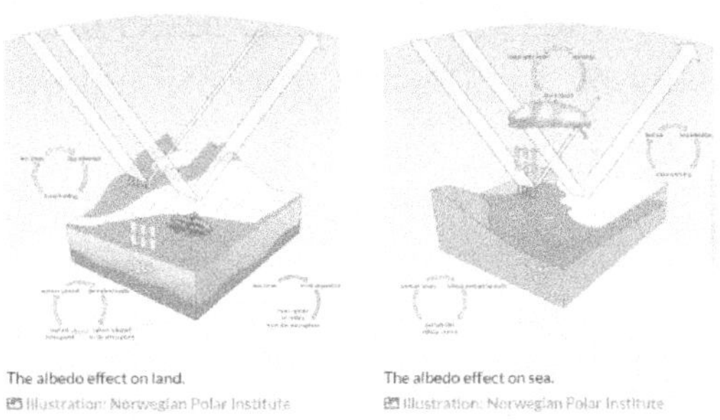

Decrease in dark surfaces leads to higher uptake of energy and, hence, warming.

Diagram and Text Source: Norwegian Polar Institute, Norway

The numbering that you see in Example 77 title has been automatically generated by AsciiDoctor in continuation to other examples that appear prior to this example in this book chapter.

As long as a block is contiguous i.e. it does not have any blank line, you can create an example block by placing the style directive `[example]` on top that paragraph as shown in Example 78. The example block will include all the following contiguous lines till a blank line in encountered.

Example 78. Example block created by style name

```
.What is Albedo ?
[example]
Albedo is an expression of the ability of surfaces to reflect sunlight (heat from the
sun). Light-coloured surfaces return a large part of the sunrays back to the
atmosphere (high albedo).
                    ①
_This line will not be part of the example block as it is separated  from the
previous text by a blank line._
```

① Blank line — Everything below this line will not be part of the example block and will be treated like normal text outside the example block.

Will be rendered as...

Example 79. What is Albedo ?

Albedo is an expression of the ability of surfaces to reflect sunlight (heat from the sun). Light-colored surfaces return a large part of the sun rays back to the atmosphere (high albedo).

This line will not be part of the example block as it is separated from the previous text by a blank line.

The line above in italics is not part of the example block. Also notice that the numbering for Example 79 has been generated automatically by AsciiDoctor in continuation to the previous examples in this book chapter.

7.7. Sidebar Block

The *sidebar block* is one of the most versatile blocks in AsciiDoc. The sidebar block can be created by enclosing the content that you wish to highlight between a starting and ending line of **** (four stars). A sidebar block is rendered in a slightly darker gray background. Any title associated with a sidebar block is *centered* and *not numbered* by AsciiDoctor as is the case with the example block. But the sidebar block distinguishes itself from other blocks by the fact that it can include or *nest* within it, all other types of blocks. So in a manner of speaking, the sidebar block can be termed as the *King of the blocks* ! Example 80 demonstrates how we can create a simple sidebar block.

If you want to include a title for the sidebar block, you can do so by placing a title on the line immediately above the opening delimiter line of the sidebar block. The title should start with a '.' and there should be no space between the '.' and the title text as seen in callout 1 of Example 80.

AsciiDoc Markup

Example 80. A Simple Sidebar Block

```
.The Viral Spread of Misinformation and Disinformation  ①
****    ②
Misinformation is false or inaccurate information—getting the facts wrong.
Disinformation is false
information which is deliberately intended to mislead—intentionally misstating the
facts.   ③

The spread of misinformation and disinformation has affected our ability to improve
public health,
address climate change, maintain a stable democracy, and more.

[small]_Source: American Psychological Association._

****    ④
```

① Title for the sidebar block. This is not auto-numbered by AsciiDoctor

② Start of the sidebar block (the four stars are called delimiters)

③ Block content (Text)

④ End of the sidebar block

Will be rendered as...

The Viral Spread of Misinformation and Disinformation

Misinformation is false or inaccurate information—getting the facts wrong. Disinformation is false information which is deliberately intended to mislead—intentionally misstating the facts. The spread of misinformation and disinformation has affected our ability to improve public health, address climate change, maintain a stable democracy, and more.

Source: American Psychological Association

7.7.1. Nesting Other Blocks Inside Sidebar a Block

Let's now see how we can nest other blocks inside a sidebar block. Example 81 shows an instance of a sidebar block within which we have nested four different types of blocks.

AsciiDoc Markup

Example 81. Single Sidebar block with four nested blocks

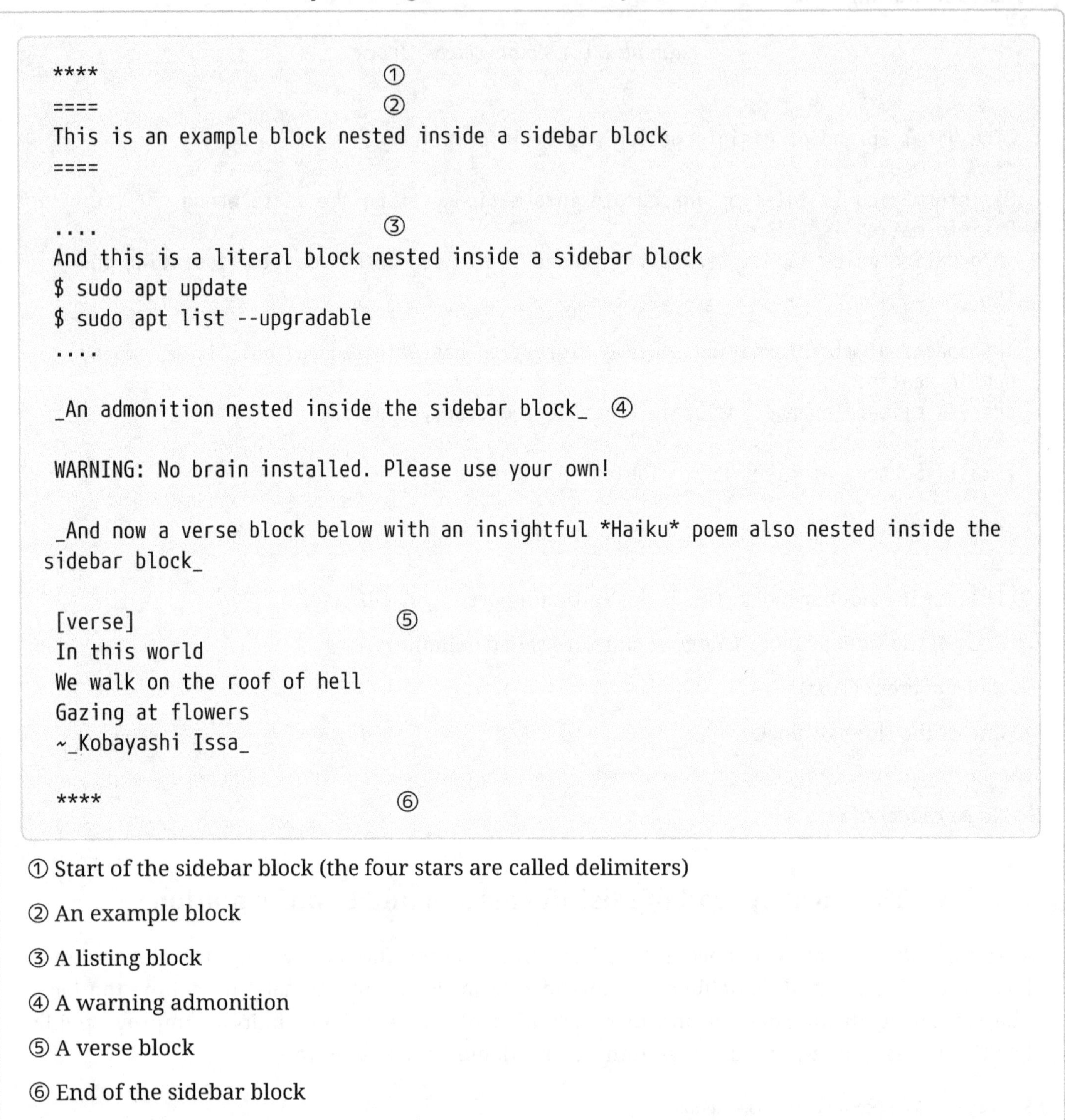

```
****                                 ①
====                                 ②
This is an example block nested inside a sidebar block
====

....                                 ③
And this is a literal block nested inside a sidebar block
$ sudo apt update
$ sudo apt list --upgradable
....

_An admonition nested inside the sidebar block_  ④

WARNING: No brain installed. Please use your own!

_And now a verse block below with an insightful *Haiku* poem also nested inside the
sidebar block_

[verse]                              ⑤
In this world
We walk on the roof of hell
Gazing at flowers
~_Kobayashi Issa_

****                                 ⑥
```

① Start of the sidebar block (the four stars are called delimiters)

② An example block

③ A listing block

④ A warning admonition

⑤ A verse block

⑥ End of the sidebar block

Will be rendered as...

Single Sidebar block with four nested blocks

This is an example block nested inside a sidebar block

```
And this is a literal block nested inside a sidebar block
$ sudo apt update
$ sudo apt list --upgradable
```

A warning admonition below nested inside the sidebar block

No brain installed. Please use your own!

*And now a verse block below with an insightful **Haiku** poem also nested inside the sidebar block*

In this world
We walk on the roof of hell
Gazing at flowers
~Kobayashi Issa

We can also nest a *source code* block to display code and a *passthrough* block to display equations inside a sidebar block. Both these blocks are discussed in the following sections.

The sidebar block is therefore a very versatile block structure that virtually provides you with an empty canvas and the freedom to create a variety of *block mashups* as required in your document.

7.8. Passthrough Block

The `passthrough` block is created by enclosing a chunk of content between opening and closing lines with `++++` i.e. with four plus symbols. This kind of block is typically used when you write mathematical equations using either AsciiMath or LaTeX Math markup. It can also be used to pass HTML content in a document. The passthrough block permits equation markup to be interpreted by software such as *AsciiDoctor-Mathematical* and display nicely formatted equations in the output. We discuss equations later in Chapter 14. However, as it might immediately not be apparent what a passthrough block really does, let's see how we can create a passthrough block and examine its behavior. Example 82 shows a line of text that has an HTML tag. When we put this line inside a listing block or just type it in running text, it is rendered exactly as it is as shown in Example 82 i.e. with the `<u>` and `</u>` opening and closing HTML tags visible (but not underlining the text they enclose).

Example 82. HTML tags inside AsciiDoc text

HTML tags can be <u>inserted</u> in text but will they will be processed?

As can be seen in Example 82, the HTML tags are not processed and the text appears as it was typed. This is because AsciiDoc does not interpret HTML tags in running text or inside a listing block.

However, if we put the same line of text inside a passthrough block, the HTML tags are allowed to *pass through* and get interpreted resulting in the word *inserted* being underlined (Example 83).

AsciiDoc Markup

Example 83. Passthrough block

```
++++
HTML tags can be <u>inserted in text</u> and they will be processed in this
passthrough block.
++++
```

Will be rendered as...

HTML tags can be inserted in text and they will be processed in this passthrough block.

The passthrough block demonstrated in Example 83 is rendered only in HTML output. We have used it here as a simple demonstrator to illustrate the concept of a passthrough block. We will revisit the passthrough block in more detail in Chapter 14.

You can also have passthrough in inline text i.e. running text to help deal with some infrequently encountered issues. Let's take the following example where in a running text sentence, we wish to communicate that we need four plus signs to start and end a passthrough block in AsciiDoc. So we write this normally in our AsciiDoc text as shown in Example 84.

AsciiDoc Markup

Example 84. Typing ++++ symbols directly in text leads to AsciiDoctor removing them from text

```
If you wish to create a delimited passthrough block, you can do so by enclosing the
desired content inside a starting and closing line comprising of ++++ signs.
```

Will be rendered as…

If you wish to create a delimited passthrough block, you can do so by enclosing the desired content inside a starting and closing line comprising of signs.

Notice in the rendered output, the four plus signs are missing as they are being interpreted by AsciiDoctor. To let those four plus signs *pass through*, we can use the inline version of passthrough as shown in Example 85.

AsciiDoc Markup

Example 85. Inline Passthrough syntax

```
If you wish to create a delimited passthrough block, you can do so by enclosing the
desired content inside a starting and closing line comprising of pass:[++++] signs.
```

Will be rendered as…

If you wish to create a delimited passthrough block, you can do so by enclosing the desired content inside a starting and closing line comprising of ++++ signs.

However, in scientific or academic writing, the most important use of the passthrough block is to display equations using AsciiMath or LaTeX Math markup. As this is a very important topic for many researchers and students, I have dealt with this separately in Chapter 14.

7.9. Source or Code Blocks

One of the major use of blocks in technical writing, particularly for developers, is to highlight code blocks such that code and its constituent syntax in a given programming language stands out from the rest of the text. This is accomplished in AsciiDoc using *syntax highlighter* software. I cover this in detail in Chapter 10.

7.10. Chapter Summary

Key learnings in this chapter are:

- Blocks are a very important feature of AsciiDoc as they help to highlight portions of text in special ways and make it stand out.
- We have seen how to create and use many different blocks in this chapter. Some of the blocks that we have covered include:
  - Comment Block — For multi-line comments.
  - Verse Block — Highlight multiple lines respecting line breaks.
  - Listing Block — Used for including source code listing or other preformatted text and can be highlighted using a syntax highlighter.
  - Literal Block — Displays the text exactly as it is written in the source, preserving formatting such as fixed-width font and end lines, and only replacing special characters and callouts. Used typically for displaying terminal outputs.
  - Example Block — Numbered block title and a prominent shaded border.
  - Sidebar Block — Can nest other blocks.
  - Passthrough Block — Permits markdown to pass through and get interpreted.
- We can also annotate listing blocks, literal blocks and source code blocks — together also referred to as *verbatim blocks* with callouts and annotations. See Section 7.3.1 for a recap.
- We discuss code highlighting using listing blocks in Chapter 10.

7.11. Try it Yourself

The exercise file for this chapter — *blockse.adoc* — can be found in the exercise packet. Refer to chapter sections for help on the following exercises.

1. Open *blockse.adoc* and create various blocks as mentioned inside the file.
2. Render *blockse.adoc* both as HTML and PDF to see how blocks display in rendered output and spot any differences in how blocks and callouts appear in HTML and PDF.

Chapter 8. Conditional Processing

"Nothing is more difficult, and therefore more precious, than to be able to decide." ~Napoleon Bonaparte

---

In this chapter we will see how to include or exclude text or images in rendered HTML or PDF output based on certain conditions being true or false. This capability gives us the flexibility to create different versions of the same document or create documents to address different audiences using the same AsciiDoc file. Conditional processing can also help avoid processing errors in certain situations like rendering AsciiDoc files to EPUB3.

8.1. Why Conditional Processing ?

Conditional processing in AsciiDoc takes document creation and customization to a whole new level. It provides a decision making structure inside your AsciiDoc file to include (or exclude) content based on a condition being true. This AsciiDoc feature, among other things, provides the following two very valuable capabilities to the document creator:

1. To be able to create different versions of the same document through conditional processing based on set attributes or their values.
2. To be able to customize the same content for on-screen reading (HTML rendering of AsciiDoc files) or print versions (PDF rendering of AsciiDoc files).

In this chapter we will see how we can use conditional directives in AsciiDoc to selectively add content to documents.

8.2. Conditional Directives in AsciiDoc

8.2.1. The ifdef, ifndef Directives

Let's take a simple use case to understand how conditional directives can be helpful. Let's say we want to create a general note on computer programming but need to include code examples from different programming languages targeting different audiences — say one group learning python and the other, Ruby. To do this, we (a) need to define or *set* an attribute and (b) write a conditional statement testing if that attribute has been *set* or not.

8.2.1.1. Defining or Setting up an Attribute

To define or set an attribute, all we need to do is to choose a name for the attribute and put it in the header of the document as shown in Example 86.

AsciiDoc Markup

Example 86. Defining an attribute called langruby

```
= Introduction to Programming
:doctype: book
:icons: font
:langruby:
```

In Example 86, we added an attribute called `:langruby:` which means that this attribute has been *set* even though it does not have a value in front of it. Compare this with the `:icons: font` attribute in which the *icons* attribute has its value set to *font*. We can surely give a value to my `:langruby:` attribute but we will come to that later. For now, let's say we have just included it in the document header which means that it has been set.

8.2.1.2. Writing the Conditional Directive with ifdef

With the `:langruby:` attribute declared in the header, we can now write conditional statements. The `ifdef::` directive *tests* whether an attribute is set. If the result of this test is *true* meaning that yes it is *set*, we can include additional lines of text in the document. However if this test fails i.e. the attribute is *not set*, the additional lines of text will not be included in the document. Figure 66 depicts a conceptual representation of how the conditional *ifdef* directive works.

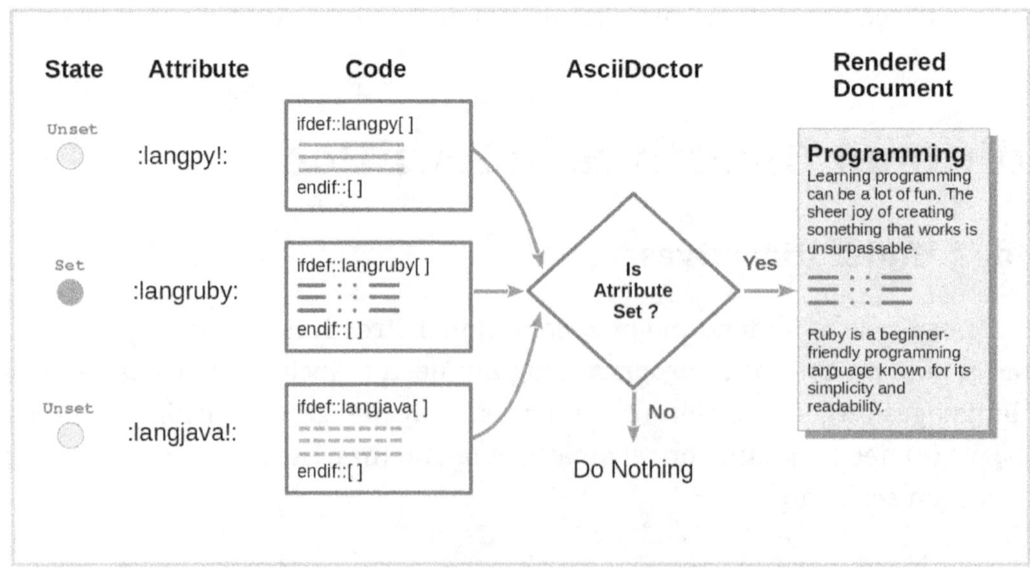

Figure 66. Conceptual diagram illustrating the ifdef conditional directive

As can be seen in Figure 66, based on whether an attribute is set or unset (the trailing `!` unsets the attribute), we can include AsciiDoc markup — represented as colored lines between the *ifdef* and *endif* statements (under the code column) — in the final rendered document. In Figure 66, `:langruby:` is the only attribute that is *set*. So when AsciiDoctor performs the *ifdef* set / unset conditional test while rendering, `:langruby:` passes the test and lines between `ifdef::langruby[]` and `endif[]` are added to the rendered HTML or PDF file. The other two attributes fail the test as they are *unset* and therefore no content is contributed by them to the rendered output.

Let's see this in context of an example similar to what has been represented in Figure 66. In the AsciiDoc markup shown in Example 87, we test if the attribute `langruby` is set and if it is, insert everything between the `ifdef::` and the `endif::[]` in the document.

AsciiDoc Markup

Example 87. Conditional ifdef syntax

```
// This sample AsciiDoc file is saved as ifdefdemo.adoc

= Programming Fundamentals
:Author: Prof. Chinmaya S Rathore
:langruby:          ①

== Functions
Let's try to learn why functions are important in computer programming and how to
write functions.

[%hardbreaks]          ②
ifdef::langruby[] ③
Functions permit us to reuse code and prevent errors. The following example shows how
we can write a function in Ruby to convert temperature in Celsius to Fahrenheit.

  def celsius_to_fahrenheit(celsius)  ④
    (celsius * 9 / 5) + 32
  end

endif::[]              ⑤
```

① Set the `:langruby:` attribute in the document header

② Ensures that every statement is on a separate line.

③ The *ifdef* directive starts by testing if the attribute *langruby* is set. In this case, it is.

④ Note that lines of code are indented by one space.

⑤ The *ifdef* directive ends with *endif.*

The conditional directive, which evaluates to be TRUE as `:langruby:` attribute is set, results in printing lines between the *ifdef* and *endif.* If you are using VS Code live preview, you can see the results instantly. Otherwise you will have to render the AsciiDoc file using *AsciiDoctor* or *AsciiDoctor-PDF* to see the results. To see how conditional statements in our example AsciiDoc file *ifdefdemo.adoc* shown in Example 87 are processed by AsciiDoctor, we issue the command shown in Example 88 from the terminal to render our file as HTML .

AsciiDoc Markup

Example 88. Rendering the AsciiDoc file to see results of the ifdef conditional statement

```
$ asciidoctor ifdefdemo.adoc
```

Will be rendered as...

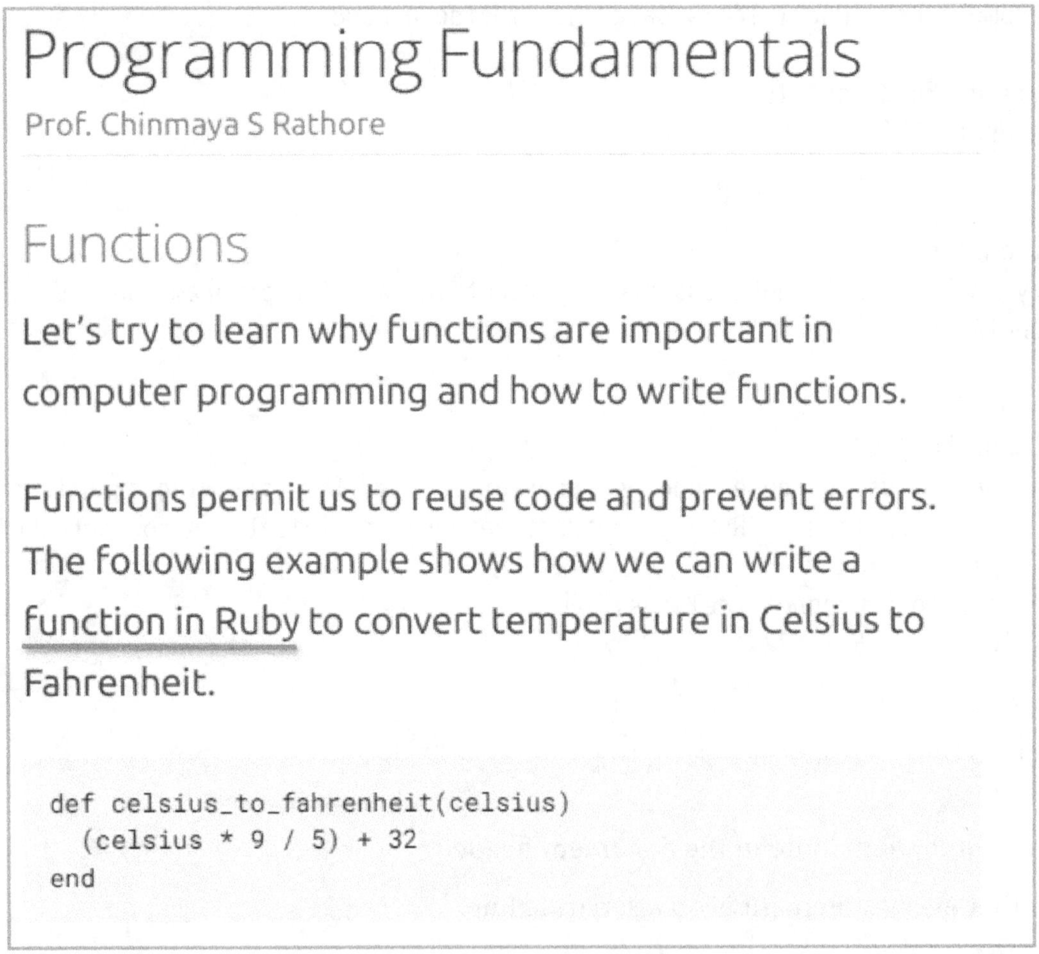

```
def celsius_to_fahrenheit(celsius)
  (celsius * 9 / 5) + 32
end
```

Figure 67. When ifdef condition evaluates to be true, the ifdef directive prints the Ruby function

If the `:langruby:` attribute was not included in the document header or if the attribute was unset by suffixing the attribute with an exclamation mark in the header (`:langruby!:`), all lines between *ifdef* and *endif* would be omitted from the text (Figure 68) as the *ifdef* directive would evaluate to be *false*.

Programming Fundamentals

Prof. Chinmaya S Rathore

Functions

Let's try to learn why functions are important in computer programming and how to write functions.

Figure 68. Output when ifdef evaluates to be false

8.2.1.3. Writing the Conditional Directive with ifndef

The `ifndef::` directive is the logical opposite of the `ifdef::` directive. It tests if an attribute is *not set or defined*. In Example 87, let's say if we wanted to include a Python function and if the *langruby* attribute was *not* set (i.e. `:langruby!:`), we could add an `ifndef::` directive to the AsciiDoc file shown as shown in Example 89.

Example 89. Conditional ifndef Directive Syntax

```
= Programming Fundamentals
:Author: Prof. Chinmaya S Rathore
:langruby!:              ①

== Functions
Let's try to learn why functions are important in computer programming and how to
write functions.

[%hardbreaks]
ifdef::langruby[]      ②
Functions permit us to reuse code and prevent errors. The following example shows how
we can write a function in Ruby to convert temperature in Celsius to Fahrenheit.

def celsius_to_fahrenheit(celsius)
```

```
  (celsius * 9/5) + 32
end
endif::[]

// We add an ifndef conditional directive below to add python code if :langruby:
attribute is missing or unset

[%hardbreaks]
ifndef::langruby[]     ③
Functions permit us to reuse code and prevent errors. The following example shows how
we can write a function in Python to convert temperature in Celsius to Fahrenheit.

def celsius_to_fahrenheit(celsius):
 return (celsius * 9 / 5) + 32
endif::[]
```

① The attribute :langruby!: is unset

② Test using *ifdef* is :langruby: is set

③ Test using *ifndef* is :langruby: is unset

In Example 89, as the attribute *langruby* is unset (callout 1), the *ifdef* conditional will evaluate to *false* and ruby lines will be omitted, while the *ifndef* conditional will evaluate to be *true* (as attribute *langruby* is unset) and the Python code will be inserted in the document as shown in Figure 69.

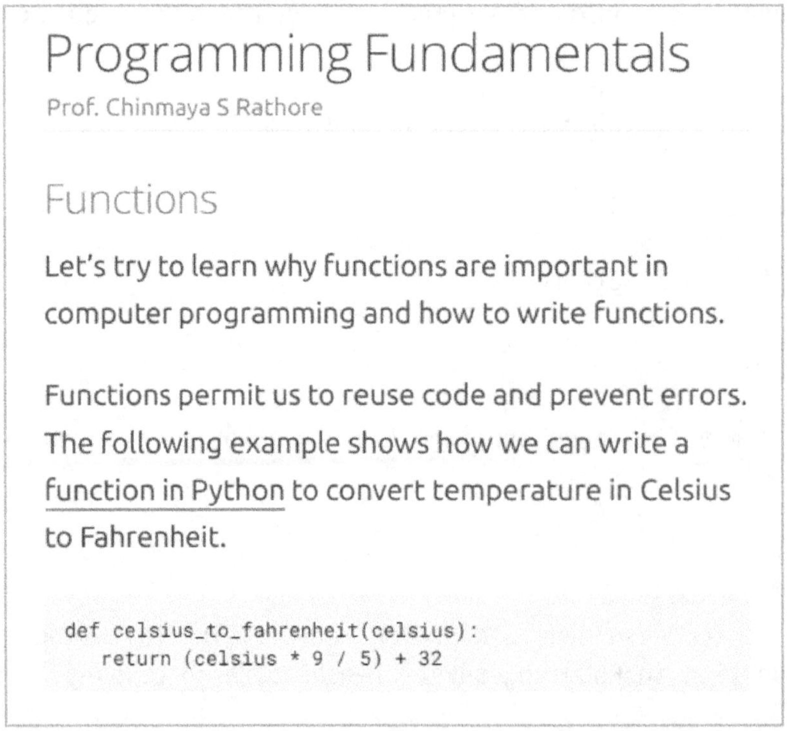

Figure 69. The ifndef conditional evaluates to be true and includes the Python code

If you were to remove the unset exclamation mark from `:langruby!:` attribute and make it `:langruby:`, you will get the code for Ruby again as shown in Figure 67.

8.2.2. Combining More than One Conditions

Both *ifdef* and *ifndef* permit combining multiple conditional statements which can be written in two formats as shown in Example 90 and Example 91.

AsciiDoc Markup

Example 90. The OR conditionals

```
ifdef::attribute1,attribute2[] ①
Lines to include
endif::[]
```

① Attributes separated by ',' means that if *ANY* one of these attributes is set (equivalent to an OR clause) — ifdef will evaluate as *True*.

Example 91. The AND conditionals

```
ifdef::attribute1+attribute2[] ①
Lines to include
endif::[]
```

① Attributes separated by '+' means that *All* of these attributes **must be set** (equivalent to an AND clause) for *ifdef* to evaluate as *True*.

Let's explore this with a simple example that extends the AsciiDoc markup in Example 87. We introduce another attribute called `:rubyskill-starter:` which indicates the programming skill level of learners. Example 92 shows this addition and the modified *ifdef* conditional testing that now tests for two conditions.

Example 92. Multiple Attribute Conditionals Equivalent to the OR Clause

```
= Programming Fundamentals
:Author: Prof. Chinmaya S Rathore
:langruby!:         ①
:rubyskill-starter:    ②
```

```
== Functions
Let's try to learn why functions are important in computer programming and how to
write functions.

[%hardbreaks]
ifdef::langruby,rubyskill-starter[] ③
Functions permit us to reuse code and prevent errors. The following example shows how
we can write a function in Ruby to convert temperature in Celsius to Fahrenheit.

  def celsius_to_fahrenheit(celsius)
    (celsius * 9 / 5) + 32
  end
\endif::[]
```

① The `:langruby:` attribute is *unset* in the document header (`:langruby!:`)

② We add a new attribute called :rubyskill-starter: (which is *set*).

③ Create a *ifdef* conditional with two attributes separated by a ',' meaning A *OR* B . You can have more than two attributes also.

By putting a comma in between the two attributes in the conditional directive as shown in Example 92, we are essentially saying that if *any* one of the attributes in the conditional line is set , *idef* will evaluate the conditional expression as *true* and you will get the output as shown in Figure 67. Only when both attributes are *unset* or missing from the header will you get the output shown in Figure 68. If even one attribute in an OR clause is *set*, the *ifdef* directive will pass the conditionality test.

If you replace the comma in Example 92 at callout 3 with a '+' as shown in Example 93, you get an AND conditional directive where *both* `:langruby:` and `:rubyskill-starter:` *must be set* to get an output shown in Figure 67.

AsciiDoc Markup

Example 93. The Multi Attribute AND Clause

```
ifdef::langruby+rubyskill-starter[]
```

If any one of these attributes — *langruby* or *rubyskill-starter* — is unset or missing from the header, then the *ifdef* clause will evaluate to *false* and you will see the output shown in Figure 68. *All* attributes in an AND clause must be *set* for the *ifdef* directive to pass the conditionality test.

8.2.3. Conditional Inclusions using Backends

Apart from the above, the *ifdef* and *ifndef* conditional directives can be very handy in including and excluding content based on whether the AsciiDoc file is being rendered as HTML (HTML5 Backend) or PDF (PDF Backend). We discuss this in detail in Chapter 17.

8.2.4. The ifeval Conditional Directive

Let's now see how we can use the `ifeval::` conditional directive. While `ifdef::` and `ifndef::` directives test wether an attribute has been *set* or *unset*, the `ifeval::` conditional directive tests the values of attributes (rather than their being set or unset) permitting more expansive conditional logic testing. With the `ifeval::` conditional directive, we compare the left hand side of the expression being evaluated with the value on the right hand side using *operators*. The generic syntax of the conditional directive is shown in Example 94. If the conditional test evaluates to be *true*, lines between `ifeval::` and `endif` get included in the text.

Example 94. The ifeval conditional generic syntax

```
ifeval:: ["{attribute}" == "value"}]
Content to Include
endif:[]
```

The == operator tests for equality. A full list of operators that can be used in `ifeval::` conditional expressions is shown in Table 2.

Table 2. Operators that can be used in ifeval conditional expressions

Operator	Name	Expression Evaluates
==	Equal To — Example A == B	True if values on either side are equal
!=	Not Equal To — Example A != B	True if values on either side are *not* equal
>	Greater Than — Example A > B	True if A is greater than B
<	Less Than — Example A < B	True if A is less than B
>=	Greater Than or Equal To — Example A >= B	True if A is greater than or equal to B
<=	Less Than or Equal To — Example A <= B	True if A is less than or equal to B

Let's try to see `ifeval::` in action using a small example. Let's add two new attributes — `:langname:` and `:langcode:` to the header in the *ifdefdemo.adoc* AsciiDoc file that we used in Example 87 and give them a value as illustrated below in Example 95.

AsciiDoc Markup

Example 95. Assigning values to attributes

```
:langname: python  ①
:langcode: 1       ②
```

① Attribute has text value = 'python'

② Integer or numerical value = 1

Let's now see how the `ifeval::` conditional can be used to test for both text and number values.

8.2.4.1. Using *ifeval* to Test for Strings or Text Values

Example 96 shows how we can use `ifeval:` to test for an attribute having a text value.

Example 96. Conditional ifeval to test text values of attributes

```
= Programming Fundamentals
:Author: Prof. Chinmaya S Rathore
:langname: python        ①
:langcode: 1             ②

== Functions
Let's try to learn why functions are important in computer programming and how to
write functions.

[%hardbreaks]
ifeval::[ "{langname}" == "python" ]  ③
Functions permit us to reuse code and prevent errors. The following example shows how
we can write a function in Python to convert temperature in Celsius to Fahrenheit.

 def celsius_to_fahrenheit(celsius):
     return (celsius * 9 / 5) + 32

endif::[]            ④
```

① Attibute having a text value

② Attibute having a numerical value

③ Using *ifeval* to test for text value in *langname* attribute

④ End of ifeval

Figure 70 shows the resulting output when the above AsciiDoc file is rendered. As the value of the *langname* attribute is equal to 'python', the expression evaluates to be *true* and the content between *ifeval* and *endif* is added to the rendered file.

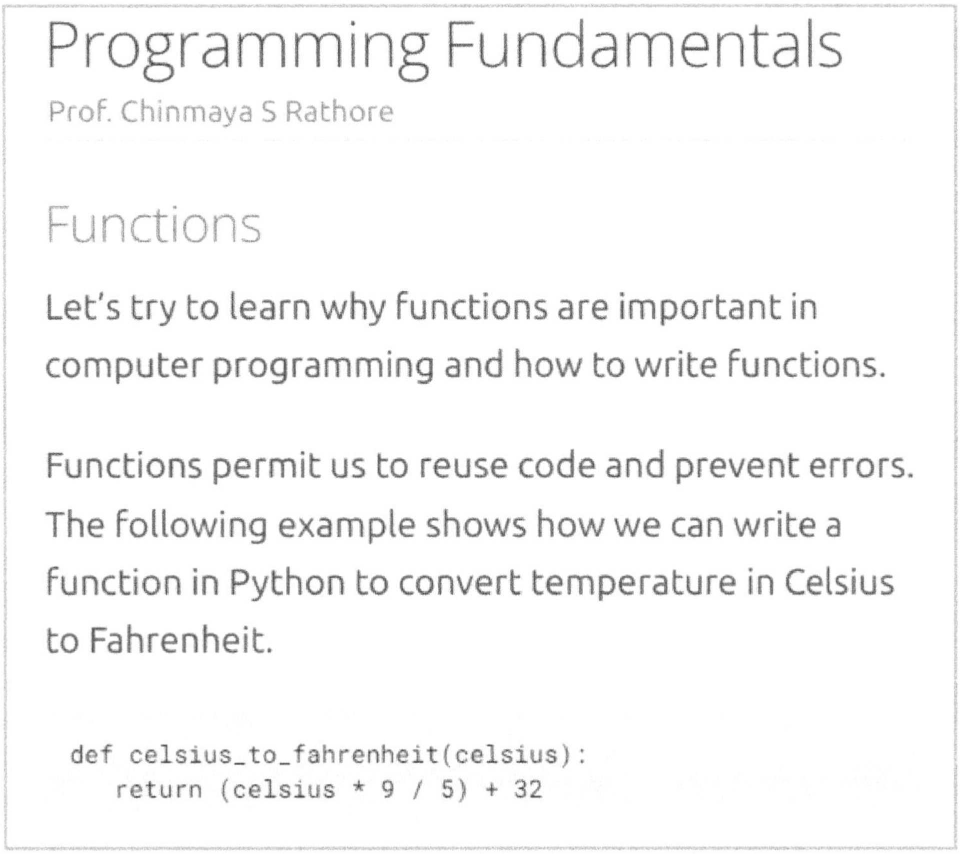

Programming Fundamentals

Prof. Chinmaya S Rathore

Functions

Let's try to learn why functions are important in computer programming and how to write functions.

Functions permit us to reuse code and prevent errors. The following example shows how we can write a function in Python to convert temperature in Celsius to Fahrenheit.

```
def celsius_to_fahrenheit(celsius):
    return (celsius * 9 / 5) + 32
```

Figure 70. Text rendered as a result of using ifeval conditional directive

8.2.4.2. Using ifeval for Testing Numbers

Similarly we can also test for integer (or decimal) values of attributes like *langcode* by replacing the *ifeval* line in Example 96 with the following line :

AsciiDoc Markup

```
ifeval::[ {langcode} == 1 ]
```

Having set the value of the langcode attribute to 1, let's use now use *ifeval* to insert an *image* rather than lines of code as we did earlier in Example 96. The images that we are using here are screenshots of highlighted code but they can actually be any image.

Let's say for example, we wish to use the same document to show the IF statement (in computer programming) in Ruby if the *langcode attribute* is equal to 1 and in Python if the *langcode attribute* is equal to 2. Example 97 shows how we can set up our AsciiDoc file where the first part is common to both versions but the second part will depend on the value assigned to the *langcode* attribute.

AsciiDoc Markup

Example 97. Using the ifeval conditional test to create two versions of the same AsciiDoc file

```
= Programming Fundamentals
:author: Prof. Chinmaya S Rathore
:langcode: 1

// Common content for both versions

== The IF Statement
An if statement in programming languages is a control flow statement that allows the
program to execute different blocks of code based on whether a specified condition
evaluates to true or false.  ①

//Ruby screenshot image will get included if langcode=1

\ifeval::[ {langcode} == 1]    ②
Here is an example of how the IF statement is written in Ruby:

.If Statement in Ruby
image::ifruby.png[]            ③
endif::[]

// Python screenshot image will get included if langcode=2

\ifeval::[ {langcode} == 2]    ④
Here is an example of how the IF statement is written in Python:

.If Statement in Python
image::ifpython.png[]          ⑤
endif::[]
```

① This part is common to both versions

② The first ifeval test — *is langcode = 1 ?* ⇒ True

③ The Ruby screenshot image is included

④ The second ifeval test — *is langcode = 2 ?* ⇒ False

⑤ The Python screenshot image is not included.

Figure 71 shows Ruby content being included in the rendred document when `langcode=1`.

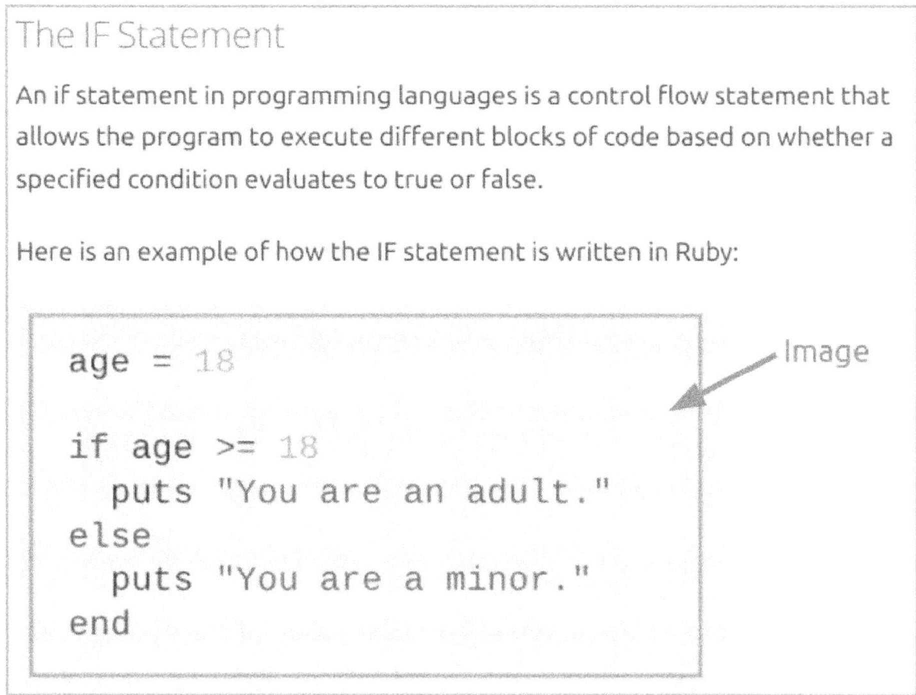

Figure 71. Content inclusion based on the langcode value — showing Ruby code being included as langcode=1

Figure 72 shows Python code being included in the same rendered document when `langcode=2`.

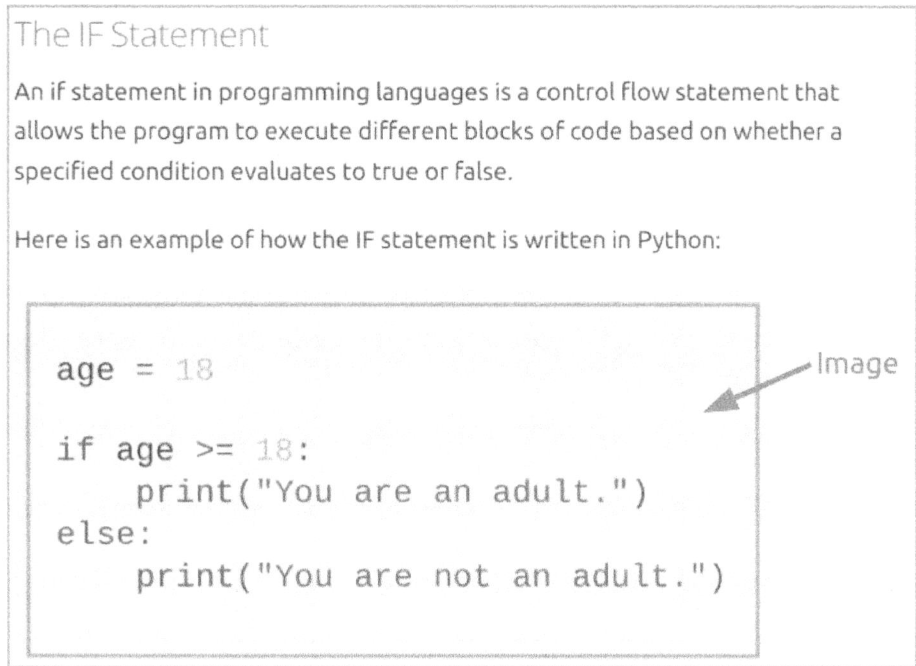

Figure 72. Content inclusion based on the langcode value — showing Python code being included as langcode=2

It will be worthwhile to reiterate once again that in Example 97, we have inserted an *image* and not text based on the conditional test. This can be any image based on the context of the document. Similarly we can add the `include::` macro in place of the `image::` macro to add external files.

8.3. Testing for System Defined Attributes

Apart from user defined attributes as demonstrated in this chapter, you can also use conditional directives to test for system defined or *built-in attributes*. Built-in attributes such as *sectnums, doctype, media, revnumber, revdate* etc. can also be similarly tested by conditional directives and content can be included or excluded based on the result of these conditionality tests.

8.4. Important Considerations while Writing Conditionals

Conditional processing to include or exclude content based on attributes and their values is a very powerful feature of Asciidoc. It opens up a host of exciting possibilities in creation and customization of documents. While working with conditional directives in AsciiDoc is quite easy, keeping the following in mind will help avoid errors:

1. With reference to the `ifeval::` conditional directive, it is important to remember that whenever you wish to test an attribute that has a text value, you need to enclose the attribute on the left hand side of the operator within braces and quotes (like `"{langname}"` — see Example 96). For numbers, you should not use quotes (like `{langcode}` — see Example 97).
2. Unlike `ifdef::` and `ifndef::` directives, the `ifeval::` conditional directive *does not* support evaluating multiple conditions in a single directive statement. This means you *cannot* write an *ifeval* statement with multiple conditions in the generic format like — `A == B AND C > D` etc. If you need to do this, you will have to write a separate ifeval — endif block for each condition.
3. AsciiDoc supports *number counters* which we discuss in [chapmatheqmain]. Conditional directives have *not* been designed to work with AsciiDoc counter variables and therefore it is good practice *not* to use them in *ifeval* expressions.

To know more about conditional processing in AsciiDoc, please visit the AsciiDoctor Documentation page on conditionals [https://docs.asciidoctor.org/asciidoc/latest/directives/conditionals/].

8.5. Chapter Summary

Key learnings in this chapter are:

- In this chapter we have seen how to use conditional directives to include or exclude content at any place in our documents.
- We can do this using three conditional directives — *ifdef* , *ifndef* and *ifeval* — that can test for the presence or absence of an attribute or its value and include lines of Asciidoc markup if the conditional test evaluates to be TRUE.
- The *ifdef* directive tests whether an attribute is *set* and if it does, AsciiDoc markup or text between the *ifdef* and *end if* statements is included in the document. Multiple conditions can be used in one directive for logical OR / logical AND testing. Please see Section 8.2.1.2 for a quick recap on how to use the *ifdef* conditional directive and Section 8.2.2 to recap how to create OR / AND expressions.
- The *ifndef* directive is the logical opposite of the *ifdef* directive and tests if an attribute is *unset* and if true, includes AsciiDoc markup between the *ifndef* and *end if* statements in the document. Multiple conditions can be used in one directive for logical OR / logical AND testing. Please see Section 8.2.1.3 for a quick recap on how to use the *ifndef* conditional directive.
- While the *ifdef* and *ifndef* conditional directives test for presence or absence of an attribute, the *ifeval* directive tests values of attributes and provides more complex conditional testing using operators =, != , > , >=, <, <= comparing left hand side to the right hand side in conditional expressions. Unlike *ifdef* and *ifndef*, you cannot test for multiple values in *ifeval* conditional expressions. Please see Section 8.2.4.1 for a quick recap on how to use the *ifeval* conditional directives.

8.6. Try it Yourself

The files used to illustrate conditional directives in this chapter can be downloaded from the chapter folder in the exercise packet.

1. Open the *ifdefdemo.adoc* file and explore how the *ifdef* directive has been used to insert selective content based on attribute testing as described in Section 8.2.1.2 of this chapter. Examine the attributes in the document. Notice that there is an attribute called `:langruby:` in the header. Render this file as HTML or PDF issuing the *asciidoctor* or *asciidoctor-pdf* command. Will the file contain the Ruby function or the Python function ?

2. Add an attribute called `:langpy:` to the header and unset the `:langruby:` attribute by adding an exclamation mark at the end of the attribute — `:langruby!:`(! ⇒ unsets). Render the file again as HTML or PDF and examine the output. Do you see the Python code or the Ruby code ?
3. With the `:langruby!:` attribute unset, change the `ifdef::langruby[]` to `ifndef::langruby[]` and render the document in HTML or PDF. Why is the code for Ruby being included even when `:langruby:` is unset ? (Hint: When does the *ifndef* test evaluates to TRUE ?)
4. Can you create an ifdef statement where if either `:rubyskill-starter:` OR `:langruby:` are unset (that is one attribute set and one unset), the Ruby code is still included in the rendered document ? (Hint: You need to use to use multiple test conditions using the OR clause (See Section 8.2.2 for help).
5. Can you bring the above ifdef directive in an AND clause ? (see Section 8.2.2 for help). How does the output change and why ?
6. Open the *imginsert.adoc* file and examine it to review how the *ifeval* conditional directive is being used to include content ?
7. Render the document in HTML and PDF and examine what is included in the document and why ?
8. Can you render a document in which both images mentioned in the the *imginsert.adoc* file are included ? (Hint: At Line 22, just after the first *endif*, enter — :langcode: 2 (in the body of the document)
9. Can you, in the *imginsert.adoc* file, add a third *ifeval* directive to the file for Java or any other programming language that adds content when the *langcode* attribute is set to a value of 3 ?
10. Can you create an AsciiDoc file that adds different content based on the skill level of the user by introducing a new attribute called :skillset: which can have a value of either beginner, intermediate or advanced ?
11. In the above example, if you set the value of the *skillset* attribute as *:skillset: beginner* in the header of document , can you change it to *:skillset: intermediate* at another place (in the body of the document) in the same AsciiDoc file ? (Hint: just paste *:skillset: intermediate* anywhere in the document and then test using an *ifeval* statement).

Chapter 9. Using Icons in Your Document

"Crap... Someone knocked over my recycle bin... There's icons all over my desktop." ~Unknown

---

Icons are great fun and can really enhance the presentation of your documents. In this chapter, we will see different ways in which we can insert and format icons in AsciiDoc.

9.1. Working with Icons

The job of the `:icons: font` attribute that we declare in the header of the document, is not just to provide icons for admonitions. It is rather a full and vast icon set of over 675 icons that can be called into service at any place inside the document. All we need to do is to just type in `icon:name[]` where *name* is the listed name of the icon in the icon set.

To illustrate the idea, Example 98 shows the basic markup to insert some interesting icons in our text:

AsciiDoc Markup

Example 98. Icon List AsciiDoc Markup

```
icon:cog[] Showing a widget or setting ①

icon:map-marker[] Depicting Location ②

icon:thermometer-three-quarters[] Thermometer ③

icon:leaf[] Leaf ④

icon:microphone-slash[] Muted Microphone ⑤
```

① icon *name* is cog

② icon *name* is map-marker

③ icon *name* is thermometer-three-quarters

④ icon *name* is leaf

⑤ icon *name* microphone-slash

Will be rendered as...

Showing a widget or setting

Depicting Location

Thermometer

Leaf

Muted Microphone

If you are wondering from where did I get all these icon names, read along. When we add the `:icons: font` attribute to the header (for admonitions), we implicitly state that we will be using the default AsciiDoctor icon set called *Font Awesome or fa.* You can visit https://fontawesome.com/v4/icons/ for a full list of the default *Font Awesome or fa* icons and their assigned names. I got the icon names used in Example 98 from this list. So from this list, you can use any icon in your text just by typing `icon:<name>[]` — replacing <name> with the exact icon name followed by `[]` as seen in Example 98.

One other great source of Font Awesome icon names is https://www.w3schools.com/icons/default.asp. On this site, the left pane has icon categories. Click on one and use just the name of the chosen icon from the list. For example the 'Alert' category has an icon listed as `fas fa-exclamation-triangle`. So ignore the fas fa part and just use the name part i.e. *exclamation-triangle* as `icon:exclamation-triangle[]` and you will see in your text. Most icon names will work (smile-o). Some may not! (frown-o)

9.2. Altering the Size of Icons

You can also easily enlarge the size of any icon just by adding the *size* attribute to the syntax shown in Example 98. The size attribute extension to `icon:` is shown in Example 99.

Example 99. Resizing icons

```
icon:leaf[size=2x]
```

When rendered Default size :

Two times enlargement : 

You can replace 2x with 3x, 4x or 5x for incrementally larger sizes or just use `lg` (`icon:leaf[lg]`) for a larger than default icon. The above icon enlargements work for both HTML and PDF.

9.3. Altering the Color of Icons (only for HTML Output)

In addition to changing the size of the icon, you can also change the color of the icon but at the time of writing, I found this to work only for HTML and *not* for PDF output. To do this, use the syntax shown in Example 100.

Example 100. Changing icon color in HTML output

```
icon:leaf[size=2x,role=red]
```

This will be rendered in red color but the colored icon can only seen in HTML output and not if you are reading this book as a PDF or a printed copy.

You could also abbreviate the markup in Example 100 to `icon:leaf[role=red]` if you wanted to see the icon in red color but in its default size.

9.4. Using Icons as Bullets in a List

If we wish to use icons to create bullet points for an unordered list, we can do so using the *fw or fixed width* size markup shown in Example 101.

AsciiDoc Markup

Example 101. Using Icons as Bullet Points

```
[%hardbreaks]     ①
icon:paw[fw] We must conserve the planets biodiversity.
icon:paw[fw] We must make efforts to prevent cruelty to animals.
icon:paw[fw] We must invest in wildlife research
```

① This styling directive ensures that every bullet points appears on a new line

Will be rendered as…

We must conserve the planets biodiversity.
We must make efforts to prevent cruelty to animals.
We must invest in wildlife research

9.5. Flipping and Rotating Icons (HTML Only)

You can also flip and rotate icons in a number of different ways using the markup in Example 102.

AsciiDoc Markup

Example 102. Rotating and Flipping Bullet Point Icons

```
icon:paw[]               ①
icon:paw[rotate=90]      ②
icon:paw[flip=vertical]  ③
icon:paw[2x,rotate=270]  ④
```

① Default size and orientation

② Other values 180,270

③ Other value — horizontal

④ Can combine attributes

Will be rendered as...

Default:

Rotate 90°:

Flip Vertical:

Size 2x and Rotate 270°:

Icon Rotation is Not Visible in PDF Output

Icon rotations, as described above work only for HTML output but not when the document is rendered as PDF. At the time of writing (July, 2025), icon rotations are supported only by AsciiDoctor (HTML) and AsciiDoctor-EPUB3 (EPUB3) but not by AsciiDoctor-PDF. A possible work around could be to use icon images that are already rotated to a desired angle using some image editing software or use a screen grab of a rotated icon from the AsciiDoctor HTML output as shown above.

9.6. Icons from Other Libraries (Only for PDF Output)

Now it so happens that Font Awesome default is not the only icon library that you can tap in AsciiDoc. You can also use icons from the following other font libraries:

- fas ⇒ Font Awesome Solid (Solid or filled icons)
- fab ⇒ Font Awesome Brands (Business Brand Icons)
- far ⇒ Font Awesome Regular
- fi ⇒ Foundation Icons

To use one of the above icon libraries, you just have to prefix the library name to an icon name (listed in that library) for it to appear in the rendered PDF. The syntax to do this is shown in Example 103.

Example 103. Using an icon from the fas or fab font icon sets

```
icon:fas-lightbulb[]
OR
icon:fab-squarespace[]
```

When rendered, the above markup will show the following icons in the PDF output:

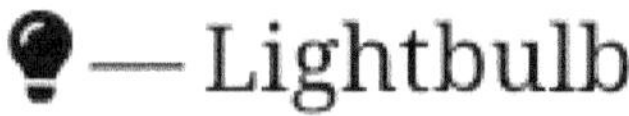

— Squarespace

Whenever you prefix the icon name with the library name as shown above, you can access icons from that library. This way you can use multiple icon libraries in one document.

Please note that if you do not prefix the icon name with the font library name (like fas, or fab etc.) and just provide the icon name as shown in Example 100, you use the default icon library — `fa`.

9.6.1. Setting a New Icon Library as Your Default (Only for PDF Output)

We can easily change the default icon set by adding the `:icon-set:` attribute to the document header as illustrated in Example 104.

Example 104. Setting the default icon set to `fas`

```
:icon-set: fas       ①
```

① You can replace *fas* with other icon libraries like *fab* or *fi* or *far*

After setting up your icon library like above for a document, whenever you type just the name of an icon like — `icon:kiwi-bird[]`, it will be assumed by AsciiDoctor that the icon is from the library defined by the `icon-set:` attribute. If the icon name is not in the icon library or icon set specified by you, AsciiDoctor-PDF will inform you that it could not find that icon in the *set* library with the following warning message:

```
WARNING: square-minus is not a valid icon name in the fas icon set
```

If you encounter such an error even though the name appears in the chosen icon-set, check if the icon name has been spelled correctly in your AsciiDoc file. Ultimately, if the icon still does not appear in spite of being spelled correctly (and yes this might happen), my advise is don't spend time troubleshooting — find something else that works!

9.6.2. Getting Icon Names for Different Icon Sets

How do you get the names of icons from other icon sets like FAS, FI or FAB ? You can visit the following websites which list icons that you can use freely in your documents.

9.6.2.1.FAS Icon Names

You can use names from the following FAS icon list:

https://fontawesome.com/v6/icons?o=r&ic=free&s=solid

When you reach this page, scroll down to the *categories section* and double click on a category like animals, automotive , alert, arrows etc. and scroll down to see the icons that you can use in that category. For example, Figure 73 shows FAS icons for the category *animals*:

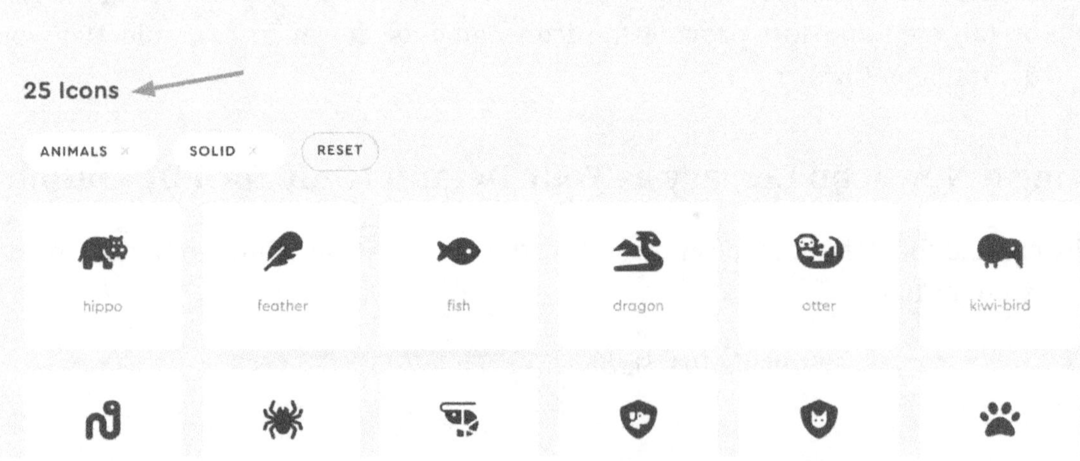

Figure 73. Free FAS icons for category 'Animals'

To use any named icon here in your PDF, use the markup shown in Example 105.

Example 105. Prefixing icon name with the icon set name

`icon:fas-kiwi-bird[]` (visible only in PDF output)

9.6.2.2. FAB Icon Names

For FAB brand icons names, please visit the Font Awesome FAB list at the following URL:

https://fontawesome.com/search?o=r&ip=brands

To use any named icon here in your PDF, use the markup shown in Example 106.

Example 106. Using FAB icons

```
icon:fab-apple[size=2em]        ①
icon:fab-linkedin[size=2em]
```

① Visible only in PDF output

Will be rendered as...

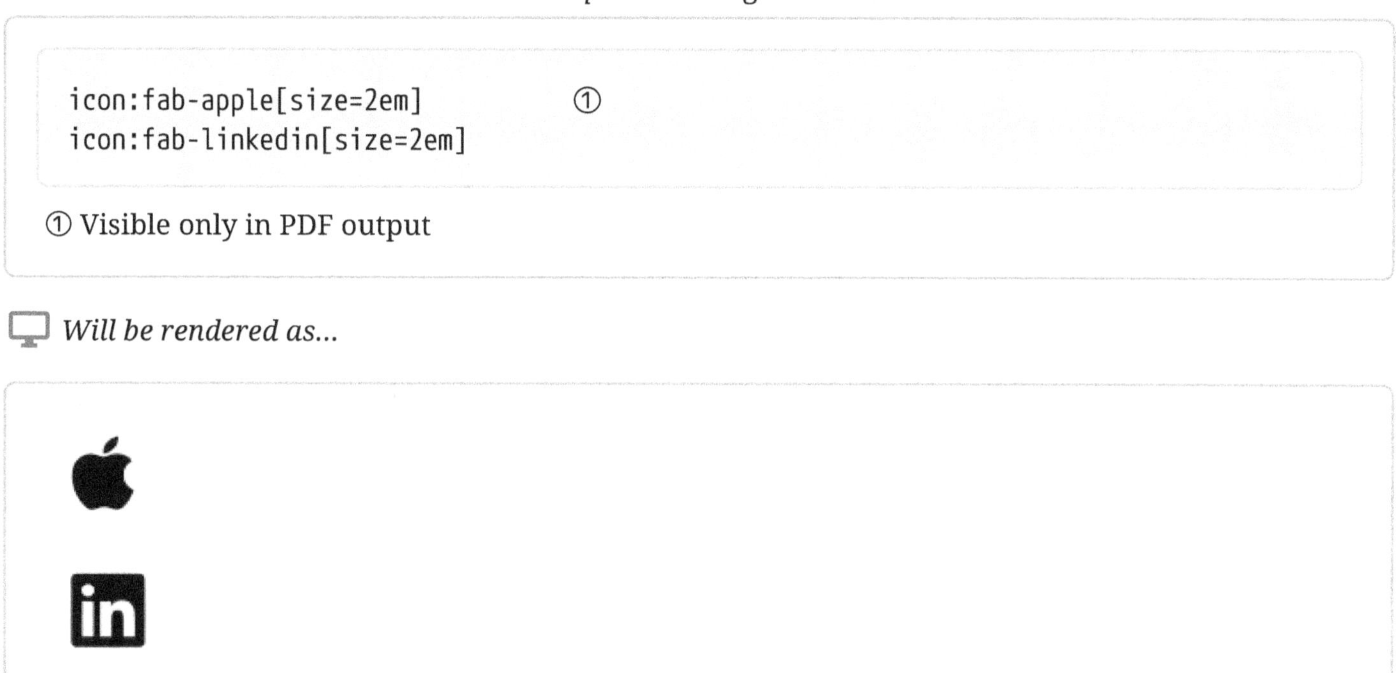

The above icons are visible only in PDF output and not in HTML output.

9.7. FI Icon Names

For Fi or Foundation icons , visit the following site for a list of icons names that you can use in your PDF output:

https://zurb.com/playground/foundation-icon-fonts-3

To use any named icon from the fi icon set in your PDF, use the markup shown in Example 107.

Example 107. Using 'fi' icons

```
icon:fi-html5[size=2em]        ①
icon:fi-elevator[size=2em]
```

① Visible only in PDF output

Will be rendered as...

If you use the above icons from fas, fab or fi icon sets, you will not see them in the HTML output. You must render a PDF file to see these icons. If you produce an HTML output using *AsciiDoctor* (and not AsciiDoctor-PDF) and don't see these icons on the HTML page, you might erroneously think that statements shown in examples like Example 106 and Example 107 don't work when they actually *do*. It's just that their output is visible when you create a PDF using the *asciidoctor-pdf* command on your AsciiDoc file.

9.8. Using your own Image Icons

9.8.1. Using Inline Images

In addition to supporting font icons, AsciiDoctor also supports image icons. What this means in practical terms is that if you need an icon that you are unable to find in the above icon-sets, you can download and use you own. Image icons work in both HTML and PDF outputs and therefore can be super useful.

Image icons can be inserted in many ways and I will first explain the *easiest* with an example. Let's say I need a fingerprint icon for my document that I am unable to find in the above mentioned icon-sets (fa,fas,fi etc.) and I also want it to be visible in *both HTML and PDF outputs*. I use the following workflow to solve the problem:

1. Visit https://fonts.google.com/icons where we can find and download a ton of outstanding icons which are completely free to use.

2. Next choose an icon and adjust its color, size etc. and download it as an *svg* file as shown by the callout sequence 1-6 in Figure 74.

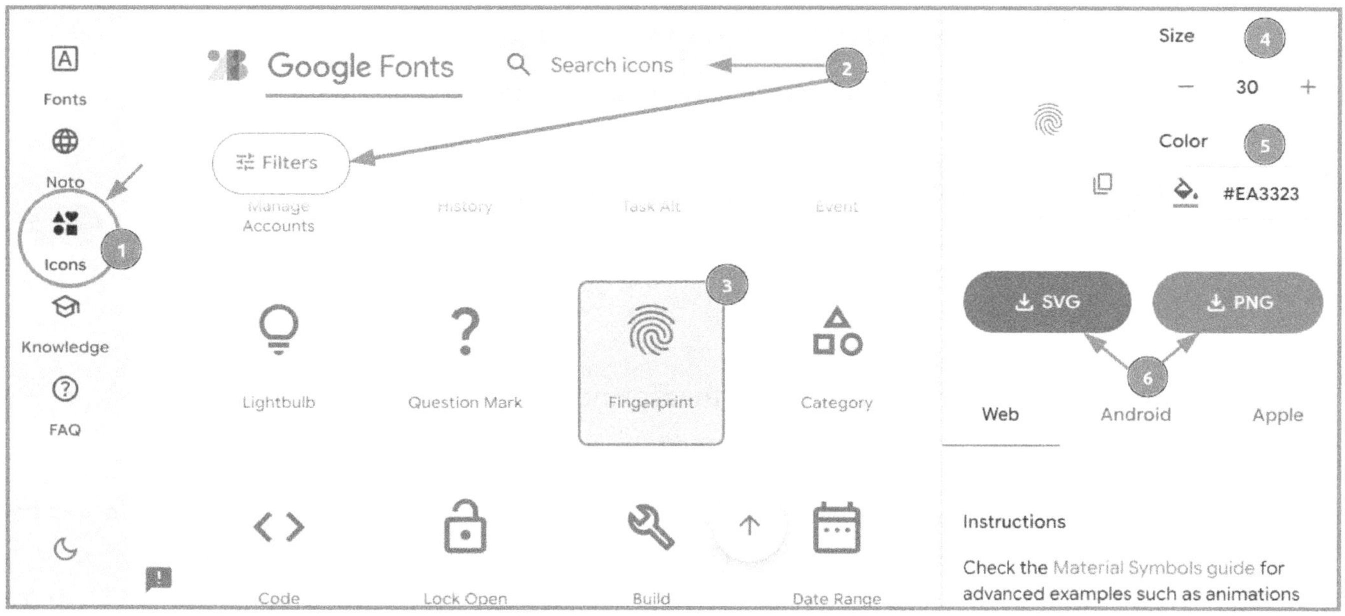

Figure 74. Icons at Google Fonts

3. Move the downloaded icon svg file to your `:imagesdir:` folder or the folder of the AsciiDoc file and just use an inline image macro to show the downloaded icon as illustrated in Example 108.

AsciiDoc Markup

Example 108. Inserting an Image Icon which is Placed in the images folder of the Current Directory

```
:imagesdir: images

Please verify your identity by your image:finger_print.svg[] fingerprint.
```

Will be rendered as...

Please verify your identity by your fingerprint.

You can also alter the size of the icon by extending the markup in Example 108 as shown in Example 109.

AsciiDoc Markup

Example 109. Altering the Size of the Image Icon

```
Please verify your identity by your image:finger_print.svg[50,50] fingerprint.
```

Will be rendered as...

Please verify your identity by your  fingerprint.

There are many other sites like https://feathericons.com/ that you can tap to get free image icons. You can also check out https://jpswalsh.github.io/academicons/ to download free academic icons as svg files. Another great site that hosts over 5600 free icons is https://tablericons.com/. Just reach this site, set the icon size , color and stroke width and copy the svg code. You can then open a text editor, paste the copied code and save the file as *name.svg* and you have an image icon just like that !

9.8.2. Setting Images Icons as Default

If for some reason, we plan to use only downloaded icons and not font icons for a document, we can *explicitly* declare this in the document header as seen in Example 110.

AsciiDoc Markup

Example 110. Declaring Image Icons and Type as Default

```
:icons: image
:icontype: svg    ①
```

① svg can be replaced by png, jpg, or gif if required.

The `:icontype: svg:` attribute indicates that all icons that will be used will be in *svg* format unless explicitly specified otherwise .

Now to make this work, the steps given below need to be followed:

1. Make sure that you have an *images folder* inside your current folder (the one in which your AsciiDoc file is residing). This is usually the folder that we specify for the `:imagesdir:` attribute.

Inside the images folder create another folder called *icons* and place all your downloaded icons that you wish to use inside the *icons* folder.

2. Once this is done, you can insert icons using the *icons macro* as shown in Example 111.

AsciiDoc Markup

Example 111. Inserting Image Icons Placed in Icons Folder

```
:icons: image
:icontype: svg


The mapping software shows this icon icon:pin[] to indicate your location.
```

Will be rendered as...

The mapping software shows this icon to indicate your location.

Specifying an Icons Directory

You can also specify any directory as icons directory by using the `:iconsdir: directory path|url` attribute as follows:

```
:iconsdir: myicons
```

With this statement, you are telling AsciiDoctor to find all icons in the *myicons* folder which is inside your current folder i.e. the folder that has your AsciiDoc file. If you do not specify this folder explicitly as mentioned above, you need to create the images/icons folder and keep your downloaded icons in that folder for this to work.

Resetting the :icons: Attribute for Admonitions

When you set the `:icons: image` attribute, you need to be aware that any admonitions following this point in your document will not show the default font based icons. If you want to use font based icons for admonitions, you need to reset the `:icons:` attribute back to `:icons: font` in your document after your requirement for image based icons is over.

You can also alternate between font icons and image icons in the same document as shown in Example 112.

AsciiDoc Markup

Example 112. Mixing Image and Font Library Icons

```
// Using a font based icon - leaf

:icons: font

icon: leaf[] Sustainability is a core value in the design of  all business processes
in our company.

// Now using a image based icon in the same document by resetting the :icons:
attribute to image

:icons: image
:icontype: svg

icon:wind_power[] All our data center energy requirements are met using electricity
generated using wind power.

// Now back again to font based icons in the same document by resetting the :icons:
attribute back again to fonts

:icons: font

icon:paw[] All materials sourced and produced by our company are free from animal
cruelty.
```

Will be rendered as...

Sustainability is a core value in the design of all business processes in our company.

All our data center energy requirements are met using electricity generated using wind power.

All materials sourced and produced by our company are free from animal cruelty.

This might appear to be a slightly more complicated method but this way, you can enjoy the best of both worlds without committing to a global `:icons:` value. <<<

9.9. Missing Icons !

Sometimes, you may experience a perplexing situation when you add icons to the text and yet icons are not visible! This can be a very frustrating situation as everything apparently appears in order and yet somehow, icons do not appear in the text.

Well it so happens that this problem is caused by an issue that has nothing to do with icons! Icons do not appear if you start your document header with a level 1 heading i.e. ==. Example 113 illustrates this situation where the header starts with a level 1 heading — `My Favourite icons`. When rendered, icons are not visible as seen in Figure 75.

Example 113. Starting a document with Level 1 heading in the header

```
== My Favorite Icons      ①
:icons: font

I just love icons.

Here are two of my favorite icons:

icon:recycle[] -- Recycle whatever you can!

icon:industry[] -- Say no to fossil fuels!
```

① Starting with a level 1 heading in the *header* hides icons.

Will be rendered as...

Figure 75. Icons are not visible as pointed by arrow

To resolve this situation you need to start with a Level 0 heading or the document title in the header (and not a level 1 heading) as shown in Example 114. Your other headings (level 1, level 2 etc.) start appearing in the body of the document i.e. after the blank line where the header finishes.

Example 114. Add a level 0 heading in the header

```
= Icons                 ①
:icons: font

== My Favourite Icons   ②

I just love icons.

Here are two of my favorite icons:

icon:recycle[] -- Recycle whatever you can!

icon:industry[] -- Say no to fossil fuels!
```

① Start with a level 0 heading in the header.

② The level 1 headings start from the body.

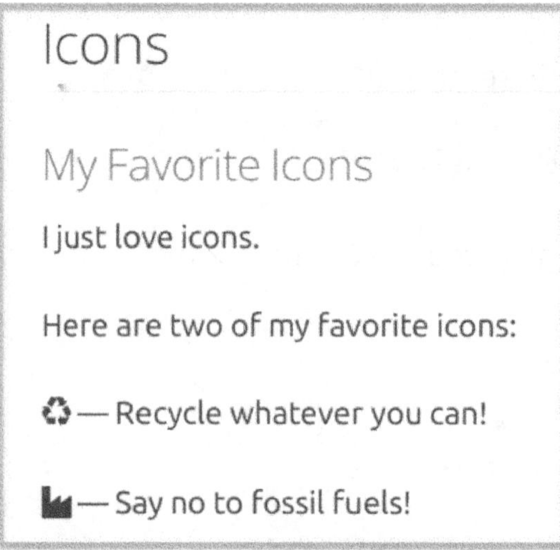

Figure 76. Icons are visible when headings are in order

For additional information on this topic with particular reference to PDF output, please visit the AsciiDoctor PDF Documentation on Icons [https://docs.asciidoctor.org/pdf-converter/latest/icons/] .

9.10. Chapter Summary

Key learnings in this chapter are:

- The default icon set — Font Awesome is activated by including the :icons: font attribute in the header of the document.
- The default icon set has many more icons in addition to the ones used for admonitions which can be used in the document text.
- To insert icons at any place in the text, use the icon:<name> macro. For example, the icon:cog[] inserts the gear icon
- To increase the size, add the size attribute — icon:cog[size=2em] which will show the icon in double its original size —
- For PDF versions of your documents, you can also use icon sets other than the default. Available icon sets include fas, fab, far, and fi. See section Section 9.6 for a recap.
- To insert an icon from a specific icon set, prefix the listed name of the icon with the name of the icon set. For example to use the lightbulb icon from the fas icon, set type — icon:fas-lightbulb[].
- To get the names of icons for different icon sets, you can visit their respective websites as mentioned in Section 9.6.2.1.
- You can also download icons as images (like SVG, PNG) from website like Google Font [https://fonts.google.com/icons] and insert it anywhere using the image:<imagename> macro. For example, to insert an image based fingerprint icon, use the markup — image:finger_print.svg[] which will display the icon. Image based icons work for all types of rendered outputs.

9.11. Try it Yourself

You will need the file *iconse.adoc* from the exercise folder for the first task below. Make sure you work from inside the *Chapter-9-Icons* folder that has an *images* folder (which in turn has an *icons* folder). Render files in AsciiDoctor and AsciiDoctor-PDF to see results.

1. Open the *iconse.adoc* and perform tasks listed in the file.
2. Open https://tablericons.com/ and you will see the following screen:

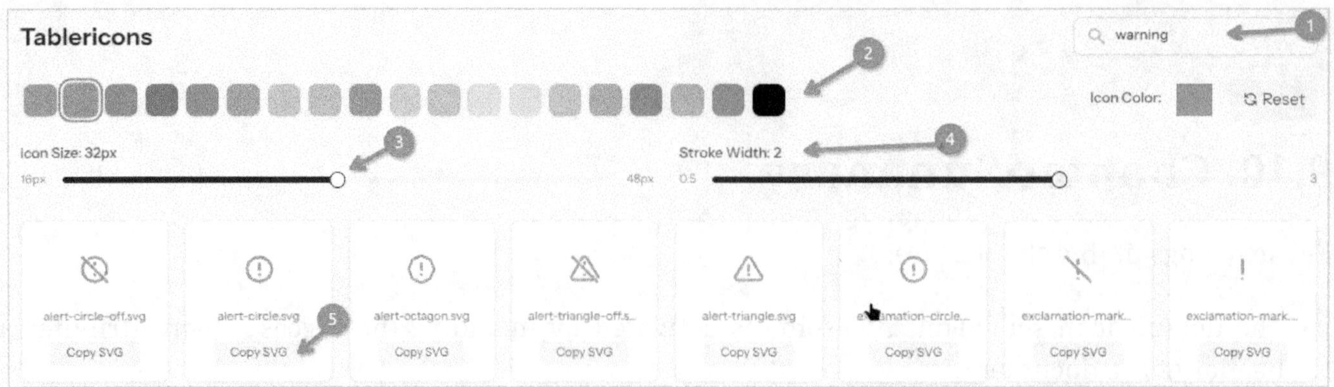

You can search for an icon category (1), alter its color (2), alter its size (3), alter the stroke width (4), and copy the SVG code (5) — which copies some code to your clipboard. Open a text editor, paste the code and save the file as _alert-circle.svg (5) or any other name. You should now see an SVG icon file that you can use as an image icon as discussed in Section 9.8.

3. Similarly, try to download some SVG icons from https://fonts.google.com/icons and use them in your AsciiDoc document as discussed in Section 9.8 and Example 108.
4. Visit https://www.w3schools.com/icons/default.asp and try to use some icons from different catw3schoolsegories in your AsciiDoc documents. Use only the name part (like `icon:exclamation-triangle[]`) seen underlined in the screenshot below:

Chapter 10. Syntax Highlighting for Code

"Any fool can write code that a computer can understand. Good programmers write code that humans can understand."
~ Martin Fowler

One of the major strengths of AsciiDoc is its ability to beautifully integrate computer code in documents. In this chapter, we will see how AsciiDoc permits you to create highly readable code blocks using different syntax highlighters. We will explore how to use Pygments, Rouge and CodeRay to highlight syntax.

10.1. A Touch of Class!

If the project that you are working on involves explaining or showcasing computer code, AsciiDoc has your back like none other. To highlight code, all you literally need to do is to paste your code block in an AsciiDoc document, choose a syntax highlighter, and *voila*— your code block is transformed into an *object of art* with all the syntax of the code block highlighted in color. This piece of magic that AsciiDoctor does with sublime ease not only makes the code highly readable, it adds tons of polish to your documents. To do this, we need to install an additional piece of software called a *Syntax Highlighter* and then we are all set to go. In fact AsciiDoc spoils us for choice and offers us more than one syntax highlighters permitting us to explore code highlighting with different highlighters and choose the one that works best in a particular situation.

As they say, a picture is worth a thousand words and Figure 77 shows what syntax highlighting can do to a normal vanilla flavored block of code. (*If you are reading a printed version of this book, you will not be able to see highlighted code in color*).

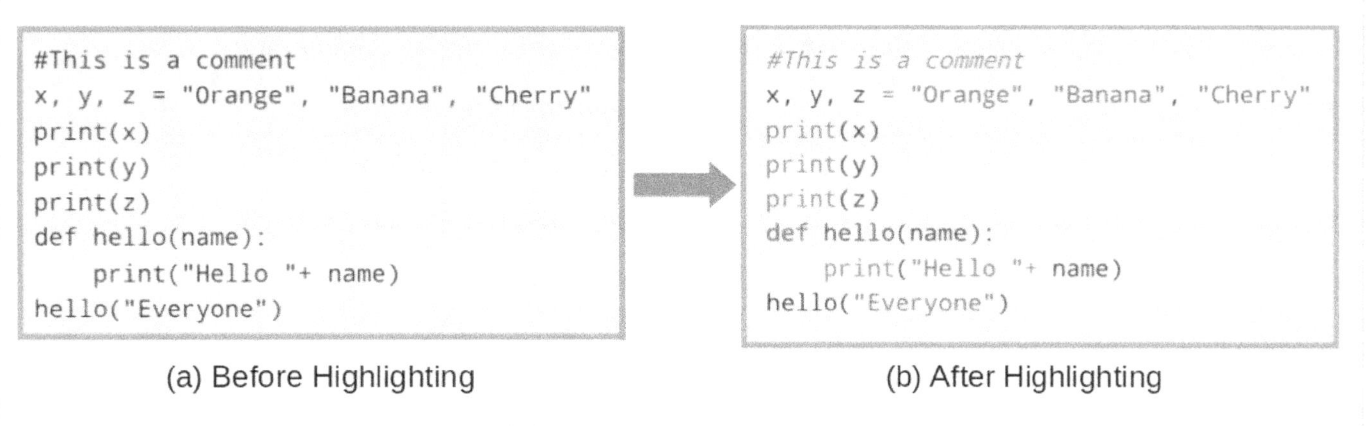

```
#This is a comment
x, y, z = "Orange", "Banana", "Cherry"
print(x)
print(y)
print(z)
def hello(name):
    print("Hello "+ name)
hello("Everyone")
```

(a) Before Highlighting

```
#This is a comment
x, y, z = "Orange", "Banana", "Cherry"
print(x)
print(y)
print(z)
def hello(name):
    print("Hello "+ name)
hello("Everyone")
```

(b) After Highlighting

Figure 77. A code block (a) without syntax highlighting and (b) with syntax highlighting

So without further ado, let's dive into the details.

10.2. The Syntax Highlighting Sequence

To highlight code, we need to execute the following steps in sequence:

1. Install one or more syntax or source highlighter/s (details in Section 10.3.1). This is a *one time install* and once done, you don't need to repeat this step.

Subsequent to installation of source highlighters, every time we need to highlight code in our document, we need to repeat the following steps:

2. Insert the `:source-highlighter:` attribute in the AsciiDoc document header and set it to a highlighter of your choice. (Section 10.4)
3. Mark a block of code with `[source,python]` syntax indicating the programming language like python in this example. (Section 10.5)
4. Run AsciiDoctor or AsciDoctor-PDF to get HTML or PDF output.
5. Open the rendered documents to check if highlighted code meets your expectations and if not, repeat steps 2-4 choosing a different source highlighter.

These steps are described in more detail in the following sections.

10.3. Installing Syntax Highlighters

Syntax highlighters, in a manner of speaking, *understand* programming languages and their syntax and highlight code based on styling rules accordingly. Installing syntax highlighter software (technically called *libraries*) gives us one more important capability — *adding line numbers* to code blocks which can be super helpful if you are trying to explain code in your document. Table 3 shows syntax-highlighters supported by AsciiDoc.

Table 3. Syntax Highlighter Options (Source: AsciiDoctor Documentation)

Syntax Highlighter	Compatible Converters
Rouge	HTML, PDF, EPUB3, Reveal.js
Coderay	HTML, PDF, EPUB3, Reveal.js
Pygments	HTML, PDF, EPUB3, Reveal.js
Highlight.js	HTML, Reveal.js

10.3.1. Syntax Highlighters in the AsciiDoctor Docker Image

If you are using the AsciiDoctor Docker image, you don't need to install anything. Rouge, Coderay and Pygments syntax highlighters come pre-installed with the Docker AsciiDoctor image. You can ignore the installation steps in Section 10.3.2 below and jump straight to Section 10.4.

10.3.2. Direct Installation of Rouge and other Syntax Highlighters

In this text we will be installing and using the *Rouge* syntax-highlighter which can highlight syntax for a large number of computer languages and scripts (225 languages and counting!). Some of the Popular languages and scripts supported by Rouge are presented in Table 4. You can visit https://rouge.jneen.net/ to know more about the languages that *Rouge* supports and also try out some syntax highlighting online for fun in your favorite programming languages.

Table 4. Partial list of computer languages and scripts supported by Rouge (Source: Rouge website)

C	C++	C#	Clojure
Shell	Swift	ERB	Go
Haskell	Groovy	HTML	Java
JavaScript	JSON	Lua	PHP
Python	Ruby	Sass	SQL
JSON	CSS	YAML	Typescript

Rouge is installed as a Ruby gem. Based on your Linux distribution, issue any one command shown in Example 115 from the terminal to install Rouge.

Terminal Command

Example 115. Installing the Rouge Syntax Highlighter on Different Linux Distros

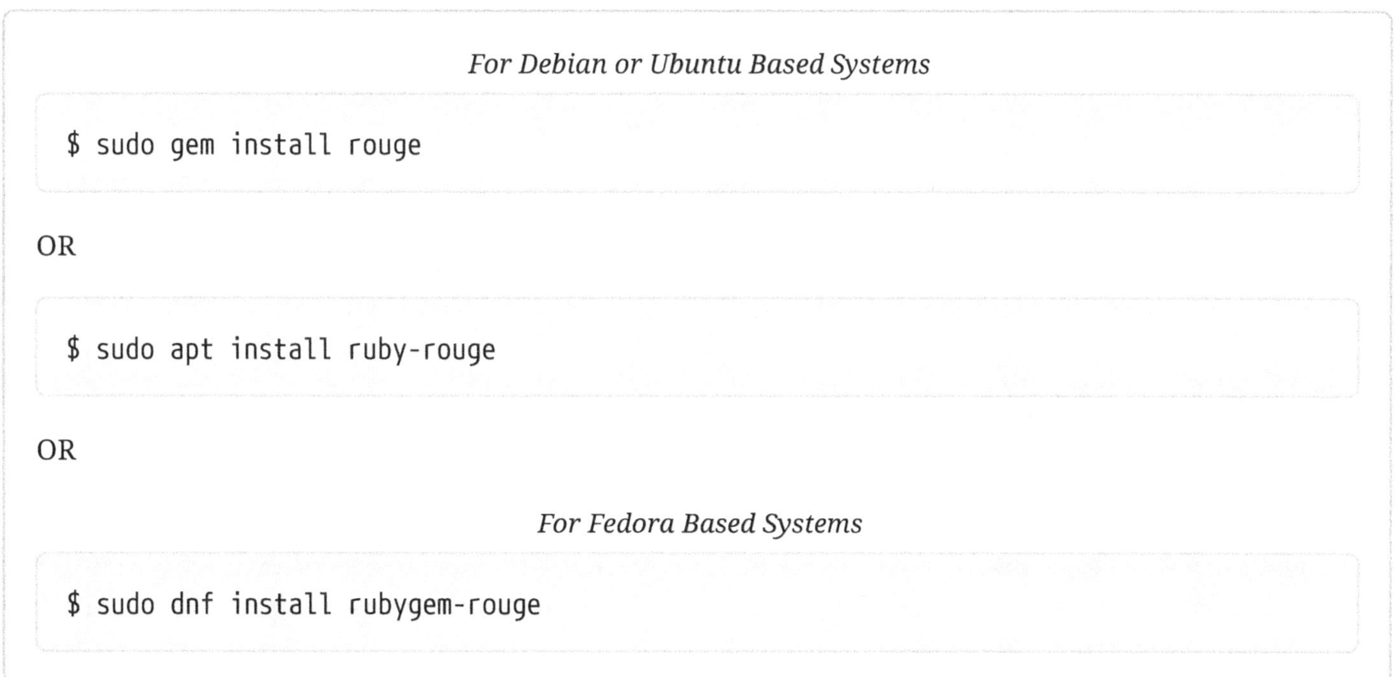

For Debian or Ubuntu Based Systems

```
$ sudo gem install rouge
```

OR

```
$ sudo apt install ruby-rouge
```

OR

For Fedora Based Systems

```
$ sudo dnf install rubygem-rouge
```

Windows and Mac users can install *Rouge* by issuing the following command from their command prompt or terminal:

```
gem install rouge
```

This is a one time install and after installation, we can start using *Rouge* in our documents for highlighting syntax of any programming language listed in the Table 4.

10.3.3. Optional Install of Other Highlighters

If you do a lot of technical writing and your documents require frequent references to code blocks, it might be worthwhile to similarly install *coderay* and *pygments* highlighters as shown. With these three highlighters installed, you can choose which highlighter works best for you.

10.3.3.1. Installing CodeRay

Like for *rouge* , you can easily install coderay using the command shown in Example 116 from your terminal (same command for Linux, Windows, Mac).

Terminal Command

Example 116. Installing the CodeRay Syntax Highlighter

```
$ gem install coderay
```

10.3.3.2. Installing Pygments

Pygments requires Python 3. Most linux systems have Python 3. You can check if Python is installed by issuing the command shown in Example 117 from your terminal.

Terminal Command

Example 117. Verifying that Python is Installed

```
$ python3 --version
```

If Python 3 is installed on your system (which should be the case as we have been using AsciiDoctor), you should see a response like `Python 3.12.3` telling you the installed version of Python. We can now issue the command shown in Example 118 from the terminal to install *pygments* syntax highlighter (same command for Linux, Windows and Mac).

Terminal Command

Example 118. Installing Pygments source highlighter

```
$ gem install pygments.rb
```

10.4. Adding the Syntax Highlighter Attribute

Once *rouge* (or any other highlighter) is installed, we need to put the `:source-highlighter:` attribute in the header of our document as shown in Example 119.

AsciiDoc Markup

Example 119. Installing the CodeRay Syntax Highlighter

```
:source-highlighter: rouge     ①
```

① Use pygments or coderay in place of rouge if you want to use those.

10.5. Adding Code Blocks in Running Text

We can add code blocks by specifying the programming language of choice using the AsciiDoc markup shown in Example 120.

AsciiDoc Markup

Example 120. Creating Code Block with Embedded Python Code

```
[source,python]  ①
#This is a comment
x, y, z = "Orange", "Banana", "Cherry"
print(x)
print(y)
print(z)
def hello(name):
    print("Hello "+ name)
hello("Everyone")
```

① We specify here that the following block is source code and its written in the Python programming language. Python can be replaced by any other programming language name.

That's it. With the *syntax highlighter* attribute set and with a code block *specifying the computer programming language*, we are all set to render syntax highlighted code blocks!

10.6. Rendering the AsciiDoc File with Highlighted Code

With the value of the `:source-highlighter:` attribute set to *rouge* or *coderay* or *pygments* , whenever you insert a code block in your AsciiDoc file, its syntax will get automatically highlighted as you render the file to HTML or PDF. Figure 78, Figure 79 and Figure 80 show the PDF output from different syntax highlighters using the same sample Python code. These outputs have been created by simply running AsciiDoctor or AsciiDoctor-PDF on the AsciiDoc file (*$ asciidoctor-pdf myfile.adoc*), that had the block of Python code shown in Example 120.

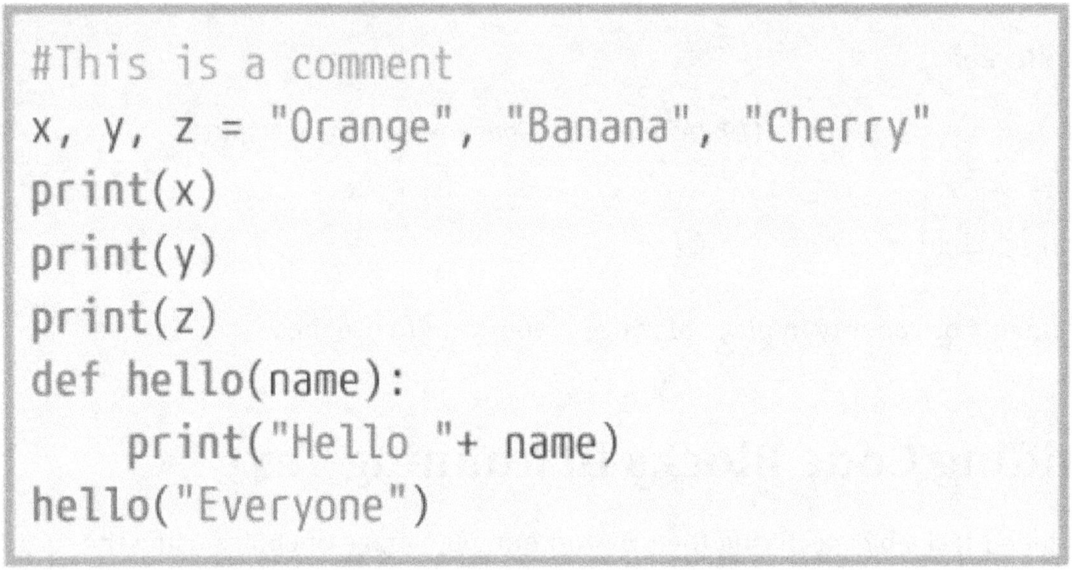

```
#This is a comment
x, y, z = "Orange", "Banana", "Cherry"
print(x)
print(y)
print(z)
def hello(name):
    print("Hello "+ name)
hello("Everyone")
```

Figure 78. Source Code Highlighted in PDF using Rouge

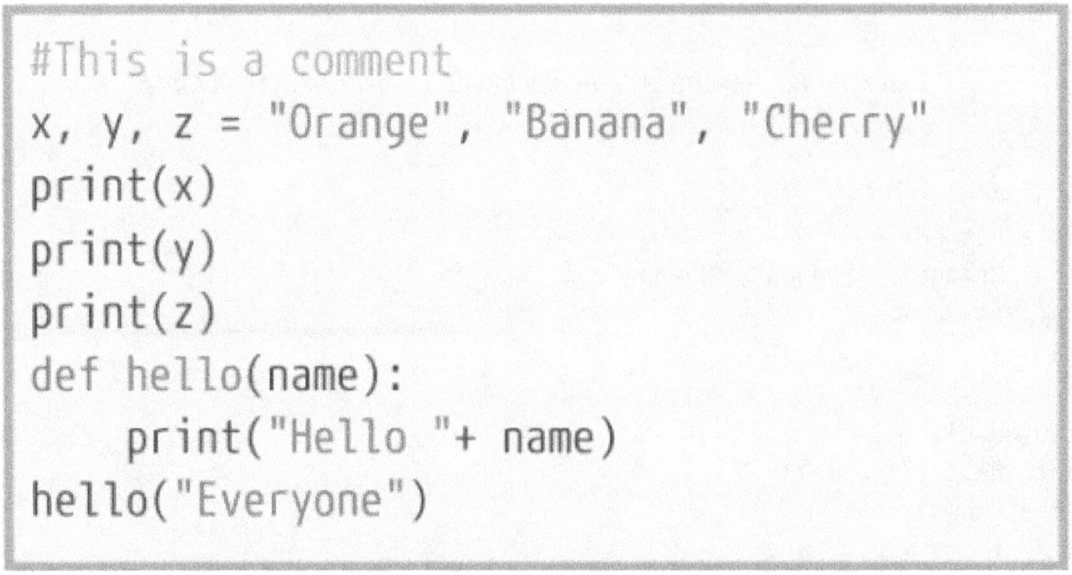

```
#This is a comment
x, y, z = "Orange", "Banana", "Cherry"
print(x)
print(y)
print(z)
def hello(name):
    print("Hello "+ name)
hello("Everyone")
```

Figure 79. Source Code Highlighted in PDF using Coderay

```
#This is a comment
x, y, z = "Orange", "Banana", "Cherry"
print(x)
print(y)
print(z)
def hello(name):
    print("Hello "+ name)
hello("Everyone")
```

Figure 80. Source Code Highlighted using Pygments

Differences Between PDF and HTML

Oftentimes while creating a document, only HTML outputs are rendered for preview. The assumption that if it works for HTML, it will also work for PDF might always not be accurate. Syntax highlighting may not render the exact same for HTML and PDF versions of your document.

It is also pertinent to point out here that code highlighting works quite differently when AsciiDoc files are rendered in EPUB 3 format (See Chapter 18). This is discussed in detail in Section 10.8.

It is therefore a good practice to always render in the targeted format and check what works best for that format!

10.7. Adding line numbers to code blocks

To add line numbers to code blocks, we will use the same code block shown in Example 120. However this time around, we will add line numbers to the code block by adding just one small keyword in the block syntax as shown in Example 121.

Line numbers are useful to refer to sections within code blocks

Adding line numbers to code blocks can be particularly useful when you are explaining code in your document and want to refer to specific lines of code. If the code block is long, it can be difficult to refer to a specific line or segment of code without line numbers.

AsciiDoc Markup

Example 121. Adding Line Numbers to a Code Block

```
[source,python,linenums] ①
#This is a comment
x, y, z = "Orange", "Banana", "Cherry"
print(x)
print(y)
print(z)
def hello(name):
    print("Hello "+ name)
hello("Everyone")
```

① We just added **linenums** here to the previous AsciiDoc source markup which will now display line numbers in addition to syntax highlighting as can be seen in the output below. This will also work when rendering PDF documents generated by AsciiDoctor.

Will be rendered as...

```python
#This is a comment
x, y, z = "Orange", "Banana", "Cherry"
print(x)
print(y)
print(z)
def hello(name):
    print("Hello "+ name)
hello("Everyone")
```

Syntax highlighting and the line numbers are automatically taken care of by Rouge and other highlighters (see note on Line numbers in code blocks in PDF Output below). Similarly , you can also try highlighting code using pygments and *coderay* by just replacing *rouge* in the `:source-highlighter:` attribute to *pygments* or *coderay*.

Line numbers in code blocks in PDF Output

The line numbering of code blocks *for PDF Output* as demonstrated in Example 121 above, *did not* work for the *Coderay* source-highlighter at the time of writing this book. However it *does work* nicely for both *Rouge* and *Pygments*. The line numbers that are visible above (not a screenshot image) were generated by AsciiDoctor-PDF using the *Rouge* highlighter. In the past, some users have reported not being able to get line numbers on code blocks in the PDF output but I could get them in PDF output without any issues or additional code.

10.7.1. Highlighting Selected Lines of a Code Block

It is possible to highlight certain lines of code in a code block by adding the `highlight` attribute as shown in Example 122.

AsciiDoc Markup

Example 122. Highlighting selected lines of code

```
[source,python,linenums,highlight='3..5'] ①
#This is a comment
x, y, z = "Orange", "Banana", "Cherry"
print(x)
print(y)
print(z)
def hello(name):
    print("Hello "+ name)
hello("Everyone")
```

① The highlight attribute value can be written as highlight='3..5' or highlight='3-5' — both formats work. They represent a *range* of lines to highlight. In this example, it highlights lines 3,4,5 or lines 3 to 5 in the code block in light yellow highlighter color.

Will be rendered as...

```
1 #This is a comment
2 x, y, z = "Orange", "Banana", "Cherry"
3 print(x)
4 print(y)
5 print(z)
6 def hello(name):
7     print("Hello "+ name)
8 hello("Everyone")
```

10.8. Code Highlighting in EPUB3

When an asciidoc file is rendered in EPUB 3 using *AsciiDoctor-EPUB3*, code blocks, unlike HTML and PDF are rendered in black and white (style name *bw*) by default even if the `:source-highlighter:` attribute is set. This is a smart default setting for epubs as it ensures that code blocks are visible in dark, white and sepia modes which most epub readers support. If you wish to show code syntax highlighted differently, you need to add the `:<highlighter>-style: <value>` attribute to the header where '<highlighter>' is replaced by either *rouge*, *pygments* or *coderay* depending on the syntax highlighter declared by the :source-highlighter: attribute. The `<value>` part is replaced by a style name. For *rouge* this is shown in Example 123 using the *pastie* style.

Example 123. Defining the pastie style sheet for the rouge syntax highlighter

```
:source-highlighter:rouge
:rouge-style: pastie
```

You can try out other Rouge styles on this live theme review page [https://spsarolkar.github.io/rouge-theme-preview/]. Click on *select theme* and replace *pastie* in the *rouge-style* attribute with any name in the list. For example, we could use the Rouge *thankful_eyes* style instead of *pastie* for coloured syntax highlights on a dark background as shown in Example 124.

Example 124. Defining the thankful-eyes style sheet for the rouge syntax highlighter

```
:source-highlighter:rouge
:rouge-style: thankful_eyes
```

Similarly if you were using *Pygments* as your source highlighter, you could set the attributes as shown in Example 125.

Example 125. Defining the colorful style sheet for the pygments syntax highlighter

```
:source-highlighter:pygments
:pygments-style: colorful
```

You can pick up names for various Pygments styles (like monokai, xcode, colorful, murphy etc.) from this Pygments Styles Page [https://pygments.org/styles/] as per your preference. Once these two attributes are set, rendering your AsciiDoc document to EPUB 3 using *asciidoctor-epub3* will result in code blocks being highlighted in color as per the chosen style.

Test your EPUBs on a Few Popular Readers

If you choose to use syntax highlighting for code blocks in EPUB3, it will be wise to view the rendered file on a few popular epub readers on mobile devices to ensure that they are readable in light, dark and sepia modes. You might also find variation in the display of EPUB content from one epub reader to another. So testing highlighted code on various devices (phones, tablets, desktops) and epub-readers will give you a heads up on any potential issues and ensure a consistent reading experience.

10.8.1. Syntax Highlighters are Not All the Same

Working with syntax highlighters might give an impression that they are all the same and the only difference is the manner in which code is coloured or highlighted. This is not correct. The number of programming and markup languages supported by different syntax highlighters can vary by a lot. It is quite possible that the code of the programming language that you are trying to highlight is not supported by a particular syntax highlighter. So do visit Pygments website [https://pygments.org/], Rouge's GitHub Page [https://github.com/rouge-ruby/rouge?tab=readme-ov-file] and the Coderay website [http://coderay.rubychan.de/] for more information about these highlighters and the programming languages they support.

10.9. Chapter Summary

Key learnings in this chapter are:

- Code can be easily highlighted in AsciiDoc documents using syntax highlighters.
- Three popular syntax highlighters that are commonly used in AsciiDoc to highlight code are — *rouge*, *pygments* and *coderay*.
- Syntax highlighters can be easily installed on Linux, Windows and Mac systems. Please see Section 10.3 for a quick recap on how to install them.
- If you are using the AsciiDoctor Docker image, you *do not* have to perform any installation as all syntax highlighters are included in the AsciiDoctor Docker image. You can just go ahead and start using them as described in this chapter.
- To highlight code in your AsciiDoc file, all you need to do is to insert the *source-highlighter* attribute in your document header (see Section 10.4) and mark a code block with `[source,python]` styling (see Section 10.5). Any code that you insert will now get highlighted in color when you render your document as HTML or PDF.
- To use a different highlighter, just replace *rouge* (as seen in Section 10.4) with another highlighter name like *pygments* or *coderay* in the `:source-highlighter:` attribute. To use another programming language, replace *Python* (as seen in Section 10.5 with the programming language of your code block like — `[source,ruby]`.
- To have code highlighting in color in EPUB files, you need to add another attribute — `:rouge-style:` to the header and set its value to a style sheet like *pastie* as shown in Example 123. See Section 10.8 for a full discussion and some more options. It is best to test your EPUBs on popular mobile and desktop EPUB reader apps to ensure that the highlighted code is being displayed as intended.

10.10. Try it Yourself

Some code samples for practice are available in the *code-hl.adoc* file in the exercises folder of this chapter. You will need to have Rouge, Pygments and / or Coderay installed on your system for these exercises (See Section 10.3 on how to install). You will need to render *code-hl.adoc* into HTML and PDF using AsciiDoctor and AsciiDoctor-PDF. Try both outputs for each example.

1. Highlight the following Python code snippet in *code-hl.adoc* using the rouge and *pygments* source highlighters (see Section 10.4 and Section 10.5 for help).

```
#This is a comment
x, y, z = "Orange", "Banana", "Cherry"
print(x)
print(y)
print(z)
def hello(name):
   print("Hello "+ name)
hello("Everyone")
```

2. Can you add line numbers to the above code snippet. See Example 121 for help.
3. Can you similarly highlight the C++ code block seen in *code-hl.adoc* and introduce line numbers ?
4. Extend the markup to highlight selected lines in any of the above code blocks (see Section 10.7.1).
5. Render your AsciiDoc file using AsciiDoctor-PDF to test if you can get line numbers and line highlighting in PDF output. (see note on see note on Line numbers in code blocks in PDF Output in Section 10.7).

Chapter 11. Tables

"Show me your flowcharts and conceal your tables, and I shall continue to be mystified. Show me your tables, and I won't usually need your flowcharts; they'll be obvious."
~Fred Brooks

In this chapter, will learn how to create tables using AsciiDoc markup. At first sight, the markup to create table might appear a bit cumbersome, but as you work with it, you will find that the markup gives you complete control in creating and formatting tables as per your requirements. In the chapter summary section, I pick two easy methods of creating and inserting tables that I use all of the time.

Tables are a powerful way to organize and present information in a clear and structured manner. They allow you to display data, compare values, and convey complex relationships in a concise and visually appealing format. Whether you're a writer, a researcher, or a professional in any field, incorporating well-designed tables into your documents can be a powerful way to improve clarity, organization, and overall effectiveness of your written communication.

One of the key advantages of using tables is their ability to help readers quickly and easily digest complex information. By arranging data in a tabular format, you can make it easier for your audience to identify patterns, trends, and relationships that might not be as apparent in a plain text format. This can be especially useful when dealing with large amounts of numerical data.

Tables can be easily created or imported in AsciiDoc using simple markup syntax. However, it is important to note that the process of creating tables using markup code may initially appear a bit tedious and confusing as people are not usually familiar with creation of tables using markup code. However, with a little practice, the process becomes much more intuitive and efficient. Once you get the hang of it, you'll be able to quickly and easily incorporate well-designed tables into your documents.

Let's get straight into it and try to create a basic table using AsciiDoc.

11.1. Basic Table Syntax

The AsciiDoc markup in Example 126 shows how to easily create a basic table. Broadly, the AsciiDoc markup in Example 126 starts with a table title (callout 1), followed by `|===` to indicate the start of a table (callout 2), a header row (callout 3), a blank line (callout 4), rows of data cells separated by the `|` symbol (callout 5) and finally ending the table with the same `|===` sequence that was used to start the table (callout 6).

AsciiDoc Markup

Example 126. AsciiDoc Markup for a Equal Column Width Basic Table

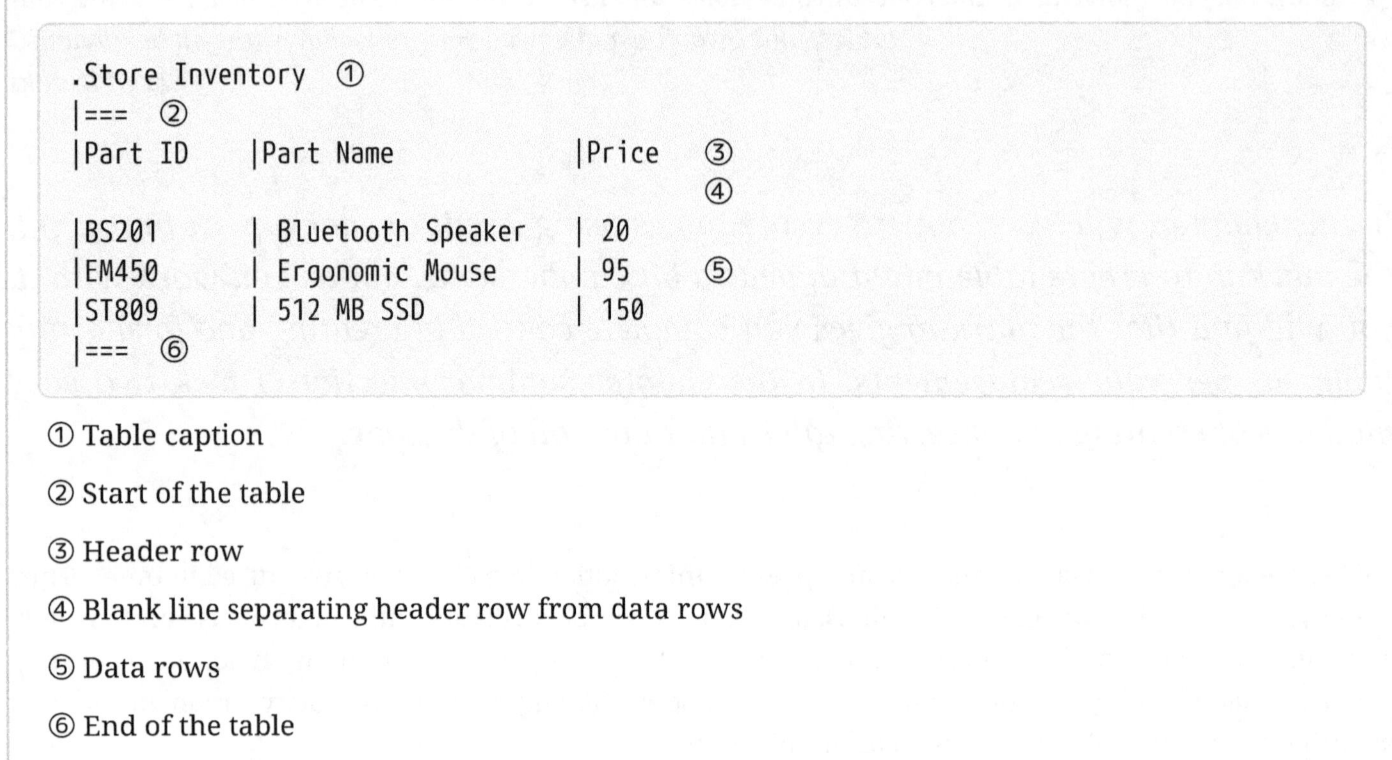

```
.Store Inventory  ①
|===  ②
|Part ID    |Part Name             |Price   ③
                                            ④
|BS201      | Bluetooth Speaker    | 20
|EM450      | Ergonomic Mouse      | 95     ⑤
|ST809      | 512 MB SSD           | 150
|===  ⑥
```

① Table caption

② Start of the table

③ Header row

④ Blank line separating header row from data rows

⑤ Data rows

⑥ End of the table

Will be rendered as...

Table 5. Store Inventory

Part ID	Part Name	Price
BS201	Bluetooth Speaker	20
EM450	Ergonomic Mouse	95
ST809	512 MB SSD	150

The above table spans the width of the page and all columns are of equal width. We can easily manipulate that by using the *width* and *cols* styling directives before the start of the table. To see these styling directives in action, let's reproduce a bigger table from the AsciiDoctor documentation as shown in Example 127. While all other elements are the same as in Example 126, notice that the *width* directive highlighted by callout 2 alters the width of the table while the *cols* directive alters the width of individual columns.

AsciiDoc Markup

Example 127. Altering Table Width and Column Widths

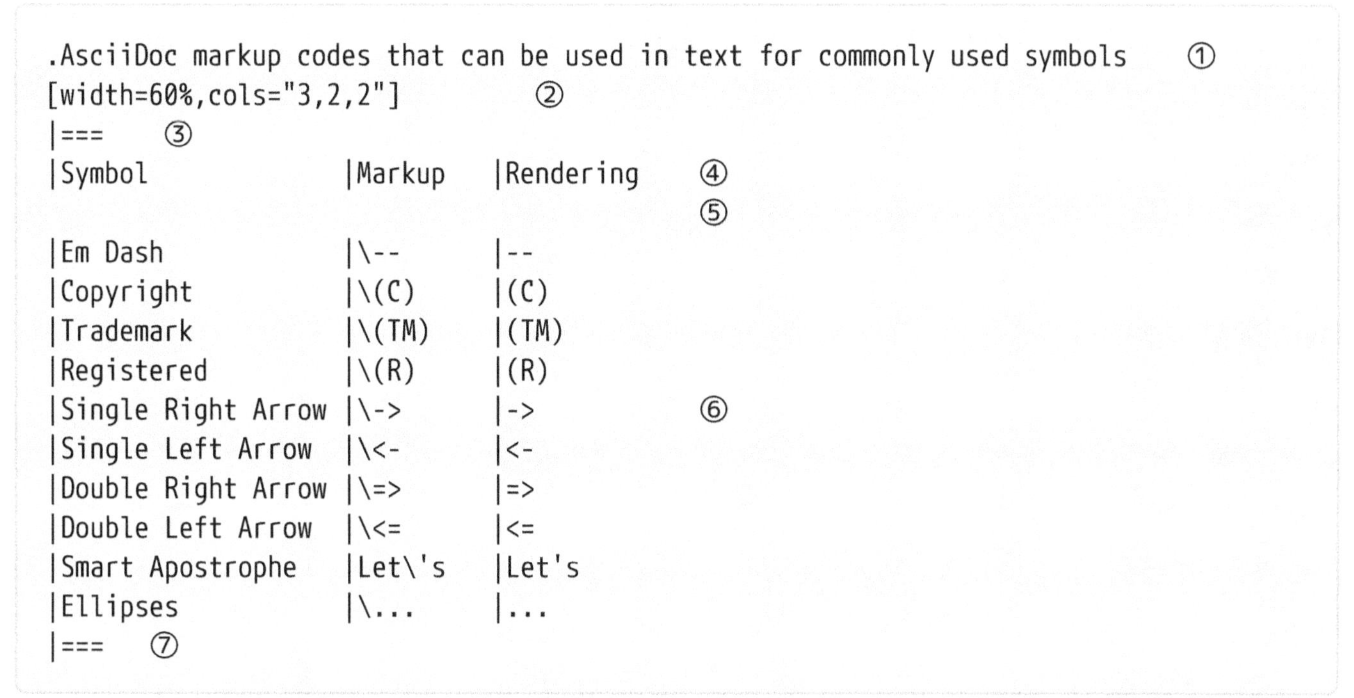

```
.AsciiDoc markup codes that can be used in text for commonly used symbols    ①
[width=60%,cols="3,2,2"]        ②
|===    ③
|Symbol              |Markup   |Rendering    ④
                                             ⑤
|Em Dash             |\--      |--
|Copyright           |\(C)     |(C)
|Trademark           |\(TM)    |(TM)
|Registered          |\(R)     |(R)
|Single Right Arrow  |\->      |->           ⑥
|Single Left Arrow   |\<-      |<-
|Double Right Arrow  |\=>      |=>
|Double Left Arrow   |\<=      |<=
|Smart Apostrophe    |Let\'s   |Let's
|Ellipses            |\...     |...
|===   ⑦
```

① Table caption or title

② Controls width of the table, number of columns and the relative width of each column (For more explanation, please see Section 11.2.

③ Start the table — table starts here.

④ The header row — Three columns with cell contents

⑤ A blank line to separate header row from data rows. If there is no blank line, the header row will be the same as other rows in the table.

⑥ The data rows — *ten rows* in all

⑦ Close the table — table ends here.

The backslash that you see preceding characters in column 2 is called the *escape character*. It has been put there to tell AsciiDoctor not to interpret or process the characters that follow the backslash. This is to ensure that you see the AsciiDoc markup syntax in column 2. Notice that in terms of cell contents, column 3 (titled *Rendering*) is an exact replica of column 2 except for the missing backslashes. As a result, when the table is rendered, AsciiDoctor interprets the markup in column 3 and column 3 displays interpreted symbols.

Will be rendered as...

Table 6. AsciiDoc markup codes that can be used in text for commonly used symbols

Symbol	Markup	Rendering
Em Dash	--	—
Copyright	(C)	©
Trademark	(TM)	™
Registered	(R)	®
Single Right Arrow	->	→
Single Left Arrow	<-	←
Double Right Arrow	=>	⇒
Double Left Arrow	<=	⇐
Smart Apostrophe	Let's	Let’s
Ellipses	...	…

There are two important things to notice about the above table:

1. The table spans only 60% of the page width
2. In addition to the header row, this table has 10 data rows — a total of 11 rows.
3. The blank line between the header row and the data rows does not manifest as a blank line in the rendered table. What it does is that it highlights the header row by rendering the header row text in bold and filling its cells with a light gray background color. If you remove the blank line, the table will still print nicely but the header row will not be highlighted and will have the same appearance as the other rows.
4. The table receives automatic numbering which is in continuation to the previous table. This happens because we have given the table a caption starting with a dot. Tables created after this table in the document will continue to get incremental numbering automatically. We don’t have to manually number each table as long as we provide a caption to the table.

Markup for Special Symbols

The above table while demonstrating how tables are created in AsciiDoc also presents *valid markup syntax* for symbols commonly used in everyday writing. Use the code under the *Markup* column in your text to display symbols under the *Rendering* column. While we have used this table for some practice and demonstration here, it is actually a very useful table that you can bookmark and refer to later on.

11.2. Controlling the Table Width and Column Widths

Let's dive a little deeper to understand the table and column width syntax demonstrated in the Example 127. You can add the `[width=60%,cols="3,2,2"]` line after creation of a table to adjust the table and column widths suiting data populated in table cells. The keyword **width=60%** means the table will be occupying 60% of page width. If you omit this, the table uses full width of the page and spreads columns evenly across the width of the page. The keyword **cols=3,2,2** means that the first column will be 1 times larger than the other two columns which will be of equal width. You can use other numbers to alter relative width of columns in a similar manner.

11.3. Justifying Table Cell Contents

You can align or justify content inside the cells as *left*, *center* or *right* justified by using the following extra symbols in the `cols` flag as shown in Example 128.

AsciiDoc Markup

Example 128. Justifying Cell Content

```
.Employees        ① ② ③
[width=60%,cols="<3,^2,>2"]
|===
|Name    |Age    |Salary

|Brenda | 25    | 1800
|John   | 35    | 5000
|Keith  | 29    | 2500
|===
```

① < The first column content will be left justified

② ^ The second column contents will be in the center of the cell

③ > The third column contents will be right justified.

Will be rendered as...

Table 7. Employees

Name	Age	Salary
Brenda	25	1800
John	35	5000
Keith	29	2500

As can be seen in Example 128, the left column content — under the *Name* column — is left justified i.e. aligned to the left border of each cell, the content under the *Age* column is in the center of each cell and the content under the *Salary* column is aligned to the right border of each cell.

11.4. CSV Format for Tables and Some Other Handy Tricks

If the above seems a bit complicated, simple tables can be *very easily* created in another way using Comma Separated Values (CSV). This, according to me, is by far the *fastest and simplest method* of creating simple tables in AsciiDoc. Example 129 shows the AsciiDoc markup to create tables using CSV notation which are in practice, quite intuitive to visualize tabular data.

AsciiDoc Markup

Example 129. Creating Tables using CSV Notation

```
.Employee Table         ①
,===                    ②
Name, Age, Department   ③
                        ④
Oliver,25,Marketing
Cynthia,32,IT           ⑤

,===                    ⑥
```

① Table caption

② Start the table with a , (comma) followed by three = (equal to) signs.

③ Header row with column titles - there must be *no blank line* above the header row.

④ Blank line below header row.

⑤ Data rows with column data separated by a comma.

⑥ Close the table with a , (comma) followed by three = (equal to) signs.

Will be rendered as…

Table 8. Employee Table

Name	Age	Department
Oliver	25	Marketing
Cynthia	32	IT

The CSV table starts and ends with `,===` and column values in each data row are separated by *commas* hence CSV.

If you want more control of CSV tables, you can do so with a little more markup. In Example 130, we see how we can create a header and footer in a table.

AsciiDoc Markup

Example 130. CSV Format Table Entry Markup

```
[%header%footer,width=60%,cols="<,^,^,^",format=csv,grid=all] ①②③④⑤⑥
,===
Product,Unit Rate,Quantity,Cost
Mars,2,10,20
Snickers,3,12,36
Twix,1,8,8                              ⑦
Toblerone,5,20,100
Total,,50,164
,===
```

① %header is shorthand notation to make first row as header

② %footer is shorthand notation to make last row as footer

③ width=60% means table will be 60% wide relative to page width

④ cols="<, ^ , ^ , ^" is justification of text cells in each column - column 1 → left other columns → center

⑤ format=csv is comma separated values. If tab separated, use TSV

⑥ grid=all — draws all table grid lines. Other options that can replace all: row /cols / none

⑦ Row data given as comma separated values because we said format is CSV

Table 9. Stock inventory

Product	Unit Rate	Quantity	Cost
Mars	2	10	20
Snickers	3	12	36
Twix	1	8	8
Toblerone	5	20	100
Total		50	164

Notice that the last row — *Total* is designated as the footer row and is shaded. Also notice that as the last row is presenting totals, I left the first column — *Unit Price* intentionally blank by putting nothing between two commas after Total (not much sense in providing the total of all unit prices!). How did I get the totals ? I calculated it using a calculator as at the time of writing, there is nothing like an Excel `sum()` function in AsciiDoc! If you feel troubled at the prospect of manually adding some numbers, the next section should relieve that anxiety !

11.5. Importing a Excel CSV File

If you have tables in MS Excel, LibreOffice Calc, Google Sheets or Numbers, you can save them as .csv files and directly import that csv file inside your AsciiDoc document. For demonstration purposes, I have created a small 5 row csv file in Excel — *species.csv* — that has the IUCN red list status of 4 species. In the markup below, I have used an additional option called *stripes* which can have values *even* or *odd* (commonly used striping options) and which results in a striped table with even or odd rows striped or shaded as per the chosen striping option. If however you do not wish to have stripes, delete the stripes option in the markup and use %header as we have done in the previous examples. Example 131 shows AsciiDoc markup for importing a csv file with every even row, striped.

AsciiDoc Markup

Example 131. Importing a CSV File

```
[width=75%,format=csv,options=header,stripes=even]
|===
include::species.csv[]
|===
```

Will be rendered as...

Table 10. IUCN Conservation Status of Select Species

Common Name	Scientific Name	Status
Elephant	Elephas maximus	Endangered
White Shark	Carcharodon carcharias	Vulnerable
Papyrus Whisp	Agriocnemis palaeforma	Vulnerable
Asiatic Lion	Panthera leo	Endangered

Please note that adding the `options=header` attribute in Example 131 ensures that the first row of the *imported or included* csv file (*species.csv in this case*) will be treated as a header row which has its text in bold. This styling can be seen in the first row of Table 10.

Tables are really easy to create using AsciiDoc markup once you get the hang of it!

11.6. Chapter Summary

Key learnings in this chapter are:

1. We have explored different ways of creating and populating tables in AsciiDoc documents.
2. To create a basic table — start and end the table with `|===`, insert rows by typing in column headings or data — separating each column by a `|` symbol. Revisit Section 11.1 for a quick recap.
3. Use the *CSV notation* to easily and intuitively create tables in AsciiDoc. Start and end the table with `,===` and insert rows by typing in column headings or data values — separating each column by a ',' or comma symbol. Please see Section 11.4 for a quick recap on how to create tables using CSV notation.
4. Import an Excel table in CSV format using the markup shown in Section 11.5.

11.7. Try it Yourself

You will need the *species.csv* file from the exercise folder of this chapter to complete the last exercise.

1. Try creating the following table *with a header row* using AsciiDoc Markup (Please see Section 11.1 for help).

Fruit	January	February	March
Avacado	300	350	500
Orange	200	400	800
Apples	800	600	300
Pears	200	150	250

2. In the above table, can you ensure that the table occupies 80% of page width and that numbers under January, February and March Columns are aligned to the center of the cell ? (Please see Section 11.3 for help).

3. In the above table, can you add markup to ensure that the table occupies the full page width and that the first column is twice the width of the other three columns ?
4. Can you create the same table using CSV notation ? (Please see Section 11.4 for help).
5. Import the *species.csv* file from the exercise folder of this chapter inside your AsciiDoc document as a evenly striped table. (Please see Section 11.5 for help).
6. Try creating a simple table on your own in MS Excel or LibreOffice Calc (or any other spreadsheet), save it as a CSV file (Save as CSV) and import that file inside an AsciiDoc document as you have done for the *species.csv* file above.

Chapter 12. Inserting Citations and Creating Styled Bibliography

"Each source that I read, I would look through the bibliography and the footnotes, and use that as a map for the next thing I would read." ~ Alexander Chee

---

In this chapter, we will explore how to cite references and create a unified bibliography for your AsciiDoc document. This is an absolutely mandatory requirement for academic and scholastic writing and no document creation tool can call itself complete unless it can properly cite literature sources and amalgamate the cited literature into a nicely formatted bibliography using standard citation styles.

12.1. A Little Background

Anybody who has engaged in academic writing like writing an essay, research paper, report or thesis would know that citing sources literature in these documents is not only a mandatory requirement, it is also quite laborious and time consuming to accomplish. In my career as an academic, I have seen many instances when a research paper or thesis has been sent back to the author for revision because literature had not been properly cited. Great attention is paid to this and scholarly work almost never passes muster unless it cites literature and includes a bibliography as per some prescribed style guide. Thankfully, it is possible to cite literature and create a nicely formatted bibliography in AsciiDoc with some external help.

In this chapter, I demonstrate how to use a BibTeX [https://en.wikipedia.org/wiki/BibTeX] bibliography file to cite references in your AsciiDoc document and then insert a properly styled bibliography as per IEEE, APA , Harvard, MLA, Chicago or other popular style guides. We will accomplish this using the following broad workflow:

1. Use an external free and open source reference manager software called *Zotero* to create a BibTex file
2. Use the *AsciiDoctor-BibTex extension* to generate the Bibliography from the BibTex file in our AsciiDoc Document.

If the above sounds a bit confusing at this stage, don't worry at all. I assure you its quite simple to do and I will explain this workflow step by step in the following sections.

12.2. Installs

To create a bibliography in an AsciiDoc document, we need to install the *AsciiDoctor-BibTex* extension. If you are using the AsciiDoctor Docker container image, you *do not* need any installation — the AsciiDoctor-BibTex extension is part of the AsciiDoctor Docker image and is available for instant use.

In summary, the following install is applicable only if you are not using *AsciiDoctor Docker Container Image* and assumes that *AsciiDoctor* and *AsciiDoctor-PDF* have already been installed on your system.

12.2.1. Installing AsciiDoctor-BibTeX Extension on Linux

The AsciiDoctor BibTeX extension adds BibTex citation support for AsciiDoc documents. More details about the AsciiDoctor-BibTex extension can be found on the project's GitHub page at https://github.com/asciidoctor/asciidoctor-bibtex.

The AsciiDoctor-BibTex extension requires two additional pieces of software to work — *ruby-dev* and *libxslt1-dev*. Ruby should already be installed on your computer after the installation of AsciiDoctor. If you unsure about Ruby, you can check its version using the following command.

Terminal Command

Checking The Ruby Version

```
$ ruby --version
```

If Ruby is installed, the Ruby version command returns the following response (Figure 81) showing the version of Ruby installed on your system. The version of Ruby seen in Figure 81 may be different in your case.

```
$ ruby --version
ruby 3.1.2p20 (2022-04-12 revision 4491bb740a) [i386-linux-gnu]
```

Figure 81. Ruby Version Check Output on Terminal

After checking the ruby version, issue the following commands in the order as they appear in Example 132 to complete the installation of the AsciiDoctor-BibTex extension.

Terminal Command

Example 132. Installing the AsciiDoctor-Bibtex extension along with its prerequisites

```
$ sudo apt-get install ruby-dev
```

```
$ sudo apt-get install libxslt1-dev
```

```
$ sudo gem install asciidoctor-bibtex
```

If all goes well, you should receive no error messages after issuing these commands.

So with this out of the way, we are all set to use the AsciiDoctor-BibTeX extension with AsciiDoctor.

AsciiDoctor-BibTeX is Already Available on the AsciiDoctor Docker Image

It does not hurt to reiterate that if you are using the *AsciiDoctor Docker image*, AsciiDoctor-BibTeX is already installed and you ***do not*** need to engage in the above installation.

12.2.2. Installing AsciiDoctor-BibTeX Extension on Windows

The install of AsciiDoctor-BibTeX extension on windows is very straightforward. Assuming that you already have AsciiDoctor installed on your computer, all you have to do is to issue a single command shown in Example 133 from the Windows command prompt.

Example 133. Installing AsciiDoctor-BibTex on Windows

```
gem install asciidoctor-bibtex
```

This installs all dependencies required for AsciiDoctor-BibTex and then installs the AsciiDoctor-BibTex extension itself as shown in Figure 82.

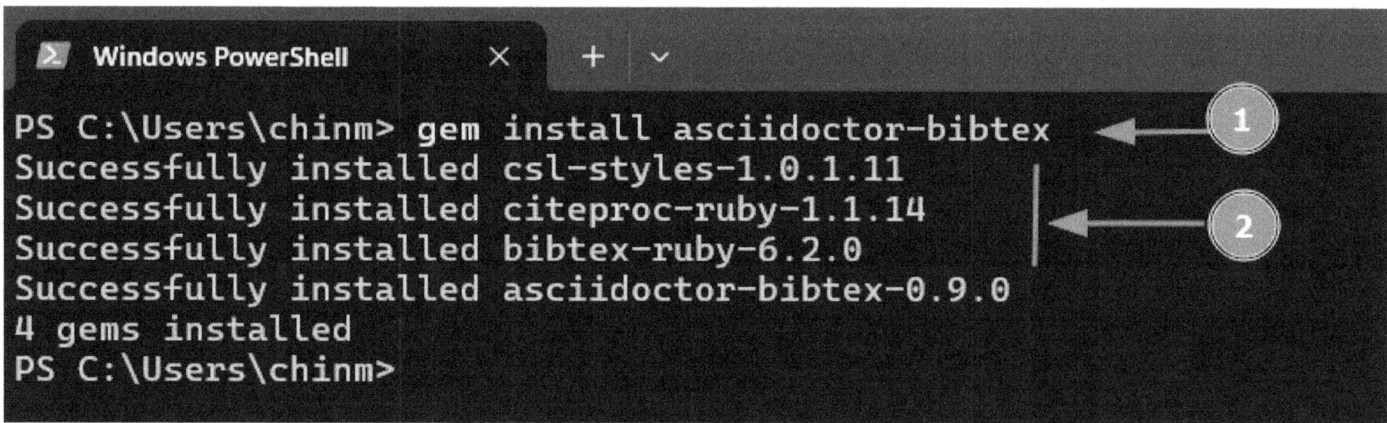

Figure 82. Windows installation of AsciiDoc-BibTex (1) the install command (2) system messages during installation showing installation of dependencies

As can be seen in Figure 82-(2), the required dependencies are installed before the installation of *AsciiDoctor_BibTex*. The installation of dependencies is automatically triggered. Please note that the number of dependencies installed could vary from what is visible in the figure (may be more) on different computers. The key message however is the last one that says — *Successfully installed asciidoctor-bibtex-0.9.0* (version may vary). That's all there is to it ! You can now start citing literature and creating bibliography as explained in the next section.

☞ The **Mac** install is also similar ⇒ Install the asciidoctor-bibtex Ruby gem from the terminal using the command shown in Example 133 (assuming that AsciiDoctor is installed). In case you face any issues with dependencies, you can try installing them manually using the following command:

```
gem install bibtex-ruby citeproc-ruby csl-styles
```

12.3. Creating a BibTeX File in Zotero

To run the BibTeX extension, we need a BibTeX file. In my opinion, the easiest way to create a BibTeX file is by using Zotero [https://www.zotero.org/], the open source , free and highly popular reference manager. However, Zotero is not the only reference manager out there and if you are using Mendeley or any other reference manager that can export a collection to a BibTeX file — use that software. As explained later, for our purposes here, all we need is a BibTeX file and it really does not matter which software is used to create it.

Coming back to Zotero, I would like to mention upfront that I have made no attempt in this text to explain how to use Zotero. If you are new to Zotero or reference management, you can view the following YouTube playlist that I have created to use Zotero.

▶ https://www.youtube.com/watch?v=jU3Qspe0JFk *(YouTube video)*

Many people are already aware of Zotero but if you haven't heard about it, the following info box explains the overall idea of using Zotero in the present context.

Let's say we need to cite 10 references in our document. So we start Zotero, create a new collection comprising of those 10 references and export that collection as a BibTeX file. We can later on add to this BibTeX file if required by bringing in more references to this collection, exporting the collection again as BibTeX and replacing the BibTeX file referred to in our AsciiDoc document with the updated file.

Once you have a collection of references that you wish to cite inside Zotero, all you need to do is to export that collection in the BibTeX file format. Figure 83 shows how to export a reference collection from Zotero to a BibTeX file.

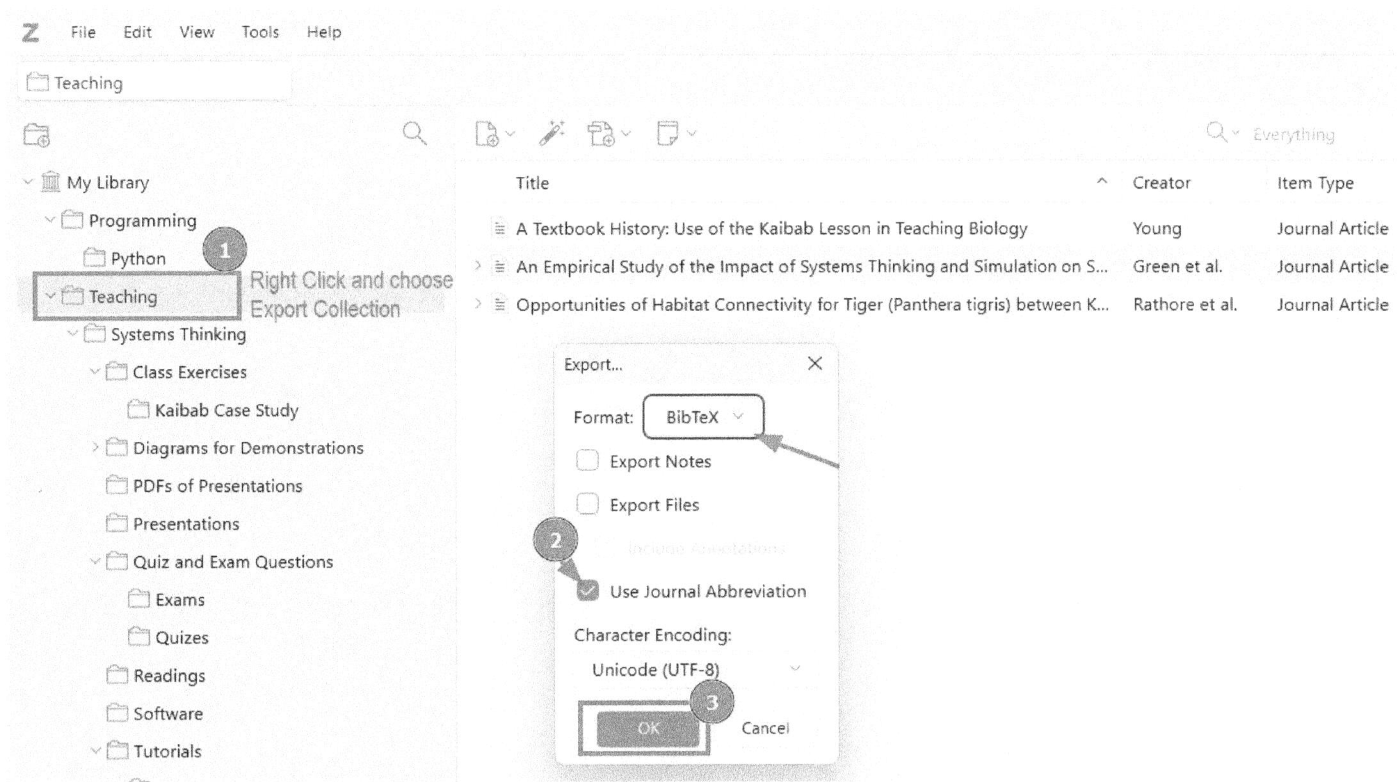

Figure 83. Exporting a collection as BibTeX from Zotero

The above export operation will result in a BibTeX file like *refs.bib*. BibTeX files have a *.bib* extension. The file or files in which you wish to insert citations must be in the same folder as the BibTeX file such that we do not have to provide any long path names to AsciiDoctor when we use the AsciiDoctor-BibTeX extension. So drop your BibTeX file in the same folder where you have your AsciiDoc files in which you plan to cite references.

12.4. Adding Attributes

Now that we have everything in place, we can start inserting citations in our *.adoc* file. We start by making two attribute declarations in the document header. These two attributes are (a) `:bibtext-file: <filename>` and (b) `:bibtext-style: <stylename>` . In the above attributes, *filename* will have to be substituted with the actual BibTeX file name that we created above using Zotero or any other reference manager. *Stylename* is the name of the style guide whose rules will be followed by the *asciidoctor-bibtex* extension to format the styled bibliography.

Figure 84 reproduced from the AsciiDoctor-BibTex documentation [https://github.com/asciidoctor/asciidoctor-bibtex] shows these two attributes and their possible valid values highlighted in red rectangles.

Attribute Name	Description	Valid Values	Default Value
bibtex-file ①	Bibtex database file	any string, or empty	Automatic searching
bibtex-style ②	Reference formatting style	any style supported by csl-styles	ieee
bibtex-order	Order of citations	`appearance` or `alphabetical`	`appearance`
bibtex-format	Formatting of citations and bibliography	`asciidoc`, `bibtex` or `biblatex`	`asciidoc`
bibtex-locale	Locale used to render the bibliography	strings supported by CSL	`en-US`
bibtex-throw	Throw an error on unknown references	`true` or `false`	`false`
bibtex-citation-template	Custom citation template for numeric style	Any string matching `/(.?)\$id(.)/`	`[$id]`

Figure 84. BibTeX extension attributes and their descriptions (source: AsciiDoctor-BibTeX project)

So let's say our bibliography BibTeX file that we exported from Zotero was named *refs.bib* and we wish to style our citations and bibliography in the **Chicago** style, the attributes that we will include in the *.adoc* file header will be as shown in Example 134.

AsciiDoc Markup

Example 134. The BibTeX File and Style Attributes

```
:bibtex-file: refs.bib  ①
:bibtex-style: chicago-author-date   ②
```

① The name of the BibTeX file. It should be in the same folder as other files.

② The name of the style guide in which we wish to format our references. IEEE is default , you can use APA or chicago-author-date or any other named CLS Style (see https://github.com/citation-style-language/styles/blob/master/din-1505-2-numeric-alphabetical.csl for citation style names. To get a name, scroll down in the left pane, click on a stylename.csl entry (1) and copy the name just before .csl (2) — example *acta-adriatica.csl — you can use _acta-adriatica* in the bibtex-style attribute as shown in Figure 85.

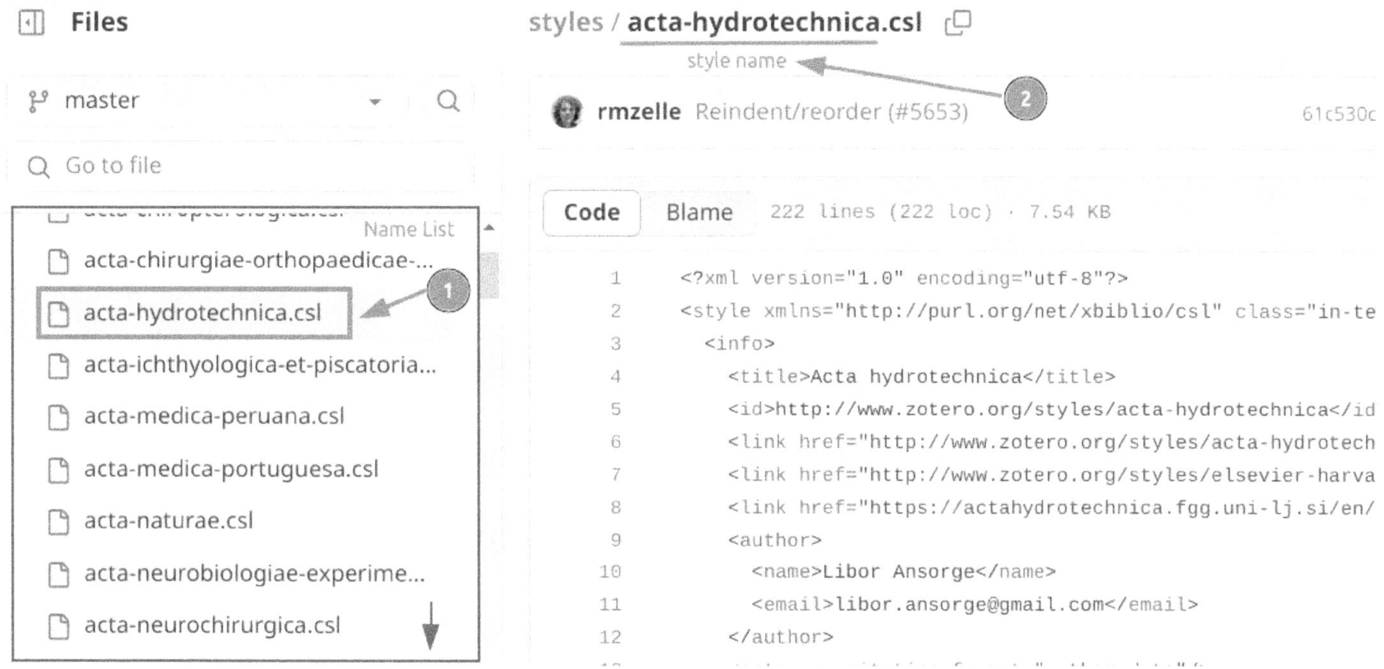

Figure 85. Style Names

12.5. Inserting Keys in a BibTeX File

To actually cite references in text, we will use the reference keys in the BibTeX file. Just double click on the *.bib* file (*refs.bib* in our example) that has all references that we wish to include in the bibliography. Now with the BibTeX file open in a text editor, we can copy the reference key from a reference that we wish to cite and paste it at the appropriate place in the document text. Figure 86 — using *refs.bib* as an example — shows two reference keys that we will use to place references in the running text of our document.

About BibTeX Reference Keys

BibTeX reference keys, also known as *labels*, are used to identify and reference entries in a BibTeX database. These keys are typically short strings of characters, usually alphanumeric with underscores, and are used to cite specific sources in a document.

A BibTeX reference key is specified at the beginning of each entry in the BibTeX file, preceded by the @ symbol, followed by the entry type (e.g., article, book, proceedings). For example:

@article{smith2020, author = {John Smith}, title = {A Study on Research}, journal = {Journal of Research}, year = {2020}, }

In this example, smith2020 is the BibTeX reference key.

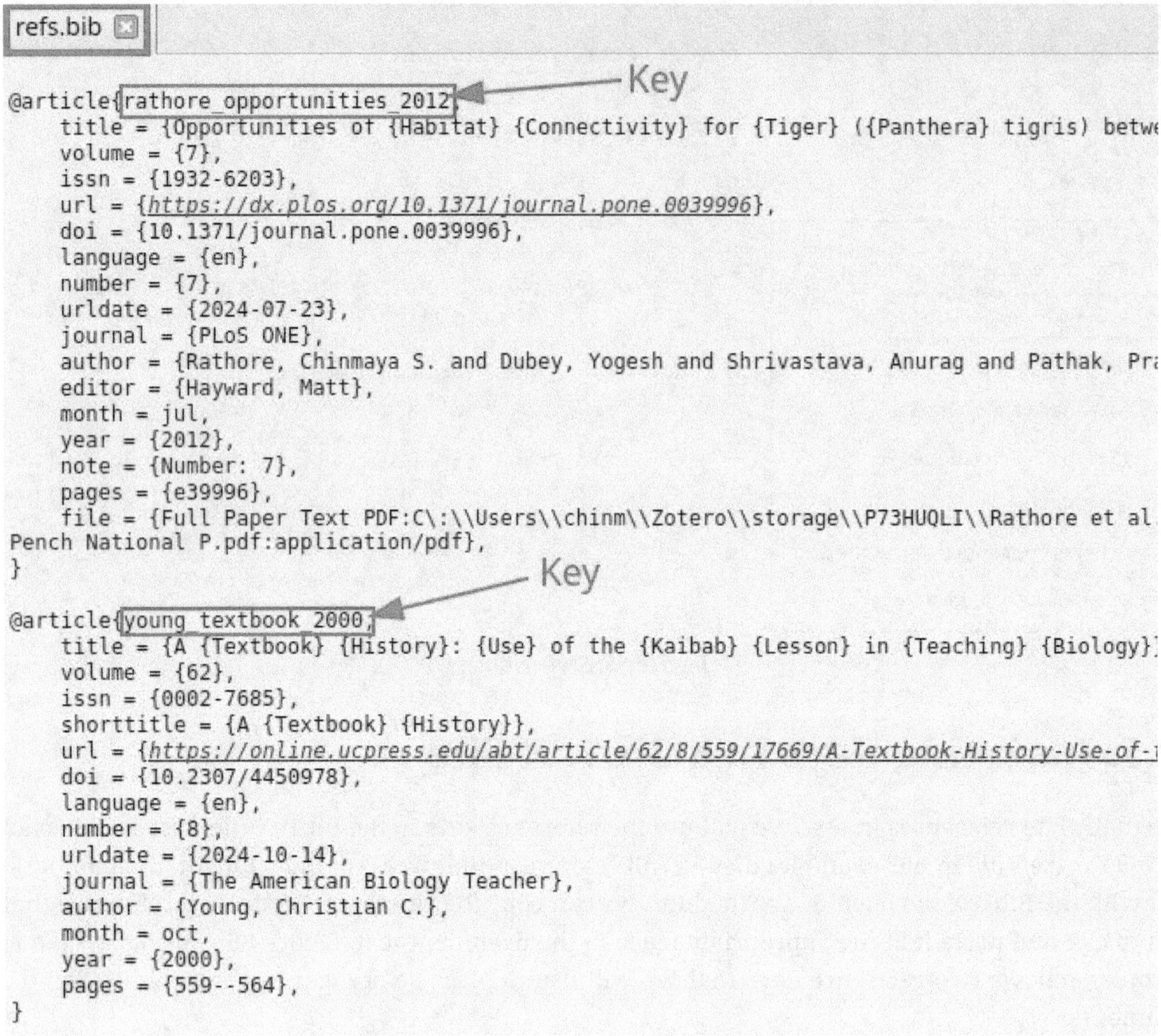

refs.bib

Key

```
@article{rathore_opportunities_2012,
    title = {Opportunities of {Habitat} {Connectivity} for {Tiger} ({Panthera} tigris) betw
    volume = {7},
    issn = {1932-6203},
    url = {https://dx.plos.org/10.1371/journal.pone.0039996},
    doi = {10.1371/journal.pone.0039996},
    language = {en},
    number = {7},
    urldate = {2024-07-23},
    journal = {PLoS ONE},
    author = {Rathore, Chinmaya S. and Dubey, Yogesh and Shrivastava, Anurag and Pathak, Pr
    editor = {Hayward, Matt},
    month = jul,
    year = {2012},
    note = {Number: 7},
    pages = {e39996},
    file = {Full Paper Text PDF:C\:\\Users\\chinm\\Zotero\\storage\\P73HUQLI\\Rathore et al
Pench National P.pdf:application/pdf},
}
```

Key

```
@article{young_textbook_2000,
    title = {A {Textbook} {History}: {Use} of the {Kaibab} {Lesson} in {Teaching} {Biology}
    volume = {62},
    issn = {0002-7685},
    shorttitle = {A {Textbook} {History}},
    url = {https://online.ucpress.edu/abt/article/62/8/559/17669/A-Textbook-History-Use-of-
    doi = {10.2307/4450978},
    language = {en},
    number = {8},
    urldate = {2024-10-14},
    journal = {The American Biology Teacher},
    author = {Young, Christian C.},
    month = oct,
    year = {2000},
    pages = {559--564},
}
```

Figure 86. Reference keys in a BibTex File

12.6. Adding Citations

Now that we have access to the reference keys, we are ready to cite them in our document text. Let's say we have the following text paragraphs in our AsciiDoc file called *ch1.adoc* and we wish to enter these two citations in the text at locations 1 and 2 marked by callouts in Example 135.

AsciiDoc Markup

Example 135. Sample Text Showing Locations where Citations Need to be Inserted

```
Tigers are on the verge of extinction, according to WWF there are about 5,500 wild
tigers left. Tigers are threatened by poaching and habitat loss. Habitats have become
fragmented making it more difficult for one population of tigers to reach another. ①
```

```
If healthy tiger populations do not have access to one another, breeding becomes more
difficult. Tigers now only have 7% of their historic range which continues to
decline. One possible solution could be to connect fragmented habitats through
corridors. ②
```

① Citation 1 (Young) needs to appear here

② Citation 2 (Rathore et. al.) needs to appear here

To do this, we will just paste the reference key for a resource (journal article, book, web page etc.) that we wish to cite as it appears in the BibTeX file. For the two citations mentioned above, its done as shown in Example 136 using the `cite:<key>` markup pair where `<key>` is replaced by the keys from the BibTeX file.

AsciiDoc Markup

Example 136. Using the 'cite:key' markup pair for citations

```
Tigers are on the verge of extinction, according to WWF there are about 5,500 wild
tigers left. Tigers are threatened by poaching and habitat loss. Habitats have become
fragmented making it more difficult for one population of tigers to reach another
cite:[young_textbook_2000] ①

If healthy tiger populations do not have access to one another, breeding becomes more
difficult. Tigers now only have 7% of their historic range which continues to
decline. One possible solution could be to connect fragmented habitats through
corridors cite:[rathore_opportunities_2012] ②
```

① Key inserted for reference 1

② Key inserted for reference 2

As demonstrated in the Example 136, you can insert as many reference keys from your BibTeX file as required at appropriate places in your document.

12.7. Rendering Bibliography and Citations to HTML

After we have placed the citations in the text, the final step is to render a bibliography. This is done by using the *AsciiDoctor-BibTeX extension* with the AsciiDoctor command as shown in Example 137. Notice that to get the bibliography, we use the *bibliography macro* with a pair of trailing square brackets at the end of the document.

Example 137. Using the bibliography macro for creating a consolidated bibliography

```
Tigers are on the verge of extinction, according to WWF their are about 5,500 wild
tigers left. Tigers are threatened by poaching and habitat loss. Habitats have become
fragmented making it more difficult for one population of tigers to reach another
cite:[young_textbook_2000] ①

If healthy tiger populations do not have access to one another, breeding becomes more
difficult. Tigers now only have 7% of their historic range which continues to
decline. One possible solution could be to connect fragmented habitats through
corridors cite:[rathore_opportunities_2012] ②

*Bibliography*
                          ③
bibliography::[]          ④
```

① BibTeX reference key insert for the first reference

② BibTeX reference key insert for the second reference

③ Blank line between the title and the bibliography macro.

④ This statement needs to be added at the end of the document. It inserts the bibliography when the document is rendered by AsciiDoctor or AsciiDoctor-PDF in conjugation with the AsciiDoctor-BibTeX extension.

To render the bibliography, we issue the command shown in Example 138 from the terminal.

Terminal Command

Example 138. Using AsciiDoctor-BibTeX with AsciiDoctor to render Bibliography

```
$ asciidoctor -r asciidoctor-bibtex test.adoc
```

Notice that we are including the *asciidoctor-bibtex* extension reference with the *asciidoctor* command. The -r flag in the command is to load a Ruby library which is what *asciidoctor-bibtex* technically is.

The output of running this command can be seen in Figure 87.

Will be rendered as...

Tigers are on the verge of extinction, according to WWF their are about 5,500 wild tigers left. Tigers are threatened by poaching and habitat loss. Habitats have become fragmented making it more difficult for one population of tigers to reach another (Young 2000) **Link leads to the reference in Bibliography**

If healthy tiger populations do not have access to one another, breeding becomes more difficult. Tigers now only have 7% of their historic range which continues to decline. One possible solution could be to connect fragmented habitats through corridors (Rathore et al. 2012)

Bibliography

Rathore, Chinmaya S., Yogesh Dubey, Anurag Shrivastava, Prasad Pathak, and Vinayak Patil. 2012. "Opportunities of Habitat Connectivity for Tiger (Panthera Tigris) between Kanha and Pench National Parks in Madhya Pradesh, India." Edited by Matt Hayward. *PLoS ONE* 7 (7): e39996. https://doi.org/10.1371/journal.pone.0039996.

Young, Christian C. 2000. "A Textbook History: Use of the Kaibab Lesson in Teaching Biology." *The American Biology Teacher* 62 (8): 559–64. https://doi.org/10.2307/4450978.

Figure 87. Bibliography generated by AsciiDoctor from citations in text after rendering to HTML & PDF

The above command may take time to finish depending on the number of references and the size of the document. So once you have entered the command, please wait for it to finish. It should terminate silently without any errors returning back to the $ prompt in the terminal.

12.8. Some Important cite:<key> Markup Variations

In the above example we have used the **cite-key** pair to cite a reference. As per documentation of the AsciiDoctor-BibTeX extension, we can also use some variants of *cite:* or *citenp:* with the following effects when using the *chicago-author-date* style:

`cite:[Lane12]` is displayed as **(Lane 2012)**
`citenp:[Lane12]` is displayed as **Lane (2012)**
`cite:[Lane12(59)]` is displayed as **(Lane 2012, 59)**

Using the above markup with styles other than *chicago-author-date* style will create different results.

12.9. Rendering to PDF

To render to PDF in place of HTML as perviously shown in Example 138, use the command shown in Example 139. The command may take some time to finish. So please be patient and let the command do its job.

Terminal Command

Example 139. Render Bibliography to PDF

```
$ asciidoctor-pdf -r asciidoctor-bibtex biblio.adoc
```

Inserting Citations in Text Using the Free Zoterobib Online Tool

If you do not wish to install Zotero and you are working with fewer references, you can also use the free Zotero Online Bibliography creator tool from https://zbib.org/ to create a Bibliography and export it as a BibTeX file. You can use this tool without logging in or downloading any software. Figure 88 shows the sequence of steps to do this.

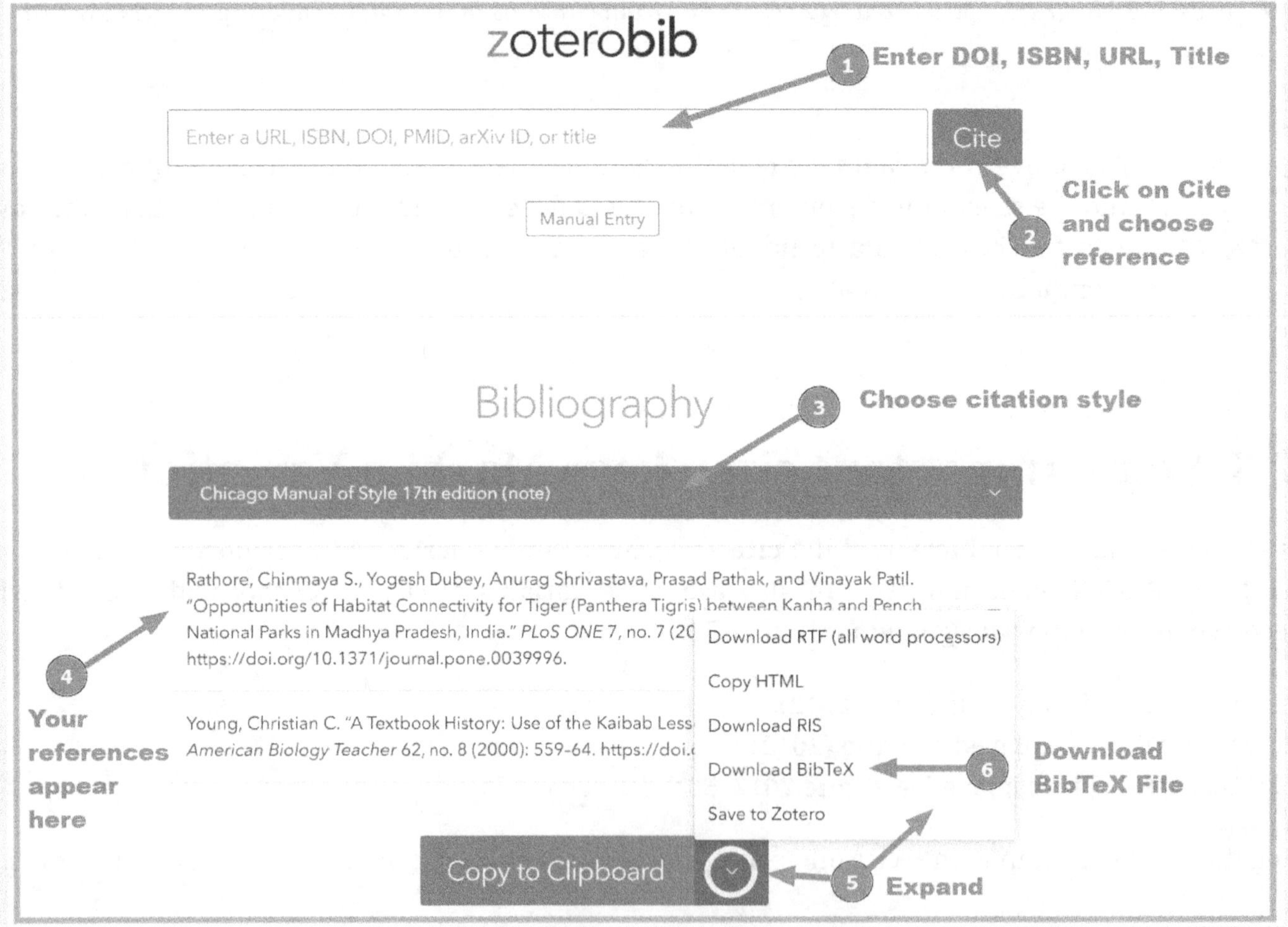

Figure 88. Using Zoteorbib online

You can also visit Zotero Bib FAQ [https://zbib.org/faq#usage] for help on this free online tool.

12.10. Single Bibliography from Multiple AsciiDoc Documents

When you write books or long reports in AsciiDoc, it is usually the case that your content is spread across many AsciiDoc files like separate files for different chapters (*ch1.adoc, ch2.adoc, ch3.adoc* etc.). So if we keep inserting citations from a BibTeX file in different AsciiDoc file using the `cite:<key>` syntax, how do we get one bibliography at the end of the merged or consolidated document? Well as it turns out, nothing special needs to be done to achieve this. Continuing the example above of *ch1.adoc*, let's say I create another document called *ch2.adoc* and I wish to cite some references from my master bibliography BibTeX file called *refs.bib* (recall I have already cited 2 references in ch1.adoc). So I can just use the key of any reference in *refs.bib* file as we have done in Example 137 and place it at appropriate places in the text of *ch2.adoc*.

If you plan to combine *ch1.adoc* and *ch2.adoc* into one document (like say a book or a report), just create a third *.adoc* file — say *book.adoc* — which must start with *bibtex-style:* and *bibtex-file* attributes, then include in that file both *ch1.adoc* and *ch2.adoc* and then end with the bibliography macro. As you are putting these attributes in a common *master* file *book.adoc*, chapter files that are being combined (*ch1.adoc*, *ch2.adoc*) *should not* have the *bibtex-file* and *bibtex-style* attributes in them. The individual chapter files can start just with their titles. As the *refs.bib* file is common to all chapters, all chapter files can use it to cite references and then we can have a consolidated bibliography at the end of the document. A small example of the contents of *book.adoc* is given in Example 140.

AsciiDoc Markup

Example 140. Basic AsciiDoc markdown for combining individual files and create a common bibliography

```
 :bibtex-file: refs.bib
 :bibtex-style:   chicago-author-date
 :toc:

 = How to Insert Citations and Add a Styled Bibliography in AsciiDoc Books and
Articles

 include::ch1.adoc[]
 include::ch2.adoc[]

_Bibliography_
                  ①
 bibliography::[]
```

① Blank Line

To render a single book file from above *book.adoc* as HTML or PDF, we can issue the command shown in [chbib-ex9-comb] from the terminal.

Terminal Command

Example 141. Creating bibliography in a single document by combining multiple files

For HTML

```
$ asciidoctor -r asciidoctor-bibtex book.adoc
```

For PDF

```
$ asciidoctor-pdf -r asciidoctor-bibtex book.adoc
```

The `include::` statements seen in Example 141 insert the content of a file in the consolidated document. We will discuss the `include::` macro in detail in Chapter 17.

This way you can use the same BibTeX file and cite references in many individual documents and combine them to have a common styled bibliography at the end of the unified document.

12.11. Chapter Summary

Key learnings in this chapter are:

1. You can insert a bibliography in AsciiDoc using the *AsciiDoctor_BibTeX extension* which needs to be installed if you are not using the AsciiDoctor Docker Image. Please see Section 12.2.1 for a quick recap on how to install this extension.
2. All the references that you plan to cite need to be in a BibTeX file which can be created using a reference manager software Like Zotero, Mendeley, EndNote , PaperPile etc. These software permit you to use a style guide like MLA, Chicago, APA, IEEE, Harvard etc. and then export your reference collection as a BibTeX file which has a *.bib* extension. Please see Section 12.3 for quick reference.
3. You can also use a free online tool called ZoteroBib [https://zbib.org/] to collect all references that you wish to cite and export them as a BibTeX file.
4. Once you have a BibTeX file and have chosen a citation style, you need to put the following in the document header (*file and style names below need to be replaced with your file and style name*):

```
:bibtex-file:refs.bib
:bibtex-style: chicago-author-date
```

The *bibtex-style* attribute can be set to a different citation style.

5. You can then open the BibTeX file containing the references you wish to cite and paste their respective BibTeX 'reference keys' at places where a reference needs to be cited in the text using the `cite:<key>` pair markup. Please see Section 12.6 for quick reference.
6. With all your citations inserted in the text, you can now generate a bibliography by placing the `bibliography::[]` macro at the end of your document. Execute the following AsciiDoctor or AsciiDoctor-PDF command on your AsciiDoc file (say *myfile.adoc*) which will generate a nicely formatted bibliography in the rendered document:

   $ asciidoctor -r asciidoctor-bibtex myfile.adoc

   or

   $ asciidoctor-pdf -r asciidoctor-bibtex myfile.adoc

7. You can also insert citations using the `cite:<key>` pair markup in individual chapter files and create a consolidated document with a single bibliography. Please see Section 12.10 for a quick recap.
8. Inserting citations and a bibliography requires patience and familiarity with citation styles and bibliographic formatting conventions. If you are not familiar with these, please spend some time to familiarize yourself. There are a lot of resources available on the Internet on how to cite references.

12.12. Try it Yourself

You will need the *refs.bib* file from the exercises folder of this chapter.

1. Try inserting the citations in this file in your document and generate a bibliography at the end of your document as demonstrated.
2. Using the free online Zoterobib tool at https://zbib.org/, try collecting some references from the web and export the collection as a BibTeX file.
3. Use this exported BibTeX file to cite some references in any AsciiDoc file that you might have.

4. While citing references, try out some variations of the `cite:` attribute as discussed in Section 12.8. What is the difference between `cite:[key]` and `citenp:[key]`? Where is this difference seen — in the text citation or in the bibliography ?

5. Try generating a bibliography in IEEE, MLA and Harvard styles. You can visit https://github.com/citation-style-language/styles/blob/master/din-1505-2-numeric-alphabetical.csl for a comprehensive list of citation styles that can be used to generate a bibliography (See Example 134 for help).

6. Referring to Section 12.10, can you add references from the same BibTeX file in two documents (ch1.adoc and ch2.adoc) and then create a third document to generate a unified bibliography? You can use the markup shown in Example 140 and study the output.

7. If you need to cite literature very often in your writing and have not used a reference manager before, you can give Zotero [https://www.zotero.org/] a try. It's open source and free and you can start by creating a small collection of references, export that collection as a BibTeX file and use it inside an AsciiDoc document to cite references and create a bibliography. See Section 12.3 for some introductory help.

Chapter 13. Creating a Book Index

"A good index is like a map, it helps you find your way, it helps you understand the territory, and it helps you discover new things." ~Peter Morville

In this chapter we learn how to create a book index by marking primary, secondary and tertiary index terms and then generating an alphabetically sorted index that is placed at the end of the document. This chapter has some long example passages that have been used to illustrate how indexing works. These long example passages were required to show how marked terms are positioned in indexes when they are contiguous or when they are some pages apart. As index creation has its fair share of nuances, a quick summary of Index related AsciiDoc markup has been included at the end of this chapter for ready reference.

13.1. Some Starting Notes

Book indexes have been around since printed books have been published. They provide readers an easy way to search and reach topics of interest. With the dawn of the internet era and availability of books in digital form, documents can now be searched fully and one can navigate to topics directly using hyperlinks. So the utility of book indexes has been a bit obfuscated — particularly when consuming digital content. However indexes have not been out of vouge either. They are very much there and most printed books still have them as an important tool for the readers to reach desired content. So if you plan to publish a book in PDF format, it might be very helpful to create an index at the end of the book, particularly if that book is likely to be printed on paper. AsciiDoc and AsciiDoctor-PDF permit you to natively create simple book indexes like the one shown in Figure 89 and Figure 93 quite easily.

As you might have guessed and in the backdrop of the above discussion, index creation is not available (and not required) for HTML output i.e. you can't create indexes when using *AsciiDoctor* which renders AsciiDoc files to HTML.

Creating a book index in AsciiDoc for PDF outputs does *not* require installation of any extension and is natively supported by *AsciiDoctor-PDF*. It is accomplished in the following two steps:

1. Marking Index Entries or Index Words in the AsciiDoc file/s . This has to be done *manually* **for each occurrence of the word to be indexed**.
2. Generating the index when the document is rendered as PDF.

Before we move forward, I would like to point out that the current version of `AsciiDoctor-PDF (2.3.19)` available at the time of writing this book **does not** support `see` and `see-also` syntax in creation of indexes. You can have up to three levels of sub-entries — primary, secondary, and tertiary as shown in Figure 89.

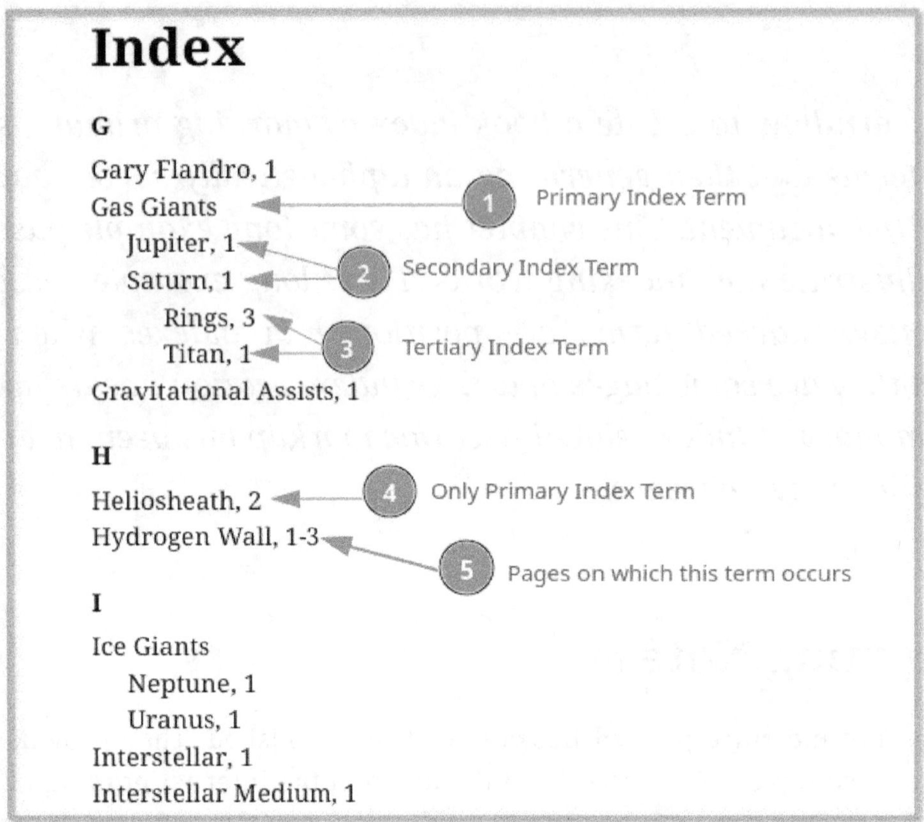

Figure 89. Primary, secondary and tertiary index term levels

13.2. Creating an Index

Before we start creating an Index, a few points need to be noted upfront :

1. Indexes are *not rendered* in HTML output. They are only rendered in PDF output.
2. Unlike the word processing environment where you can mark a term and press a button to mark all occurrences of that term, you will have to manually (or using find-replace or some other tool) mark all occurrences of that term in your document.
3. While simple indexes — which are sufficient in most cases — can be easily generated in AsciiDoc, it may not be possible to include more complex indexing nuances that you might see in some printed books.
4. So while the idea of creating an index is easy and straightforward in AsciiDoc, if you set out to do this for a real book, you should be patient and be prepared to engage in a somewhat laborious pursuit.

With that out of the way, let's see, step-by-step, how we can create an index in AsciiDoc. The index that you see at the end of this book has been created using these exact same steps.

13.2.1. Step 1 — Marking Index Entries

This step involves marking words in your document that need to appear in the book's index. This is best done at the same time as you type your content. However, even though it might be a lot of work, you can also do it once you have finished writing. You can mark index entries in multiple ways as you type or after you have created the document.

To illustrate how to mark index terms in running text, we will use some sample text about the legendary Voyager Mission taken from the Voyager Programme page on Wikipedia [https://en.wikipedia.org/wiki/Voyager_program]. These excerpts can be seen in Example 142 and we will try to mark some index terms on these passages and generate a well formatted and alphabetically sorted index at the end of the document. Referring to Example 142, let's assume for the sake of illustration, that the text is spread over *two pages*. As you read the following sections, feel free to refer to Figure 89 for a visual appreciation of indexing terminology.

Example 142 shows how we can use *nested parenthesis* markup in running text to designate primary, secondary and tertiary terms to be included in the index.

AsciiDoc Markup

Example 142. Inline Index Entry for Primary Terms (Text Source — Wikipedia, Voyager Program)

```
---Page 1
== The Voyager Program

The Voyager program is an American scientific program under Aegis of ((NASA)) ①
that employs two space probes,
(((Voyager Program,Voyager 1))) Voyager 1 and (((Voyager Program,Voyager 2))) Voyager
2. ②
They were launched in 1977 to take advantage of a favorable (((Planetary)))planetary
alignment to explore the two gas giants ③
(((Gas Giants,Jupiter)))Jupiter and (((Gas Giants,Saturn)))Saturn  ④
and potentially also the ice giants, Uranus and Neptune -
to fly near them while collecting data for transmission back to ((Earth)). After
Voyager 1 successfully completed its flyby of Saturn and its moon
(((Gas Giants,Saturn,Titan)))Titan,  ⑤
it was decided to send Voyager 2 on flybys of Uranus and Neptune.

---Page 2

On 25 August 2012, data from (((Voyager Program,Voyager 1)))Voyager 1
indicated that it had entered interstellar space. On 5 November 2019,
```

```
data from (((Voyager Program,Voyager 2)))Voyager 2
indicated that it also had entered interstellar space.              ⑥
On 4 November 2019, scientists reported that on 5 November 2018,
the (((Voyager Program,Voyager 2)))Voyager 2  had reached a region of
outer space beyond the influence of the solar wind, as did
(((Voyager Program,Voyager 1)))Voyager 1 in 2012. In August 2018,
((NASA)) confirmed, based on results by the New Horizons spacecraft,
the existence of a "Hydrogen Wall" at the outer edges of the ((Solar System)) that
was first detected in 1992 by the two Voyager spacecraft.

Text Source:Wikipedia, Voyager Program
```

① Primary Index Term — The word inside the double parenthesis will appear in the Index without parenthesis and will also continue to be visible in the running text when rendered.

② Primary (P) and Secondary (S) index terms defined using (((P,S))) — Everything inside the 3 pairs of parenthesis will NOT be visible in the running text when rendered.

③ Primary term — the indexed word will appear with a first letter in sentence case.

④ Primary term and secondary term, as seen at callout 2 ((P,S))

⑤ Primary (P) Secondary (S) and Tertiary (T) index terms defined using (((P,S,T)))

⑥ Every instance of index terms marked on page 1 must also be marked on subsequent pages for them to be reflected on the page numbers on which they appear in the rendered index.

13.2.1.1. Marking Primary Index Term

There are two methods for marking a primary (meaning single) index term. Both these methods achieve the exact same result and you can choose whichever one you find easy to work with.

Method 1 — Enclosing the Term in Double Parenthesis

To mark any word for index entry, just enclose it inside two opening and two closing parenthesis like — `((term))`. This can be seen in the Example 142 at callout 1. Here the term NASA is part of our running text and we want to include it in the index. To do that we just enclose it inside two pairs of parenthesis. Whenever we enclose the word inside two pairs of parenthesis, it appears in the running text when rendered as PDF without the parenthesis as it would normally. It also appears in the index once we create it in Section 13.2.6 described later. This type of index term — marked using two pairs of parenthesis — is called *flow text* or *visible* index term because whatever is inside the parenthesis, is *visible* in the rendered document. You can see in Figure 89 how primary index terms marked within two sets of parenthesis appear in the rendered index. In Example 142 — 'Earth' and 'Solar System' are both examples of *visible* primary index terms. The *visible* primary index term is also case sensitive which means that if the word enclosed inside a double parenthesis was `((nasa))`, it would appear in the index as *nasa* i.e. in *lower case*. Later on, we will see a way to overcome this.

The term 'Hydrogen Wall' in Figure 89 is also an example of this *flow text* primary index term. However, because this term was found on more than one page — in this case consecutive pages, its occurrence therefore is shown as a page range 1-3 meaning that this term has appeared on page 1, page 2 and page 3 of the book. This brings us to an important question — "If we marked a term on its first occurrence and the term appears on many pages subsequently in the text, will the presence of this term on other pages in the document be automatically reflected at the time of creating the index ?" And the short answer is — *No* — it will not be automatically reflected. Let's explore this question with a practical example.

To illustrate the above question in reference to Example 142, we see that we marked NASA as an indexed term in the first paragraph, but as can be seen, NASA also appears on page 2 of our example (and may possibly occur on other pages if there were more pages in the document). So the question is — do we have to mark every instance of NASA by enclosing it inside a set of parenthesis for it to be mentioned in the index or will just marking it once be enough ? And the answer is *yes, we do* have to mark *all* instances! Now before you start panicking and pulling your hair in frustration, this might not be a very difficult job to do in your text editor as you can just use *find* — `NASA` and *replace it with* — `((NASA))`. So essentially this hack involves that you mark a word for indexing and use your text editor's *find and replace feature* to mark all occurrences of that word in your entire document. If an indexed word appears on a page and you do not mark it as an indexed term i.e. not enclose it inside a double parenthesis, that page will not appear in front of that indexed term when the index is created.

There is one more variation of marking a primary index term using a concealed entry. Say our running text has a word 'heliosheath' and we wish to mark it as an index term. As done before, we enclose *heliosheath* inside a pair of parenthesis like — `((heliosheath))` to mark it as an index term. However, marking the term in this manner creates an issue for us. This entry in the index will appear exactly as it was marked — *heliosheath* with a lower case *h*. Usually however, index words appear with the first letter in capital. Now as you might have guessed, to rectify this issue we could just make the first letter of that word as capital in the running text before marking it as an indexed term but that could be grammatically wrong — as it would show a capitalized word mid-sentence in our running text. Once again, AsciiDoc comes to our rescue. AsciiDoc has a brilliant solution for such a situation when you want the marked index word to appear with its first letter capitalized in the index but *not* in the running text. If we want *heliosheath* to appear as *Heliosheath* in the index, we need to enter the capitalized word inside a *double pair* of parenthesis just preceding 'heliosheath' in the running matter. This is markup is shown in Example 143.

AsciiDoc Markup

Example 143. Capitalizing the first letter of an indexed term

```
...and entered the ((Heliosheath))heliosheath, where the solar wind is compressed....
```

When the document is rendered in PDF by *AsciiDoctor-PDF*, the term inside the double pair of parenthesis — the one with the first letter capitalized — will become invisible in the running text but will magically appear in the index.

Method 2 — Using the *indexterm2* syntax

If you are uncomfortable with using and balancing parenthesis, you can do the exact same thing by using the *indexterm2* keyword as shown in Example 144.

Example 144. Using 'indexterm2' to mark primary index terms in place of parenthesis

```
The Voyager program is an American scientific program under Aegis of ((NASA))
```

is the same as

```
The Voyager program is an American scientific program under Aegis of indexerm2:[NASA]
①
```

① The term inside the square bracket after *indexterm2* will be visible in the running text and will also appear in the index as is the case with the double parenthesis. The keyword *indexterm2:* itself will not be visible in the running text.

13.2.2. Marking Primary , Secondary and Tertiary Index Terms

Book indexes also carry grouped indexed items where a primary indexed term has sub-entries under it, bunched up in a group. You can see this in Figure 90(c) under the entry for 'Voyager Program'. There is no page number in front of the index entry — 'Voyager Program'. However it has two sub or secondary entries — Voyager 1 and Voyager 2 under it which have page numbers. To create an index term with primary and secondary entries, enclose primary and secondary terms within three pairs of parentheses as shown in the Example 142 just above callout (2). Rather than enclose the term Voyager 1 and Voyager 2 directly in the running text as in the previous case, we insert the indexing terms just before the word Voyager 1 and Voyager 2 in the text, as shown in Example 145 (you can put a space between the text term and the term inside three parenthesis).

AsciiDoc Markup

Example 145. Putting primary, secondary and tertiary terms just before the terms to be indexed

```
(((Voyager Program,Voyager 1))) Voyager 1 and (((Voyager Program,Voyager 2)))
Voyager 2.
```

This creates a grouped sub-entry term in the index. When the text is rendered by AsciiDoctor-PDF, the index terms inside the three pairs of parenthesis *do not show up* in the running text i.e. they remain invisible thereby maintaining the flow of the text. However, they do appear as a group in the index. This whole sequence of marking in AsciiDoc, appearance in running text in PDF after rendering and entry in the index is shown in Figure 90.

Figure 90. (a) Inserting raw AsciiDoc primary and secondary index terms (b) How it shows up in the PDF in the running text matter after rendering (c) How it shows up in the index. Note that NASA was marked as a primary index entry in the previous section.

This method — using three pairs of parentheses — is also called *concealed* because whatever you type inside the three parenthesis pairs does not appear in the running text and is just used for creating the index entry. Like before , you need to mark every occurrence of Voyager 1 and Voyager 2 in your document in a similar fashion i.e. precede it with `(((Voyager Program,Voyager 1)))` and `(((Voyager Program,Voyager 2)))` as the case may be wherever they appear in your text.

13.2.3. Grouping at Tertiary Level

The sub-entry grouping can be taken down to a third level. An instance of this can be seen in the Figure 89 under 'G — Gas Giants' where the index terms Rings and Titan appear under Saturn which in turn appears under Gas Giants. In this example, Rings and Titan — occurring at level 3 — are both *tertiary* index terms, Saturn is the *secondary* index term and 'Gas Giants' is the *primary* index term. In such a index grouping, only the secondary and tertiary terms carry page numbers. There is no page number on the primary term.

To create *tertiary* index terms as in the example above, the markup is identical to the previous markup except that we extend it by another term. We use the markup `(((Gas Giants,Saturn,Rings)))` and `(((Gas Giants,Saturn,Titan)))` just before the word Rings and Titan in the running text to indicate that terms Rings and Titan will appear under Gas Giants → Saturn (Example 142, Callout 5). Once again, every occurrence of Titan and Rings in the document must be preceded with this markup for these terms wherever they occur in the document text.

13.2.4. Marking Secondary and Tertiary Terms using *Indexterm* Syntax

Just like *indexterm2* is used as an alternative to marking primary terms using a pair of double parenthesis, if you feel overwhelmed by using 3 pairs of parenthesis, you can use `indexterm:[P,S,T]` to primary (P), secondary (S) and tertiary (T) index terms. For the above mentioned example of Saturn → Rings and Titan, we can use the following to insert the exact same tertiary index entry as shown in Example 146.

AsciiDoc Markup

Example 146. The indexterm: syntax is the same as three parenthesis syntax for primary, secondary and tertiary index term entry

```
After Voyager 1 successfully completed its flyby of Saturn and its moon (((Gas
Giants,Saturn,Titan)))Titan
it was decided to send Voyager 2 on flybys of Uranus and Neptune. Voyager 2 also
obtained high-resolution pictures of Saturn's (((Gas Giants,Saturn,Rings)))rings on
Aug. 22 1981.
```

is the same as

```
After Voyager 1 successfully completed its flyby of Saturn and its moon
indexterm:[Gas Giants,Saturn,Titan] Titan
it was decided to send Voyager 2 on flybys of Uranus and Neptune. Voyager 2 also
obtained high-resolution pictures of Saturn's indexterm:[Gas Giants,Saturn,Rings]
rings on Aug. 22 1981.
```

Figure 91 shows the results of the above indexterm syntax in running text and index after the AsciiDoc file is rendered as PDF.

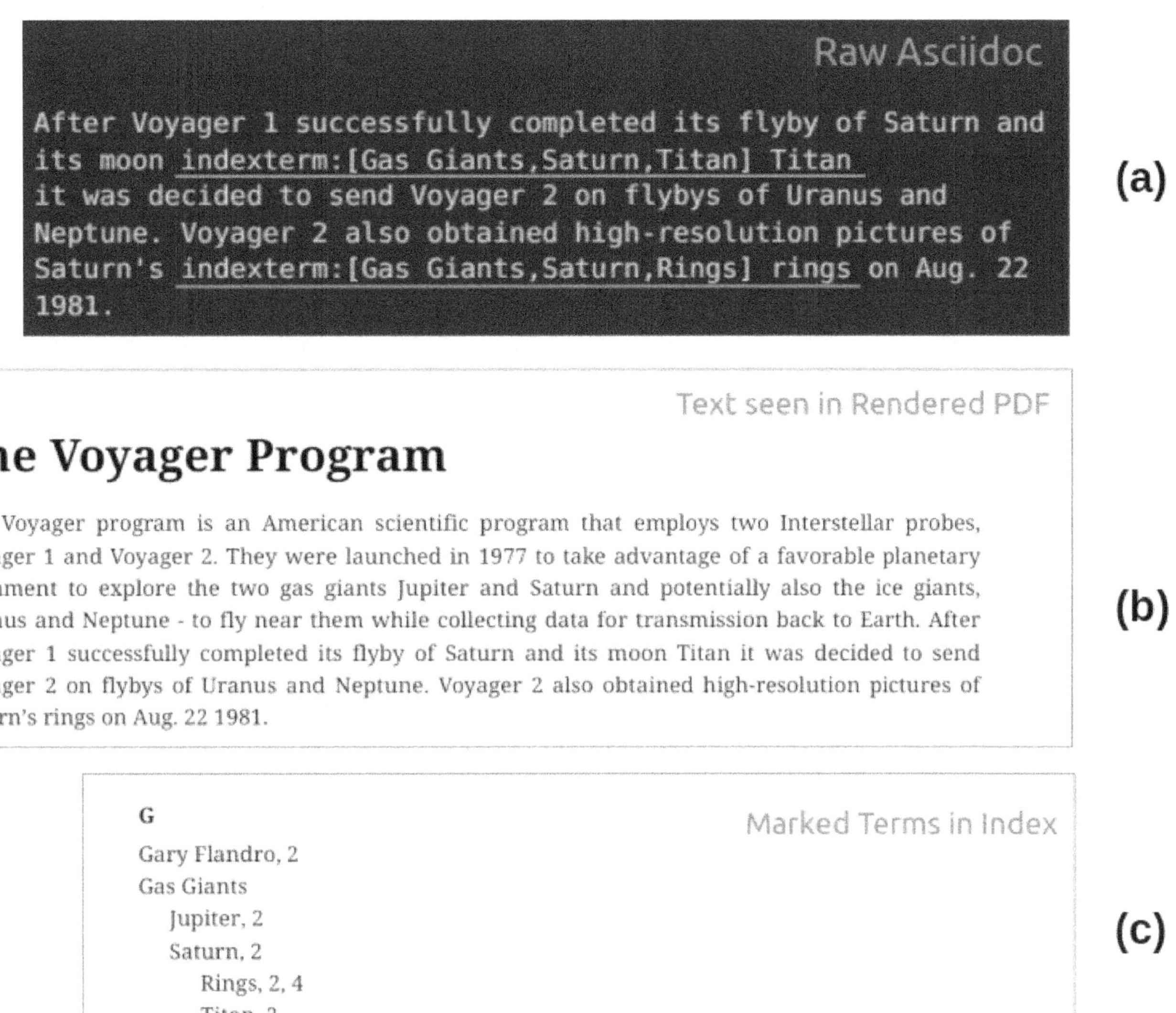

Figure 91. (a) Asciidoc showing indexterm markup (b) Markup rendered in PDF as running text (c) Markup entries in (a) appearing in Index after rendering showing Rings and Titan under Saturn which is under Gas Giants.

As can be seen, the *indexterm:[]* and anything contained inside the square brackets does not appear in the running text and is *concealed* or *invisible* appearing only in the index.

13.2.5. Using Indexterm Over Paragraphs

Two quick points with reference to the usage of the `indexterm:[P,S,T]` (Primary, Secondary and Tertiary) markup as demonstrated in Section 13.2.4.

1. We can also use indexterm:[] to define primary index terms for example like `indexterm:[NASA]`

NASA. As the term inside the square bracket will be invisible, we need to place it before the actual word. There can be a space between the indexterm entry and the word being indexed.

2. We can place the indexterm[] insert on top of paragraphs or text blocks *making sure that there is no empty line between the terms and the text block* as shown in Figure 92.

```
indexterm:[Discoveries,Hydrogen Wall]
indexterm:[Interstellar Medium]
indexterm:[Solar Wind]
After the planetary flybys were complete, decisions were made to keep the probes in operation
to explore interstellar space and the outer regions of the solar system. On 25 August 2012,
data from (((Voyager Program,Voyager 1)))Voyager 1 indicated that it had entered interstellar
space. On 5 November 2019, data from (((Voyager Program,Voyager 2)))Voyager 2 indicated that
it also had entered interstellar space.On 4 November 2019, scientists reported that on 5
November 2018, the (((Voyager Program,Voyager 2)))Voyager 2 probe had officially reached the
Interstellar medium (ISM), a region of outer space beyond the influence of the solar wind, as
did (((Voyager Program,Voyager 1)))Voyager 1 in 2012. In August 2018, NASA confirmed, based
on results by the ((New Horizons)) spacecraft, the existence of a "Hydrogen Wall" at the
outer edges of the Solar System that was first detected in 1992 by the two Voyager
spacecraft. This was a phenominal discovery by the Voyager Program.
```


Figure 92. Placing indexterm:[] index entry on top of a text block — all these terms will appear in the index referring to this page

Indexterm placement above Section Titles

Please note that the above placement of indexterm applies to paragraphs or blocks of text that do not have a section title above them. If there is a section title over a text block, the placement of indexterm requires a blank line in between as explained later in the discussion on common indexing errors — Section 13.5.1.

So how can this be useful? This can be helpful if say you wish to mark some terms occurring on a para or a page without making all instances of that word on that page. If a term appears multiple times on one page, it will appear only once in the index. So if you mark it on top of one paragraph on that page, it will be included in the index. You can stack multiple terms but you must make sure they must all appear in the text block underneath (or on that page) otherwise the index generated will carry inaccurate page numbers resulting in readers being mislead.

Placing the indexterm above the section title separated by a blank line as described above might in certain cases, introduce blank lines in the text. Please refer to Section 13.5.2 for helpful tips to deal with such a situation.

13.2.6. Step 2 — Generating the Book Index

Once all Index terms have been marked in the document text, we can proceed to generate the index. However we need to complete a couple of tasks before generating the PDF that will render the document and create the index.

(1) The first thing to do is to add the markup shown in Example 147 at the end of the document i.e. where you want the index to physically appear in the book.

AsciiDoc Markup

Example 147. Generating an index at the end of the document

```
[index]
== Index
```

(2) In Example 147, it is important to note that the heading **Index** *must* be either a Level 0 (=) or a Level 1(==) heading.

(3) To ensure that index entries are sensibly presented — like page numbers are not being repeated if a term is present more than once on the same page and clubbing entries in *page ranges* if a term is present on consecutive pages — we need to add the *media* attribute and set it's value in the header of the document as shown in Example 148. Please see Chapter 20 — Section 20.5 to know more about *print* and *prepress* modes.

AsciiDoc Markup

Example 148. Setting the value of the media attribute in the document header

```
:media: print
```

or

```
:media: prepress
```

After the above are added, we just use AsciiDoctor-PDF to convert the AsciiDoc file (say *mybook.adoc*) to PDF as follows:

Terminal Command

```
$ asciidoctor-pdf mybook.adoc
```

You should now see a well formatted and alphabetically sorted index at the end of your generated PDF like the excerpt shown in Figure 93.

Index

D

Discoveries
    Hydrogen Wall, 2, 5

G

Gary Flandro, 1
Gas Giants
    Jupiter, 1
    Saturn, 1
        Rings, 1, 3
        Titan, 1
Gravitational Assists, 1

H

Heliosheath, 2
Hydrogen Wall, 1-4

Figure 93. An excerpt from a full index

And that's how you can create a book index in AsciiDoc.

13.3. Hyperlinked Index

If you are creating a PDF just for online circulation i.e. the media is not for printing or publication as a hard copy, you can have your index with page numbers acting as active hyperlinks or *back links* as can be seen in Figure 94. In such an index, when you click on any page number in front of an index entry, you are taken directly to the page where that index term appears.

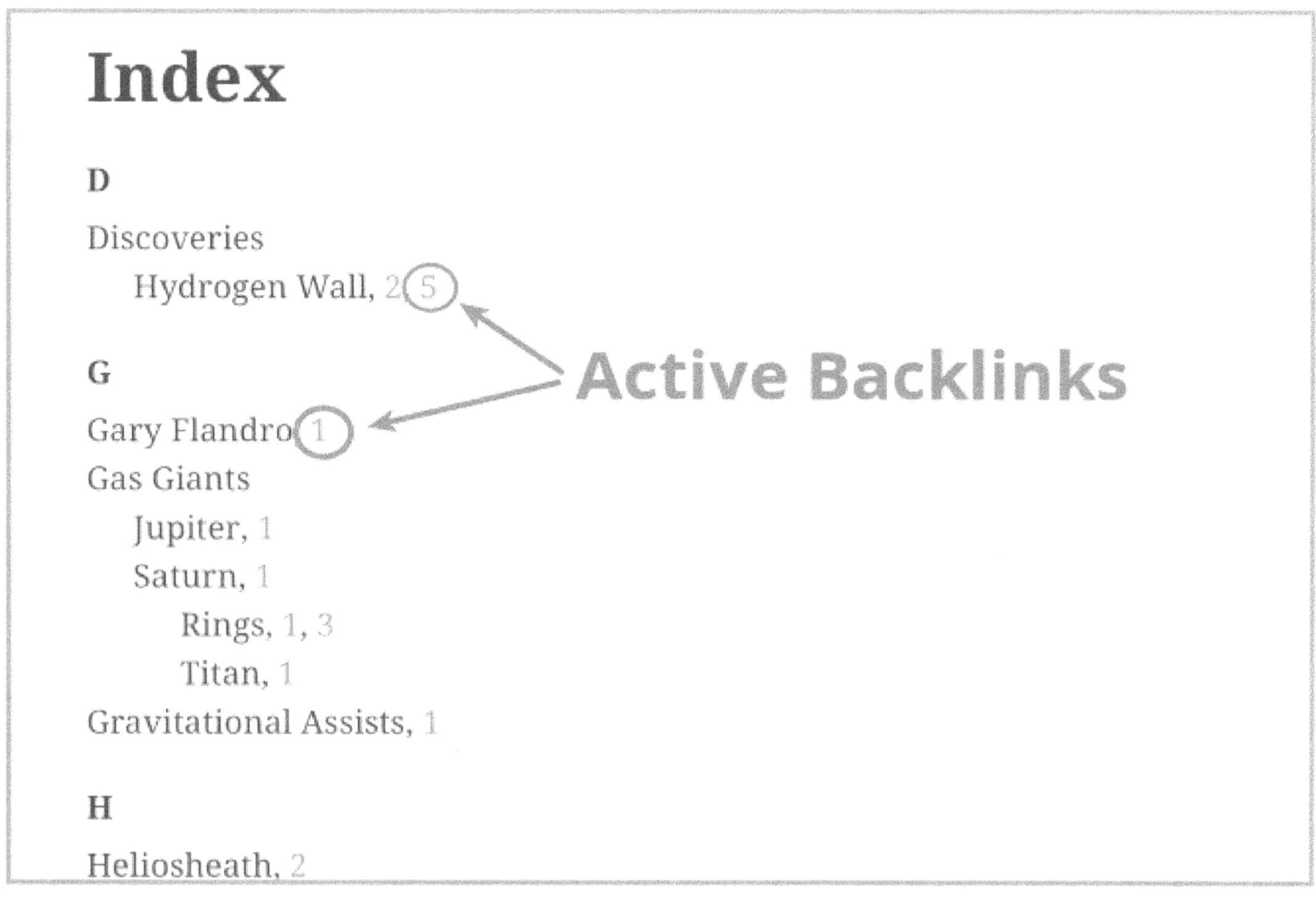

Figure 94. Linked index with active backlinks

To achieve this, all you need to do is to ***omit*** the `:media: print` or `:media: prepress` and the `:doctype: book` attributes from your header. When these attributes are absent and you render your file simply using *asciidoctor-pdf <yourfile.adoc>*, a *hyperlinked index* in the generated PDF as shown in Figure 94.

13.4. Creating a Composite Index Across Multiple AsciiDoc Files

The examples mentioned in this chapter so far have used a single AsciiDoc file and created an index at the end of that file. However when you take up a book writing project, it is unfair and impractical to assume that your entire book will be written in a single AsciiDoc file. It is more likely that you would have at the least, a separate file for every chapter in your book. So an important question without which this chapter would be incomplete is — "if I marked index entries using double or triple parenthesis in individual chapter files, can I still get a single index at the end of my book when the book is compiled ? "

The answer to that question is — *Yes absolutely!*

All you have to do is to move the above mentioned index insertion markup shown in Example 147 to your *main* AsciiDoc file — the file that has all the chapter include statements (see Chapter 17 for more) and add `:media: print` (or `:media: prepress`) in the header of your *main* AsciiDoc file.

I illustrate this with a small simulated example. Let's say we have our content spread across two files — *v1.adoc* and *v2.adoc* (rather than a single file). Each file starts with a level 1 (`==`) chapter heading and has primary, secondary and tertiary index terms marked in them. I collate both these chapter files using the *v0.adoc* file (I refer to this as the main file) using the markup shown in Example 149.

Example 149. Contents of Main AsciiDoc file — v0.adoc

```
// This file is saved as v0.adoc

= Creating an Index for PDF Book
:icons: font
:doctype: book
:sectnums:
:media: print         ①

include::v1.adoc[]
include::v2.adoc[]    ②

[index]
== Index              ③
```

① Added the attribute — :media: print (can also use `:media: prepress:`) — and any other needed attributes only in the main file and not in the chapter files v1 and v2.

② The include attributes will bring in contents of v1.adoc and v2.adoc here

③ The [index] styling and Index level 1 (==) title has also been included in the main file (v0) only.

To bring all these chapters and the consolidated index in one PDF, just run *asciidoctor-pdf* on *v0.adoc* as follows:

```
$ asciidoctor-pdf v0.adoc
```

You should now have a file name *v0.pdf* which will have a cover page, contents of both chapters with large chapter headings and a consolidated index which is the same index that you generated with the single file *voyager.adoc.*

This way you can add as many chapters to your PDF and end up with a consolidated index in the final PDF file.

13.5. Some Common Sources of Errors While Creating a Book Index

When you create a book index, you might encounter the following common errors.

13.5.1. Problem 1 : Messed up Section Titles

When you use the `indexterm:[]` directly above a *section heading*, it prevents the section heading to be displayed in default heading style. This not only messes up the text at that point resulting in the section title appearing as normal text, it also results in the term not being indexed. Figure 95(a) shows default styling for section heading while Figure 95(b) shows the section heading appearing as normal text caused due to the indexterm being placed directly above the section heading.

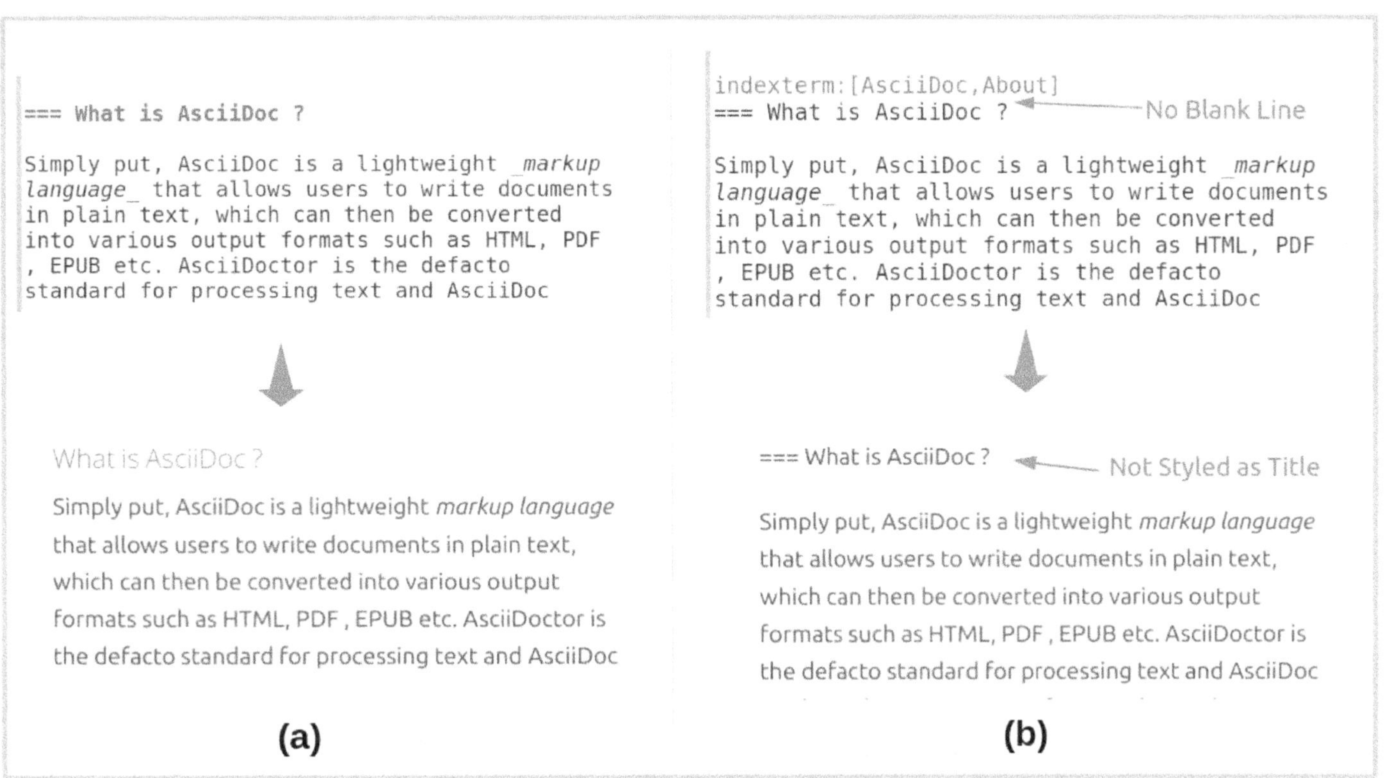

Figure 95. Indexterm problem: (a) Normal section title and styling (b) indexterm:[] directive placed on top of section title results in badly styled section title and term not included in index.

How to Avoid this Error: The solution is to bring the *indexterm* directive *under* the section title as shown in Figure 96.

```
=== What is AsciiDoc ?
indexterm:[AsciiDoc,About]
Simply put, AsciiDoc is a lightweight _markup
language_ that allows users to write documents
in plain text, which can then be converted
into various output formats such as HTML, PDF
, EPUB etc. AsciiDoctor is the defacto
standard for processing text and AsciiDoc
```

Move indexterm under the title

What is AsciiDoc ?

Simply put, AsciiDoc is a lightweight *markup language* that allows users to write documents in plain text, which can then be converted into various output formats such as HTML, PDF , EPUB etc. AsciiDoctor is the defacto standard for processing text and AsciiDoc

Figure 96. Indexterm solution: Introducing a blank line between section title and the 'indexterm:[]' directive solves the problem

If you leave the indexterm on top of the title and introduce a blank line between it and the title, you will get back the default section heading styling but a blank line will get added on top of the section title when the document is rendered as PDF by *AsciiDoctor-PDF*.

13.5.2. Problem 2: Multiple Index Entries for the Same Index Term

Let's suppose you are scanning a few pages to mark index terms. On Page 1, you find a term appearing in `Sentence Case`, and you mark it for index entry. Subsequently you find that the same term appears on page 2, but on this page it *appears in italics*, which you again mark for index entry. Moving ahead, on page 3, you find the same term spelled in *lower case letters* and mark it for index entry. This situation is illustrated in example Figure 97.

```
=== Moving Beyond Word Processing Software

In word processing programs like ((MS Word)), ((Google Docs)), ((LibreOffice Writer))
and others, the content i.e the text you type in and the presentation of that text
i.e. all the styling etc. are done by one software. Which means when you write an
article say in ((_LibreOffice Writer_)), you not only need to type in the text for
your article but you als  eed to know various software operations that style and
format text. These optio   as many might be well aware, include things like choosing
fonts, setting up margins, inserting page numbers, headers, footers, adjusting line
spacing and many other styling changes! In short, the burden of both writing and
styling a document is on you. Learning to use software such as ((libreoffice writer))
to its full potential takes a lot of time and effort and practically lock  ou with
```

Figure 97. Index term marking for a term that has been styled or capitalized differently (1) Normal Styling (2) in italics and (3) spelled in lower case letters.

The question is — will the index show one entry for LibreOffice writer with different page numbers in front or will the index show *three* separate entries ? Well as it turns out, the same word styled or capitalized differently (at the time of writing) is treated as a separate index entity. The above situation will manifest in the index as three *separate index terms* even though they are *spelled exactly the same*. This is shown in Figure 98.

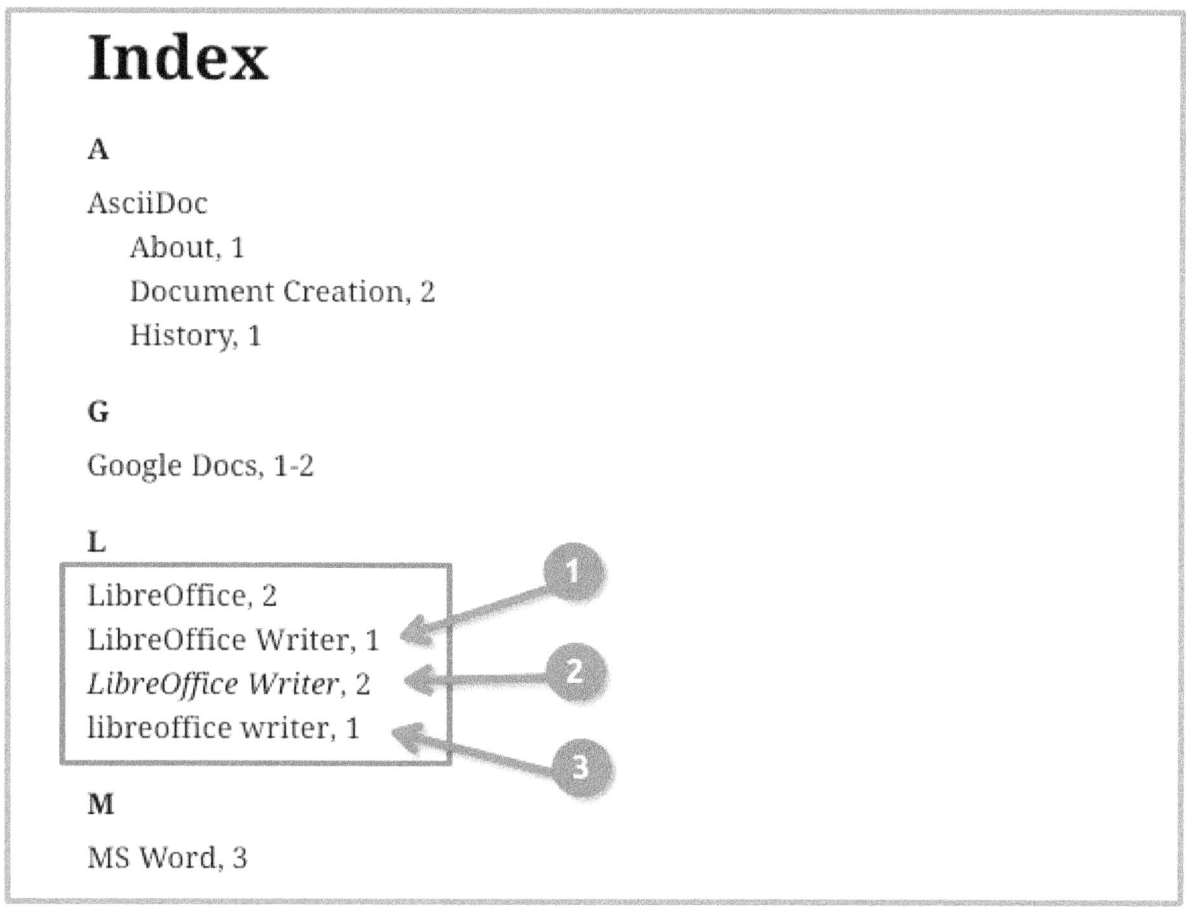

Figure 98. Three separate index entries for differently styled or capitalized words.

How to Avoid this Error: Just make sure that the word is not styled or capitalized differently or if a different styling or capitalization of the word is required, use a three bracket hidden index term preceding the term to be indexed. For the above example—`(((LibreOffice Writer))) _LibreOffice Writer_` and `(((LibreOffice Writer))) libreoffice writer`—will ensure that the term is indexed once with styling or capitalization being retained in the running text.

13.5.3. Problem 3: Index Does Not Appear in Document

Sometimes in spite of marking all index terms correctly, the index may not appear at the end of the document. This might happen because no space was given between the Level 1 heading markup symbols `==` and the word `Index` as shown in Figure 99 (a).

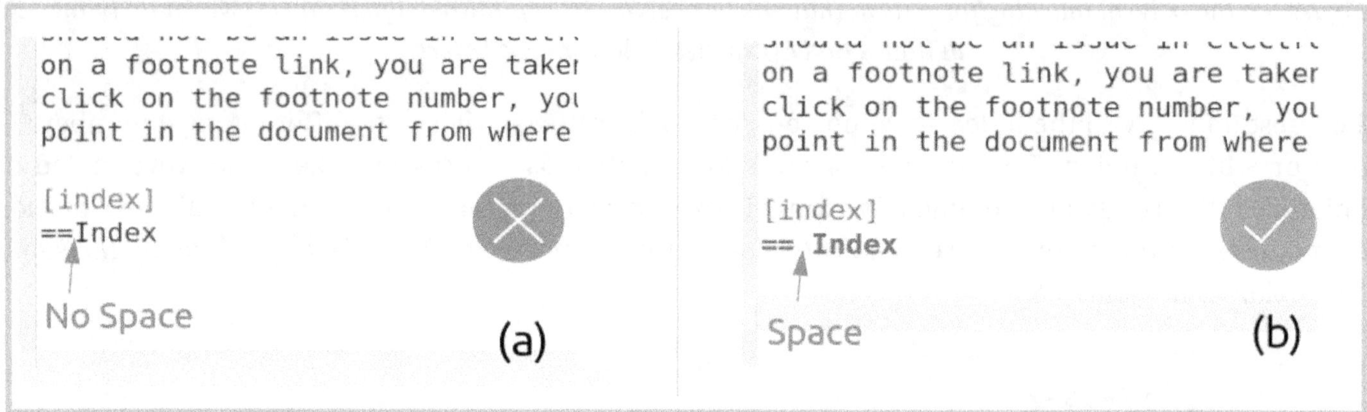

Figure 99. Index does not appear (a) missing space (b) solution is to add a space

How to Avoid this Error: Just insert a space between the chapter heading markup symbol `==` and the word `Index` as shown in Figure 99(b).

13.6. Chapter Summary

Key learnings in this chapter are:

1. In this chapter we have seen how to create a simple book index in AsciiDoc. The content in this chapter might seem a bit overwhelming due to the many nuances involved in creation of a book index. Essentially however, there are four key markup sequences that we need to remember in order to create a book index:
2. You can mark any word to be included as a primary index entry by enclosing it inside a pair of

parenthesis like — `((NASA))` or by using markup `indexterm2:[NASA]`

3. You can mark primary, secondary or tertiary terms by prefixing the term with three pairs of parenthesis like `(((Gas Giants,Saturn,Titan))) Titan` or by using `indexterm:[Gas Giants,Saturn,Titan]` Titan
4. You can generate an index by placing the following markup at the end of your document `[index]` `== Index` and the following markup in the header of your document `:doctype: book` and `:media: print` or `:media: prepress`. If you want index entries to be hyperlinked like for online reading of PDF, omit all these attributes from the header before rendering to PDF.
5. You can generate the PDF with the index by issuing the following command from the terminal (replacing *mybook.adoc* with your file name): `$ asciidoctor-pdf mybook.adoc`

13.7. Try Out Yourself

Sample files required for the tasks below can be accessed from the chapter's folder in the exercise packet.

1. Examine the *voyager.adoc* file in the examples folder of this chapter and see how index entries have been marked. Take your time to study the markup. You can mark some more words to be included if you like in the index.
2. Run *AsciiDoctor-PDF* on this file and see if you can generate a PDF version with an index by issuing the following command from the terminal:

```
$ asciidoctor-pdf voyager.adoc
```

3. The file *voyager.adoc* has been split into two individual chapter file — *v1.adoc* and *v2.adoc*. Examine both these files and locate indexed words and terms. Now open the *v0.adoc* file and examine it. Notice how the two chapters have been integrated into one document using *include* directives and the index is at the end of these two chapters. Now run *asciidoctor-pdf* on *v0.adoc* and see if you can create a single PDF file with a common unified index for both these chapters as discussed in Section 13.4.

4. Make a copy of the *voyager_clean.adoc* file and mark index words primary , secondary and tertiary index terms yourself in that file (please see the chapter summary for quick reference). Use both `((term))` and *indexterm* syntax. Do not forget to insert `:media: print` or `:media: prepress` in the header of the document and the following markup at the end of the document:
   ```
   [index]
   == Index
   ```
   Finally run Asciidoctor-PDF on your AsciiDoc file to create an PDF with a book index.
5. For reference, you can check the *Voyager.pdf* file in the exercise folder to check if you got the same or similar index as me !

Chapter 14. Math Equations

"Politics is for the present, but an equation is for eternity." ~ Albert Einstein

In this chapter we see how we can create and include properly formatted equations in AsciiDoc. We will learn how to use an AsciiDoctor extension called AsciiDoctor-Mathematical. We will also explore LaTeX (pronounced as "Lah-tech" or "Lay-tech") which is a technical typesetting system. It defines markup codes that are, among other things, particularly suited for writing equations.

14.1. Writing Math Equations

Writing equations *properly* in your documents — even if you are using a word processor like MS word or LibreOffice Writer — can be quite challenging. Thankfully most people don't have to worry about them at all in their daily communications or in their writing for regular office work. If however you are an educator, a researcher or a student pursuing Science-Technology-Engineering-Mathematics (STEM) courses, it is more than likely that you will, sooner or later, find yourself wanting to include equations or mathematical formulae in your documents. This brings you into the world of a new markup vocabulary that specializes in rendering well formatted equations. To illustrate the point, let's say we wish to reproduce the equation seen in Figure 100 — written on your class whiteboard, in your digital document.

$$\sigma = \sqrt{\frac{\sum(x_i - \mu)^2}{N}}$$

Figure 100. Image of Formula for Population Standard Deviation

As you can infer, it is practically impossible to render the above formula in your document using your laptop's keyboard. But if you knew a bit of LaTex markup — which can be easily typed on the keyboard, you can easily render the formula exactly as seen above in your document. Example 150 shows LaTeX markup that captures and reproduces the population standard deviation equation (Figure 100) in your AsciiDoc document.

LaTeX Markup

Example 150. LaTeX markup for the equation in figure 1 which can be typed on your keyboard !

```
\sigma=\sqrt{\frac{\sum{(x_{i}-\mu)^2}}{N}}
```

The LaTex Math markup in Example 150 will be interpreted and rendered by AsciiDoctor and AsciiDoctor-Mathematical as follows:

Will be rendered as...

$$\sigma = \sqrt{\frac{\sum(x_i - \mu)^2}{N}}$$

If you are thinking that all this LaTeX markup appears too complicated to learn, I would say *I hear you* but would also like to say not to worry as we have some easy workarounds at hand. There are many online converters like — https://latexeditor.lagrida.com/ — that can help you visualize your equations using math symbols and which write LaTeX markup for you which you can then simply paste in your AsciiDoc documents. They are also great learning tools that can help you get familiarized with LaTeX math markup. You will notice that once you get comfortable with the syntax, you can start typing LaTeX markup yourself without external assistance!

AsciiDoctor supports both AsciiMath [https://asciimath.org/] or LatexMath [https://www.cmor-faculty.rice.edu/~heinken/latex/symbols.pdf] (LaTeX) markup out of the box rendering to HTML. No additional software is required. However generating PDF output that needs to include mathematical equations requires installation of additional packages. In the subsequent examples, I will be using LaTeX which is widely used in academia for writing equations and which I recommend you try. There is another reason why I am choosing to use LaTeX markup here (over AsciiMath) and that is because if you choose to create a PDF version of a document that has equations, AsciiDoctor, via an extension called *AsciiDoctor-Mathematical* (explained later), supports only LaTeX markup.

You can choose to use AsciiMath, which is similar to LaTeX math and in some ways, easier to learn and recall. The AsciiMath Website [https://asciimath.org/] has a comprehensive cheatsheet of AsciiMath markup that you can explore. However please be aware that if you choose to use AsciiMath for equations in AsciiDoc documents, you can (at the time of writing this) render equations only in HTML output and *not* PDF. LaTeX math however, renders in both!

The following sections do not attempt to serve as an exhaustive tutorial on how to write equations in AsciiMath or LaTeX for which many good resources are available on the Internet. Rather, we will see how we can create beautifully formatted equations using LaTeX math, rendering them as both HTML and PDF. If you haven't used LaTeX math markup before for equations, the examples below will help you get started.

14.2. Creating HTML Output for Equations using AsciiDoctor

To write and render equations using LaTeX markup, we need to place the `:stem:` attribute with `latexmath` as its value, in the header of the AsciiDoc document as shown in Example 151.

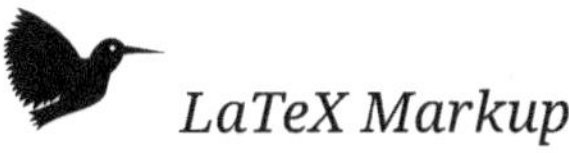

LaTeX Markup

Example 151. The stem attribute

```
:stem: latexmath
```

The space between `:stem:` and `latexmath` is important. So make sure you don't omit or overlook that space ! Also if no value is provided, i.e only `:stem:` is mentioned, the default is taken as `asciimath`. So if you plan to use LaTeX math markup, make sure you provide `:stem: latexmath` in the header of your document.

Next we will start a block with `[latexmath]` styling and inside a passthrough block starting and ending with `++++` (four `+` signs without spaces), we will write our equation using LaTeX math markup as shown in the Example 152.

Example 152. A Basic LaTex math equation block

```
[latexmath]   ①
++++          ②
e^{i\pi}+1=0  ③
++++          ④
```

① Declare *latexmath* styling for content that follows

② Start of passthrough block

③ Your equation / equations come here written in LaTeX markup

④ End of passthrough block

Will be rendered as...

$$e^{i\pi} + 1 = 0$$

14.2.1. Writing Inline Equations

We can also add equations inline i.e. in running text using the `stem:` *macro* as as shown in Example 153.

Example 153. Inline equation macro inserts equations in running text

```
The Pythagorean theorem can be written as an equation like stem:[a^2 + b^2 = c^2]
which relates the three sides a, b and the hypotenuse c, of a right triangle.
```

Will be rendered as...

The Pythagorean theorem can be written as an equation like $a^2 + b^2 = c^2$ which relates the three sides a, b and the hypotenuse c, of a right triangle.

14.2.1.1. Automatically Adding Equation Numbers (HTML)

It is possible to automatically add numbers to equations. To do that we will have to do the following two things :

1. Qualify the start and end of every equation with extra lines of LaTeX Math markup.
2. Add the `:eqnum:` attribute to the header of the document.

Let's see this in Example 154 which shows the contents of a sample *.adoc* file with three equations. Notice in Example 154 how we extend the `[latexmath]` declaration in Example 152 above by adding a # followed by an ID name. We can use this id to reference the equation wherever we want in the running text.

AsciiDoc Markup — | — *LaTeX Markup*

Example 154. Numbered Equations

```
== Some Numbered Equations
:icons: font
:doctype: book
```

```
:stem: latexmath        ①
:eqnums:                ②

[latexmath#euler]       ③
++++
\begin{equation}        ④
e^{i\pi}+1=0
\end{equation}          ⑤
++++


[latexmath#pythagorean] ⑥
++++
\begin{equation}        ⑦
 c=\sqrt{(a^2 + b^2)}
\end{equation}          ⑧
++++


[latexmath#correl]      ⑨
++++
\begin{equation}        ⑩
r=\frac{\sum(x-\bar x)(y-\bar y)}{\sqrt{\sum{(x-\bar x)^2(y-\bar y)^2}}}
\end{equation}          ⑪
++++
```

① The stem attribute at the top of the document with value latexmath indicates that we will use latex math markup

② The eqnums attribute indicates that we want the equations to be numbered

③ For equation 1, we add an id called #euler which we will use when we want to refer to this equation in the running text.

④ The begin tag indicates the start of the equation 1 (essential for correct equation numbering)

⑤ The end tag indicates the end of equation 1 (essential for correct equation numbering)

⑥ The equation 2 id is #pythagorean

⑦ Start of equation 2

⑧ End of equation 2

⑨ The equation 3 id is #correl

⑩ Start of equation 3

⑪ End of equation 3

Will be rendered as...

$$e^{i\pi} + 1 = 0 \tag{1}$$

$$c = \sqrt{(a^2 + b^2)} \tag{2}$$

$$r_{xy} = \frac{\sum_{i=1}^{n}(x - \bar{x})(y - \bar{y})}{\sqrt{\sum_{i=1}^{n}(x - \bar{x})^2}\sqrt{\sum_{i=1}^{n}(y - \bar{y})^2}} \tag{3}$$

14.2.1.2. Referring to Numbered Equations in Running Text

Once we have ids for each equation as described above, we can refer to them easily in running text as demonstrated in the following example. Notice that whenever we wish to refer to an equation we use the id inside << followed by a comma and the text that needs to appear as a clickable link — like Equation 1 (this can be any text) — and then close with >> signs as shown in Example 155.

AsciiDoc Markup

Example 155. Referring to Numbered Equations

```
        ① ②
<<#euler,Equation 1>> has been described as one of the most beautiful equations in
mathematics.
As we can see in <<#pythagorean, Equation 2>>, the Pythagorean theorem gives us a way
to calculate distance between pixels in spectral space. The Pearson's Coefficient of
Correlation (<<#correl,Equation 3>>) when applied to a sample. I have deliberately
chosen to transcribe a rather intimidating <<#correl,Equation 3>> from
https://en.wikipedia.org/wiki/Pearson_correlation_coefficient[Wikipedia^] in LaTeX
Math markup as it has a lot of elements that are commonly employed in statistical
equations and this markup can also be used to get familiarized with LaTeX Math.
```

① Equation ID

② Clickable text (internal link) that appears wherever we insert it linking to that equation number as seen in the output below.

Will be rendered as...

Equation 1 has been described as one of the most beautiful equations in mathematics. As we can see in Equation 2, the Pythagorean theorem gives us a way to calculate distance between pixels in spectral space. The Pearson's Coefficient of Correlation (Equation 3) when applied to a sample. I have deliberately chosen to transcribe a rather intimidating Equation 3 in Example 154 from Wikipedia [https://en.wikipedia.org/wiki/Pearson_correlation_coefficient] in LaTex Math markup as it has a lot of elements that are commonly employed in statistical equations and this markup can also be used to get familiar with LaTeX Math.

14.3. Creating PDF Output for Equations using AsciiDoctor-PDF

While inclusion of equations in HTML output just requires insertion of LaTeXMath or AsciiMath in your AsciiDoc document, including the same equations when you render to pdf requires installation of an extension called *Asciidoctor-Mathematical.* The installation of *Asciidoctor-Mathematical* (a ruby gem) is a two step process involving (a) installation of some required dependencies for *Asciidoctor-Mathematical* followed by (b) installation of the *Asciidoctor-Mathematical* extension itself. However if you are using a Docker image of AsciiDoctor, you *do not* need to install *Asciidoctor-Mathematical* as it is already included in the docker image. AsciiDoctor Docker image users can therefore skip the next section that details installation of AsciiDoctor-Mathematical. At the time of writing, *AsciiDoctor-Mathematical* was available *only for Linux* but windows and Mac users can get it if they run AsciiDoctor via the AsciiDoctor Docker container.

14.3.1. Installing AsciiDoctor-Mathematical

To install *AsciiDoctor-Mathematical*, the first requirement is to install all dependencies. On Ubuntu and Debian based systems like Linux Mint, the terminal command shown in Example 156 does that.

Terminal Command

Example 156. Installation of AsciiDoctor-Mathematical

```
$ sudo apt-get -qq -y install bison flex libffi-dev libxml2-dev libgdk-pixbuf2.0-dev
libcairo2-dev libpango1.0-dev fonts-lyx cmake
```

Please visit https://github.com/asciidoctor-contrib/asciidoctor-mathematical to copy this long command (under Ubuntu).

The execution of the above terminal command (Example 156) usually takes a little time, so please be patient and let it finish its job. When finished, we issue the command to install *AsciiDoctor-Mathematical* as shown in Example 157. This is a one time operation and once *asciidoctor-mathematical* is successfully installed, you can subsequently use it to include equations in your

AsciiDoc documents. Example 157 shows screen messages during the installation of *AsciiDoctor-Mathematical*, which culminates with a *gems installed* message.

Terminal Command

Example 157. Screen messages during the installation of the AsciiDoctor_Mathematical Gem

```
$ sudo gem install asciidoctor-mathematical

Building native extensions. This could take a while...
Successfully installed mathematical-1.6.20
Successfully installed asciidoctor-mathematical-0.3.5
Parsing documentation for mathematical-1.6.20
Installing ri documentation for mathematical-1.6.20
Parsing documentation for asciidoctor-mathematical-0.3.5
Installing ri documentation for asciidoctor-mathematical-0.3.5
Done installing documentation for mathematical, asciidoctor-mathematical after 90
seconds
2 gems installed
```

Done! We are all set to use *AsciiDoctor-Mathematical* in our documents.

14.4. Using Asciidoctor-Mathematical

Asciidoctor-mathematical parses the AsciiDoc file and converts any *LaTeX Math blocks* that it finds into formatted equation *images* and pastes them inside the PDF. To use Asciidoctor-Mathematical, we enter the terminal command shown in Example 158.

Terminal Command

Example 158. Using AsciiDoctor-Mathematical to include equations in PDF output

```
$ asciidoctor-pdf -r asciidoctor-mathematical -a mathematical-format=svg math.adoc
```

In the above command, *math.adoc* should be replaced by your .adoc file that has the LaTeX math markup. The file has to be present in the same folder from where the command is being issued otherwise the full path of the file needs to be given. The `mathematical-format=svg` part of the command forces creation of SVG images of equations which is the *preferred* option as SVG images maintain absolute clarity when zoomed. The default option however is `mathematical-format=png` . If you omit the `mathematical-format=svg` directive from the above command, the equations will be inserted as PNG images, which may pixilate when zoomed.

14.5. The Workaround to Equation Numbering in PDF Output Using AsciiDoc Markup

As we have seen above, equations are automatically numbered in HTML output. However, at the time of writing, it was noticed that automatic equation numbering, due to bugs or otherwise, did not work for PDF (all equations ended up having the same number — 1). It is quite possible that in future versions, equations are automatically numbered in rendered PDF documents as well.

However till that happens, we can deploy a small workaround that might not be conventional but in my opinion, quite workable. Instead of relying on AsciiDoctor-Mathematical to create sequential numbering of equations in PDF output, we will use AsciiDoc *counters* to do that ourselves. Example 159 shows how this workaround can be rigged up using three independent counters. The counter attribute permits us to increment a value starting with 1 using a counter name. It's pretty simple to implement and all you have to do is to choose a counter name (name must be in lowercase) and affix `counter:` to it (again all in lowercase). In Example 159, I have used three counters — *equation* , *enu* and *refnum* and created the counters using : `{counter:equation}`, `{counter:enu}` and `{counter:refnum}` markup tags. Whenever AsciiDoctor comes across a counter in the document — starting from the first to the last — the counter automatically gets incremented by one count. The braces around the counter term mean *substitution* implying that the value of the counter *enu* is being added to create an ID like `#eq1` such that we can reference this equation from anywhere in the text using the equation id like `<<#eq1>>`. At that point in the text (after rendering in PDF) we will see the `reftext` value i.e. `Equation 1` which is being set combining the word *Equation* with the value of the counter *refnum*.

Why use three counters ?

I used three counters because using the same counter more than once — for generating equation *id* or *reftext* or equation *caption* — increments the counter's numbering. Whenever AsciiDoctor encounters the statement `{counter:name}`, it just increments the named counter by 1. Hence using the same counter name thrice i.e. inserting 3 `{counter:name}` statements would mean a different incremented value each time. It may be possible to use less number of counters but I used three separate counters to keep it simple and it worked nicely for me.

In summary, the simple workaround is that whenever you need to enter an equation or a set of equations, just copy the entire block in Example 159, paste it in your document at the designated place and replace the equation line (you can have more than one equation lines) with your own equation (callout 6 in Example 159) below and you will get a numbered equation in your PDF output. Whenever you wish to reference any equation (say equation 3 for example) from anywhere in your text, just enter `<<#eq3>>` at that point and you will have a clickable link in your text to reach that equation if the PDF is being read on a computer or mobile device. With this background, just explore the markup shown in Example 159 and use it every time you wish to include a numbered equation in your PDF.

Example 159. A Makeshift Equation Block that can be repeated replacing only the equation

```
****   ①
[.text-right]    ②
*_Equation {counter:equation}_*   ③
[latexmath#eq{counter:enu},reftext='Equation {counter:refnum}']   ④
++++   ⑤
Z=\frac{O}{\sqrt{y}}    ⑥
++++   ⑦
**** ⑧
```

① Start of Sidebar Block (you can also use ==== example block here if you like)

② Text on the following line will be aligned right

③ The equation title in bold & italics with the equation number coming automatically from equation counter

④ Latexmath block extended with an id (id number coming from counter enu) and reference text (number coming from counter refnum)

⑤ Start of passthrough block

⑥ Your equation in Latex Math markup

⑦ Close of passthrough block

⑧ End of sidebar block (you can also use ==== example block here if you like)

Will be rendered as...

Equation 1

$$Z = \frac{O}{\sqrt{y}}$$

Caution

It is important to remember that the above scheme of copying an equation block works well if equations are inserted in sequence. If for some reason however, you move equations after you have added them in the document, the id number of that equation will also change. For example, if there are three equations, the first one will get an id of *#eq1*, the second one will get an id of *#eq2* and the third one will get an id of *#eq3*. Let's say that you drop a reference to equation 3 in your running text somewhere in the content and later on decide to move the equation 3 block above equation 2. As you render your PDF after this change, the earlier equation 3 will now

> automatically become equation 2 (as it has been moved at a location above equation 2) and will now get an equation id of *#eq2* while the previous equation 2, which will now become equation 3, will get a new equation ID of #eq3. So when someone clicks on your previously entered reference for equation 3, they will now be taken to what used to previously be equation 2. So if you move any equation, just make sure you also correct references to it in the running text with the new ID for that equation number. A good practice might be *not to majorly move or relocate equations in your text* after you have entered them. If you do not need to refer or provide back links to equations in running text, you can move them as much as you like. Another strategy could be to reference equations in running text only after you have finished writing your document. Remember this applies only to PDF output.

Let's create a few more sample equations which I am going to generate just by copying the above equation block and replacing only the equation line (between the opening and closing four + signs) with the new LaTeX equation markup as shown in Example 160, Example 161 and Example 162.

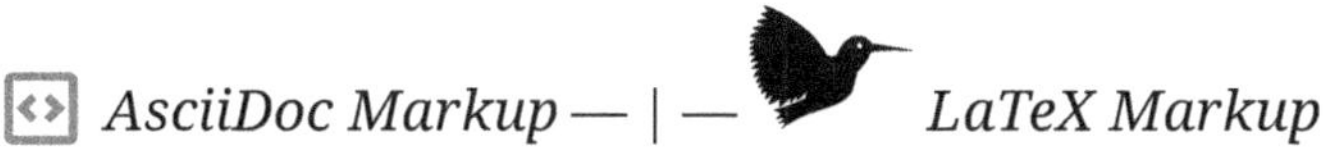

AsciiDoc Markup — | — LaTeX Markup

Example 160. Sample Equation 2

```
[.text-right]
*_Equation {counter:equation}_*
[latexmath#eq{counter:enu},reftext='Equation {counter:refnum}']
++++
a_1^2 + b_1^2 = c_1^2
++++
```

Will be rendered as...

Equation 2

$$a_1^2 + b_1^2 = c_1^2$$

AsciiDoc Markup — | — LaTeX Markup

Example 161. Sample Equation 3

```
[.text-right]
*_Equation {counter:equation}_*
```

```
[latexmath#eq{counter:enu},reftext='Equation {counter:refnum}']
++++
f(x) = \int^a_b \frac{1}{3}x^3
++++
```

Will be rendered as...

Equation 3

$$f(x) = \int^a_b \frac{1}{3}x^3$$

Example 162. Sample Equation 4

```
[.text-right]
*_Equation {counter:equation}_*
[latexmath#eq{counter:enu},reftext='Equation {counter:refnum}']
++++
E=mc^2
++++
```

Will be rendered as...

Equation 4

$$E = mc^2$$

You will notice that all these equation blocks are absolutely identical except for the equation line (between the opening and closing four + signs) and have equation numbers in sequence as they appear in the document.

14.5.1. Reference your Equations with Equation Ids in Running Text

After you have entered equations, you can also refer to your equations in running text. To refer to your equations anywhere in running text, all you have to do is to type in `<<#eq1>>` or `<<#eq2>>` or `<<#eq3>>` or `<<#eq4>>` in the running text. In this example we have just four equations but in your document, it can be any equation number (x) `<<#eqx>>`, and you can just replace the x with that number. For example if you have 10 equations in your document, you can refer to equation 10 by typing `<<#eq10>>`.

Example 163 — using some dummy text — shows how to cite the four sample equations discussed in previous examples, in the running text.

Example 163. Citing equations in running text

```
Lorem ipsum dolor sit amet, consectetur adipiscing elit. Nulla dolor diam,
condimentum ac lobortis sit amet, accumsan non est. Proin commodo (see <<#eq2>>),
nisi ac maximus euismod, erat ligula luctus leo, eu imperdiet orci sem quis elit. Nam
pulvinar sem id malesuada feugiat. In hac habitasse platea dictumst. Nulla luctus
imperdiet est quis tempus. Fusce rhoncus ante dapibus aliquam posuere. Integer mattis
malesuada. Proin non nulla nec neque pretium tempus (see <<#eq1>>).

We can see in <<#eq3>> that the term Cras eget est in nunc tincidunt dapibus.
Pellentesque dapibus justo vitae sem semper porttitor. In pellentesque lorem elit,
sed ullamcorper enim vulputate a. Sed iaculis luctus condimentum. Cras quis nisi
vitae sem pellentesque interdum ac sed nisl. Donec eget placerat augue. Sed eu
vulputate est. Nunc non euismod nibh. Aenean fringilla tincidunt. Sed ut diam non
nibh sagittis efficitur sed at nibh. <<#eq4>> neatly encapsulates postulations of the
theory of special relativity which expresses the fact that mass and energy are the
same physical entity and can be changed into each other. Vestibulum ullamcorper orci
in mi sagittis, et tincidunt neque placerat. Morbi accumsan velit et mi ornare
feugiat. Nulla ac augue nec lacus dictum gravida et at massa.
```

Will be rendered as...

Lorem ipsum dolor sit amet, consectetur adipiscing elit. Nulla dolor diam, condimentum ac lobortis sit amet, accumsan non est. Proin commodo (see Equation 1), nisi ac maximus euismod, erat ligula luctus leo, eu imperdiet orci sem quis elit. Nam pulvinar sem id malesuada feugiat. In hac habitasse platea dictumst. Nulla luctus imperdiet est quis tempus. Fusce rhoncus ante dapibus aliquam posuere. Integer mattis malesuada. Proin non nulla nec neque pretium tempus (see Equation 2).

We can see in Equation 3 that the term Cras eget est in nunc tincidunt dapibus. Pellentesque dapibus justo vitae sem semper porttitor. In pellentesque lorem elit, sed ullamcorper enim vulputate a. Sed iaculis luctus condimentum. Cras quis nisi vitae sem pellentesque interdum ac sed nisl. Donec eget placerat augue. Sed eu vulputate est. Nunc non euismod nibh. Aenean fringilla tincidunt. Sed ut diam non nibh sagittis efficitur sed at nibh. Equation 4 neatly encapsulates postulations of the theory of special relativity which expresses the fact that mass and energy are the same physical entity and can be changed into each other. Vestibulum ullamcorper orci in mi sagittis, et tincidunt neque placerat. Morbi accumsan velit et mi ornare feugiat. Nulla ac augue nec lacus dictum gravida et at massa.

And that's about it ! Please do remember that you need to make sure that whenever you are making a reference to an equation in the running text, make sure that you use the id number of that equation i.e. refer to it as <<eqx>> replacing the **x** with the number that is displayed after the word *equation* in the top right hand corner as shown in Figure 101.

Equation 3

$$f(x) = \int_b^a \frac{1}{3} x^3$$

X

Figure 101. Replace x with this number to refer to a particular equation in the running text

This is how you can have equation numbering in your equations in PDF documents.

I am hopeful that we might not need to use the workaround described above in future versions of Asciidoctor-Mathematical once this issue gets resolved.

14.6. Chapter Summary

Key learnings in this chapter are:

- We have seen how to write mathematical equations in AsciiDoc documents using LaTeX markup.
- You can insert equations in AsciiDoc documents using LaTeX markup.
- You need to learn LaTeX markup to write equations or you can write equations using online LaTeX editor tools like https://latexeditor.lagrida.com/ which convert your equations to LaTeX markup. You can then copy and paste the converted LaTeX markup in your AsciiDoc documents.
- If you are rendering to HTML or EPUB, you do not need to install any software to insert equations but if you wish to include equations in PDF output, you need to install an AsciiDoctor extension called *AsciiDoctor-Mathematical*. You can refer to Section 14.3.1 for a quick recap of how to install and use AsciiDoctor-Mathematical.

- If you are using a Docker image of AsciiDoctor, you do not need to install *AsciiDoctor-Mathematical*. It is already inlcuded in the image and you can use it directly.
- While this chapter is not a tutorial for LaTeX markup, you can refer to Section 14.2 to see some LaTeX markup examples to get started and recap how you can insert equations for HTML output in AsciiDoc documents.
- You can also write equations inline in running text matter. Please see Section 14.2.1 for a quick recap.
- To use *AsciiDoctor-Mathematical* with AsciiDoctor and AsciiDoctor-PDF, you can use terminal commands covered in Section 14.4.
- Equations are automatically numbered in HTML output. Refer to Section 14.2.1.1 for a recap.
- Equation numbering does not happen automatically in PDF output (at the time of writing). You can refer to Section 14.5 to recap a workaround and also see some more samples of LaTeX math equations.
- *AsciiDoctor-Mathematical* is available only for the Linux operating system at the time of writing this book. Windows and Mac users can have access to it if they are running AsciiDoctor using the AsciiDoctor Docker container.

14.7. Try It Yourself

1. Create a new AsciiDoc file. Try reproducing LaTeX math for equations 1-4 in this chapter shown in Example 159, Example 160, Example 161 and Example 162. Render to HTML (See Example 158).
2. Go to https://latexeditor.lagrida.com/ and try creating LaTeX markup for two equations of your choice. Copy the LaTeX markup generated by the site and paste it in your AsciiDoc file created in 1 above. Make sure that you add the `:stem: latexmath` and the `:eqnums:` attributes in the document header.
3. Use AsciiDoctor and AsciiDoctor-Mathematical to render your AsciiDoc file to HTML. Verify that your equations in the rendered HTML are properly and sequentially numbered (See Example 158).
4. Use AsciiDoctor-PDF and AsciiDoctor-Mathematical to render your AsciiDoc file to PDF. Are your equations sequentially numbered? If not, try using the counters workaround demonstrated in Example 159, Example 160, Example 161 and Example 162.

Chapter 15. Overriding the Default AsciiDoctor-PDF Theme for Some Useful Styling Tweaks

"A theme is not just a design; it's an experience that resonates with users." ~ Unknown

---

In this chapter, we will see how we can extend the default theme used by AsciiDoctor to style and output PDF documents from raw AsciiDoc files. The AsciiDoctor software provides a very elegant way to extend the default theme and provide users a mechanism to customize things such as default fonts , default styling of figures, blocks and many other presentation elements. The content presented in this chapter is specifically aimed at AsciiDoctor-PDF and rendered PDF output and does not discuss theme customizations to HTML output.

15.1. Extending or Overriding the Default AsciiDoctor-PDF Theme

All styling that you see in your rendered PDF output comes from a default theme file —*default-theme.yml* [https://github.com/asciidoctor/asciidoctor-pdf/blob/main/data/themes/default-theme.yml] . If you open this file, you can see among other things—fonts, font size, styling for lists, styling for tables, background color of delimited blocks and many other styling elements. When we use AsciiDoctor-PDF to render an AsciiDoc file to PDF, the nicely formatted PDF is produced using these styling rules tastefully curated for us in the default-theme.yml file. For example if you inspect the *default-theme.yml* file, you can see in lines 187-188 that images are styled by default to be left aligned as are captions (lines 119-120). An excerpt showing these lines can be seen in Figure 102.

About the Default PDF Styling Theme

While the link to *default-theme.yml* in Section 15.1 shows this file from the *asciidoctor-pdf GitHub repository*, this very same file is present on your computer when you install AsciiDoctor-PDF. Also if you haven't heard about a YML file, you can think of it to be somewhat like a configuration file. If you need more details, you see the Wikipedia entry on YML [https://en.wikipedia.org/wiki/YAML] for a quick summary.

```
    margin_bottom: $vertical_rhythm
  caption:
    align: left
    font_size: $base_font_size * 0.95
|
    padding: [$vertical_rhythm, $horizontal
  image:
    align: left
  prose:
```

Figure 102. An excerpt from default-theme.yml showing styling statements for image and caption alignment

While the default theme is very nice, there might be times when we might want to alter the default styling — like for example, having images and their captions aligned to the center or use a different font for our text. Well, AsciiDoctor-PDF provides a very convenient way to do this by putting our specific preferences in an external yml file which we can then use to *override* the default styling for selected elements. Whatever we want to customize, we put in the external yml file. Everything else comes from the default yml file. This way we *extend* (and not replace) the default styling. Let's look at some useful styling tweaks that might be needed from time to time in the following sections.

15.2. Centering Figures and Captions

To ensure that all figures are center aligned on the page and so are their captions, we will override the default left alignment by creating a file called *mytheme.yml* in the same folder as your *.adoc* file (say *myfile.adoc*) and add the styling attributes to it as shown in Example 164.

Example 164. YML file mytheme.yml extends the asciidoctor-pdf default theme

```
extends: default
image:
  align: center
caption:
  align: center
```

The above styling attributes extend the default theme and with it, we are elegantly able to change the image and caption alignment properties to center from the default left. By creating a YML file like the above, what we are essentially doing is telling AsciiDoctor-PDF to use the default theme but just for the image and caption properties, override the default and use the styling as given in our *mytheme.yml* instead. The indentation of elements in Example 164 is important.

With *mytheme.yml* in the same folder as our AsciiDoc file (say *myfile.adoc* for this example) we can now render our asciidoc file to PDF using the terminal command shown in Example 165.

Terminal Command

Example 165. Using an external yml file with AsciiDoctor-PDF

```
$ asciidoctor-pdf --theme mytheme.yml myfile.adoc
```

When you examine the resulting PDF, in this case say *myfile.pdf*, you will find that *all images* in the rendered PDF document along with their captions are now center aligned i.e. they are positioned in the center of the page as shown in Figure 103.

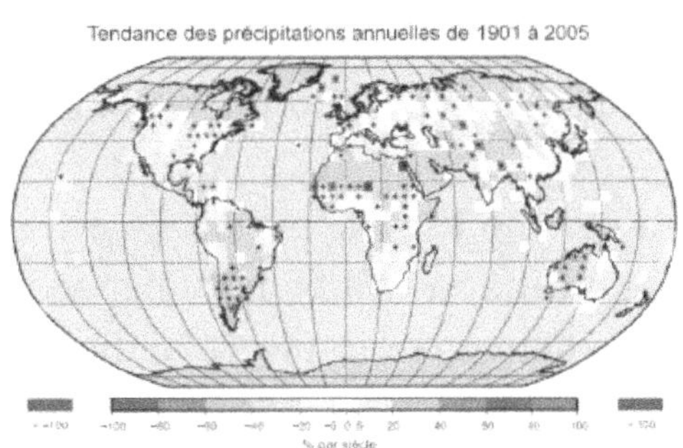

Figure 1. Annual Precipitation Trend from 1901 to 2005

Figure 103. The above figure and its caption have been centered by extending default styling through a YML file

If you want for some reason, to center some images and keep some images in left alignment, you can create a different version of *mytheme.yml* having the styling changes shown in Example 166.

Example 166. Alternate mytheme-alt.yml version

```
extends: default
image:
 caption:
  align: inherit
```

The styling in Example 166 ensures that the caption *inherits* the styling of the image i.e. if the image is left aligned, the caption will also be left aligned while if the image is center aligned or right aligned, the captions will also be aligned likewise. If we use the above *mytheme-alt.yml* version which forces the caption to inherit the alignment of the image, the alignment of the caption will now depend on how the image is aligned. Example 167 shows two ways of inserting an image in your AsciiDoc file and the caption underneath that image will inherit the alignment of the image:

Example 167. Image alignment is inherited by the caption

```
image:: picture1.png[] ①
OR
image:: picture1.png[align=center] ②
```

① If you insert an image in your document with nothing inside the brackets, image and caption will be left aligned (this is the default alignment).

② If you use [align-center], the image will be centered and the caption will *inherit* center alignment from the image.

When you make styling changes, you can save the alternate versions of *mytheme.yml* under a different name (say *mytheme-alt.yml*). You can then use the alternate yml file in place of *mytheme.yml* as shown in Example 166 when rendering to PDF.

Referring back to Figure 103, whenever you use the option shown at callout 1 (Example 167) to insert images in your content, the image and caption will be left aligned and whenever you choose to insert an image using the option shown at callout 2 (Example 167), the image and caption will be aligned in the center. To see the output, you will have to render your AsciiDoc file with the *mytheme-alt.yml* file issuing the terminal command shown in Example 166.

15.3. Adding a Rounded Border around Figures or Images

Taking this customization further, we can extend the *asciidoctor-pdf* default theme to add a rounded border around images by adding the styling attributes shown in Example 168 to the *mytheme.yml*.

Example 168. Adding a rounded border around images

```
image:
      border-color: #C0C0C0      ①
      border-width: 0.5
      border-radius: 2           ②
```

① This is the color silver — #C0C0C0 (these are Zeros not the letter O). You can choose any color value. See this colour guide [https://www.w3schools.com/tags/ref_colornames.asp]) for more color codes.

② Higher values for `border-radius` produce more rounding of border edges. A value of 0 creates a rectangular border.

With just the default theme in operation, images do not have any surrounding border as seen in Figure 104(a). With the theme extended as detailed in Example 168, all images in the rendered document get a rounded border as seen in Figure 104(b).

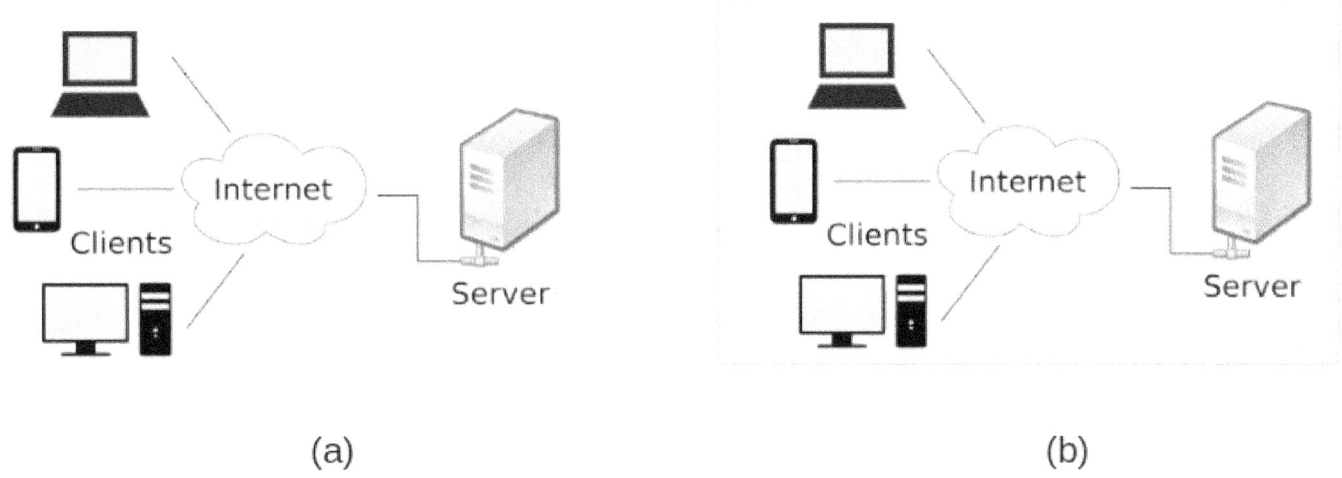

Figure 104. Image with (a) no border — default theme and rounded border (b) with extended styling for image.
`Source: David Vignoni derivative work: Calimo, LGPL, via Wikimedia`

15.4. Changing Default Base Fonts in Rendered PDF Documents

You can extend or override any styling property in the *default-theme.yml* file as shown in the examples above. A single theme file like the *mytheme.yml* created by you can contain many such *overrides* ensuring that the rendered PDF document meets your customized styling requirements. Fonts profoundly influence the visual reading experience and document design by shaping perception, readability, and emotional response. We can easily change default fonts and map these fonts to different document elements like body text, headings and code blocks.

Let's now see how we can change the default base font by examining the first 30 lines of the *default-theme.yml* [https://github.com/asciidoctor/asciidoctor-pdf/blob/main/data/themes/default-theme.yml] file which are reproduced in Example 169.

AsciiDoc Markup

Example 169. Examining the initial lines of the asciidoctor-pdf default theme

```
font:
  catalog:
    # Noto Serif supports Latin, Latin-1 Supplement, Latin Extended-A, Greek,
Cyrillic, Vietnamese & an assortment of symbols
    Noto Serif:  ②
      normal: GEM_FONTS_DIR/notoserif-regular-subset.ttf
      bold: GEM_FONTS_DIR/notoserif-bold-subset.ttf
      italic: GEM_FONTS_DIR/notoserif-italic-subset.ttf
      bold_italic: GEM_FONTS_DIR/notoserif-bold_italic-subset.ttf
    # M+ 1mn supports ASCII and the circled numbers used for conums
    M+ 1mn: ③
      normal: GEM_FONTS_DIR/mplus1mn-regular-subset.ttf
      bold: GEM_FONTS_DIR/mplus1mn-bold-subset.ttf
      italic: GEM_FONTS_DIR/mplus1mn-italic-subset.ttf
      bold_italic: GEM_FONTS_DIR/mplus1mn-bold_italic-subset.ttf
page:
  background_color: FFFFFF
  layout: portrait
  initial_zoom: FitH
  margin: [0.5in, 0.67in, 0.67in, 0.67in]
  # margin_inner and margin_outer keys are used for recto/verso print margins when
media=prepress
  margin_inner: 0.75in
  margin_outer: 0.59in
  size: A4
base:
  text_align: justify
  font_color: 333333
  font_family: Noto Serif   ①
  font_size: 10.5
  # line_height_length is really just a vertical spacing variable; its not the height
of a line
  line_height_length: 12
```

① Line 28 → base font property is set to Noto Serif

② Lines 5-9 → set location and name of Noto Serif regular, bold, italic and bold-italic font files

③ Font M+ 1mn (open source font) is used by AsciiDoctor default theme to print callout numbers (conums) like this one — 3 in the black circle.

So to change the base font, we need a replacement font and then we can create a new YML file using which we will extend the default stylesheet (as done in Example 166 for the image and caption centering) to override the default Noto Serif font.

To demonstrate this, we will download and use an open sans serif font set called Montserrat [https://fonts.google.com/specimen/Montserrat] from Google Fonts (click on the Get Font button to download). This font, being a sans serif font, is visually distinct from the default Noto Serif font which will enable us to easily see if the font substitution through our YML file works. The font is downloaded as a ZIP file. Unzip the downloaded file and you will see a *Montserrat* folder inside which there is *static* folder and inside the *static* folder — many Montserrat ttf fonts. We are mainly interested in the following *four* Montserrat font variants:

1. Montserrat-Regular.ttf
2. Montserrat-Bold.ttf
3. Montserrat-Italic.ttf
4. Montserrat-BoldItalic.ttf

Once we have located the font files of interest, We need to do the following in sequence:

1. Create a folder called *fonts* inside your project folder i.e. the folder where you have your AsciiDoc files.
2. Copy the above mentioned four fonts into the *fonts* folder. After copying the ttf files, your fonts folder will look as shown in Figure 105.

Figure 105. Contents of the fonts folder after copying the four Montserrat fonts

3. Create a new YML file (*theme-monts.yml* in my example) that changes the default base fonts shown in Example 169 to the newly downloaded Montserrat fonts as shown in Example 170.

As you examine the YML file shown in Example 170, notice that we haven't provided any path for the four font variants — we have just mentioned their names like `normal: Montserrat-Regular.ttf`. We will do that in a subsequent step (step 4 — Example 171) at the time of issuing the AsciiDoctor-PDF command.

Example 170. Contents of the theme-mont.yml that will replace the default Noto font with Montserrat

```
extends: default
font:
  catalog:
    # Montserrat ①
    Montserrat:
      normal: Montserrat-Regular.ttf        ②
      bold: Montserrat-Bold.ttf
      italic: Montserrat-Italic.ttf
      bold_italic: Montserrat-BoldItalic.ttf
      # M+ 1mn supports ASCII and the circled numbers used for conums
    M+ 1mn:  ③
      normal: GEM_FONTS_DIR/mplus1mn-regular-subset.ttf
      bold: GEM_FONTS_DIR/mplus1mn-bold-subset.ttf
      italic: GEM_FONTS_DIR/mplus1mn-italic-subset.ttf
      bold_italic: GEM_FONTS_DIR/mplus1mn-bold_italic-subset.ttf
base:
      font_family: Montserrat     ④
```

① We have replaced the Noto Serif font file with Montserrat giving absolute path to the file.

② Make sure there is a space after the :

③ We are retaining this M+ 1mn font as it is - the original lines from default-theme.yml need to be included here to avoid path errors. These lines are the same as in the default YML file.

④ We now set the base font family to Montserrat

4. With the YML created, we can now just use the command shown in Example 171 to render our PDF document and it will be rendered using the new base font, which in this case is Montserrat.

Terminal Command

Example 171. Command to render PDF document with custom base fonts

```
$ asciidoctor-pdf --theme theme-monts.yml -a pdf-fontsdir=./fonts test.adoc
```

The `-a pdf-fontsdir=./fonts` part in the above command is *important* as it is telling AsciiDoctor-PDF the location of the fonts mentioned in the *theme-monts.yml* file.

The command for the Windows users is the same except for the location of the fonts folder: `asciidoctor-pdf --theme theme-monts.yml -a pdf-fontsdir=fonts test.adoc`

Figure 106 shows the results comparing the (a) default version with base font Noto serif and (b) the version created using our above extended YML file with the new base font — Montserrat.

Creating and Using Delimited Blocks

About Delimited Blocks

Simply put, delimited blocks in AsciiDoc are chunks of content that break the normal flow of text in a document to make it standout in a special way. Delimited blocks can be used to highlight console output, code snippets, create information sidebars, example boxes, display mathematical equations and more. The figure below illustrates the concept of delimited blocks.

Blocks can be very useful elements.

(a) PDF output using default Noto Serif Font set in default theme

Creating and Using Delimited Blocks

About Delimited Blocks

Simply put, delimited blocks in AsciiDoc are chunks of content that break the normal flow of text in a document to make it standout in a special way. Delimited blocks can be used to highlight console output, code snippets, create information sidebars, example boxes, display mathematical equations and more. The figure below illustrates the concept of delimited blocks.

Blocks can be very useful elements.

(b) PDF Output using sans-serif Montserrat Font deployed via theme-monts.yml

Figure 106. Image (a) showing default Noto Serif base font (b) Montserrat base font set using external YML file

---

You can add as many fonts as you like to your fonts folder and change the base font to any chosen font as demonstrated above.

⚠ Remember that *all four font variants* — normal, bold, italics and bold italics, must be available. If your chosen font set is missing any font variant out of these four — say like italics, you can use the normal font in its place (like `italic: Montserrat-Regular.ttf`). You will then not have italics font but just the regular font whenever you mark something as italics. Remember this is just a suboptimal workaround and it is best if you choose font sets that have all the four required variants. For more information on using custom fonts, visit the AsciiDoctor-PDF manual page on using custom fonts [https://docs.asciidoctor.org/pdf-converter/latest/theme/custom-font/#configure-search-path].

The SIL Open Font License website — https://openfontlicense.org/ofl-fonts/ offers many free fonts and free font sources.

15.5. Changing Background of Blocks

Likewise, we can create another YML file (or add to the existing *mythme.yml* file) to change the background of any AsciiDoc block — like a sidebar block or a table or footer etc. In Example 172, we create a new file called *theme-sb.yml* to extend the default theme which changes the background color of a sidebar block to cyan and its border to red :

Example 172. The theme-sb.yml file gives a cyan background and a red border to sidebar blocks

```
extends: default
sidebar:
  background_color: C8F4F6
  border_color: F6213C
```

Figure 107 shows the result with the default gray background for sidebar blocks tuning into cyan with a red border.

Sidebars

Sidebars are a great way to break the flow of text

Sample Sidebar

Artificial intelligence (AI), in its broadest sense, is intelligence exhibited by machines, particularly computer systems. It is a field of research in computer science that develops and studies methods and software that enable machines to perceive their environment and use learning and intelligence to take actions that maximize their chances of achieving defined goals.

A machine with artificial general intelligence should be able to solve a wide variety of problems with breadth and versatility similar to human intelligence.

A sidebar block can contain other blocks and admonitions!

Figure 107. New Styling for Sidebar Block

15.6. Changing the Color of Headings in PDFs

All headings in PDFs rendered by *asciidoctor-pdf* are by default in black. If you are creating a PDF (like lecture notes, articles, concept notes or even books) specifically for color printing or *on-screen* reading, you can add some color to your document by changing the color of headings. This can be done quite easily by adding *font-color* key under your *heading category* in the extended theme file (like *mytheme.yml* referred earlier in the chapter). Please see Chapter 20 — Section 20.10 for a detailed discussion on this topic.

15.7. Extending Default PDF Theme for Print Documents

When you wish to create a print-ready PDF of your document — like a book printed in black & white (not color print) — you need to make many adjustments by extending the default PDF theme. These adjustments typically involve altering outer and inner margins, gutter margin to permit binding, creating headers and footers, defining the physical page or trim size, adjusting page numbering, creating decorative borders etc. All this work is done by extending the default theme. I invite you to read Chapter 20 to learn more about how to extend the default theme to meet book publishing requirements.

15.8. Chapter Summary

Key learnings in this chapter are:

- For PDF output of AsciiDoc files using AsciiDoctor-PDF, we can change many things in the default theme using which AsciiDoctor-PDF styles the PDF document.
- This can be done quite elegantly by extending the default theme using a *.yml* file and making styling changes there. Please revisit Section 15.1 for a recap.
- A YML file can be considered like a configuration file and is used to extend the AsciiDoctor-PDF default theme. Any theme customizations mentioned in the YML file override the default customizations for those elements.
- The *.yml file* containing the styling changes can be run by *AsciiDoctor-PDF* with the AsciiDoc file and the rendered PDF will replace default theme styling for those components mentioned in the *.yml file* . Example 165 shows the terminal command to run the *.yml* file with AsciiDoctor-PDF.
- We can make many styling changes like changing base fonts (Section 15.4), image and caption alignments (Section 15.2), background fills (Section 15.5) etc. by extending the default theme.

- You can download many free fonts from https://fonts.google.com/. Many free fonts are also avaiable under SIL Open Font License from https://openfontlicense.org/ofl-fonts/.
- When customizing base fonts, please make sure that you have a font (ttf) file each for normal, bold, italics and bold italics.
- More discussion about extending the default theme can be found in Chapter 20.

15.9. Try it Yourself

1. The YML files mentioned in the examples of this chapter are available in the exercises folder of this chapter. Download and try to generate PDFs using them to rework the examples in this chapter. To change the base font, you will have to download the Montserrat Font from https://fonts.google.com/specimen/Montserrat.
2. Download any other font of your choice from Google Fonts and try to change or edit and existing YML file and change the base font to that font as has been explained in Section 15.4 .
3. Can you change the the border width of an example block from the default — `border_width: 0.75` to `border_width: 1.25` ? Hint: Look for the example block styling in the default YML file https://github.com/asciidoctor/asciidoctor-pdf/blob/main/data/themes/default-theme.yml and extend the default style example block with the new border width. Alter just the border width on similar lines as we have done for centering image captions in Section 15.2.

Chapter 16. Multi-Page HTML Output

"In unity there is strength, but in division there is conquest." ~William Penn

---

In this chapter we will see how to make the HTML rendered by AsciiDoctor more readable on the web. We will discuss the use of a software extension to AsciiDoc that breaks the single HTML file that AsciiDoctor produces into a interconnected web of multiple pages through HTML chunking. This permits readers to navigate large HTML pages conveniently in smaller manageable 'chunks' with options to navigate to previous or next sections or to directly jump to a section or chapter of their choice.

16.1. Why Multi-Page ?

When we render our AsciiDoc files as HTML using *AsciiDoctor*, everything ends up in a *single HTML file*. We can include a Table of Contents (TOC) thankfully which can help us jump to a section in the HTML document directly. While this arrangement works well for smaller documents, it may not provide the best reading experience for large documents like books. For example if you have a 300 page book which has been rendered as a single HTML file using AsciiDoctor, you will have to navigate inside it in your browser using vertical scrolling. As you might imagine, reading a document in this manner can be a bit tardy and exhausting. Furthermore, very large HTML files negatively impact page load times and may create glitches for users having slow internet connections.

So if you have a particularly large HTML document and you wish to share it for online reading on a website, it might be desirable to break it down into multiple smaller HTML files that are faster to load yet remain seamlessly linked together. This also permits better navigation as we can display the document chapter wise or section wise and where the user has the option to conveniently move to the *next* or *previous* pages by clicking buttons. This process of breaking a single large HTML file into multiple smaller HTML files that remain linked together as one entity is known as *chunking* [https://www.ibm.com/architectures/papers/rag-cookbook/chunking] and we can use it to present HTML output from AsciiDoctor in a more reader friendly format.

16.2. Chunking the HTML Output from AsciiDoctor

Now that we know the benefits of *chunking* a large HTML file which we have created using AsciiDoctor, the question is — can we split this file into multiple HTML documents which can remain linked up together and display convenient buttons to move forward and backwards while reading the document ? The answer is *yes*! While AsciiDoctor does not have this functionality built-in, we can make use of the *AsciiDoctor-Multipage extension*. You can read more about about this extension and its features on the AsciiDoctor-Multipage project [https://github.com/owenh000/asciidoctor-multipage] page.

16.2.1. How Does the AsciiDoctor-Multipage Extension Chunk HTML files ?

If you just want to get the job done i.e. go directly to chunking, feel free to skip to the next section — Section 16.3. However I recommend that you spend just a few minutes to read on and get a birds-eye view of how chunking is done by *AsciiDoctor-Multipage*. This conceptual understanding will be immensely helpful in using the extension and evaluating its results. In a nutshell, *AsciiDoctor-Multipage* acts like a replacement to AsciiDoctor. When we use AsciiDoctor to render our AsciiDoc document, it produces one HTML file. In contrast, *AsciiDoctor-Multipage* takes in an AsciiDoc file and creates *many* smaller files and links them all together through a *landing page* or a main HTML file. But how does it know where to create a split ? Well, the *AsciiDoctor-Multipage* extension splits or chunks the AsciiDoc file using *chapter headings or section headings* in the document. To understand this let's refer to Figure 108 which shows a sample AsciiDoc file that has two level 1 headings — ch1 and ch2 (for chapter 1 and chapter 2). Under each of these level 1 headings, there is a second level heading — sec1 (for section 1) under ch1 and sec2 (for section 2) under ch2.

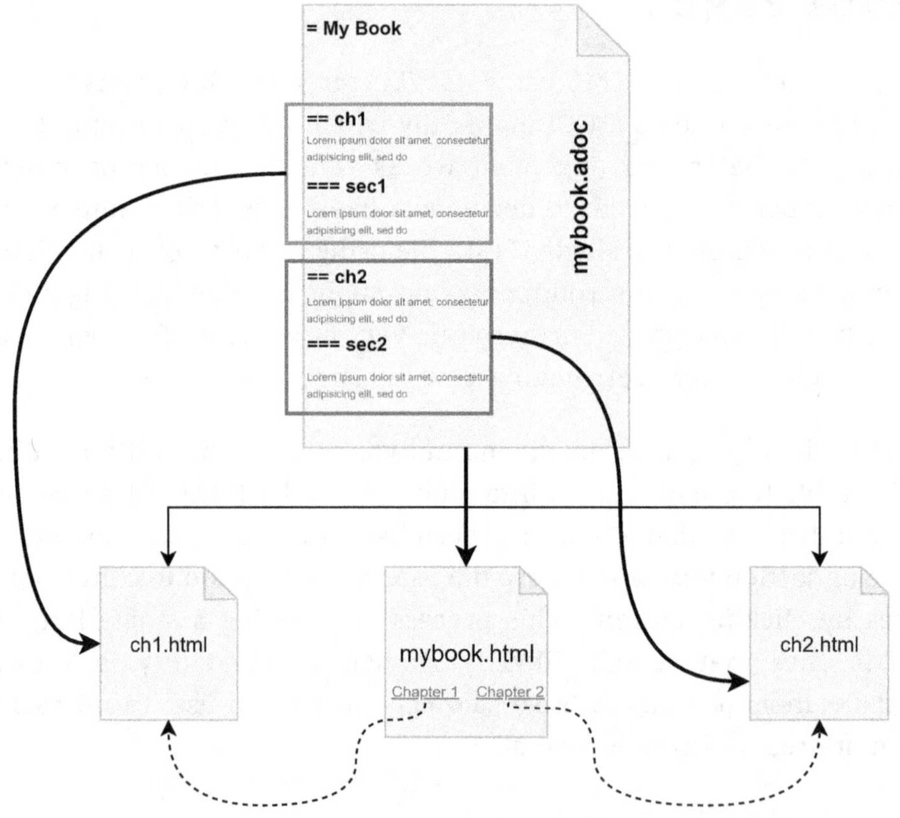

Figure 108. Default chunking at level 1 headings

When we hand over this AsciiDoc file — *mybook.adoc* to *AsciiDoctor-Multipage* (we will see how to do this shortly), the default chunking strategy is to create HTML files with all level 1 headings i.e. everything between the first level one heading (ch1 in this case) and the next level 1 heading (ch2) is written to a separate HTML file — ch1.html. Likewise all content between the next first level heading (ch2 in this case) and level 1 heading following it or the last line (no other level 1 heading after ch2 in this case) is written to another file — ch2.html. Finally a main HTML file called *mybook.html* that has links (represented by dashed lines in Figure 108) to both these files is created. So we end up with three HTML files in this case after chunking rather than a single file and for good measure, *AsciiDoctor-Multipage* adds *previous*, *next* and *home* links at the end of every HTML file for easy navigation.

An obvious question here is that can we create still smaller files - say split at *section* rather than *chapter* level i.e. at level 2 with *AsciiDoctor-Multipage* ? The answer is yes ! All that we have to do is to add the attribute `:multipage-levels:` to the header of the AsciiDoc file and set its value to the level (like 2 or 3) which we want *AsciiDoctor-Multipage* to take into consideration while chunking. Also for this to work, we must set the `:toclevels:` to a value that is *either equal to or greater than* the `:multipage-levels:` value. In Figure 109, we have just added these two attributes (to Figure 108) and set the value of both attributes to 2. As can be seen, *AsciiDoctor-Multipage* now chunks the same file quite differently.

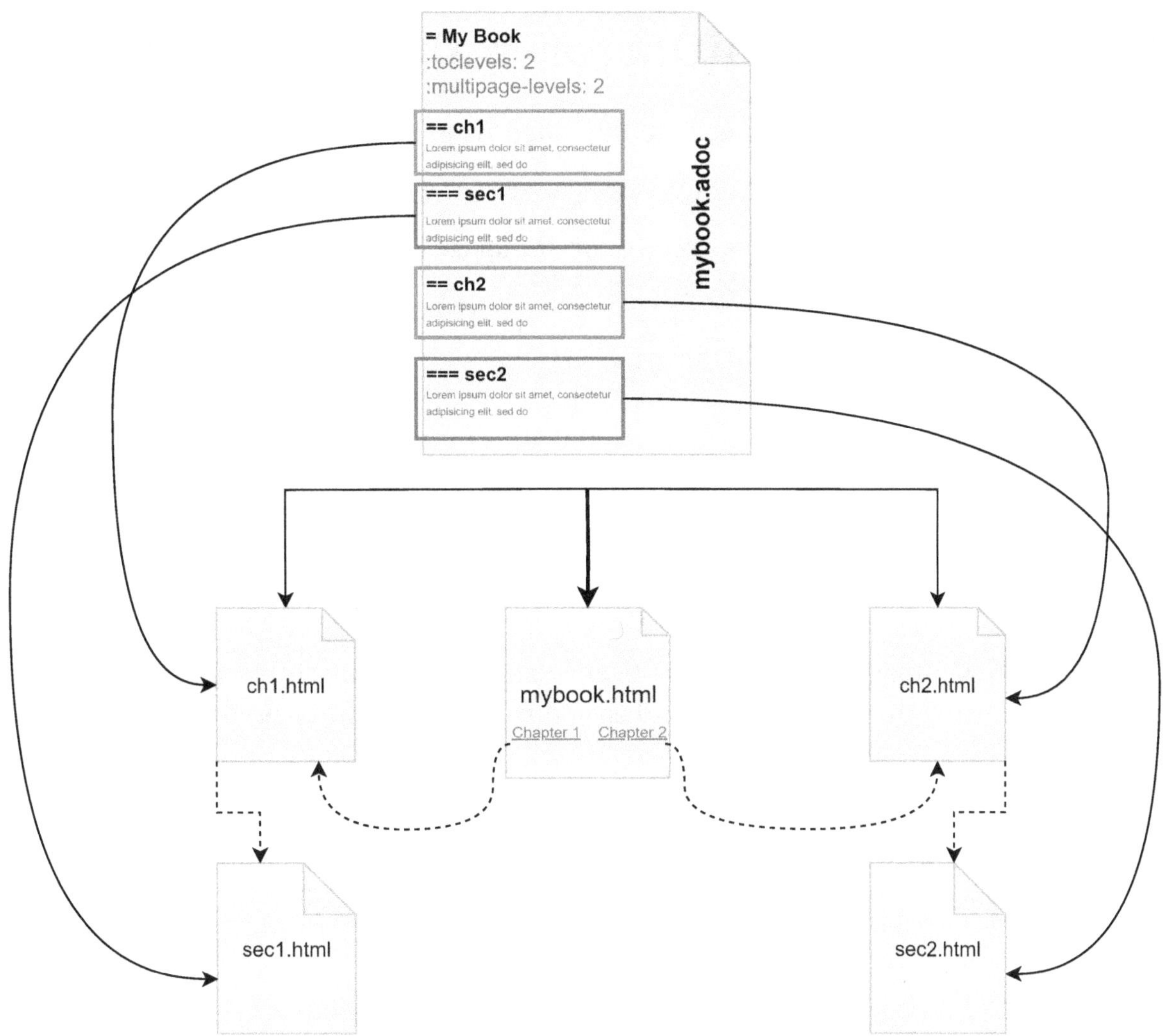

Figure 109. Chunking at level 2 headings

This time around, we end up with 5 HTML files, *ch1.html* and *ch2.html* i.e. level 1 headings but these contain content only till the start of the next level heading which in this case is sec1. So ch1.html and ch2.html are smaller files this time around as they end at the boundary where the next level heading begins. We also have two files *sec1.html* and *sec2.html* for each section having content confined to just these respective sections. The ch1.html and ch2.html files have links to sec1.html and sec2.html files as shown by the dashed lines in Figure 109. Finally, we have a main or landing page HTML file called *mybook.html* like before that has links to ch1.html and ch2.html which is also shown in Figure 109 as dashed lines. Like before, *AsciiDoctor-Multipage* adds *previous*, *next* and *home* links at the end of every HTML file for easy navigation through this new multi-page file assemblage.

That's how *AsciiDoctor-Multipage* chunks or splits content that would have otherwise been part of one single humongous HTML file. In Section 16.5, we will see this chunking in a worked example that uses a real AsciiDoc file called *haikumasters.adoc*. But before that, let's see how we can install the *AsciiDoctor-Multipage* extension and how we can use it to split content as described above from the command line.

16.3. Installing the AsciiDoctor-Multipage Extension

Example 173 shows the command that needs to be issued from the terminal to install the *AsciiDoctor-Multipage* extension.

Example 173. Installing the AsciiDoctor-Multipage Extension Gem from CLI

```
$ sudo gem install asciidoctor-multipage
```

Command for Windows is the same but without *sudo*. That's it. Installed!

16.4. Using the AsciiDoctor Multipage Extension

Once the AsciiDoctor-Multipage extension has been installed, we can chunk our AsciiDoc file into a multi-page collection using the simple command issued from the terminal as shown in Example 174.

AsciiDoc Markup

Example 174. Using AsciiDoctor-Multipage from the command line in terminal

```
$ asciidoctor-multipage -D folder myfile.adoc  ①
```

① folder is any folder (relative to the current folder) where you want the split up files to land and *myfile.adoc* is your AsciiDoc file that will be split into multiple HTML pages.

16.5. A Worked Example Showing Chunking

We have the following example AsciiDoc file — *haikumasters.adoc* — that has a Level 0 heading (document title is = Great Haiku Masters) followed by level 1 heading (Chapter heading is == for poets) and *three* level 2 headings (===) for sample Haiku Poems by each of these poets (see this web page [https://docs.asciidoctor.org/asciidoc/latest/sections/titles-and-levels/] to recap heading levels in AsciiDoc). Brief descriptions for each poet included in the following file have been reproduced from Wikipedia. Take a minute and examine the hierarchical heading structure in a sample file as shown in Example 175.

AsciiDoc Markup

Example 175. Hierarchical heading structure enforced by the multipage-level attribute

```
= Great Haiku Masters
:toc: left
:toclevels: 2
:multipage-level:2     ①

[desc="1644–1694. Edo Period Poet"]          ②
==  Matsuo Bashō                              ③
Matsuo Basho was the most famous Japanese poet of the Edo period. During his
lifetime,
Bashō was recognized for his works in the collaborative _haikai no renga_ form.
After centuries of commentary, he is recognized as the greatest master of haiku.
Two famous Haiku poems by Matsuo Bashō are featured below:

=== In Kyoto                                  ④
[verse]
In Kyoto,
hearing the cuckoo,
I long for Kyoto.

=== First Winter Rain                         ⑤
[verse]
First winter rain–
even the monkey
seems to want a raincoat.

[desc="1716–1784. Edo Era Poet and Painter"]  ⑥
== Yosa Bousan
Yosa Buson or Yosa no Buson was a Japanese poet and painter of the Edo period.
Buson is considered among the greatest poets of the Edo Period. He is also known for
completing haiga as a style of art, working with haibun prose, and experimenting with
a mixed Chinese-Japanese style of poetry.
Two famous Haiku poems by Yosa Bousan are featured below:
```

```
=== The Light of a Candle
[verse]
The light of a candle
Is transferred to another candle -
spring twilight.

=== On the one-ton temple bell
[verse]
On the one-ton temple bell
A moonmoth, folded into sleep,
Sits still.

[desc="1763–1828. Edo Period and Priest"]       ⑦
== Kobayashi Issa
Kobayashi Issa was a Japanese poet and lay Buddhist priest of the Jōdo Shinshū.
He is known for his haiku poems and journals. Reflecting the popularity and interest
in Issa as man and poet,
Japanese books on Issa outnumber those on Buson and almost equal in number those on
Bashō.
Two famous Haiku poems by Kobayashi Issa are featured below:

=== All the time I pray to Buddha
[verse]
All the time I pray to Buddha
I keep on
killing mosquitoes.

=== On a Branch
[verse]
On a branch
floating downriver
a cricket, singing.
```

① multipage-level attribute set to a value of 2 i.e. levels `==` and `===` . The toc levels attribute must also be set as >= to multipage-level. It is therefore set to 2 here.

② description *desc* provides a short description of chapter (see note below).

③ Level 1 — Chapter heading for Poet 1.

④ Level 1 — Section heading.

⑤ Level 1 — Section heading.

⑥ The structure — 2-5 above — repeats for Poet 2.

⑦ The structure — 2-5 above — repeats for Poet 3.

the [desc=text] statement seen at ❷ ❻ ❽ puts a small description in front of headings below them after rendering as can be seen in Figure 111.

Now that we have our AsciiDoc file, we have two options to render to HTML. We can use the following command from the terminal:

Terminal Command

```
$ asciidoctor haikumasters.adoc
```

This will result in creating a single HTML file called *haiku.html.*

However, if we choose to use the *AsciiDoctor-Multipage* extension, we can issue the command shown in Example 176 which will split up the content into 10 HTML files and place them inside a directory called *haiku.*

Example 176. Using the AsciiDoctor-Multipage Extension

```
                              ①
$ asciidoctor-multipage -D haiku haikumasters.adoc
```

① the `-D haiku` in the above command puts all the split files in a new directory or folder called *haiku.* If the folder does not exist, it is automatically created.

Figure 110 shows the split as a result of using the *AsciiDoctor-Multipage* on our AsciiDoc file:

Figure 110. Chunked HTML files inside the haiku folder after running above command

As expected and can be seen in the above folder (Figure 110), the result shows 10 HTML files, 2,3,4 — level 1 heading for each poet, 5,6 for two poems by Matsuo Bashō that have level 2 headings, 7,8 for two poems by Yosa Bousan — again with level 2 headings and 9,10 for the two poems by Kobayashi Issa which also have level 2 headings. File 1 that is *haikumasters.html* is the *landing page* connects to level 1 files 2,3,4 which in turn connect to the other files with level 2 headings under them. Figure 111 and Figure 112 show the output starting when we open *haikumasters.html* and then proceeding forward choosing linked content. That we end up with 10 files in this case is because of the fact that we had specified the split at heading level 2 by adding the attribute `:multipage-level:2` in our AsciiDoc file.

Figure 111 shows the landing page of our split file setup from where the reader can navigate the entire content of the AsciiDoc File using links at the bottom of the page.

Great Haiku Masters

- Matsuo Bashō – 1644—1694. Edo Period Poet
- Yosa Bousan – 1716—1784. Edo Era Poet and Painter
- Kobayashi Issa – 1763—1828. Edo Period and Priest

1 =desc["text"] puts these lines in front of links

2 Next: Matsuo Bashō →

Figure 111. The landing page — haikumasters.html

Notice in Figure 111, lines of text just after the links to the three poets. These come from the `desc["text"]` statements (1) just above each level 1 heading in the *haikumasters.asciidoc* file as seen at callouts 2,6,7 in Example 175. If these lines were missing, you would just see the links on this page. Also notice navigation link at the bottom of Figure 111 at callout (2) that provide the option to go to the next chapter or section . As we click on the next link in this case, we see the following page as shown in Figure 112 for the chosen poet.

Dynamic Navigation Links

The navigation links at callout 2 Figure 112 change depending on the page that is being viewed. If there are pages before the page that is being viewed, you get an *Up* navigation link to go back one chapter. If there are pages ahead, you also get a *Next* link to move ahead one chapter. You also get a *Home link* that takes you directly to the landing page. These navigation links can be seen in Figure 113.

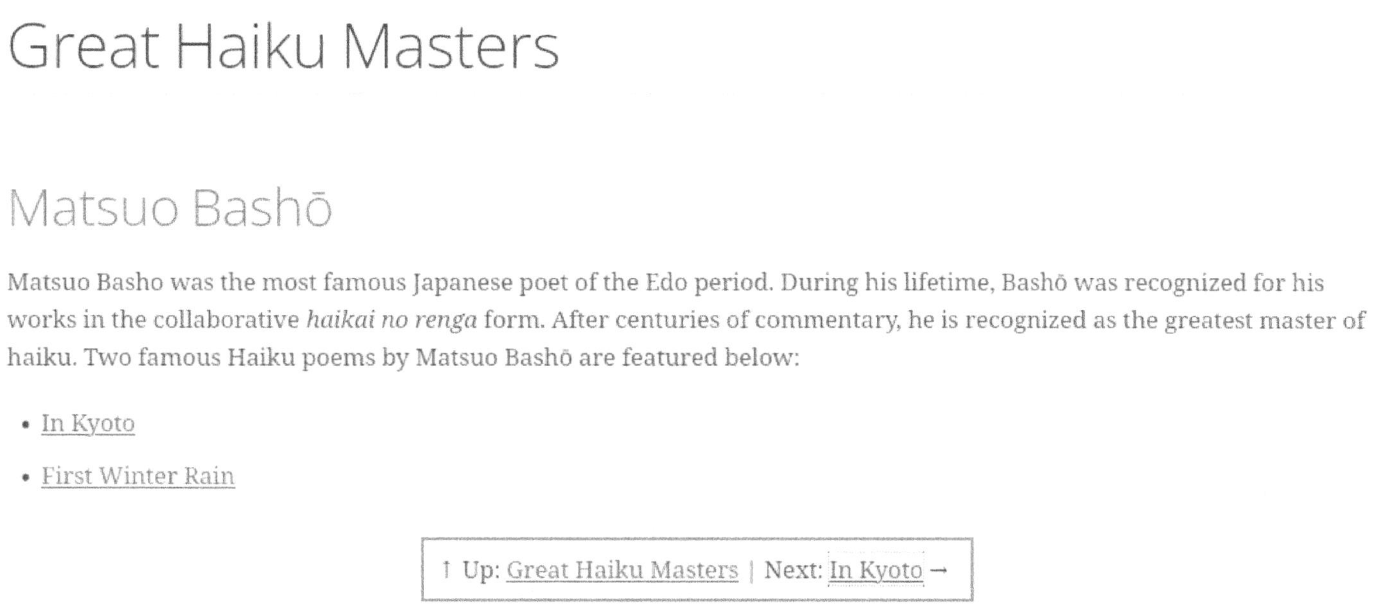

Great Haiku Masters

Matsuo Bashō

Matsuo Basho was the most famous Japanese poet of the Edo period. During his lifetime, Bashō was recognized for his works in the collaborative *haikai no renga* form. After centuries of commentary, he is recognized as the greatest master of haiku. Two famous Haiku poems by Matsuo Bashō are featured below:

- In Kyoto
- First Winter Rain

↑ Up: Great Haiku Masters | Next: In Kyoto →

Figure 112. Level 1 Page for Matsuo Basho

In Figure 112, you can see both Up (for previous) and Next navigation links. If you click next, you see the chosen poem as seen in Figure 113.

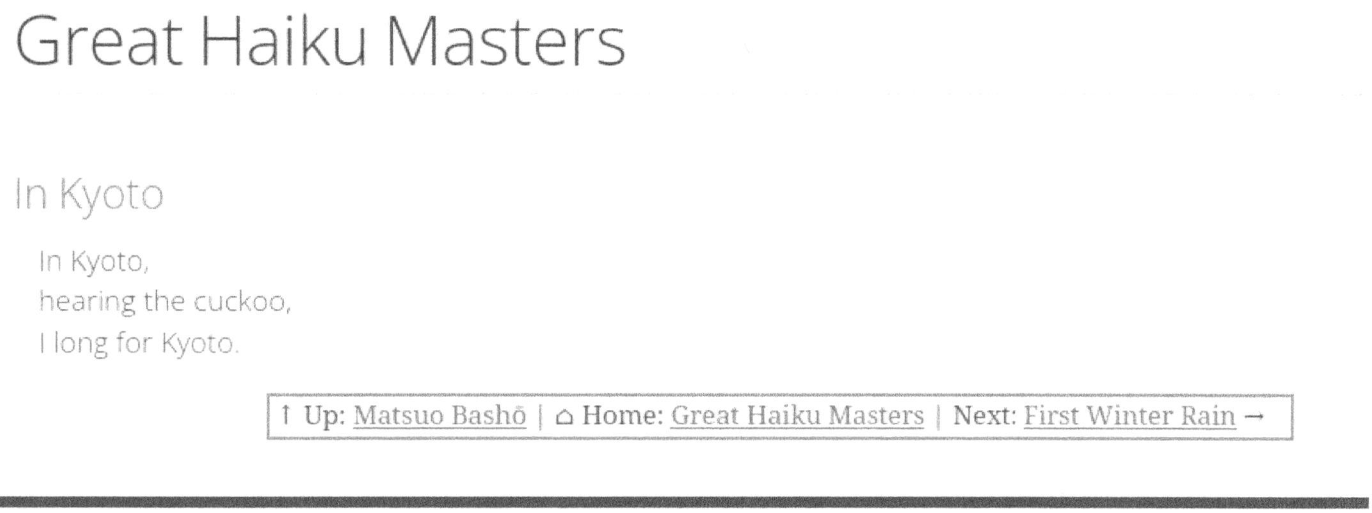

Great Haiku Masters

In Kyoto

In Kyoto,
hearing the cuckoo,
I long for Kyoto.

↑ Up: Matsuo Bashō | ⌂ Home: Great Haiku Masters | Next: First Winter Rain →

Figure 113. Level 2 Page for Matsuo Basho Poem - 'In Koyoto' with navigation links

On this page, you see Up, Home and Next links for easy navigation inserted by *AsciiDoctor-Multipage* connecting all the chunked files.

The AsciiDoctor-Multipage extension provides a simple and easy way to display your large HTML document online on a website. You can use the *AsiiDoctor-Multipage* command as shown in Example 174 to achieve this. This will render multiple interlinked HTML pages which readers can start navigating from the landing page.

16.6. Chapter Summary

Key learnings in this chapter are:

- Running AsciiDoctor on AsciiDoc files results in a single HTML file.
- While navigating this HTML file in your browser is not a problem for small files, it can be cumbersome for large files like a book.
- It is desirable to present a large document in smaller chunks like presenting content chapter or section wise to the reader to ensure a more engaging reading experience.
- We can use an extension called *AsciiDoctor-Multipage* to achieve this. If you wish to present your content in smaller chunks, *AsciiDoctor-Multipage* can be used to render HTML in place of AsciiDoctor.
- You can decide how the content will split by setting the split level using the `multipage-levels:` attribute in the header of the document. When using this attribute, it is important to also set the `:toclevels:` to a value that is *equal to or greater* than the value of the `multipage-levels:` attribute.
- After rendering, *AsciiDoctor-Multipage* splits content into multiple HTML files based on the set split level and puts them all in a folder creating a new *landing page* from where users can start navigating content.
- *AsciiDoctor-Multipage* also inserts navigation links at the bottom of pages permitting the reader to move to the next section , previous section or the landing page.

16.7. Try it Yourself

You can work through the following tasks using the example file *haikumasters.adoc* which is available in the exercises folder of this chapter.

1. Open the *haikumasters.adoc* file and examine the level 1 headings. Recall from Section 16.2.1 that these serve as split points for *AsciiDoctor-Multipage* to automatically chunk the single HTML file.
2. Notice that the header in the *haikumasters.adoc* file has the following two attributes that need to be set to indicate the level of the split (in this case till level 2):
   `:toclevels: 2` and `:multipage-level: 2`
   If the above is not provided, the default split point is at level 1 that is headings starting with ==

3. First run AsciiDoctor on *haikumasters.doc* to create a single file HTML output — *haikumasters.html.*
4. Using AsciiDoctor-Multipage, chunk *haikumasters.html* and store the interconnected chunked page structure in a folder called *haikumasters*. (See Section 16.5 for reference)
5. Navigate to the *haikumasters* folder and examine the contents of the folder (See Figure 110 for reference and file tally).
6. Click on the *haikumasters.html* file and navigate the document chapter wise using the options in the navigation bar at the bottom of the page.

Chapter 17. Creating a Single Document from Multiple AsciiDoc Files

" The magic is only in what books say, how they stitched the patches of the universe together into one garment for us "
~ Ray Bradbury

In this chapter we will learn an important skill — how to combine multiple AsciiDoc document files into one single file. This is particularly useful when you are working on big projects like writing a book and you have your content spread across many AsciiDoc files like individual chapters, code files, text files, BibTeX bibliography files and more. AsciiDoc permits you to seamlessly integrate all this scattered content and create a single PDF , HTML or EPUB3 document.

17.1. Bringing it all Together

When you create a large document like a book or a report, it is highly unlikely that you would end up having the entire document in a single AsciiDoc file. More realistically, you are likely to create an AsciiDoc file for each chapter resulting in multiple files which you would ultimately like to combine in a single document. AsciiDoctor can easily accomplish this using *include* statements for each chapter AsciiDoc file in a *master* AsciiDoc file. When we pass on this *master* AsciiDoc file to AsciiDoctor or AsciiDoctor-PDF or AsciiDoctor-EPUB3, we get a single rendered PDF or HTML or EPUB document which *stitches together* or *includes* all files mentioned in the *master* file.

Let's see how this is done with a small illustrative example. Let's say Felicity has written a book titled — Python Programming for Beginners. She has four chapters in this book, each written in a separate AsciiDoc file — *ch1_introduction.adoc, ch2_functions.adoc, ch3_loops.adoc and ch4_decisions.adoc.* She has also written a preface — *preface.adoc* and two appendices — *appendix1.adoc and _appendix2.adoc.* She uses a few images in some of these chapters and she has put all the images in a separate folder called *images*. She has also created a *master.adoc* file (discussed below) using which she will bring all the above mentioned chapter and image files into a single document. Figure 114 shows her book folder with all these files in it.

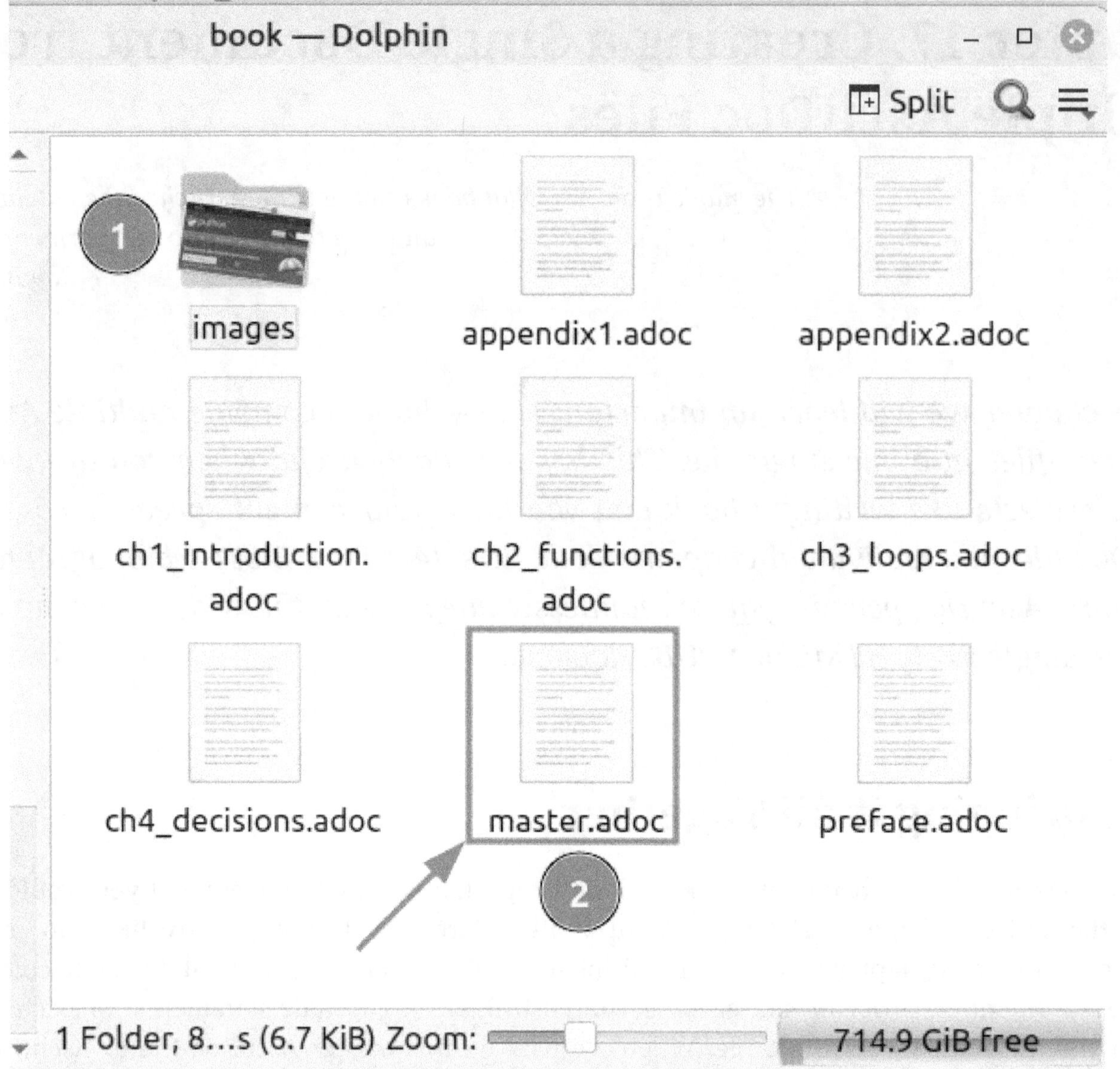

Figure 114. Contents of book project folder —(1) An image folder that has all the images used in different chapters and (2) The master file

Example 177 shows the contents of the *master.adoc* file.

AsciiDoc Markup

Example 177. Sample master.adoc file that facilitates collation of independent AsciiDoc files into a single rendered HTML, PDF or EPUB document

```
= Python Programming for Beginners
:author: Felicity Morgan
:doctype: book
:imagesdir: images   ①
:icons: font
:source-highlighter: pygments
```

```
:toc: left
:toclevels: 3
:sectnums:
:sectnumlevels: 2
:chapter-signifier: Chapter  ②
:experimental:

include::preface.adoc[]
include::introduction.adoc[]
include::ch2_functions.adoc[]
include::ch3_loops.adoc[]
include::ch4_decisions.adoc[]
include::appendix1.adoc[]
include::appendix2.adoc[]
```

① Attribute declaring the location of all images in this document

② Attribute adds the word 'Chapter' in front of every Level 1 (==) heading

Let's analyze Example 177. As can be seen, the header part of *master.adoc*, contains the book title as level 0 (=) heading followed by a selection of attributes that are *common* to *all chapters* of this book. Notice here that the attribute `:imagesdir: images` is declaring that all images mentioned in the individual AsciiDoc chapter files are inside the images folder which is located inside the current folder.

Following the header, the *master.adoc* file has multiple *include* statements that have the syntax — `include::filename.adoc[]` which point to various files that need to be included in the final document. Notice these have been sequenced by Felicity in the order in which she wants them to appear in the final document.

As *attributes* included in the *master.adoc* file are common to all chapter files, *we do not need to repeat them in chapter files which can just start with the chapter headings or maybe have some attributes that might be specific to that particular chapter.*

Important — Attributes are Global in Scope

If you set an attribute in the master file and then change its value in some *included* file later, the changed value will prevail unless you reset it to its original value again subsequently. For example, say we put the `:sectnums:` attribute in the *master.adoc* file and in the chapter 3 file, we put in the `:sectnums!:` attribute signifying no section numbering, then you will have section numbering only till chapter 2 and no section numbering in or beyond chapter 3. In short attribute settings have a *global scope*. So if you don't want section numbering to appear in one section of some document put the `:sectnums!:` attribute on top of that section and when that section ends, put back the `:sectnums:` attribute once again on the next line to restart section numbering from that point onward. And yes, you can use attributes anywhere in the document.

Also it might be best to leave the first line of all included files blank as shown in Figure 115.

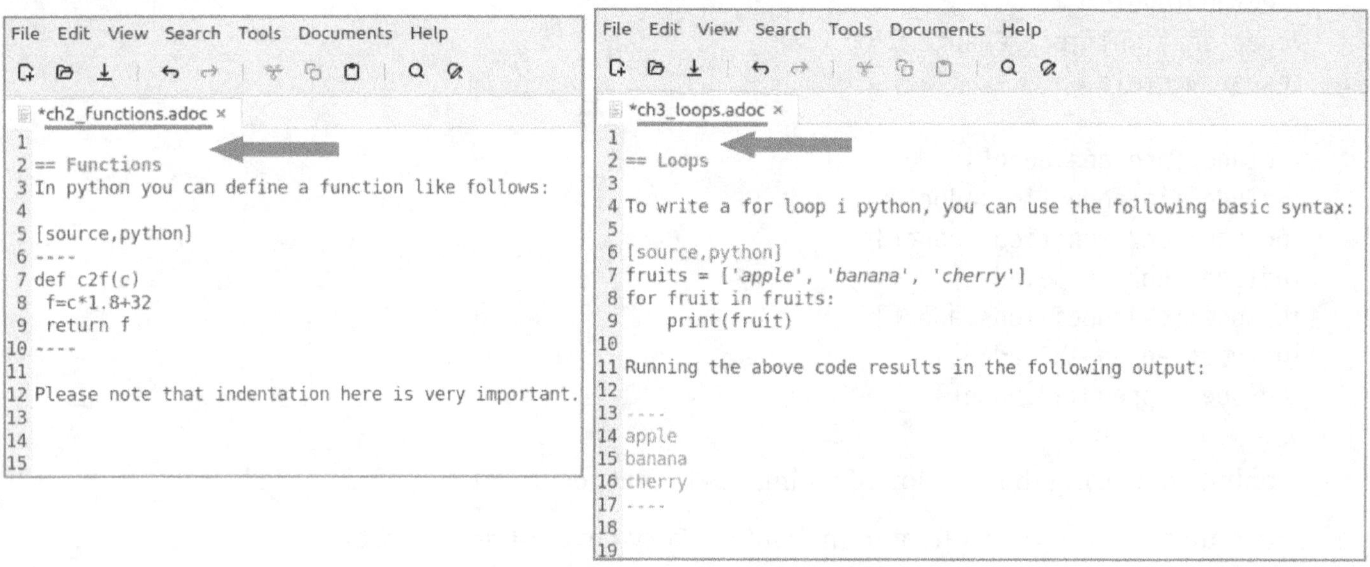

Figure 115. Sample chapter files that just start with chapter headings. Attributes included in the master file will be applicable here as well and need not be repeated. Also the big arrows indicate leaving the top line blank in individual chapter files.

Once the master.adoc file is ready, all we need to do is to run the *AsciiDoctor* or *AsciiDoctor-PDF* command as shown in Example 178 on the *master.adoc* file and we will have a *master.html* or *master.pdf* file when the commands are done processing.

Terminal Command

Example 178. Rendering AsciiDoc file as HTML or PDF

```
$ asciidoctor master.adoc

or

$ asciidoctor-pdf master.adoc
```

The result is a single HTML or PDF file that has all chapter and image files as shown in Figure 116.

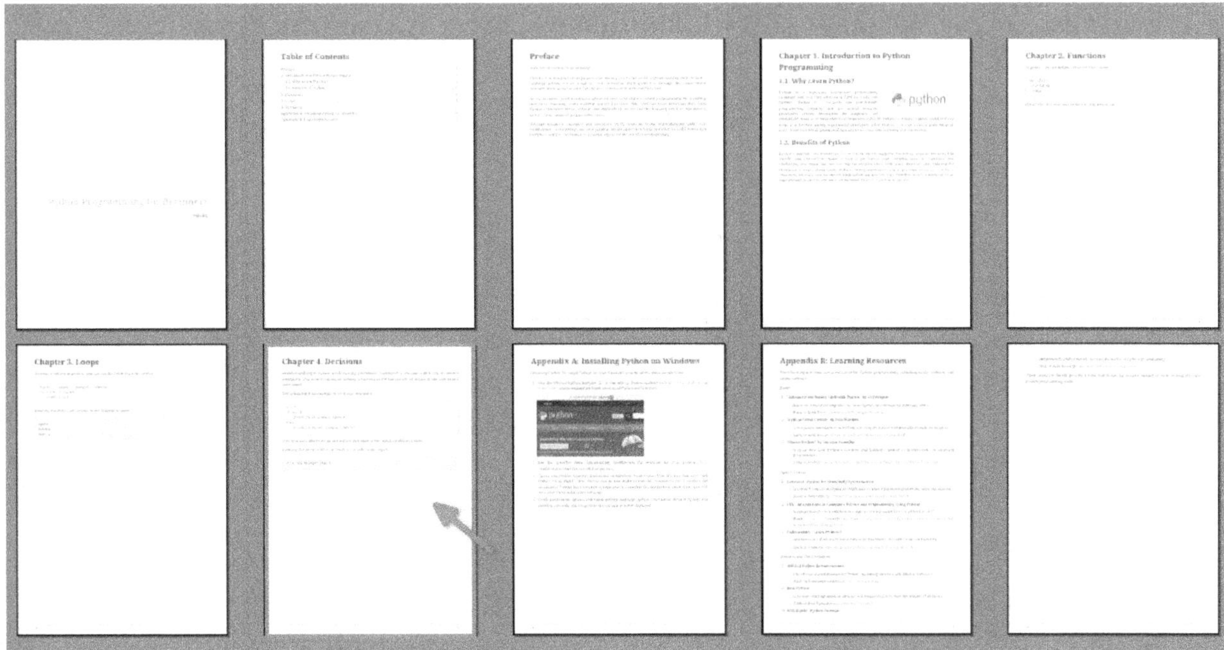

Figure 116. All chapters in a single PDF document.

In Figure 116, chapter 4 has been highlighted by a red rectangle which is shown enlarged in Figure 117.

Chapter 4. Decisions

Decision making in Python involves using conditional statements to execute code based on specific conditions. The primary decision-making structures in Python include if, if-else, if-elif, and nested statements.

The following is an example of an if-else Statement:

```
a = 3
if a > 5:
    print("a is greater than 5")
else:
    print("a is not greater than 5")
```

This structure allows for an alternative execution if the initial condition is false.

Running the above code will result in the following output:

```
a is not greater than 5
```

Figure 117. Zoom in on chapter 4 with syntax highlighting in the rendered PDF

The file *preface.adoc* starts with the styling declaration `[preface]` as shown in Figure 118.

```

[preface]
== Preface

Welcome to Python Programming!

This book is designed for beginners, int
known for its simplicity and versatility
and data types to control structures and

As you progress, you'll learn more advan
```

Figure 118. The Preface Styling Declaration

This ensures that in spite of a level 2 heading, 'Preface' does not get a chapter number automatically like the other chapters.

Likewise, *appendix1.adoc* and *appendix2.adoc* similarly start with an `[appendix]` styling declaration as shown in Figure 119 which automatically gives them an alphabetically incrementing ID like 'Appendix A' and 'Appendix B'.

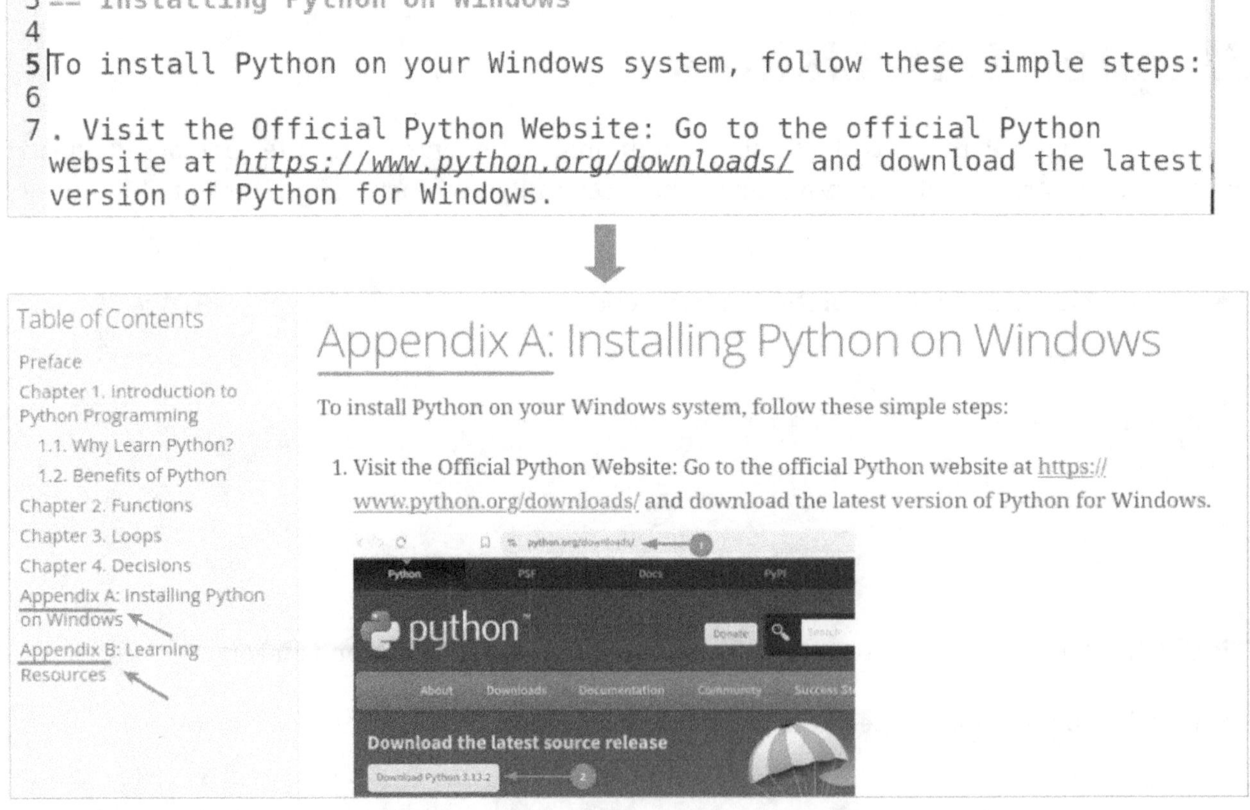

Figure 119. The [appendix] styling renders with automatic incremental alphabetical IDs for all appendices

17.2. Organizing Your Folder Structure

AsciiDoctor has you covered if you have structured your book project in a more detailed and organized way. For example, if you decide to organize your book with every chapter in its own folder (rather than in one folder as shown in Figure 114) and images for every chapter inside their individual image folders i.e. a dedicated image folder per chapter, you could have a folder structure as shown in Figure 120.

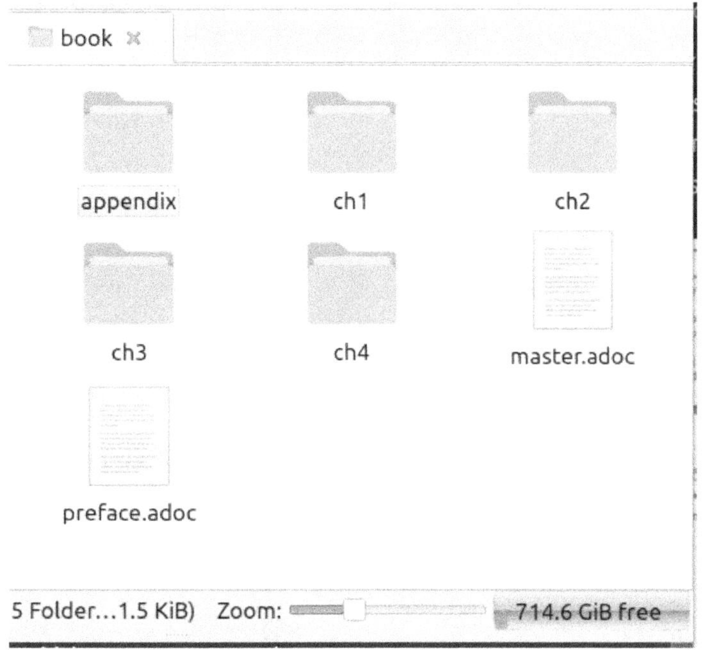

Figure 120. AsciiDoc files and images of every chapter are organized inside inside separate folders

The structure inside each folder — Chapter 1 folder or ch1 being taken as a representative example — is shown in Figure 121.

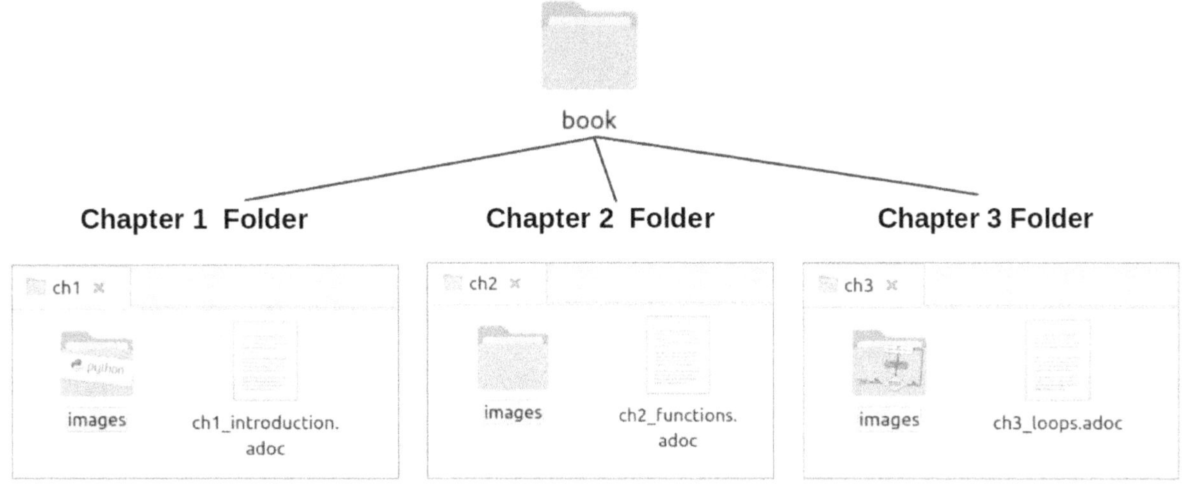

Figure 121. Contents of some chapter folders

So if you have organized your book in a structure that resembles the the structure seen in Figure 121, you can easily make some minor changes in the *master.adoc* file and have the exact same outcome i.e. render a single PDF or HTML file combining all these files. The changed *master.adoc* file contents are shown in Example 179 assuming that we are in the folder where the master.adoc is placed and other chapter folders are inside this folder.

Example 179. Sample master.adoc file that facilitates collation of independent AsciiDoc files into a single rendered HTML, PDF or EPUB document

```
= Python Programming for Beginners
:author: Felicity Morgan
:doctype: book
:icons: font
:source-highlighter: pygments
:toc: left
:toclevels: 3
:sectnums:
:sectnumlevels: 2
:chapter-signifier: Chapter
:experimental:

include::preface.adoc[]

:imagesdir: ch1/images/                          ①
include::ch1/ch1_introduction.adoc[]             ②

:imagesdir: ch2/images/
include::ch2/ch2_functions.adoc[]

:imagesdir: ch3/images/
include::ch3/ch3_loops.adoc[]

:imagesdir: ch4/images/
include::ch4/ch4_decisions.adoc[]

:imagesdir: appendix/images/
include::appendix/appendix1.adoc[]

:imagesdir: appendix/images/
include::appendix/appendix2.adoc[]
```

① imgesdir now has a relative path to chapter 1 image folder (same for other chapters).

② include now has a relative path to the chapter 1 AsciiDoc file (same for other chapters).

There are few things worth noticing in this version of *master.adoc* :

1. If you revisit the previous version of *master.adoc* in Example 177, you will find that we have deleted the attribute `:imagesdir: ./images/` from the header because in our present folder structure, we do not have a common image directory or folder for all chapters as was the case earlier. Now because each chapter is inside its own folder and has its exclusive image directory, we need to alter the *include* statements for every chapter to accurately provide the location of the chapter file and images for that chapter.
2. The base folder now only has *master.adoc* and *preface.adoc* files (Figure 121).

So as can be seen in Example 180, we are effectively saying that go inside the ch1 folder and *ch1_introduction.adoc* is available there — *include it in the final document that is being collated.* With the `:imagesdir:` attribute, we are saying that images used in *ch1_introduction.adoc* file are located inside the local *images* folder i.e. the *images* folder inside the ch1 folder.

AsciiDoc Markup

Example 180. Pointing include to chapter and image files when they are inside a folder structure

```
:imagesdir: ch1/images/
include::ch1/ch1_introduction.adoc[]
```

We insert a blank line in between each pair of *include* and *imagesdir* declarations in Example 179 for improved readability (and to avoid any code mixup). Notice that as *preface.adoc* is in the base folder where *master.adoc* itself is located, we do not provide any path for it.

Like before, we just run AsciiDoctor or AsciiDoctor-PDF on the *master.adoc* file as seen below and we get the same single HTML or PDF file that we got before:

Terminal Command

```
$ asciidoctor master.adoc
```

or if rendering to PDF…

```
$ asciidoctor-pdf master.adoc
```

So this is how you can conveniently organize your files and generate a single HTML or PDF using appropriate path references in the master.adoc file (or whatever you wish to call the main file).

17.3. Moving and Reorganizing Content is Super Easy

When you have a master document with include statements for various chapters, it becomes very easy to reorganize and move content. Referring to the revised *master.adoc* file in Example 179, let's say you decide that you need to change the sequence of chapters and feel that the current chapter 4 should actually be chapter 2 and the current chapter 2 should become chapter 4. To effect this change in chapter sequence, all you have to do is to exchange the positions of the chapter 4 and chapter 2 `include` and `imagedir` statements in your *master.adoc* file as shown in Figure 122.

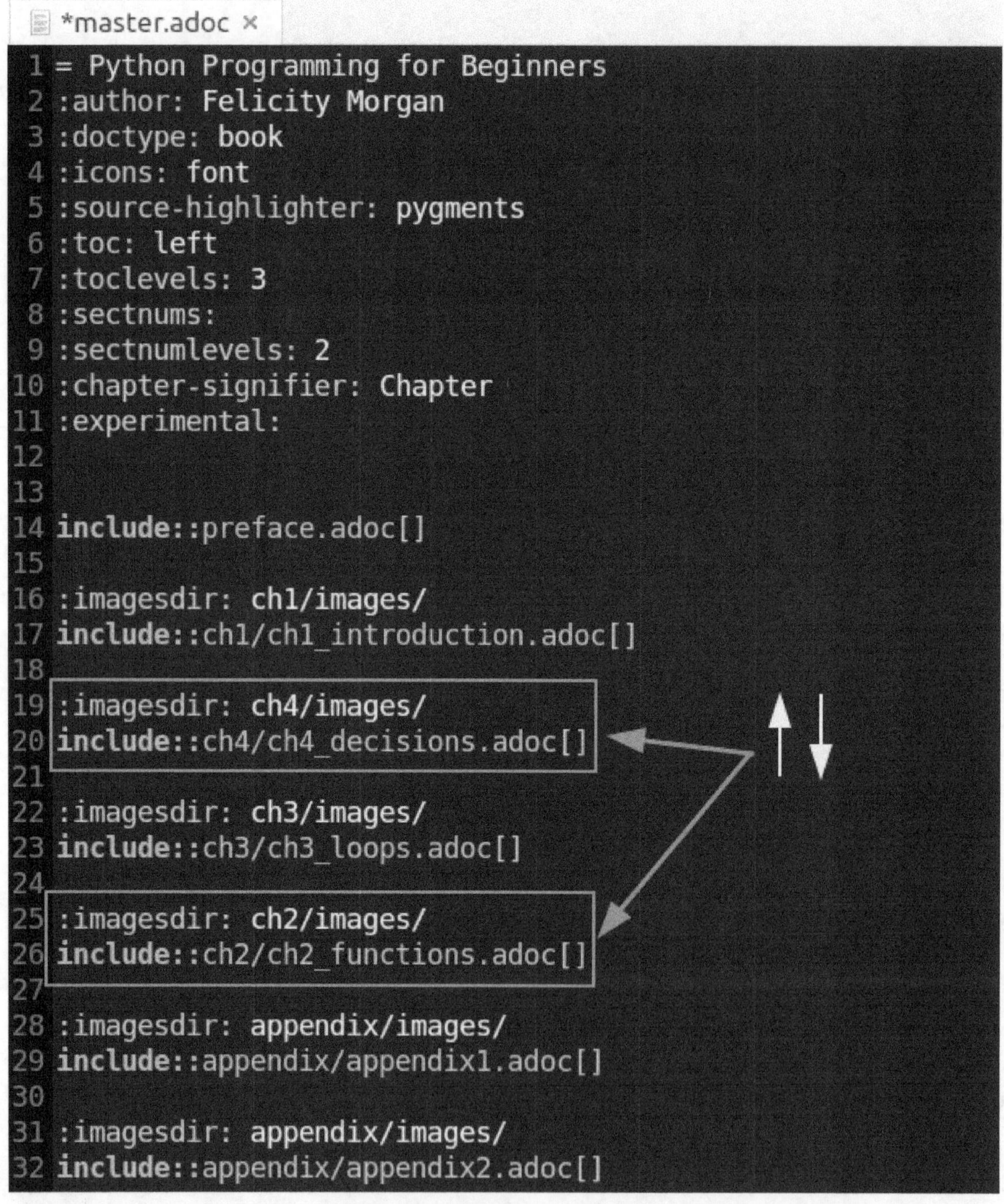

Figure 122. Reorganizing chapters by moving chapter 2 to chapter 4 position and chapter 4 to chapter 2 position

It might not be immediately apparent but none of the include AsciiDoc files in *master.adoc* have a chapter number hardwired inside them. The chapter number is assigned based on their sequential position in the *master.adoc* file. So when the book will be rendered, the contents of chapter 4 folder will be labeled as 'Chapter 2' and those of chapter 2 will be labelled as 'Chapter 4' because they appear in that sequence in the *master.adoc* file. We do not need to rename any folders or files. Just move them around in the *master.adoc* file and we are done. This provides us with tremendous flexibility and freedom to organize content.

17.4. Including External Source Code Files

The *include* macro can also be used to insert content from external files like text files or source code files. Let's take for example the *AsciiDoc* file shown in Example 181.

AsciiDoc Markup

Example 181. AsciiDoc file containing text and embedded code

We can define a function in python as demonstrated in the following code block:

```
#1 Get temperature in Celsius from user
celsius = float(input("Enter temperature in Celsius: "))

#2 Function Celsius to Fahrenheit
def c2f(c):
 f=c*1.8+32
 return f

#3 Call the Function
fahrenheit=c2f(celsius)

#4 Print the result
print(f"{celsius}°C is equal to {fahrenheit}°F")
```

When the user provides a temperature value in °C, a call is made to function c2f passing the user provided value in °C and the program prints the equivalent value in °F.

Now instead of *directly typing or pasting* the code in the AsciiDoc file as seen in the above example, we can also import the python file directly. Let's say if the Python code part in the AsciiDoc file in Example 181 is in a Python file called *c2f.py*, we can *directly* include *c2f.py* without any copying and pasting as shown in Example 182.

AsciiDoc Markup

Example 182. Inserting code in AsciiDoc file by including a Python code file

```
We can define a function in python as demonstrated in the following code block:

include::c2f.py[] ①

When the user provides a temperature value in {deg}C, a call is made to function c2f
passing the user provided value in {deg}C and the program print the equivalent value
in {deg}F.
```

① Here we are instructing AsciiDoctor to insert or *include* contents of *c2f.py* at this location.

17.5. Extracting and Including line Ranges

Continuing with the above discussion pertaining to insertion of content from an external file, if you want to include only certain lines from a particular file (i.e. not the entire file), you can do so by extending the include statement by the *lines* attribute. If we refer to Example 182 and wish to extract only lines 5-7 from the *c2f.py* file i.e. the part that is defining the function, we can do so using the *include* statement shown in Example 183.

AsciiDoc Markup

Example 183. Include only a range of lines from a file

```
[%hardbreaks]
include::c2f.py[lines=5..7]
```

As already mentioned earlier, the `[%hardbreaks]` styling directive puts each extracted statement on a new line.

The *include* macro in the above markup ensures that only lines 5, 6, and 7 — highlighted by a red rectangle in Figure 123 — are extracted from the *c2f.py* file when rendered by AsciiDoctor in HTML or PDF.

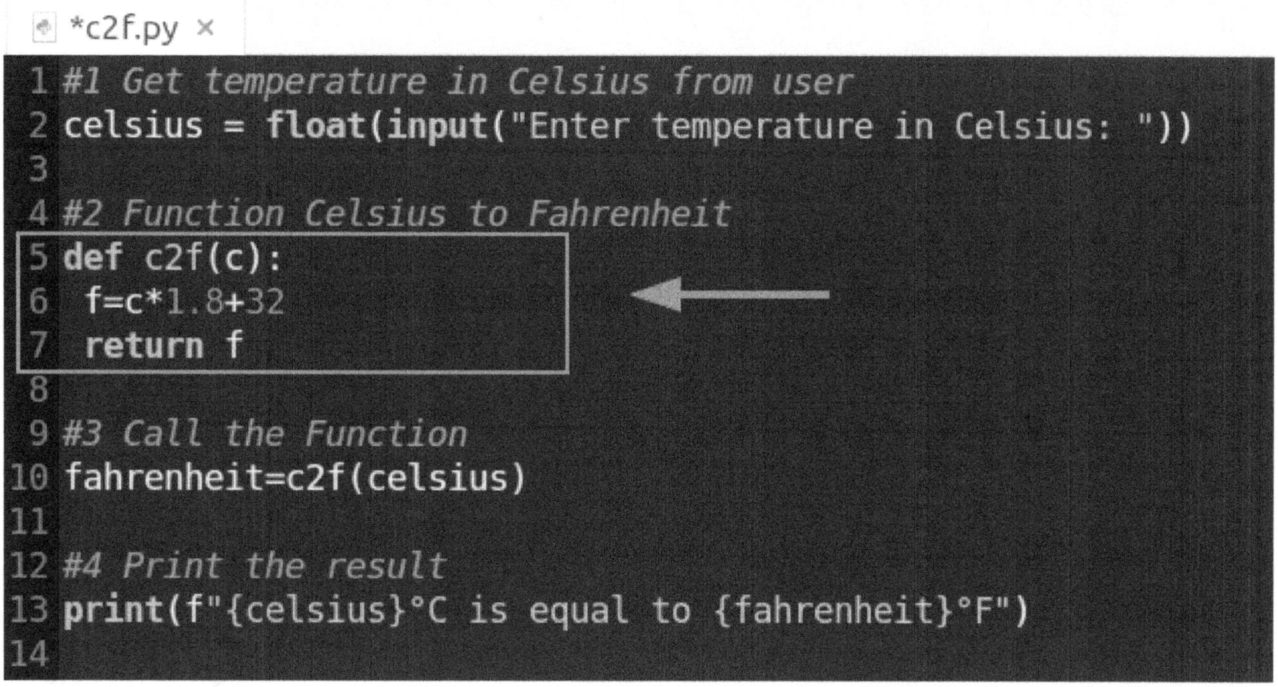

*c2f.py ×

```
#1 Get temperature in Celsius from user
celsius = float(input("Enter temperature in Celsius: "))

#2 Function Celsius to Fahrenheit
def c2f(c):
 f=c*1.8+32
 return f

#3 Call the Function
fahrenheit=c2f(celsius)

#4 Print the result
print(f"{celsius}°C is equal to {fahrenheit}°F")

```

Figure 123. Only the lines mentioned in the include 'lines' directive will be extracted and inserted

The rendered document as a result, contains only the following lines form the *c2f.py* file:

def c2f(c):
f=c*1.8+32
return f

Such *includes* inside files can be super helpful in directly adding code from source code files, text files or even other AsciiDoc files.

17.6. Conditional Includes

This might sound a bit geeky for a *beginners book* but I thought I should briefly introduce this as it is easy to do and adds a powerful capability to your *AsciiDoc repertoire*. In a nutshell, *conditional includes* permit selective additions in documents rendered by AsciiDoctor only if specific *conditions* are met. Let's take a simple hypothetical example. Let's say I have an AsciiDoc file called *adpdf.adoc* which has an admonition as shown in Example 184 explaining how footnotes will appear in the PDF document when rendered by AsciiDoctor-PDF.

Example 184. Example Admonition in adpdf.adoc

```
[IMPORTANT]
.Footnotes in PDF Documents Generated by AsciiDoctor PDF
Whenever rendering to PDF, footnotes do not appear at the end of the page where they
```

```
appear in text. Rather they appear at the end of the chapter or at the end of the
document depending on the _doctype_ . The AsciiDoctor documentation states the
following in regard to this limitation:

_"Footnotes are always displayed as endnotes (at the bottom of the last page of a
chapter for books; at the bottom of the last page of the document for all other
doctypes). Footnotes cannot be displayed at the current bottom of the page because
the PDF generator does not support content reflows."_
```

Now because this admonition concerns only PDF documents, I need to include this admonition only when I generate a PDF output of my document but not when I generate HTML or EPUB3 outputs. We can do this quite easily by adding a *conditional include* for the above stated situation in your current AsciiDoc document file as demonstrated in Example 185.

AsciiDoc Markup

Example 185. Conditional include of a file if the backend is PDF

```
ifdef::backend-pdf[]
include::adpdf.adoc[]
endif::[]
```

The conditional statement comprising of the `ifdef` — `endif` pair is essentially saying that when the document is rendered to PDF, the admonition will be included in the PDF seen in Figure 124.

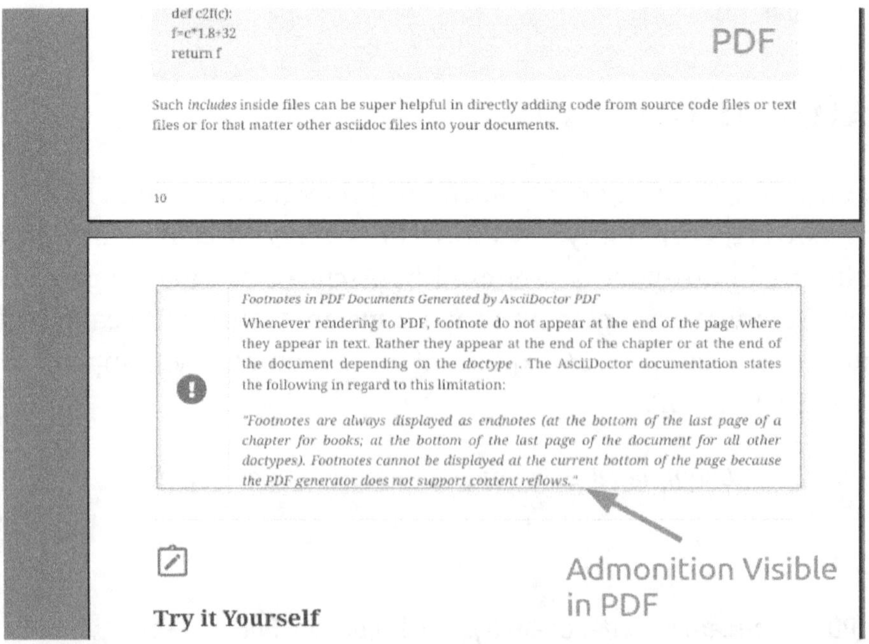

Figure 124. The PDF document contains the admonition inserted by the include adpdf.adoc statement

With reference to Example 185, you can have multiple statements between the `ifdef` — `endif` pair.

If on the other hand, you are using *AsciiDoctor* or *AsciiDoctor-EPUB3* to generate an output, you will not see this admonition in those documents as seen in the HTML output (Figure 125) because the *backend=PDF* condition is not evaluated to be true.

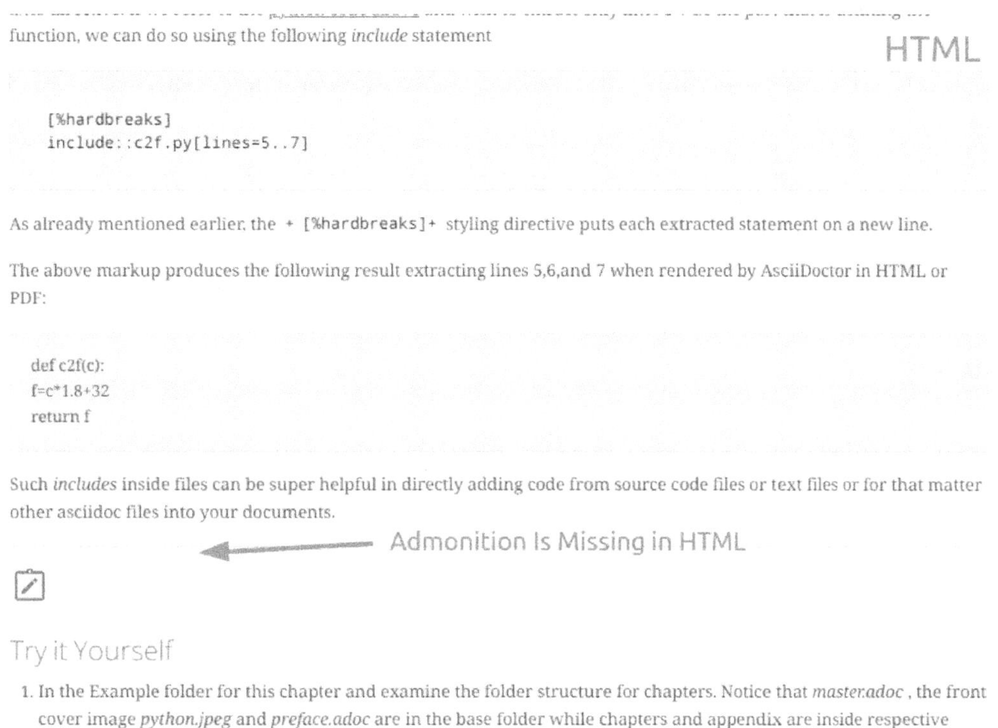

function, we can do so using the following *include* statement

```
[%hardbreaks]
include::c2f.py[lines=5..7]
```

As already mentioned earlier. the + [%hardbreaks]+ styling directive puts each extracted statement on a new line.

The above markup produces the following result extracting lines 5,6,and 7 when rendered by AsciiDoctor in HTML or PDF:

def c2f(c):
f=c*1.8+32
return f

Such *includes* inside files can be super helpful in directly adding code from source code files or text files or for that matter other asciidoc files into your documents.

Try it Yourself

1. In the Example folder for this chapter and examine the folder structure for chapters. Notice that *master.adoc* , the front cover image *python.jpeg* and *preface.adoc* are in the base folder while chapters and appendix are inside respective

Figure 125. The generated HTML does not contain the admonition as ifdef:: test fails for the PDF backend

Likewise to create a conditional directive for HTML (the default HTML backend is HTML5), we can write an *ifdef* conditional as shown in Example 186 which states that the *adhtml.adoc* file will be included in the rendered output only if the backend is HTML5.

AsciiDoc Markup

Example 186. Conditional Include of a file if the backend is HTML5

```
ifdef::backend-html5[]
include::adhtml.adoc[]
endif::[]
```

When we normally convert an AsciiDoc file to HTML using the command — `$ asciidoctor myfile.adoc`, the backend deployed by AsciiDoctor is HTML5. Hence the conditional `ifdef::` directive above tests for `backend-html5`.

17.7. Positioning the Table of Contents

AsciiDoc has special provisions for adding front matter to your book. Some important elements include, Table of Contents or TOC, Preface, Colophon and Dedication. Articles usually carry an *abstract*. Let's quickly have a look at how you can specially style or manage these sections.

17.7.1. Table of Contents

As has already been discussed earlier in Chapter 4, you can create a Table of Contents (TOC) automatically by placing the `:TOC:` attribute in the header. When rendered to HTML, the TOC is the first item to appear under the Level 0 Title. Many times however, this may not be the most desirable place for the TOC to appear. For example if you are creating a book, you want the TOC to appear at a specific point, say after the preface and initial front matter. To move TOC to a specific location in your document, you need put the following markup in the header of your document:

AsciiDoc Markup

```
:toc: macro
```

With the `:toc: macro` attribute in the header, you could place `toc::[]` as shown below after any include statement in Example 177 and the TOC will appear at that place in the rendered document.

AsciiDoc Markup

```
toc::[]
```

With the `:toc: macro` attribute in the header, you could place `toc::[]` after any include statement in Example 177 and the TOC will appear at that place in the rendered document.

This specific positioning of the TOC in your *master.adoc* (Example 177) gives you complete control over the placement of TOC when you are compiling your book or report.

Important

Please note that the `toc::[]` macro can appear *only once* in your document. Also if you forget to assign the *macro* value to the TOC attribute in the header, any reference to the `toc::[]` macro placed anywhere in the document will be ignored. So if you are using the TOC macro, make sure you comply with these conditions.

17.8. Uploading Your HTML Document on a Website

When you are all done and have a final HTML version of your document, to share it with others you will have to upload the HTML page on a website. If you are familiar with HTML, you will know that HTML documents do not embed images, video, audio etc. that are referred in the document text. These items reside in external folders. So what needs to be uploaded to your website for the document to become available online? Let's try to understand taking the example of a book project and visualizing the following two common scenarios in which your project has been organized.

17.8.1. Situation 1: All Chapter Files in One Folder

The first situation could be that we have organized our project with all our AsciiDoc chapter files in one single folder with a common image folder for all chapters. This folder structure is as illustrated in Figure 126.

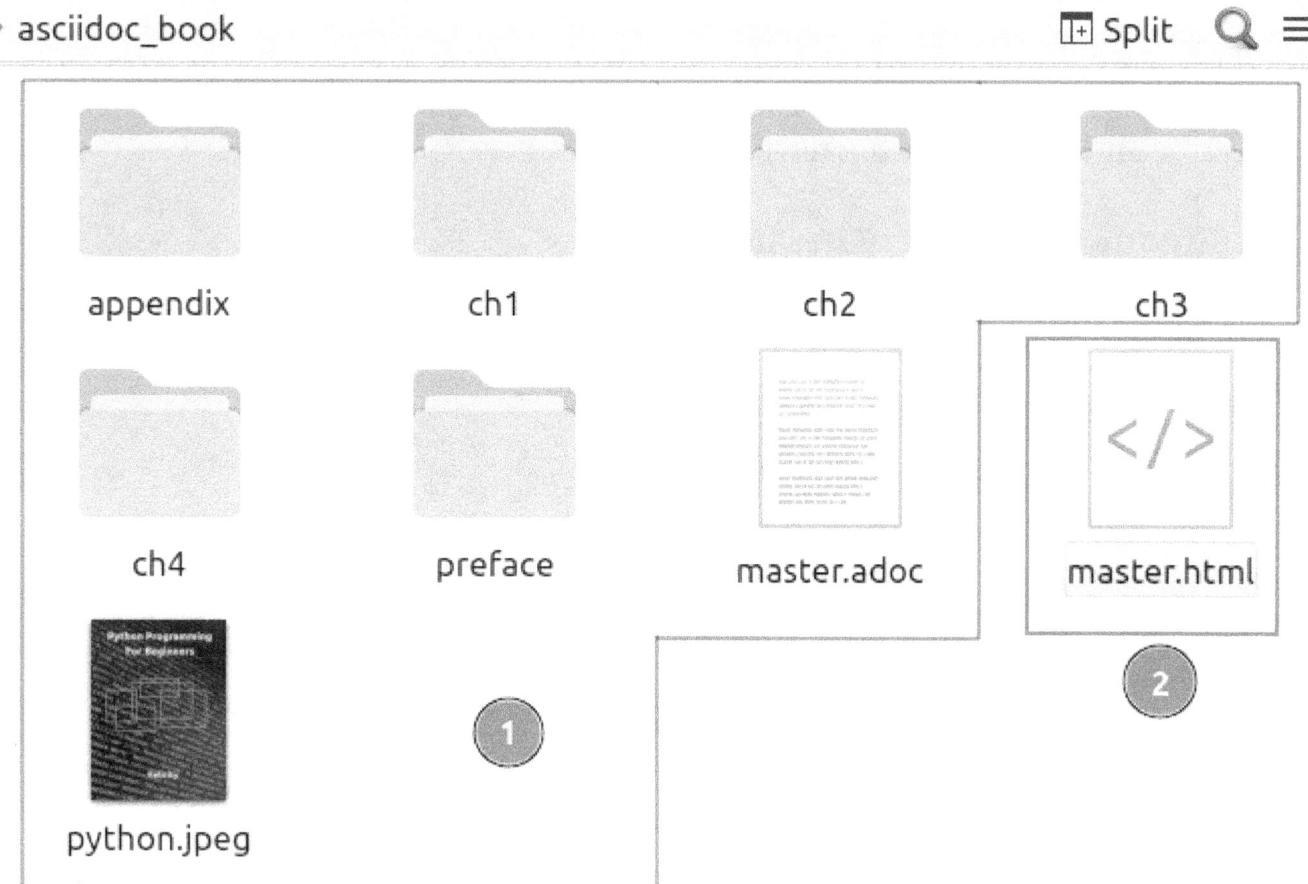

Figure 126. Situation 1 - (1) All AsciiDoc chapter files in one folder (2) all images files in one folder (3) the master.html file after running AsciiDoctor on master.adoc

As can be seen, we have a *master.adoc* file that brings together the entire book. Once we run AsciiDoctor with *master.adoc*, we will get *master.html* (callout 3 in Figure 126), which is the HTML version of this book. All AsciiDoc chapter text gets included inside this single file — *master.html* . However, all images referred in this html file are inside the *images* folder(callout 2 in Figure 126). So when you want to move this book, you will have to move *master.html* file and also the *images* folder to the server hosting your website. To avoid confusion, you can consider creating an upload folder and place in it, just those items that need to be uploaded on the web server as shown in Figure 127.

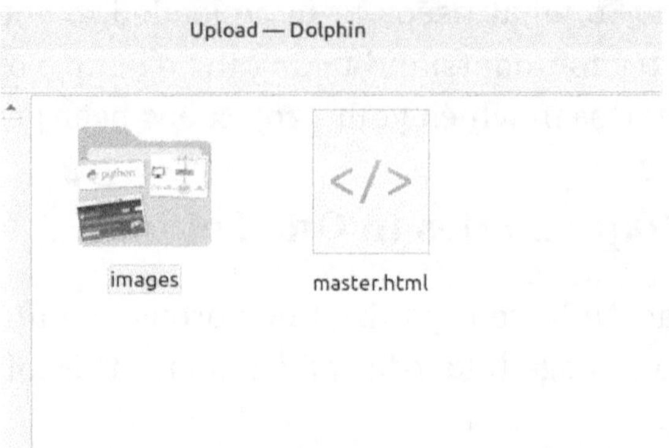

Figure 127. Contents of the upload folder which need to be moved to the web server

The AsciiDoc files do not need to be uploaded as their text content is already inside the HTML file. Once these are uploaded on your web server, you can rename *master.html* to *index.html* to get a shorter URL that you can share for others to access this book online.

17.8.2. Situation 2: Chapter Files in

The second situation involves separate folders for each chapter and a dedicated images folder within each chapter folder for images used in that folder as shown in Figure 128.

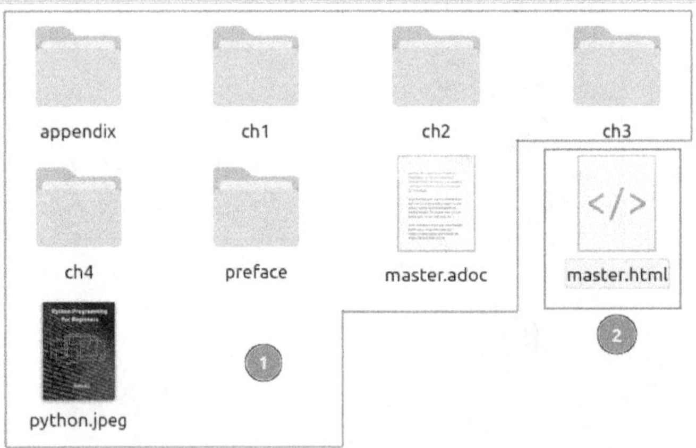

Figure 128. Situation 2 - (1) More detailed folder structure with every chapter AsciiDoc file inside their folder with an images folder inside each chapter folder and (2) HTML file after renderimg master.adoc

In this case once we get our HTML file, we will have to upload the exact same folder structure as seen in Figure 128 to your web server. From the uploaded folders, you can remove any AsciiDoc files from the main folder and chapter folders as their content has been captured in the *master.html* file. However, the *images* folder inside each chapter folder must be present. For example, in Figure 129 which shows an HTML source excerpt of my *master.html* file, the `<IMG>` tag is pointing to the location of the image *flow.png* as being inside the ch3/images/ folder. If the folder structure is therefore distrubed, images will not show up on the HTML page.

```
<p>Conceptually, the loop moves like follows:</p>
</div>
<div class="imageblock">
<div class="content">
<img src="ch3/images/flow.png" alt="flow">
</div>
</div>
</div>
</div>
<div class="sect1">
<h2 id="_decisions">Chapter 4. Decisions</h2>
<div class="sectionbody">
<div class="paragraph">
```

Figure 129. HTML excerpt showing the IMG tag and the image it points to

So when you organize your chapter files as shown in Figure 128 i.e. with different folders for every chapter and each chapter folder having an *images folder* for that chapter's image file, you need to maintain the same folder structure when you upload your HTML file otherwise your images will not show up. Once you have these files on your web server, the *master.html* file can be renamed as *index.html* for a shorter URL that you can share with others for them to access this book online.

It is important to reiterate that when you run AsciiDoctor on an AsciiDoc file, AsciiDoctor does not create any new or additional folders (like pooling all images in the included files to a new folder). AsciiDoctor renders just the HTML file and all images and files that the HTML references continue to be in the same folder structure as before. So to move your document to a web server, you need to move the entire folder structure with the HTML file in it as it is on your machine.

In conclusion, include statements in AsciiDoc provide tremendous power and control in document generation by bringing many individual files into one document. They also permit tremendous flexibility to move and reorganize content freely before the final document in generated.

17.9. Chapter Summary

Key learnings in this chapter are:

1. When you are working on large documents, you need not put all your content in one AsciiDoc file. You can put your text in multiple AsciiDoc files like a separate file for every chapter.
2. To amalgamate all these files into one single document like a book, you can create a new *master* AsciiDoc file and use *include* statements for each individual file that you wish to bring in your final document. For a quick recap on how to do this, please see Example 177.
3. Collating a document via the *master file* permits you to easily reorganize content. All you have to do is to relocate any *include* statement in your master file. Please see Section 17.3 for a quick recap.
4. With *include* statements, you can also bring in external files like text files, code files or even other AsciiDoc files inside your document. Revisit Section 17.4 for a recap.
5. AsciiDoc also permits you to *conditionally* add external content to a document. This means, you can test for the document backend and then add or omit content as per your requirement. Please revisit Section 17.6 for more on how to do this.
6. While collating large documents like books, there is a set sequence to front matter. By default, the Table of Contents or TOC is inserted just after the level 0 heading or the book heading. You can change this and position your TOC anywhere you want in the document by using the `:toc: macro` directive. For a quick recap, please revisit Section 17.7.
7. When you render your master file as HTML and wish to share it online, you need to upload the rendered HTML file along with the images folder to the web server. You don't need to upload your AsciiDoc files. Please see Section 17.8 for a recap.

17.10. Try it Yourself

1. Open the example folder for this chapter and you will find a folder called *book*. This folder has chapters of the sample book used in this chapter in separate folders and a *master.adoc* file . Explore the folder structure of the book folder and familiarize yourself with how the files have been organized.
2. Notice that *master.adoc*, the front cover image *python.jpeg* and *preface.adoc* are in the base folder (book folder) while individual chapters, images for each chapter and the two appendix documents are inside their respective folders.

3. Open *master.adoc* and examine it. Notice the sequence of chapter files and also notice that there is an empty line after include statements for every chapter.
4. Run AsciiDoctor and AsciiDoctor-PDF on *master.adoc* as shown in Example 178 and generate both HTML and PDF outputs. Examine the output to confirm that starting from the front cover to the last appendix, everything appears in the same sequence as in the *master.adoc* file. Also see that the TOC displays everything correctly as expected.
5. For chapter 2 (ch2 folder), open *ch2_functions.adoc* and notice that the code for the function *c2f* has been embedded. Can you bring the same code inside this file by inserting the *c2f.py* file available in the book folder following the discussion in Example 182. (Hint- make a copy of *ch2_functions.adoc* file and delete the code lines and replace it with an include statement pointing to c2f.py).
6. Make a copy of the *master.adoc* file. Open the copy and try exchanging the positions of Chapter 2 and Chapter 4 and then render an HTML or PDF again to see the sequence and numbering of the moved chapters (See Section 17.3).
7. Notice that the TOC in your final PDF appears above the book cover. Can you place it after the preface ? (Hint, you have to change the value of the attribute `:toc: left` to `:toc: macro` and insert `toc::[]` wherever you want the TOC to appear).

[illegible]

[illegible]

[illegible]

[illegible]

[illegible]

Chapter 18. Generating EPUB 3 Files

"You don't see people getting pulled over by the police for reading ebooks on their smartphones."
~Jason Merkoski

In this chapter we will see how to render AsciiDoc files to the latest EPUB 3 e-book format using a dedicated converter called AsciiDoctor-EPUB3. We will see step-by-step, how to install and use AsciiDoctor-EPUB3 to create EPUB 3 documents that are responsive and adjust to fit any screen on which they are viewed.

18.1. Why EPUB ?

EPUB is an open e-book file format for digital documents and publications. It has been developed by the International Digital Publishing Forum (IDBF) and is widely supported by influential publishing industry bodies like the Book Industry Study Group. The latest minor revision of the EPUB 3 specification at the time of writing is EPUB 3.3 [https://www.w3.org/publishing/epub3/]. You can read more about EPUB 3 from the IDBF website [https://idpf.org/epub/30/].

So far in this book, we have primarily discussed creating AsciiDoc documents and rendering them in HTML and PDF formats. However if we look at the devices on which people consume digital content today, mobile phones would be a clear winner. Unfortunately, it is not easy to read PDF files on a mobile phone. That's where EPUBs really excel. Once you render your document in the EPUB format, you can use an EPUB reader app on your mobile phone or tablet to very conveniently read the document. Your content inside an EPUB file is like water (to recall a Bruce Lee quote!) that is reflowable and fits any screen on which it is viewed. The epub reader app permits you to adjust the font size, the background color, highlight passages, take notes and even convert text-to-speech. Generally, EPUB files are also smaller than PDFs. The EPUB 3 specification also supports multimedia content like audio and video files and provides a very contemporary and immersive reading experience, particularly on mobile devices.

In summary, rendering your content as EPUB is a great idea as it increases reach by making documents conveniently readable on mobile devices. Fortunately, the AsciiDoctor toolchain has a dedicated EPUB 3 converter tool called *AsciiDoctor-EPUB3* that makes rendering your AsciiDoc documents to EPUB format, a breeze! Let's get into installing and using the *AsciiDoctor-EPUB3* tool.

18.2. Installing AsciiDoctor-EPUB3

18.2.1. Docker Image

If you are using the AsciiDoctor Docker Image, *no installation* is required. The *AsciiDoctor-EPUB3* tool is part of the container image and you can start using it from the container image prompt as described in subsequent sections.

18.2.2. Installing on Linux

If you are not using a Docker image however, you will have to install *AsciiDoctor-EPUB3*. The installation is simple enough from the terminal using the following command:

Terminal Command

```
$ sudo gem install asciidoctor-epub3
```

OR you can alternatively use the following alternate command for a faster install:

Terminal Command

```
$ sudo NOKOGIRI_USE_SYSTEM_LIBRARIES=1 gem install asciidoctor-epub3
```

NOKOGIRI ?

"Nokogiri is basically an open-source software library designed to parse HTML and XML in Ruby" (Wikipedia [https://en.wikipedia.org/wiki/Nokogiri_(software)]).
In the above command, the NOKOGIRI_USE_SYSTEM_LIBRARIES environment variable is set = 1 to ensure a faster install of *AsciiDoctor_EPUB3* by using some already installed required libraries rather than building them again from scratch.

18.2.3. Installing on Windows

Open an administrator terminal (command prompt) and enter the following command to install *AsciiDoctor-EPUB3* on Windows (Figure 130).

Terminal Command

```
> gem install asciidoctor-epub3
```

```
PS C:\Users\chinm> ruby -v
ruby 3.3.6 (2024-11-05 revision 75015d4c1f) [x64-mingw-ucrt]
PS C:\Users\chinm> gem install asciidoctor-epub3
```

Figure 130. Installing asciidoctor-epub3 on Windows

18.2.4. Installing on Mac

You can issue the following command in the bash terminal assuming that you have AsciiDoctor already installed.

Terminal Command

```
gem install asciidoctor-epub3
```

18.3. Verifying the Install

To verify installation after the above command has finished, type in the following command from the terminal:

Terminal Command

```
$ asciidoctor-epub3 -v
```

If everything has gone well, you should see the message shown in Figure 131 (version numbers might be different in your case).

```
Asciidoctor EPUB3 2.1.3 using Asciidoctor 2.0.23 [https://asciidoctor.org]
Runtime Environment (ruby 3.3.6 (2024-11-05 revision 75015d4c1f) [x86_64-linux-m
usl]) (lc:UTF-8 fs:UTF-8 in:UTF-8 ex:UTF-8)
```

Figure 131. Output from the asciidoctor-epub3 -v command

18.4. Creating an EPUB Using AsciiDoctor-EPUB3

Once you have *AsciiDoctor-EPUB3* installed, you can just pass on your AsciiDoc file to *AsciiDoctor-EPUB3* by issuing the following command from the terminal or AsciiDoctor docker image prompt:

Terminal Command

```
$ asciidoctor-epub3 zen.adoc
```

The above command creates the epub file — in this case *zen.epub* — in the same directory as the *adoc* file. You can replace *zen.adoc* with your own AsciiDoc file.

18.4.1. Reading on Mobile Devices

You can now copy this file to your mobile device and open it using an epub reader. Apple iPhone and iPad users can open EPUBs in the *Books* [https://apps.apple.com/us/app/apple-books/id364709193] app. Android users can try the free version of ReadEra [https://play.google.com/store/apps/details?id=org.readera] or any other app of their choice. Linux users can use the Foliate [https://johnfactotum.github.io/foliate/] ebook reader which is available as a Flatpak or as a package via software managers for all popular Linux distributions. You can also read EPUB files on your Laptops or Desktops using browser extensions like EpubReader [https://chromewebstore.google.com/detail/jhhclmfgfllimlhabjkgkeebkbiadflb] for the Chrome, Brave and Firefox [https://addons.mozilla.org/en-US/firefox/addon/epubreader/] browsers.

18.5. Piecing up an EPUB from Individual Chapters

Stitching together a single EPUB document from multiple AsciiDoc files like individual chapters kept in separate folders is essentially the same as described in Chapter 17 for creating single HTML or PDF documents from individual files. You need to create a master file that has each chapter AsciiDoc file added via an include statement (Chapter 17, Example 177) and then run *AsciiDoctor-EPUB3* from the terminal as shown in Example 187.

Terminal Command

Example 187. Running AsciiDoctor-EPUB3 on an AsciiDoc file

```
$ asciidoctor-epub3 master.adoc
```

This will result is a single epub file combining all files mentioned in the *include statements* inside the master file. For EPUB files particularly, it is good practice to include some extra attributes that add metadata to the generated epub file which is used by EPUB reader apps. Some of these attributes with sample values are given in Figure 132.

```
*zen.adoc ×
= Zen and The Art of Story Telling
:front-cover-image: cover.jpeg
:doctitle: Zen and The Art of Story Telling
:author: Chinmaya S Rathore
:description: Describes the core philosophy of Zen Bhuddhism and explores the role of
storytelling in imparting spiritual concepts.
:producer: Zen Books
:revdate: {docdate}
:revnumber: 1.0
:lang: en-US
:uuid: 10.2515/9780344858087-0114
:keywords: Zen,Parables,Bhuddhism,Philosophy
:toc: left
:toclevels: 3
```

Figure 132. Some useful attributes to include in EPUB files

The UUID attribute value can be a document identifier like DOI, ISBN, ISSN etc. Figure 133 shows how these attributes are incorporated in the EPUB file metadata when the file is opened by an ebook reader and the properties or file information, queried:

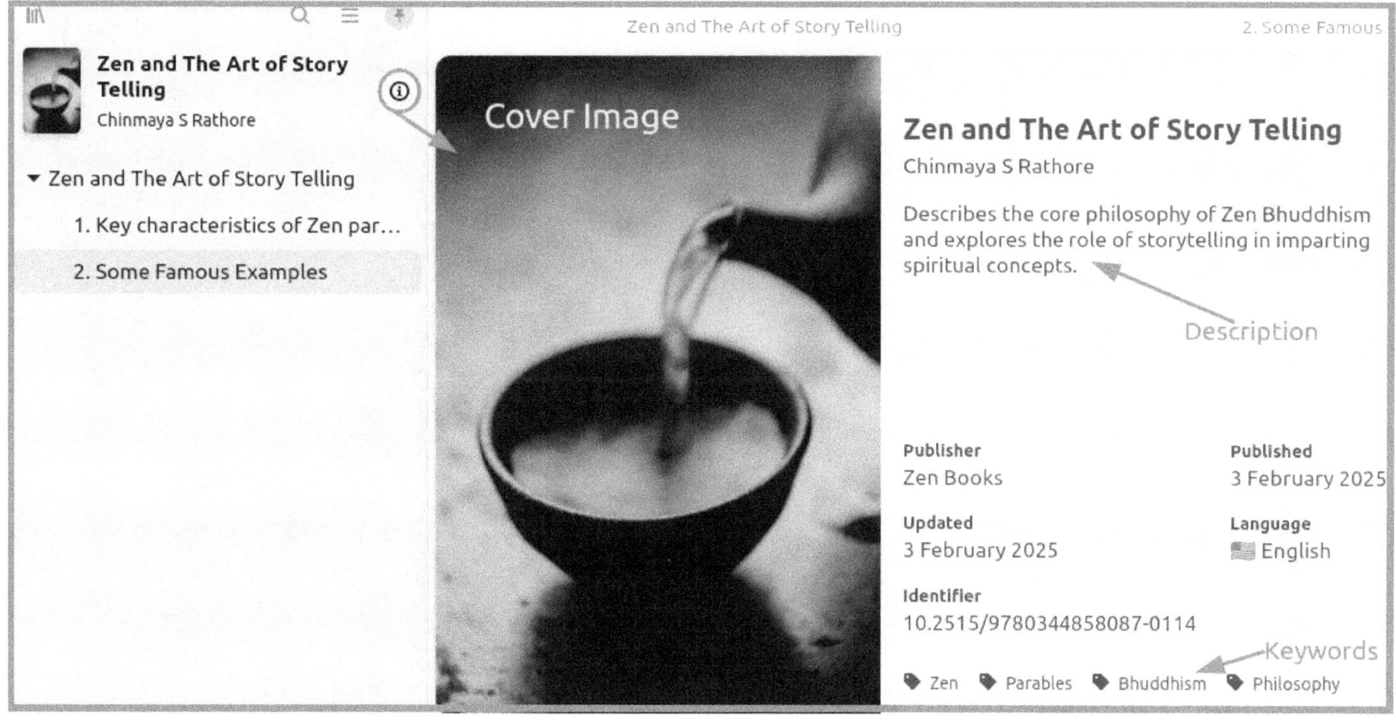

Figure 133. Epub Metadata as seen in Foliate EPUB Reader

> *The lang Attribute Value for Ebooks in Non-English Languages*
>
> With reference to the language attribute, `:lang: en` or `:lang: en-US` i.e. the language of the ebook, please visit this Oracle site [https://docs.oracle.com/cd/E13214_01/wli/docs92/xref/xqisocodes.html#wp1250778] for language codes and country codes specified by ISO 639 and ISO 3166 that can be used for setting the *lang* attribute value for languages other than English.

Let's see this in action as we try to create a single epub file from individual chapter files.

A sample set of attributes and individual chapter includes in *master.adoc* are shown Example 188.

AsciiDoc Markup

Example 188. Sample Master AsciiDoc file with Typical Attributes to Create an EPUB3 eBook

```
= Zen and The Art of Story Telling
:doctype: book
:front-cover-image: ./images/cover.jpeg
:doctitle: Zen and The Art of Story Telling
:author: Chinmaya S Rathore
:description: Describes the core philosophy of Zen Buddhism and explores the role of
storytelling in imparting spiritual concepts.
:producer: Zen Books
:revdate: {docdate}
:revnumber: 1.0
:lang: en-US
:uuid: 10.2515/9780344858087-0114
:keywords: Zen,Parables,Buddhism,Philosophy
:toc:
:toclevels: 2
:sectnums:
:sectnumlevels: 1
:imagesdir: images

// You can include any number of chapters in the sequence they need to appear

 include::chapter1.adoc[]
 include::chapter2.adoc[]
 include::chapter3.adoc[]
```

It is important to note that if you have stored your images in a separate folder like *images*, you just need to state the name of the folder in the `:imagesdir:` attribute without any / or path. Just state the name of the folder which is relative to the directory in which your AsciiDoc master document is residing as shown in Example 188.

Running AsciiDoctor-EPUB3 (Example 187) on the AsciiDoc file shown in Example 188 creates a polished EPUB3 file as seen in Figure 134.

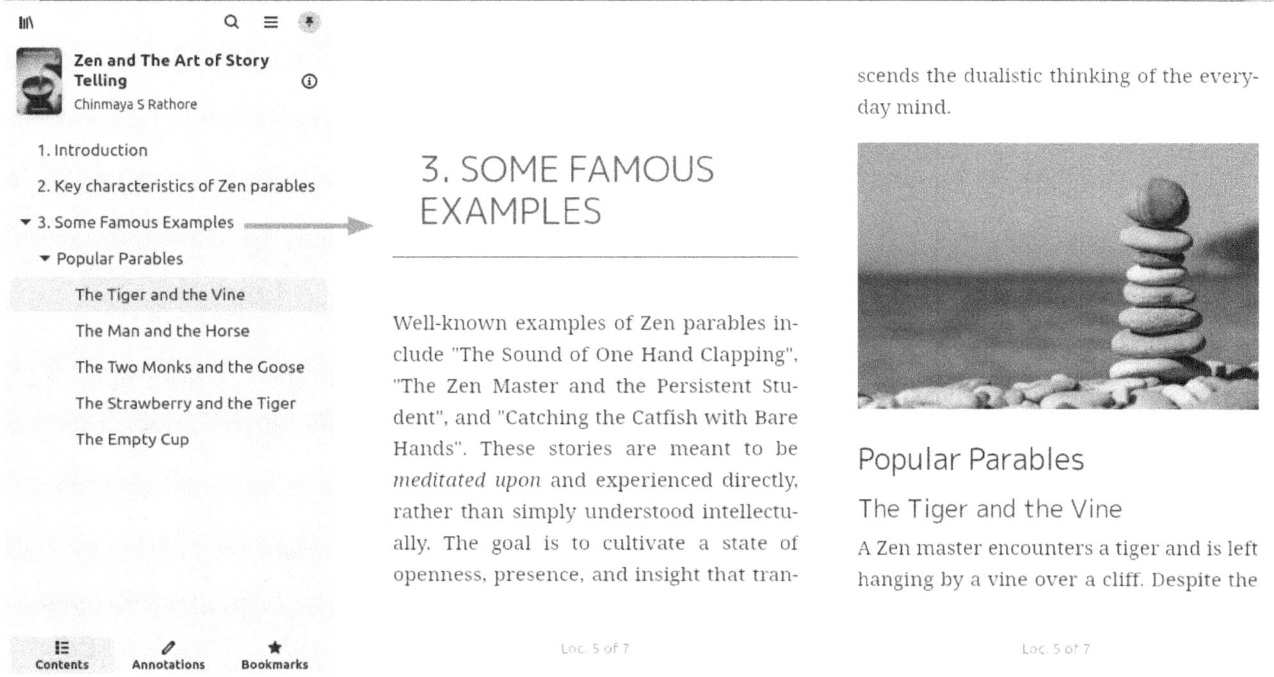

Figure 134. EPUB3 Ebook as seen on a desktop Linux computer using the Foliate Ebook Reader

The same file can also be conveniently read on a mobile phone with reformatted pages to fit the device screen as shown in Figure 135.

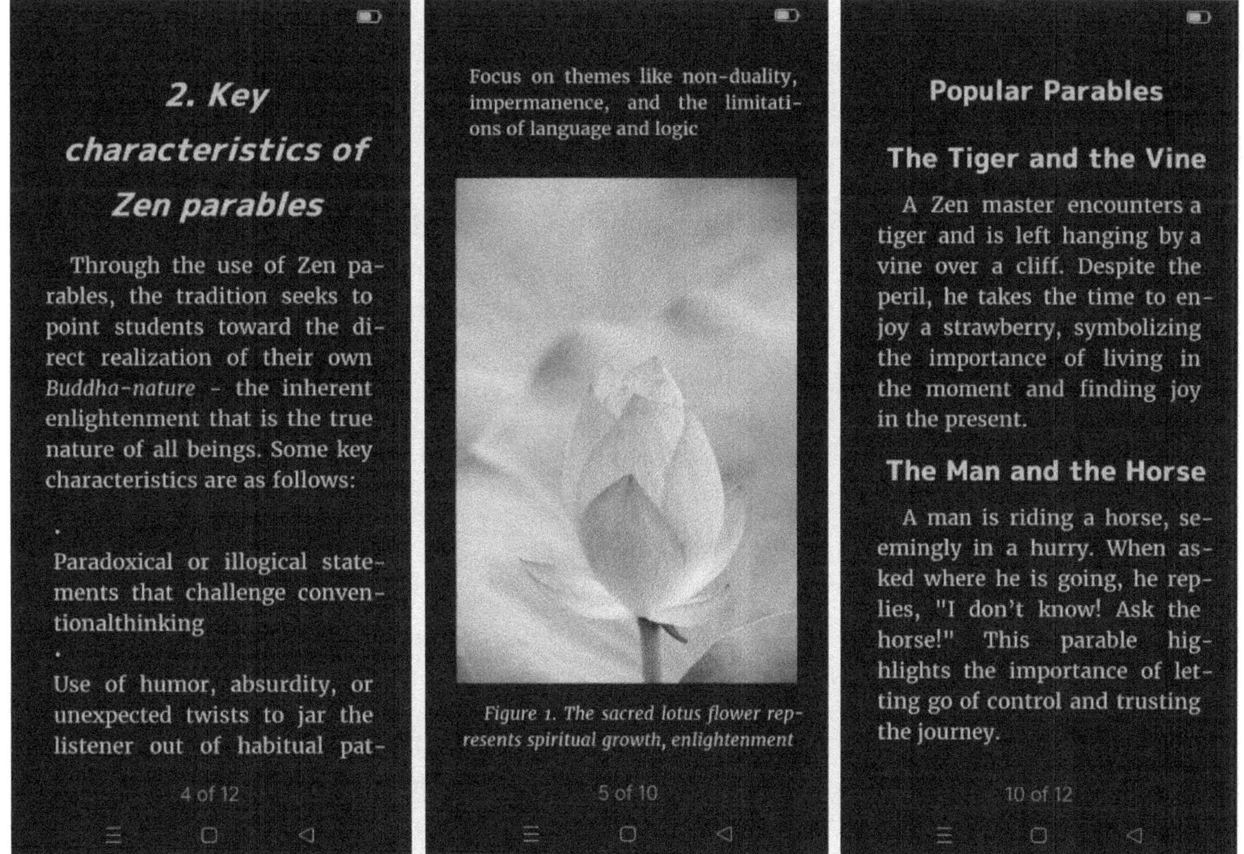

Figure 135. The Zen EPUB3 file as seen on a Android Mobile EPUB Reader (ReadEra)

18.6. Compiling EPUBs from More Detailed Folder Structures

If your chapter files reside in separate folders as has been discussed in Chapter 17, you can collate a single EPUB file by altering the master file with appropriate path details. The process is exactly the same as described in Chapter 17 (Section 17.2). See Exercise 2 at the end of this chapter for sample files that demonstrates chapter wise folders.

The same also applies to reorganizing content. You can reposition include statements in your *master.adoc* file to reorganize and rearrange your material as discussed in Section 17.3 of Chapter 17.

18.7. Editing EPUB Files

While *asciidoctor-epub3* does a fantastic job of creating polished epubs, there might be times when some quirk needs to be fixed. If you are in such a situation, you might consider using Sigil [https://sigil-ebook.com/], an open source ebook editor. If you wish to explore Sigil, I have created the following videos that will get you started in using Sigil to edit EPUBs. In these videos, you can ignore those parts that discuss creation of EPUB files and just view the part that talks about editing EPUBs.

Watch these videos on YouTube

▶ https://www.youtube.com/watch?v=SPv9jGwGcmM *(YouTube video)*

18.8. Structure of an EPUB File

On a side note, it might be of peripheral interest to know that the EPUB file is *not a single file* but essentially a zipped archive comprising of a number of files. If you wish to examine it, you can make a copy of the EPUB file (example file - zen.epub) and unzip it using the following command (Linux).

Terminal Command

```
$ unzip zen.epub -d ./zen
```

The `-d` flag in the above command ensures that the unzipped contents are placed in a directory called *zen* which will be created inside the current folder. Windows and Mac users can unzip the EPUB file using their installed file archiver apps.

When you open the *zen* folder, you will find another folder called EPUB inside which are all the files that make up the EPUB document. All metadata provided by the author is placed inside the *package.opf* file and you can click on it to open it inside a text editor and examine its contents. All content text is inside .XHTML files. The *styles* folder has the .css or stylesheet files. The *fonts* folder has the fonts that have been used. This information can be helpful in fixing some infrequently encountered problems.

18.9. Chapter Summary

Key learnings in this chapter are:

1. EPUB documents provide a great reading experience on mobile devices.
2. To convert AsciiDoc files to EPUB, we need to install *AsciiDoctor-EPUB3*. You can check out Section 18.2 for a quick recap on how to install *AsciiDoctor-EPUB3*.
3. If you are using the AsciiDoctor Docker container, you need no installation as *AsciiDoctor-EPUB3* is part of the image.
4. You can create an EPUB3 file from any AsciiDoc document by using the following command:
   `$ asciidoctor-epub3 <file.adoc>`
   where <file.adoc> is to be replaced by your file name.
5. If your content is spread across multiple folders, you can use a *master.adoc* file to combine all your content and process it though *asciidoctor-epub3* to create a single EPUB file. See Section 18.5 for a quick recap.
6. You can read EPUB3 files on your mobile devices using popular ebook reader apps. Please refer back to Section 18.4.1 for more details.

18.10. Try it Yourself

Sample files used in the following exercises can be found in the example folder for this chapter.

Exercise 1

1. Navigate to the epub exercise folder. Here you will find an AsciiDoc file called *zen.adoc* and two picture files called *cover.jpeg* and *zen_pic.jpeg*. In this exercise we assume a situation that all the files — both AsciiDoc and image are inside one folder.
2. Open the zen.adoc file in a text editor and examine it. Notice that the first attribute (line2) `:front-cover-image: cover.jpeg` directly refers to cover.jpeg as the front cover image implying that it is in the same folder.
3. Also notice that at line 49, we include an image — `image::zen_pic.jpeg` again directly referring to the image (with no path) implying that this image too is in the same folder as *zen.adoc*.
4. Now create an EPUB by issuing the following command:

```
$ asciidoctor-epub3 zen.adoc
```

or the following if you wish to store the created epub in a separate folder:

```
$ asciidoctor-epub3 -D folder-name zen.adoc
```

You should get your epub now which you can read on tablets and phones using EPUB reader apps.

Challenge

Let's assume that you wish to store all your images in an images folder rather than in the same folder. You create an *images folder* and move all your images there. Can you tweak *zen.adoc* to reflect this ?

Hint and Solution : Just add a `:imagesdir:` attribute to the header section as shown in Example 188 setting its value to `image`. You don't have to provide any / before or after to indicate a path - just the folder name. You will also have to provide the correct location of the *front-cover-image* attribute putting the path to cover.jpeg which is inside the images folder as follows:

```
:front-cover-image: images/cover.jpeg
```

After making the above two changes to *zen.adoc*, open a terminal and just run the following AsciiDoctor-EPUB3 command — *asciidoctor-epub3 master.adoc* — to render the EPUB.

Exercise 2

We can repeat the same exercise but this time with multiple chapter files spread in multiple chapters folders with a local image folder for each chapter and a *master.adoc* file to *stitch* everything together. Work through the following:

1. In the downloaded sample files, go inside the EPUB folder and then the chapters folder.
2. Examine the contents of each folder. Notice that there is an image folder inside each chapter folder.
3. Open the *master.adoc* file and examine the `:imagesdir:` and `include::` statements and see how the location of chapter and images used in that chapter have been added.
4. From the folder which has the *master.adoc* file, open a terminal and just run the AsciiDoctor-EPUB3 command — *asciidoctor-epub3 master.adoc* to render the EPUB — *master.epub*

Remember, you can organize your AsciiDoc files in whatever way works best for you. At the end of the day, to bring all these files into a seamless single EPUB, PDF or HTML document, it's just about telling AsciiDoctor, AsciiDoctor-PDF and AsciiDoctor-EPUB3 where the AsciiDoc and images files are located.

Chapter 19. Converting AsciiDoc Files to MS Word and MS Word files to AsciiDoc

"Words travel worlds. Translators do the driving."
~Anna Rusconi

In this chapter, we will see how to convert AsciiDoc files to MS Word and MS Word Files to AsciiDoc. This can be particularly useful if you need to send your AsciiDoc document to someone who uses only MS Word or for those who wish to transition to AsciiDoc but the documents that they need are in MS Word format. We will see how to use the Pandoc software to aid in this conversion process.

19.1. Converting an AsciiDoc file to MS Word

As we live in a world dominated by office software, there may periodically arise a situation when you need to send an AsciiDoc document to someone who only uses MS Word. This can be an issue as MS Word cannot directly import or convert an AsciiDoc file in MS Word format. Under the circumstances, the only option is to convert your AsciiDoc file to MS Word format before you can send it across to the recipient. Luckily, we can easily convert AsciiDoc files to MS Word and vice versa with the help of an external software called *Pandoc*. Let's dive into it.

19.2. Converting in a Normal AsciiDoctor Install (Non-Docker)

The process of converting an AsciiDoc file to an MS Word file involves the following two sequential steps:

1. We first use AsciiDoctor to convert our AsciiDoc file to *DocBook* format which is essentially an XML (E**x**tensible **M**arkup **L**anguage) file.
2. Once we have a *DocBook* XML file, we use a free and open source software called *Pandoc* — a hugely popular universal document format converter, to convert the DocBook XML file to MS Word *docx* file. Pandoc can convert documents in one format to a large number of other formats. Unfortunately, while Pandoc supports AsciiDoc as a valid *output format*, at the time of writing (Pandoc 3.6.2), it does not support AsciiDoc as a recognized *input* format. This means that while you

can use Pandoc to convert files in other formats to AsciiDoc in just one step, you *cannot directly* convert an AsciiDoc file to other formats. Hence the two step process of first converting AsciiDoc to DocBook (recognized by Pandoc as valid input) using AsciiDoctor and then using Pandoc to convert the DocBook file to MS Word. You can read more about Pandoc and its super impressive conversion list on its official website [https://pandoc.org/].

19.2.1. Installing Pandoc on Linux

To install Pandoc, just start your distro's software manager, search for *Pandoc* and install it. If you prefer the command line, just open a terminal and issue the following command:

Terminal Command

```
$ sudo apt install pandoc
```

This is usually not the latest bleeding edge version but it will do just fine. However if *latest and greatest* motivates you, just go to the Pandoc Official Download Page [https://pandoc.org/installing.html] and download and install the latest *.deb package*.

19.2.2. Installing Pandoc on Windows and Mac

To install Pandoc on Windows or Mac just visit the Pandoc Official Download Page [https://pandoc.org/installing.html]. Here you will find the latest installers for Windows (msi) and MacOS.

19.3. AsciiDoc to MS Word Conversion

Now that we have installed Pandoc, we are all set to go. So let's assume that we have an AsciiDoc file called *zen.adoc* that we wish to convert to *zen.docx* i.e. an MS Word file. Following the two step process conceptually described earlier in Section 19.2, we will in step 1, convert *zen.adoc* to DocBook format (XML) using AsciiDoctor as shown in Example 189.

AsciiDoc Markup

Example 189. Converting AsciiDoc file to DocBook Format

```
$ asciidoctor -b docbook zen.adoc
```

You should now see a file called *zen.xml* (DocBook Format) created in the folder as a result of running the above command. Notice that as we haven't provided an output file name, AsciiDoctor automatically creates the XML file with the same name as the input AsciiDoc file.

Now in step 2, we will convert *zen.xml* — the DocBook file — to MS Word *.docx* file with Pandoc using the command shown in Example 190.

 *AsciiDoc Markup*

Example 190. Converting DocBook(XML) format to MS Word using Pandoc

```
$ pandoc -r docbook -t docx -o zen.docx zen.xml
```

Done ! You should now see *zen.docx* in your folder and you can open it in MS Word, LibreOffice Writer or Google Docs.

> *A Quick Explanation of the Pandoc Command*
>
> The `-r` and `-t` options in the Pandoc command in Example 190 are used to specify the input and output file formats, respectively. The `-r` option denotes the "reader" format, which defines the format of the input file. Conversely, the `-t` option denotes the "writer" format, which defines the format of the output file. The -o option denotes the name of the output file. The DocBook XML file that is being converted appears at the end of the command.

19.3.1. Converting From Windows

The command for Windows is absolutely identical. Just open a terminal (non-admin command prompt), move to the folder where your AsciiDoc file is located and assuming that AsciiDoctor and Pandoc have been installed on your Windows machine, issue the AsciiDoc to DocBook conversion command (Example 189) followed by the docx conversion command (Example 190) shown in Figure 136 (callouts 1 & 2) — and you will have you MS Word file.

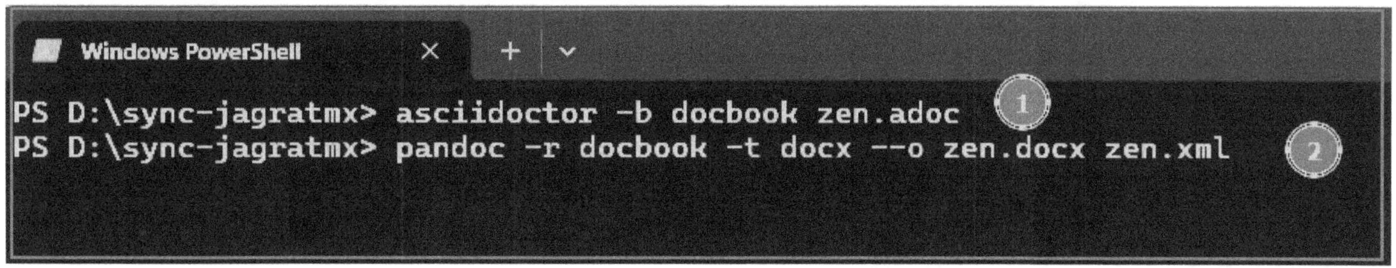

Figure 136. Converting AsciiDoc to MS Word from Windows Command

19.4. Converting from a Docker Container on Linux

If you are using the Docker AsciiDoctor container, Pandoc is *not* part of that image. What this means is that while you can use AsciiDoctor from inside the Docker container to convert your AsciiDoc file to the DocBook format, you cannot use Pandoc from the Podman (or Docker) container prompt. So first you need to install Pandoc on your computer as mentioned above and then follow the sequence given below:

1) From inside the docker image, convert your AsciiDoc file to a DocBook file using the command shown in Example 191.

Example 191. Using AsciiDoctor from inside the AsciiDoctor Docker image to convert AsciiDoc to DocBook

```
58cf050055f6:/documents# asciidoctor -b docbook zen.adoc
```

The *58cf050055f6:/documents#* above is the Docker image prompt. The command itself starts with *AsciiDoctor*. Once AsciiDoctor is finished, you should now see an *zen.xml* file created in the folder.

2) Now *exit* the docker container by typing *exit* at the command prompt as shown below:

```
58cf050055f6:/documents# exit
```

Once you have exited the container and assuming you have already installed Pandoc, issue the following command as previously demonstrated:

Terminal Command

```
$ pandoc -r docbook -t docx -o zen.docx zen.xml
```

This should create a word document that you can open in word , LibreOffice and Google Docs.

So in summary, the commands are identical — just that the conversion of the AsciiDoc file to DocBook format happens *inside* the container and the conversion of the DocBook File to the MS Word *docx* files happens *outside* the container in your regular terminal assuming that you have installed Pandoc on your machine.

19.5. AsciiDoc to MS Word or MS Word to AsciiDoc Using Pandoc Docker Image

Earlier I had suggested that you can install *Pandoc* on you machine as it is a pretty useful software. However if you do not wish to install Pandoc and are a container fan, you can run the Pandoc commands mentioned above using the *Pandoc Core Docker image* via the Podman AsciiDoc ⇒ MS Word and Podman MS Word ⇒ to AsciiDoc commands discussed below in Section 19.5.1 and Section 19.5.2.

19.5.1. Podman AsciiDoc to MS Word

You must first use AsciiDoctor from the Docker AsciiDoctor image prompt to get the DocBook XML file as has shown in Example 191. In this example, once you get *zen.xml*, converting the DocBook XML (*zen.xml*) to MS Word *docx* (in this example *zen.docx*) can then proceed using the Docker Pandoc Image using the Podman command shown in Example 192. This is assuming that you are in the directory where your XML file—*zen.xml in this case*—is located and you have Podman already installed on your computer.

Terminal Command

Example 192. Podman command to convert DocBook(XML) to MS Word using the Docker Pandoc container image

```
$sudo podman run --rm --volume "$PWD:/data" --user `id -u`:`id -g` pandoc/core
zen.xml -f docbook -t docx -o zen.docx
```

19.5.2. MS Word to AsciiDoc

As mentioned earlier, Pandoc recognizes MS Word as a valid input format and AsciiDoc as a valid output format. So running the Podman command shown is Example 193 will convert a MS Word file (*zen.docx in this example*) to AsciiDoc (*zen.adoc in this example*):

Terminal Command

Example 193. Podman command to convert MS Word file to AsciiDoc using the Docker Pandoc container image

```
$ podman run --rm --volume "$PWD:/data" --user `id -u`:`id -g` pandoc/core zen.docx
-f docx -t asciidoc --wrap=none --markdown-headings=atx --extract-media=media -o
zen.adoc
```

Please note that the above command is a *single unbroken line*—you can just copy and paste in a terminal window. You can also see Appendix C(Section C.3) for running via Podman Desktop.

Docker Users

If you use Docker instead of Podman, just replace the word 'podman' with 'docker' in the command shown in Example 193.

I prefer installing Pandoc and running Pandoc in the normal mode (i.e. not as a container) for reasons of simplicity. Pandoc is a pretty handy software to have on your computer anyway!

19.6. Dealing with Possible Pandoc Generated Errors

Figure 137 shows an error that I encountered in one of my files while running the Pandoc command to convert a DocBook file to MS Word file.

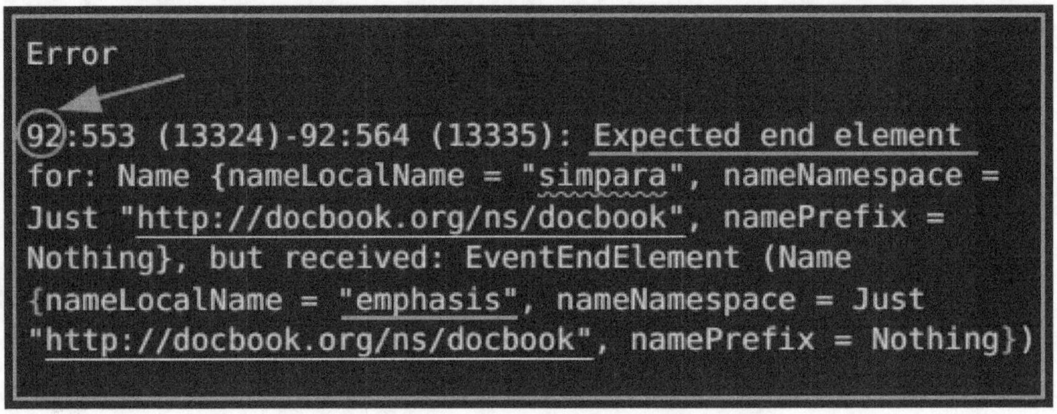

```
Error

92:553 (13324)-92:564 (13335): Expected end element
for: Name {nameLocalName = "simpara", nameNamespace =
Just "http://docbook.org/ns/docbook", namePrefix =
Nothing}, but received: EventEndElement (Name
{nameLocalName = "emphasis", nameNamespace = Just
"http://docbook.org/ns/docbook", namePrefix = Nothing})
```

Figure 137. Pandoc Error Message

As can be seen in Figure 137, Pandoc has pointed out the line number in my input AsciiDoc file to which it is objecting i.e. line 92. We can open the XML file in a text editor and examine line 92 to spot and fix the issue seen in Figure 138.

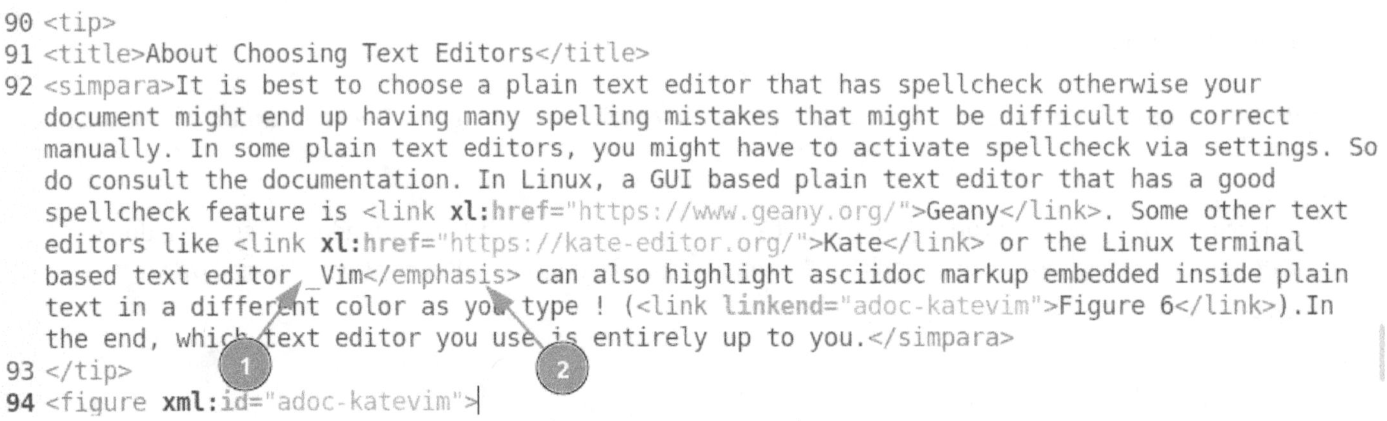

```
90 <tip>
91 <title>About Choosing Text Editors</title>
92 <simpara>It is best to choose a plain text editor that has spellcheck otherwise your
   document might end up having many spelling mistakes that might be difficult to correct
   manually. In some plain text editors, you might have to activate spellcheck via settings. So
   do consult the documentation. In Linux, a GUI based plain text editor that has a good
   spellcheck feature is <link xl:href="https://www.geany.org/">Geany</link>. Some other text
   editors like <link xl:href="https://kate-editor.org/">Kate</link> or the Linux terminal
   based text editor _Vim</emphasis> can also highlight asciidoc markup embedded inside plain
   text in a different color as you type ! (<link linkend="adoc-katevim">Figure 6</link>).In
   the end, which text editor you use is entirely up to you.</simpara>
93 </tip>
94 <figure xml:id="adoc-katevim">
```

Figure 138. Missing Opening Tag for Emphasis

A closer look at line 92 reveals the problem. We can see in the above figure that at callout (2), while there is a closing `</emphasis>` tag, there is no opening `<emphasis>` tag at callout (1) to emphasize the word *'Vim'*. This must have happened when AsciiDoctor converted the AsciiDoc file *zen.adoc* to DocBook XML format, possibly due to some oddity in the AsciiDoc file that AsciiDoctor could not resolve correctly. So the solution is to just insert an opening *emphasis* tag as shown in Figure 139.

```
<tip>
<title>About Choosing Text Editors</title>
<simpara>It is best to choose a plain text editor that has spellcheck otherwise your document might end up having many spelling mistakes that might be difficult to correct manually. In some plain text editors, you might have to activate spellcheck via settings. So do consult the documentation. In Linux, a GUI based plain text editor that has a good spellcheck feature is <link xl:href="https://www.geany.org/">Geany</link>. Some other text editors like <link xl:href="https://kate-editor.org/">Kate</link> or the Linux terminal based text editor <emphasis>Vim</emphasis> can also highlight asciidoc markup embedded inside plain text in a different color as you type ! (<link linkend="adoc-katevim">Figure 6</link>).In the end, which text editor you use is entirely up to you.</simpara>
</tip>
<figure xml:id="adoc-katevim">
```

Figure 139. Adding the opening tag for emphasis

If there were other similar errors listed in Figure 137, we would need to locate and fix them as well.

Once the corrections have been made, we can save the file and re-run the command shown in Example 190 to convert XML to docx and the command should execute without any error.

In summary, if you get such an error (which usually triggers more errors in other lines under it), it is likely caused by some missing tag. Deal with the first error, save and run and the other errors might just vanish away because they were being triggered by the first error. If you still get an error message, examine and rectify it as described above and try to run the Pandoc conversion command again.

19.7. Converting Word Documents to AsciiDoc

The requirement to convert Word documents to AsciiDoc could materialize under the following two situations:

1. You would like to *migrate* to AsciiDoc and would like to convert some of your existing MS Word documents to AsciiDoc.
2. You created something in MS Word (or LibreOffice or Google Docs) but would like to continue that work in AsciiDoc.

Thankfully, this is much simpler to do as we already know that Pandoc recognizes AsciiDoc as a valid output format and can directly convert any MS Word file to AsciiDoc. Let's say we have an example MS Word file called *zen.docx* the contents of which are shown in Figure 140.

Zen and the Art of Storytelling

Dr. Chinmaya S Rathore

Zen parables are short stories or anecdotes used in Zen Buddhism to illustrate spiritual principles and provoke deeper understanding. These parables often feature simple, everyday situations and characters, but contain profound lessons about the nature of reality, the self, and the **path to enlightenment**.

Key characteristics of Zen parables

Through the use of Zen parables, the tradition seeks to point students toward the direct realization of their own *Buddha-nature* - the inherent enlightenment that is the true nature of all beings. Some key characteristics are as follows:

- Paradoxical or illogical statements that challenge conventional thinking
- Use of humor, absurdity, or unexpected twists to jar the listener out of habitual patterns of thought
- Emphasis on direct experience over abstract concepts or *intellectual analysis*
- Focus on themes like non-duality, impermanence, and the limitations of language and logic

Some Famous Examples

Well-known examples of Zen parables include "The Sound of One Hand Clapping", "The Zen Master and the Persistent Student", and "Catching the Catfish with Bare Hands". These stories are meant to be *meditated upon* and experienced directly, rather than simply understood intellectually. The goal is to cultivate a state of openness, presence, and insight that transcends the dualistic thinking of the everyday mind.

For more information, see this Wikipedia page : https://en.wikipedia.org/wiki/Zen

Figure 140. A Word File for Conversion to AsciiDoc

To convert this Word file (*zen.docx*) to AsciiDoc, all we have to do is to type the Pandoc command shown in Example 194 from our terminal.

Example 194. Word to AsciiDoc direct conversion using Pandoc

```
$ pandoc zen.docx -f docx -t asciidoc --wrap=none --markdown-headings=atx --extract
-media=media -o zen.adoc
```

Explanation of the above Command

In the above command, we have used some flags which are described below:

- `--wrap=none` means that there will be no word wrapping even if the original word document has it. This is not needed in AsciiDoc anyway however if you wish to retain it , you can use `wrap=preserve` which retains word wrapping.
- `markdown-headings=atx` refers to *atx style* heading conversion i.e. headings of different levels in the word file will be represented as `= or == or ===` in the converted AsciiDoc document. This is opposed to the other option `setext` headings which are represented by underlining headings by `========` or `---------` line under the heading text.
- `--extract-media=media` indicates where the images extracted from the word file will be placed — in this case inside a new folder called *media* which will be created in the current folder, if not present.

Done ! You will now have an *adoc* file with the same name in your current folder — in this case *zen.adoc*. The contents of the converted *zen.adoc* file are shown in Figure 141.

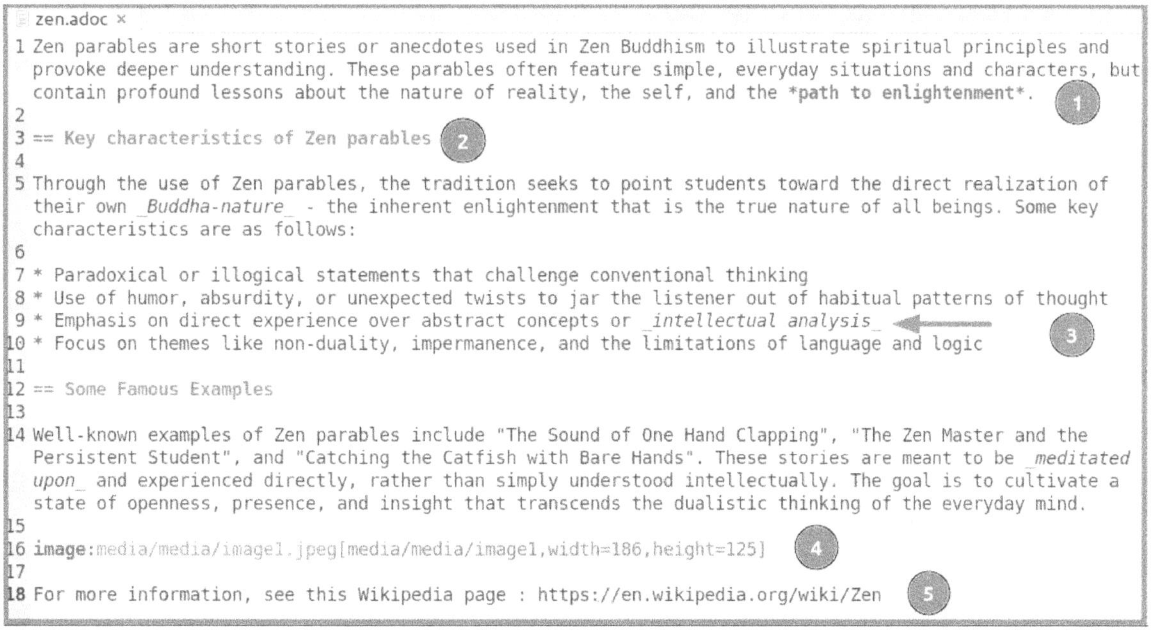

```
zen.adoc ×
Zen parables are short stories or anecdotes used in Zen Buddhism to illustrate spiritual principles and provoke deeper understanding. These parables often feature simple, everyday situations and characters, but contain profound lessons about the nature of reality, the self, and the *path to enlightenment*. (1)

== Key characteristics of Zen parables (2)

Through the use of Zen parables, the tradition seeks to point students toward the direct realization of their own _Buddha-nature_ - the inherent enlightenment that is the true nature of all beings. Some key characteristics are as follows:

* Paradoxical or illogical statements that challenge conventional thinking
* Use of humor, absurdity, or unexpected twists to jar the listener out of habitual patterns of thought
* Emphasis on direct experience over abstract concepts or _intellectual analysis_ (3)
* Focus on themes like non-duality, impermanence, and the limitations of language and logic

== Some Famous Examples

Well-known examples of Zen parables include "The Sound of One Hand Clapping", "The Zen Master and the Persistent Student", and "Catching the Catfish with Bare Hands". These stories are meant to be _meditated upon_ and experienced directly, rather than simply understood intellectually. The goal is to cultivate a state of openness, presence, and insight that transcends the dualistic thinking of the everyday mind.

image:media/media/image1.jpeg[media/media/image1,width=186,height=125] (4)

For more information, see this Wikipedia page : https://en.wikipedia.org/wiki/Zen (5)
```

Figure 141. AsciiDoc File created by Pandoc from a MS Word File

19.8. Evaluating Conversion Accuracy from MS Word to AsciiDoc

When we compare the converted AsciiDoc file in Figure 141 with the original word file shown in Figure 140, it can be seen that Pandoc has nailed the conversion getting most of the things right. The red callouts in Figure 141 explain some key document markup elements that have been translated into AsciiDoc. The numbers below refer to each numbered callout in Figure 141.

1. Bold text highlighted in orange, has the correct AsciiDoc markup for bold text as observed in `*path to enlightenment*`.
2. Level 1 headings have been correctly translated with the == markup.
3. Unordered list has been correctly marked with the * character for each bullet point. Also italics have been correctly identified and marked with the _(underscore) character.
4. The image has also been tagged correctly and placed inside the extracted-media/media folder. However the conversion has been done for an inline image and we can just add a semicolon here to make it `image::image1.jpeg` to restore it to a block image.
5. The link has been brought in intact. Furthermore, even if some text was hyperlinked to a URL rather than a direct URL as shown here, that will also be correctly translated by Pandoc (I have separately tested this on Pandoc 3.6.2 and it works).

However, it must be understood that file conversions cannot be 100% accurate and file conversions can and will always have issues. For example, in Figure 141, the level zero heading — `Zen and the art of Story Telling`-- is missing and so we will have to insert markup to correctly reflect that. Also we might need to manually add, in the header, any specific attributes that we would like to make available in the document. We might also simplify the image markup (resulting from conversion) if we wanted to.

☞ *So one important point to remember is that after we get the converted AsciiDoc file from Pandoc, it is highly recommended that you browse the converted file and manually correct any AsciiDoc markup issues that you can spot.*

Points to remember While Converting Word Files to AsciiDoc

While MS Word to AsciiDoc conversions by Pandoc are good, results can vary depending on what is inside the word file. It is important to understand that Pandoc *may not be able convert* everything inside a word document. So it is recommended that before proceeding with this conversion, the word document be simplified retaining only those elements that you reasonably expect to see in the AsciiDoc File. Please refer to the AsciiDoctor Documentation [https://docs.asciidoctor.org/asciidoctor/latest/migrate/ms-word/] if you need more information on Word to AsciiDoc Conversions.

19.9. Pandoc on Linux on 32 Bit Machines

The above mentioned AsciiDoctor and Pandoc commands can be run on 32 bit Linux distros. I have tested this on an MX Linux 23.5 32 bit Xfce Install and I was very easily able to convert DocBook XML files created using AsciiDoctor to MS Word docx (and from docx to AsciiDoc), using the exact same Pandoc commands described in the sections above. Pandoc 2.17 is available (at the time of writing) from the enabled repos on MX Linux Software Installer as shown in Figure 142.It should also be similarly available on other 32 bit Linux distros.

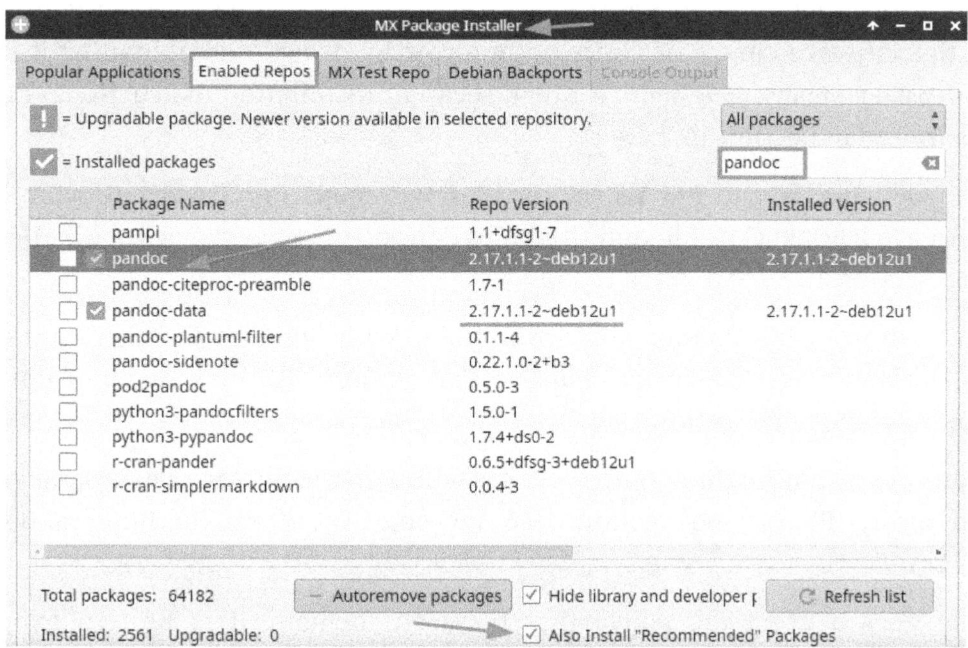

Figure 142. MX Package installer on MX Linux 32 bit Xfce 23.5 showing availability of Pandoc

In conclusion, you can use AsciiDoctor and Pandoc to convert between AsciiDoc and MS Word and vice versa with ease. Pandoc can accurately convert in both directions but if you are converting MS Word to AsciiDoc, it might be best if you simplify your word document to retain what you need in terms of formatting *before* performing the conversion.

Pandoc is a great software to have on your computer as it can perform all kinds of document conversions. It's free, it's open source and it's the Swiss army knife of document conversion. If you are interested to explore some other document conversion options that Pandoc can offer, you can checkout the demos page [https://pandoc.org/demos.html] on the Pandoc website.

Converted Documents Can Have Errors

Remember, conversions are usually never perfect. While Pandoc does a great job converting between formats, it is best to always examine converted documents and make any manual corrections in case something did not work. This may involve checking the formatting, headings, lists, images, links and other elements in the converted document and fixing any broken AsciiDoc markup.

19.10. Chapter Summary

Key learnings in this chapter are:

- You can convert AsciiDoc documents to MS Word Documents and Vice Versa quite easily.
- For conversions, we need an external free and open source software called Pandoc which can be installed via the software centre of your computer or by directly downloading it from the Pandoc website [https://pandoc.org/installing.html]. A quick recap of installation instructions for your operating system can be found in Section 19.2.1.
- The conversion of AsciiDoc to MS Word involves two steps (a) Use AsciiDoctor to convert your AsciiDoc file to a DocBook XML file and (b) using Pandoc to convert DocBook XML file to MS Word file. Please see Section 19.3 for a quick recap.
- If you do not wish to install Pandoc and are familiar with Podman / Docker, you can also use the Pandoc Core Docker Image to perform PanDoc Conversions. A quick recap of how to use Pandoc Docker image is available in Section 19.4.
- Some common errors that might pop up working with Pandoc during conversions can be examined and rectified easily. Please see Section 19.6 for some pointers on how to deal with typical conversion errors.
- While Pandoc does a great job converting between formats, it is best to examine converted documents and make any manual corrections in case something did not work. It is best to simplify MS Word files in terms of formatting before converting to AsciiDoc using Pandoc. Please see Section 19.8 for some pointers.

19.11. Try it Yourself

1. Navigate to the example file folder for this chapter — *conversions* — and open the *zen.adoc* file. Browse this file and make note of the AsciiDoc Markup in this file. We will convert this file to MS Word format.
2. Run AsciiDoctor on the *zen.adoc* file to convert it to DocBook or XML format using the terminal command — `asciidoctor -b docbook zen.adoc` — discussed earlier. This should result in *zen.xml* file in your current folder.
3. Use Pandoc to convert the XML file created in step 2 to MS Word using the Pandoc command — `$ pandoc -r docbook -t docx -o zen.docx zen.xml` — explained earlier. You should now see an MS

Word file *zen.docx* in your current folder.

4. If you are running Pandoc via a docker image, follow the discussion in Section 19.4 to accomplish steps 2 and 3 above.
5. Now to convert a Word file to AsciiDoc. The example folder for this chapter has a sample MS Word file *zenstory.docx* or you can use any MS Word file that you might have on your computer. Convert the MS Word file directly to AsciiDoc following the discussion in Section 19.7 and using the Pandoc command discussed in Section 19.7.
6. Open and examine the converted AsciiDoc file and analyze the accuracy of conversion and spot and correct any conversion issues.

Chapter 20. Book Writing in AsciiDoc

"There's nothing like a printed book; the weight, the woody scent, the feel, the look." ~ E.A. Bucchianeri

This final chapter is devoted to highlighting some important considerations that need to be taken into account when embarking on a book writing project, particularly one that aims at producing a printed book. Unlike content that will be read on a screen, a printed book requires you to define a page or trim size, outer and inner margins, a gutter margin in the center such that the book can be bound properly, headers, footers, mirrored facing pages, just to name a few. Being aware of these requirements and how to address them at the start of your project can save a ton of time and frustration when you want to create a print ready copy of your book. While AsciiDoc is not a book publishing software, it has a number of features that can help create a print ready copy of your book with ease and elegance. While this chapter specifically addresses issues related to book writing and printed books, it also has some important tips that are generally very helpful in working with large documents.

20.1. Citing Figures, Tables , Examples and Sections

20.1.1. The Problem

When you are writing a book, it is most likely that you have a separate AsciiDoc file for every chapter. Once you are done writing, you would then compile the book using a *master* AsciiDoc file that has an include statement for every chapter as discussed in Chapter 17. When you are writing your individual chapters though, numbering of figures, tables, examples and sections starts afresh from 1 in each chapter file — figure 1, table 1, example 1 and so on. However when you compile the book bringing all chapters together, figures get sequentially numbered in context of *the entire book*. So a figure in chapter 2, seen individually, might be numbered figure 2 (with the first figure in the chapter numbered figure 1), but it's number changes to say figure 4 when compiled or rendered into a single PDF combined with chapter 1. Now a problem arises due to a mismatch between figure numbers and how they have been cited in the text. So for example, while writing chapter 2, you made a reference to a figure in the text as *figure 2*, you notice that in the combined PDF, the figure number, preceded by figures from chapter 1, has now been numbered in sequence as *figure 4* even though the text continues to refer to it as *figure 2* (your typed words don't change!) . This situation is conceptually illustrated in Figure 143 with the arrow showing text referring to a wrong figure number after rendering all chapters in a single file.

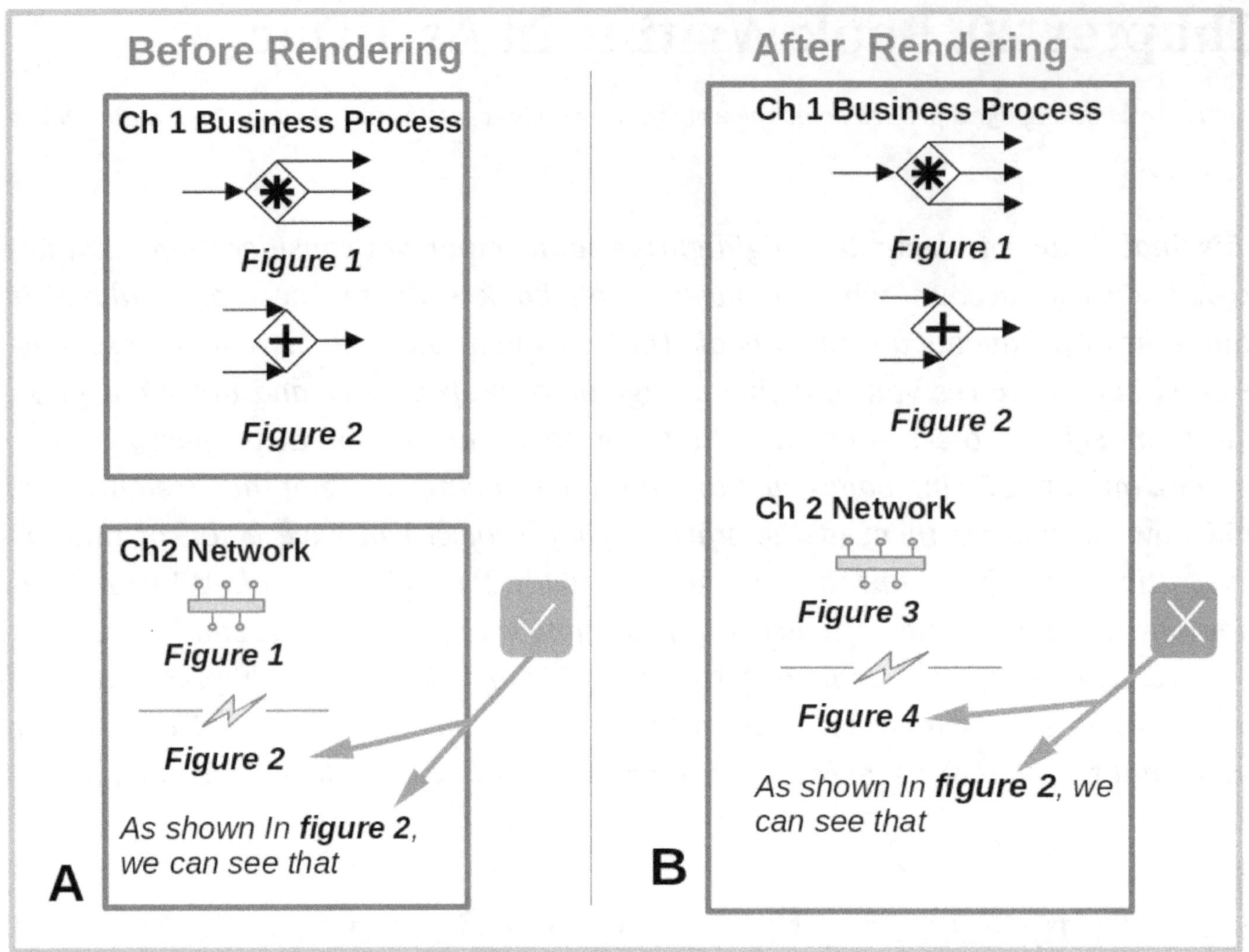

Figure 143. Citing figures (a) figure numbers inside each chapter individually (b) changed figure numbers but same text citation when chapters are brought together and rendered in a single file

As it is not practically possible to guess before hand or keep track of the actual figure, section, example or table number when the book will be rendered into a single file, the question is how do we cite these figures, sections, examples or tables in our running text when we are writing individual chapters? Referring to Figure 143 again, when I am writing chapter 2, a practical problem that I face is how to refer to figure 2 in the text of that chapter — as figure 2 or as figure 4 ? And say later on if I add a few more figures to chapter 1, however I cite this figure in chapter 2 will automatically stand in error as this figure will get a still different number when all chapters are compiled.

Well as it happens, AsciiDoc has a *brilliant* solution for this problem that involves zero number tracking on your part and which guarantees that the citation that you put in text for a figure will always match the actual figure number after compilation. Even when figures, examples, tables and sections are added or deleted or moved, the citations in the text will always be correct. Knowing and using this solution as you start your book or large document project can save you days of mind numbing work later on. In fact, I would go on to say that this might be the *single most valuable practical tip for book writers* that solves a really critical problem.

20.1.2. The Solution

The following steps solve this problem:

1. Add an attribute called `:xrefstyle: short` to the document header. Also add the `:sectnums:` attribute to the header if you wish to refer to section numbers in your running text.
2. Whenever you add a figure, section, table or example, add a *unique anchor* (think bookmark) in the format `[#ch1fig1]` — i.e. hash followed by some unique text — right on top of the figure title (without any blank line). Similarly, you can add an anchor right above any section heading, example title or table title.
3. Now whenever you want to refer to this figure in the running text, just insert `<<#ch1fig1>>` and this will be replaced in rendered text as 'Figure 1' (or whatever is the correct figure number). The same stands true for examples, sections and tables. Never type — 'Figure 1. , 'Table 2', 'Section 1.2.2' or 'Example 1' — instead just use the *anchor* (or bookmark if you prefer to call it that)!

Example 195 shows how to *anchor* and *cite* figures & sections using a sample AsciiDoc file.

AsciiDoc Markup

Example 195. Example AsciiDoc Markup showing anchors for figures and sections

```
= Programming for Beginners
:author: Prof. Chinmaya S Rathore
:xrefstyle: short  ①
:sectnums:         ②

[#ch1sec1]         ③
== Programming is Fun
Programming is fun because you create from scratch and see your ideas come to
life.<<#ch1fig1>> is a loud proclamation to that fact !

[#ch1fig1]         ④
.Programming is Fun
image::progisfun.png[]

[#ch1sec2]         ⑤
== Debugging
While programming is fun (See <<#ch1sec1>>) , it may not be always easy. Fixing bugs
is a pain (<<#ch1fig2>>) but in the end, it is a rewarding experience.

[#ch1fig2]         ⑥
.All those bugs that I let loose!
image::debug.png[]
```

① Set the `:xrefstyle:` attribute to *short* in the header.

② Set the `:sectnums:` attribute in the header for section numbering.

③ Anchor `[#ch1sec1]` on top of section 1 heading and then refer to it in text using `<<#ch1sec1>>`

④ Anchor `[#ch1fig1]` on top of the figure title and then refer to it in text as `<<#ch1fig1>>`

⑤ Anchor `[#ch1sec2]` on top of section 2 heading and refer to it in text as `<<#ch1sec2>>`

⑥ Anchor `[#ch1fig2]` on top of the figure title and then refer to it in text as `<<#ch1fig2>>`

You can now render your AsciiDoc document to PDF or HTML using one of the following commands from the terminal.

```
$ asciidoctor-pdf mybook.adoc
OR
$ asciidoctor mybook.adoc
```

Figure 144 shows how cited figures and sections are shown once the AsciiDoc markup shown in Example 195 is rendered by *AsciiDoctor* or *AsciiDoctor-PDF*. You don't have to worry about numbering as AsciiDoctor takes care of it automatically!

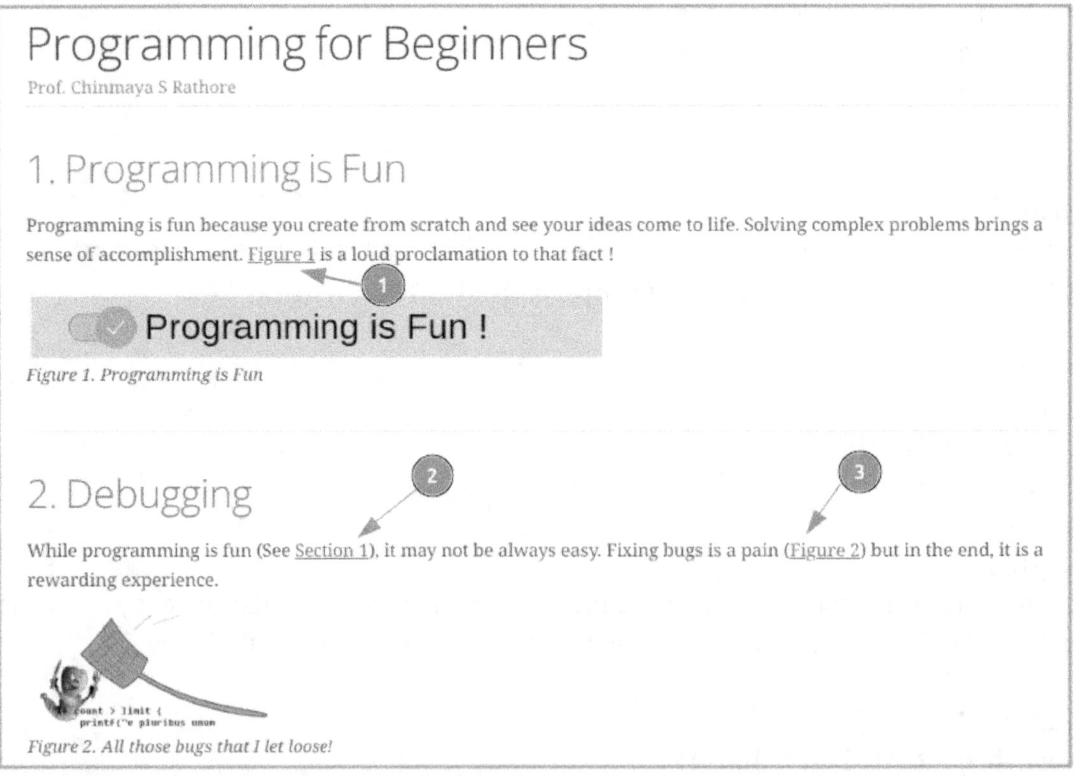

Figure 144. Rendered output showing how cited figures and sections appear in rendered output— (1), (2) and (3) highlight how anchor references in AsciiDoc file appear in output

If you keep anchoring and citing figures, tables, examples and sections in this manner as you write your individual chapters, you will always have correctly numbered references to them in your running text when you render all chapters to HTML, PDF or EPUB3. All numbering is done automatically by AsciiDoctor. You can add or delete any number of figures from anywhere in your document, but in the final compilation, numbering everywhere is guaranteed to remain in correct sequence. How cool is that!

20.2. Setting up a Page Size for your Print Copy

The page size of the book — also called *trim size* — is the actual size of the book after printing and trimming (edges cut by a paper guillotine!). Some standard trim sizes for different types of books can be seen on this informative reedsystudio page [https://reedsy.com/studio/resources/standard-book-sizes]. The default page size or trim size set in AsciiDoctor is A4 which is 210 x 297 mm or 8.27 x 11.69 inches. So how do you set a custom page size for your book once you have decided on one ? All you need to do is to include the `:pdf-page-size:` attribute in your document header and assign it width and height measurements as shown in Example 196.

Example 196. Defining the trim size of the book

```
:pdf-page-size: 8in x 10in
```

The page size above is given in *inches* but you can use other units of measurement [https://docs.asciidoctor.org/pdf-converter/latest/theme/measurement-units/] like mm or cm replacing the 'in' or inches part in the attribute value. In Example 196, the first value — *8in* — is the width (X axis of the book ☺) and the second value — *10in* is the height (the Y axis of the book). This way you can set your book page size to any dimension. Knowing this before you start work can save you a ton of time later adjusting content on pages because when page size changes, you need to readjust content accordingly!

Trim Size Guidelines on Kindle Direct Publishing

Kindle Direct Publishing (KDP) by Amazon is a popular platform for self-publishing books in print and eBook formats. When you are publishing a book on KDP, you need to set the trim size of the book as per KDP guidelines. KDP has a number of standard trim sizes that you can choose from. These include 5" x 8", 6" x 9", 7" x 10", 8.5" x 11" among others.

You can visit the Kindle Direct Publishing website Kindle Direct Publishing website [https://kdp.amazon.com/en_US/help/topic/GVBQ3CMEQW3W2VL6#trimsize] to know more about trim size and standard trim sizes for paperbacks, hardcover and eBooks.

20.3. Setting up Margins for Printed Books

For a printed book, setting up your margins correctly is very important. This is best done by extending the default AsciiDoctor-PDF theme — a topic that we have discussed in detail in Chapter 15. As explained in Chapter 15, we need to create a *yml* file (*mytheme.yml* for this example) and set up top, right, bottom and left margins as shown in Example 197.

Example 197. Defining margins in our mytheme.yml file

```
# custom theme- mytheme.yml
extends: default

page:
  margin: [1in, 1in, 1in, 1in]   ①
  margin-inner: 0.75in           ②
  margin-outer: 0.5in            ③
```

① Sets all four margins — top, right, bottom, left to 1 inch.

② Sets the inner margin to 0.75 inch. Comes into effect only when `media: prepress` attribute is included in the document header. You need to change this value as per guidelines of your book publisher.

③ Sets the outer margin to 0.5 inch. Comes into effect only when `media: prepress` attribute is included in the document header.You need to change this value as per guidelines of your book publisher.

Keep an eye on the mytheme.yml file that we have created in this example. We will expand it further in Example 3 to include headers and footers.

If you plan to distribute the PDF version of your book for on screen reading (not printed), all four margins set as shown in callout 1 (Example 197) is maybe all that you need. However if you plan to print this book on paper, statements at callouts 2 and 3 will replace the left and right margins in statement 1 (callout 1) leaving the top and bottom margins to what they have been set in the statement at callout 1 i.e 1 inch. This is because a printed book needs to be bound and we have to leave enough blank space for binding in the spine area of the book. However this gets a bit tricky when you examine a single page or leaf of the book which is printed on both sides — front and back. On the front side (called *Recto*), the inner margin (towards the spine of the book) is the *left margin*. When you face the back side of the page (called *Verso*), the inner margin (in reference to the book spine) is on the right side of the page. As the margins that meet on the spine are located differently on recto and verso sides (or pages), we need to ensure that the inner margin setting is applied to the side of the page which is meeting at the spine. Figure 145 illustrates recto and verso sides with inner and outer margins.

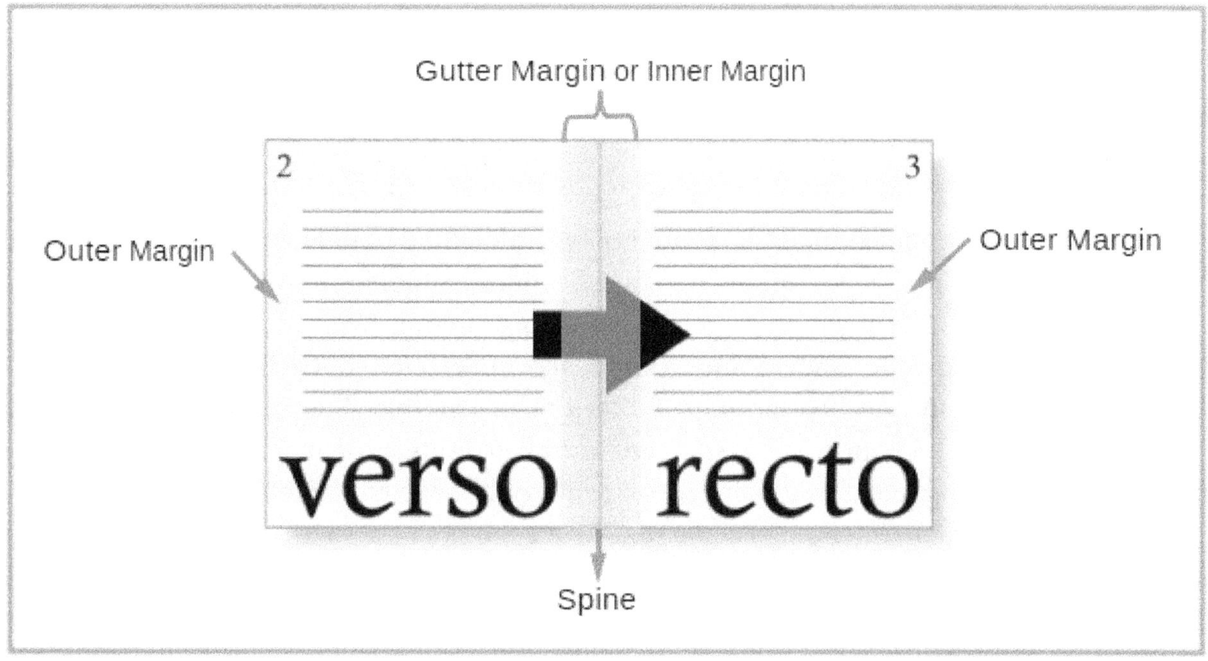

Figure 145. Facing verso and recto pages of a book (adapted from original by Tkgd2007, Wikipedia)

The area of the spine where both verso and recto inner margins meet is also called the *gutter margin* (the gray band in the center — Figure 145). How much inner margin you need for the book to be bound properly depends on the number of pages in the book and also on the thickness of paper (70 GSM paper, 80 GSM paper, 100 GSM paper etc). KDP recommendations for inner or gutter margin based on the number of book pages can be seen on this KDP page [https://kdp.amazon.com/en_US/help/topic/GVBQ3CMEQW3W2VL6]. To ensure that the inner margin is correctly applied to both verso and recto pages, AsciiDoctor automatically implements *margin mirroring*. What mirroring essentially means is that on verso pages, the inner margin value is applied to the right of the page and on recto pages it is applied to the left side of the page, provisioning a wide gutter margin at the center for proper binding. If the gutter margin is not sufficient, readers will have a hard time reading content close to the spine of the book (with some bending the book like Beckham!). Revisiting Example 197, when the `media: prepress` attribute is included in header, the recto and verso page margins *automatically operate* as conceptually illustrated in Example 198 (you don't need to set this).

Example 198. How mirror margins work for printed books in AsciiDoc

Read the margin figures inside the brackets in sequence — [Top, Right, Bottom, Left]. Notice how the inner and outer margin (think left and right) measurements — 0.75 and 0.5 — alternate or mirror on recto and verso pages, both meeting at the spine of the book which is utilized for binding.

```
recto page margin
[1in, 0.5in, 1in, 0.75in]

verso page margin
[1in, 0.75in, 1in, 0.5in]
```

20.4. Headers and Footers

If you pick up a book from your book shelf, you will notice that printed books have peculiar header and footers. Depending on the genre of the book, you might see the chapter title and the book title alternating on recto and verso pages. In some books, page numbers appear in the header area (common in technical text books) while in some other books, they appear in the footer area (common in novels). In some other books, you might not find headers or footers at all. Controlling headers and footers is therefore an important aspect of printed book production. We can insert headers and footers easily by extending our custom theme file — *mytheme.yml* discussed earlier in Example 197. Let's revert back to that file and add headers and footers to it. For this illustration, I am going to add a header that alternates the book title on verso pages and the chapter title on the recto pages of the book. The header will also show page numbers in the extreme right or extreme left of the page in the header area. If you are reading the printed or PDF version of this book — the header as it appears in the book (with no footer), has been created by adding the header and footer sections to the *mytheme.yml* file as shown in Example 199.

Example 199. Extending mytheme.yml to add headers and footers

```
# custom theme- mytheme.yml
extends: default

page:
  margin: [1in, 1in, 1in, 1in]
  margin-inner: 0.75in
  margin-outer: 0.5in

  header:
    height: $base_line_height_length * 3   ①
    margin: [0.25in]                       ②
   #border-color: #D3D3D3
   #border-width: 0.1                      ③
    recto:                                 ④
      right:
        content: '_{chapter-title}_   | *{page-number}*'
    verso: ⑤
      left:
        content: '*{page-number}* |   _{document-title}_'
  #footer:    ⑥
    #height: 15mm
    #columns: =100%
    #recto:
      #center:
        #content: '({page-number})'
    #verso:
```

```
    #center:
      #content: '({page-number})'
```

① Sets the height of the header in reference to the base font size. Multiplying with higher numbers increases the header height.

② Sets the margin of the header.

③ If you want the border of the header to be visible (like a line separator), you can set the border line width and color. Uncomment these lines (remove #).

④ Sets recto pages to display chapter title and page number on the right side

⑤ Sets verso pages to display book title and page numbers on the left side

⑥ If you want page numbers to appear in the footer center, uncomment these lines. Remove page number reference | `*{page-number}*` from header content key for both recto and verso pages.

The *indentations* in the above YML file are important and must be reproduced as shown. Also many links that have been commented in Example 199 extend header and footer styling and can be used by uncommenting them. They have been described later in the chapter.

The above *mytheme.yml* file when run with AsciiDoctor-PDF on the AsciiDoc file (see note Running a YML file with AsciiDoctor below) renders as shown in Figure 146.

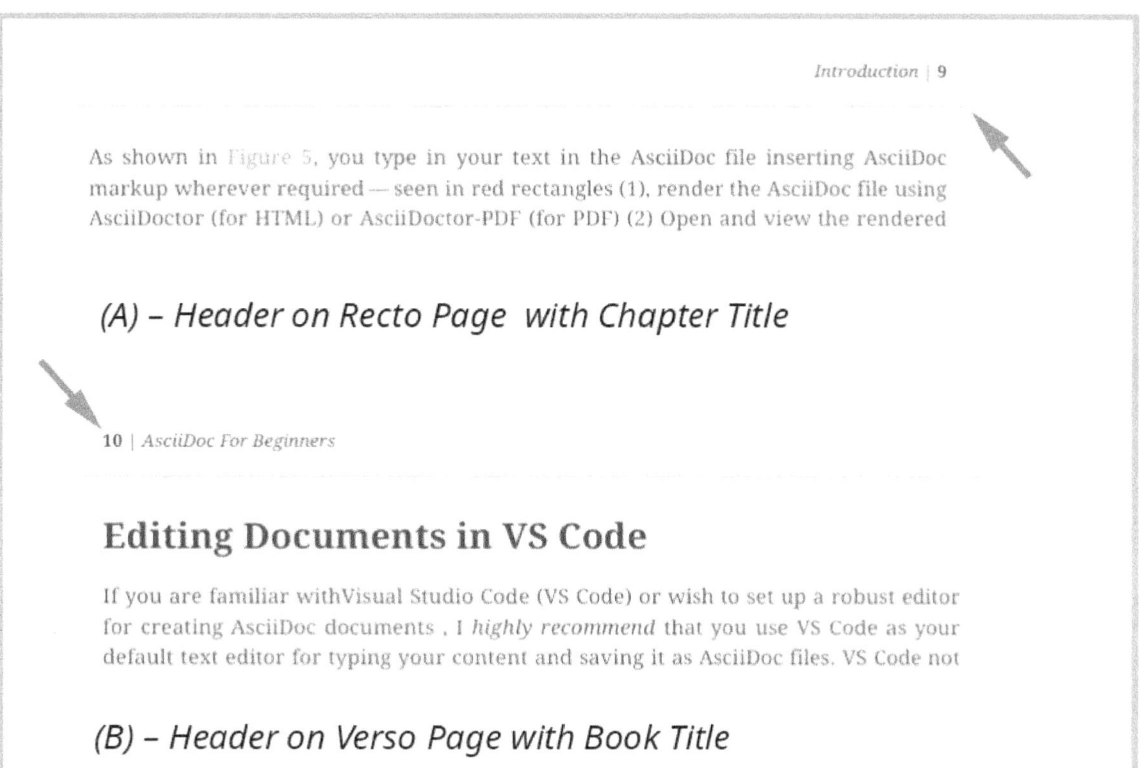

Figure 146. (a) Header as it appears on recto pages and (b) Header as it appears on verso pages

Running a YML file with AsciiDoctor

Quick Recap: To run a yml file like *mytheme.yml* while rendering your AsciiDoc document (say *introduction.adoc*), use the following command from the terminal:
$ asciidoctor-pdf --theme mytheme.yml introduction.adoc

20.4.1. Moving the Header Margin from Page Edge

In Example 199, callout 2 shows the header margin setting as follows:

```
margin: [0.25in]
```

If you set this margin as 0, the header moves closer to the top of the page i.e. where the top page margin lies. A value of 0.25in (inches) pulls the header away from the top edge. You can play with this number to get the desired header distance from the top of the page. This adjustment can be particularly useful in situations where text at the top of the page is in danger of getting chopped off when the printed book is trimmed.

20.4.2. Ensuring that Header or Footer Borders Match Text Borders

If you choose to show a header border in light gray color as shown in callout 3 of Example 199 i.e. uncomment the *border-color* and *border-width* keys, you will see a border separating the header and the body text in *light gray* color. However you will notice that the left and right edges of the border extend to the edge of the page or the page margins rather than the body text margins. To make sure that the border matches the text margin, you can set the margin key under header at callout 2 in Example 199 (*mytheme.yml* file) file as follows:

```
margin: [0, inherit]
```

If you want to move the header margin some distance away from the physical edge of the paper (to avoid paper trim), you can replace the 0 with a distance value as follows:

```
margin: [0.25in, inherit]
```

Figure 147 (a) illustrates the extended border issue and (b) the solution after setting the header margin as described above.

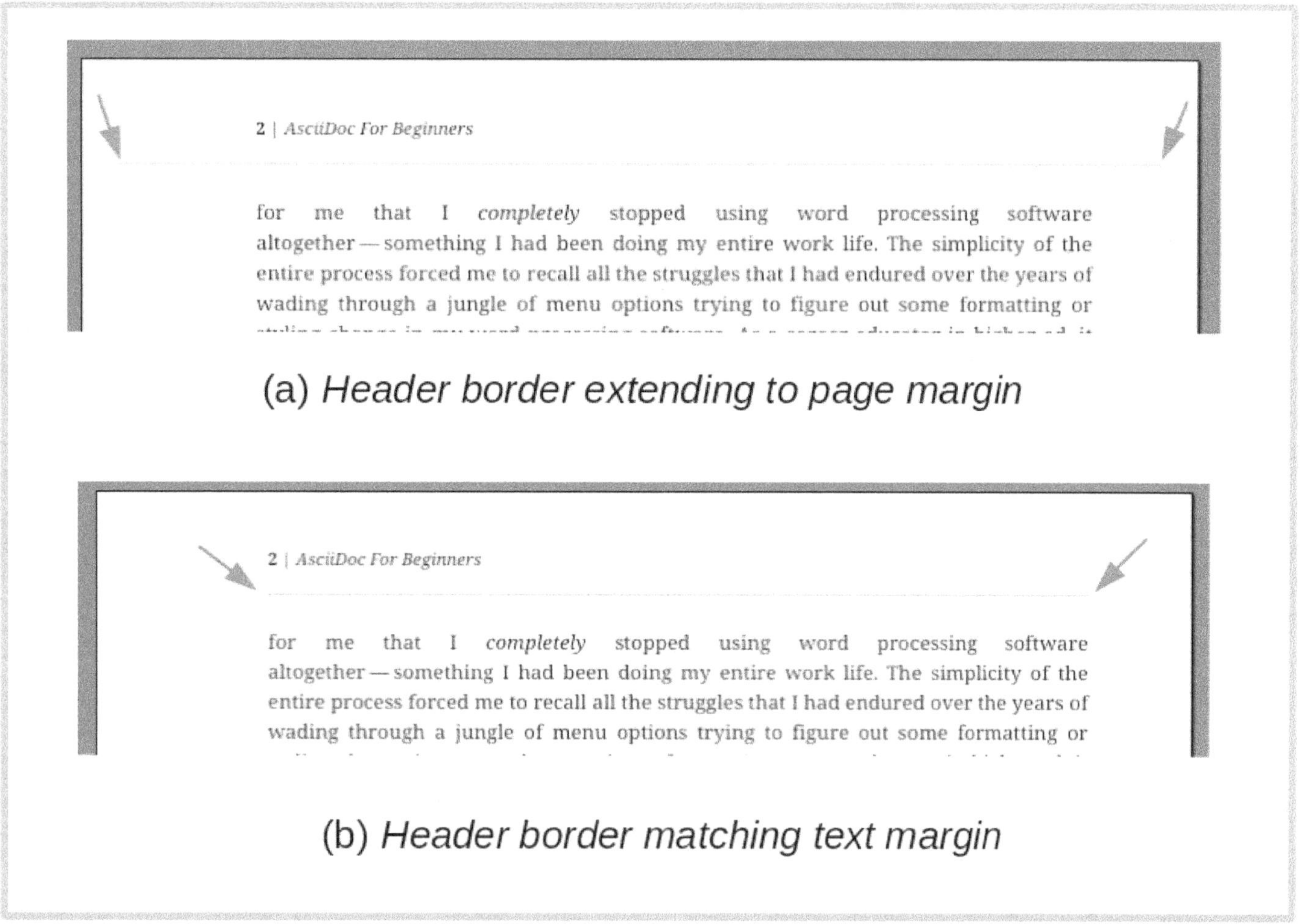

(a) *Header border extending to page margin*

(b) *Header border matching text margin*

Figure 147. Header borders (a) touching page margin (b) matching text margin after margin inherit setting

Header Border Color Values

A widely accepted border color for header border is #D3D3D3 i.e HTML *LightGray*. If you wish to make the header border a tad darker, you can try some of these HTML colors `#D0D0D0`, `#C0C0C0`, `#BEBEBE`, `#B0B0B0`, `#A9A9A9` and `#A8A8A8` — in increasing order of darkness. For a full list of HTML gray color shades, visit the W3Schools HTML color shades page [https://www.w3schools.com/colors/colors_shades.asp].

20.4.3. No Headers and Footers

If for some reason, you do not want the header or footer to appear in your document, place the `:noheader:` or `:nofooter:` attribute in the header of your *AsciiDoc* document. This will make sure that the header or footer will not appear in the book.

20.5. Screen, Print and Prepress Modes

When you are rendering your document, say a book in PDF, you can include the `:media:` attribute and set its value to either *screen, print,* or *prepress.* Each of these renders the PDF in a different way. Let's have a quick look at the *screen, print,* and *prepress* modes.

20.5.1. Screen

Screen is the default *media* mode in AsciiDoctor. When you render a PDF with `:media: screen` set in your document header (or even exclude it entirely from the header), the PDF is, by default, rendered for screen viewing. All links and cross references in your document work — i.e. you can jump to an external or internal link clicking on the link as can be seen in Figure 148. If you have included an index in the book, the page numbers in front of index entries are also hyperlinked and clicking on them takes you directly to that page as shown in Figure 149.

In summary, AsciiDoc is super easy to learn and once you get the big picture of the AsciiDoc document creation process, you can get going in just a few minutes and start creating beautifully formatted documents in a plain text editor of your choice.

For More Information on the need and utility of AsciiDoc, you can read this insightful page on the AsciiDoctor website.

External Link

How does AsciiDoc Document Creation Work ?

Internal Link

Lets now have a quick overview of how the AsciiDoc based document creation process works. Figure 3 presents a summary of the simple three step process involved in document creation using AsciiDoc and AsciiDoctor.

Figure 148. Live external and internal links in screen mode

T

Text Editors

Geany, 9

Kate, 9

Live Preview, 10

Vim, 9

Visual Studio Code, 10

Click here to reach page

V

VS Code, 10

Figure 149. Index page numbers are hyperlinked to pages

20.5.2. Print

When the *media* attribute is set to `:media: print`, the print mode gets activated. In this mode, it is assumed that the content will be read *offline*, in hard copy. As readers cannot click on a hyperlink on printed page, the print mode displays full *URLs* in brackets (Figure 150) next to the hyperlinked text such that readers can type the URL in their web browsers if they wish to access that resource. The hyperlink itself is not deactivated permitting online reading of the text as well. The index page links which were active in the screen mode (Figure 149) are deactivated in the print mode for the same reason and if an index term appears on successive pages, it is shown as a page range like 2-4 rather than as individual pages in the format — 2,3,4.

In summary, AsciiDoc is super easy to learn and once you get the big picture of the AsciiDoc document creation process, you can get going in just a few minutes and start creating beautifully formatted documents in a plain text editor of your choice.

For More Information on the need and utility of AsciiDoc, you can read this insightful page [https://AsciiDoctor.org/docs/what-is-AsciiDoc/] on the AsciiDoctor website.

How does AsciiDoc Document Creation Work ?

Lets now have a quick overview of how the AsciiDoc based document creation process works. Figure 3 presents a summary of the simple three step process involved in

Figure 150. Print mode — URL being displayed in front of external links which remain active

20.5.3. Prepress

The `prepress` mode — `:media: prepress` — further fine tunes the PDF for publishing. It takes the print mode forward and makes the PDF compatible for printing. In addition to what the print mode does, it introduces the following two behaviors in the generated PDF:

1. Page Mirroring (already discussed in Section 20.3)
2. Automatic Facing Pages

The Automatic facing pages feature ensures that the title page, table of contents, the first page of your book text and chapters (and also parts if your book if it has been segmented into parts) — all start on the *recto or right page*. The `prepress` attribute does this by inserting a *blank page* wherever required. Figure 151 shows key differences between *print* and *prepress* modes and how mirroring and automatic facing pages manifest in the output rendered in the *prepress* mode.

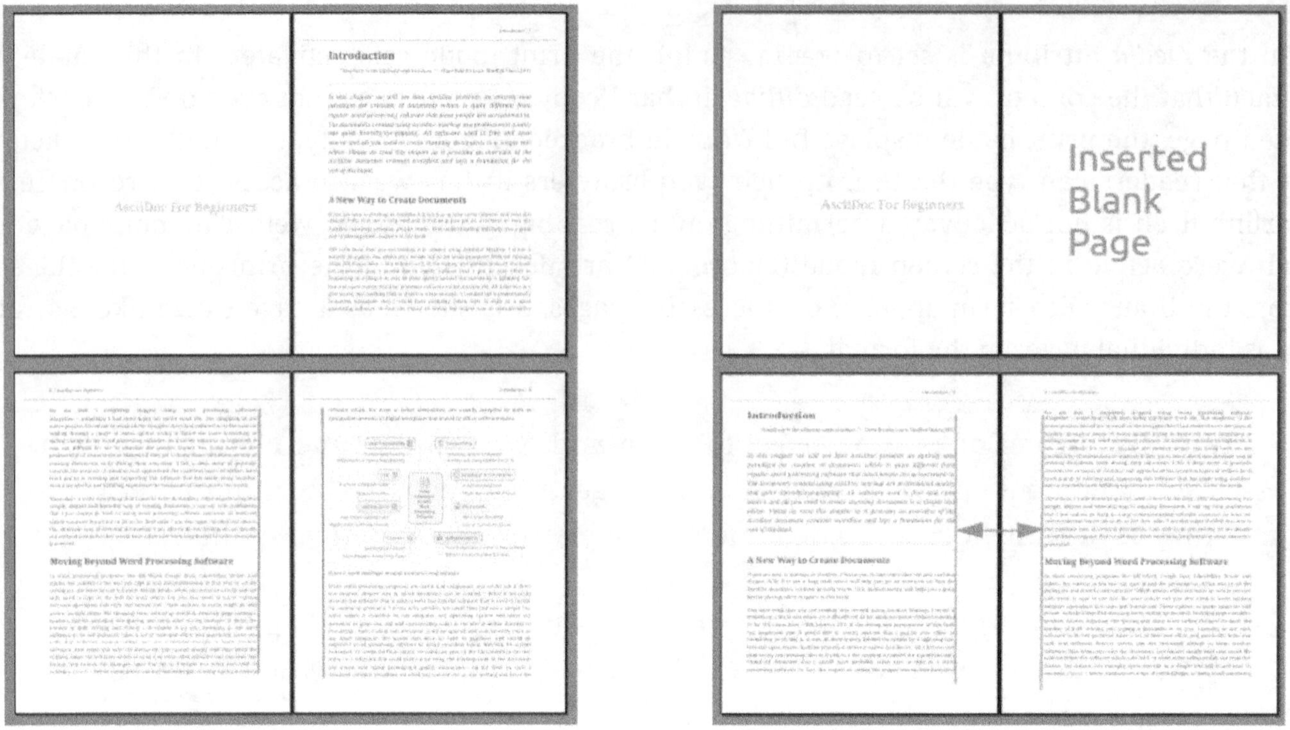

Figure 151. Print and prepress with extended theme (a) Print mode output with standard margins (b) Prepress mode with automatic facing pages which inserts blank pages to ensure that new content starts on recto pages and mirroring which ensures adequate binding space in the spine area.

It is important to note in Figure 151(a) that as printing will happen on both sides of a page, the first page of chapter *introduction* would normally start on the back side of the first page or the *title page*. In Figure 151(b), by inserting a blank page (which is the back side of the title page), *introduction* now starts on a right or recto page. This positioning of the first page of every chapter is much easier to locate for the reader when compared to looking for it behind another page.

So if you have set `:media: prepress` in your header, don't be surprised to see blank pages forcing chapters or sections starting on a recto page!

> *Why are Blank Pages Inserted Anyway ?*
>
> Inserting blank pages to start a new chapter on a recto page is largely an aesthetic decision that has become a mainstream tradition in book publishing. If you don't want a chapter to start from the facing recto page, use the following AsciiDoc markup just above the chapter title to disable automatic facing pages for *that chapter*.

```
[%nonfacing]
== Chapter 2 - Installation
```

In summary, if you wish to create a PDF for only screen viewing, you can ignore the media attribute or use `:media: screen`. If you plan for a hybrid viewing scenario i.e. both online and offline, you can explore `:media: print`. However if you wish to create a *print ready* copy meant exclusively for reading as a printed book, use `:media: prepress`.

You need to set the *doctype* attribute to *book* i.e. `:doctype: book` for the *print* and *prepress* modes to work.

20.6. Asciidoc PDF Theme for Darker Font Color for Printing

When we opt to print our book in Black & White (as opposed to the very expensive colored option), the default AsciiDoctor-PDF theme may not provide the sharpest gray color contrast in font color. Many heading or title styles in the default theme are also a bit light for printed output as they are optimized for online reading. To ensure the sharpest black and white output is delivered for printing, we need to use an alternate theme or extend the default theme to print everything in high contrast black and white. Luckily, the AsciiDoctor-PDF documentation suggests one theme called *default-for-print-theme.yml* which does exactly that. You can download this theme from the AsciiDoctor-PDF GitHub page [https://github.com/asciidoctor/asciidoctor-pdf/blob/main/data/themes/default-for-print-theme.yml]. Move the downloaded file in your project folder where your *master* AsciiDoc file resides. Now we need to do the following in sequence to use this file in conjugation with our *mytheme.yml* file (which is also in the same folder) to get a darker output along with all our header, footer and margin customizations:

1. Just open the *default-for-print-theme.yml* and copy lines 2 to the last and paste the contents at the bottom of the mytheme.yml file and save it. Don't copy the first line — `extends: default` — as it is already present in our *mytheme.yml* file.
2. Now just issue the following command from the terminal to render the AsciiDoc file to PDF:
   `$ asciidoctor-pdf --theme mytheme.yml master.adoc`

The rendered pdf will have much darker text and titles which are more suitable for printing and ensure a crisp and sharp reading experience.

As an alternative to the above, we can also do the following for the exact same result:

1. Add the theme attribute to your master AsciiDoc document header `:theme: default-for-print-theme.yml` and *save*.
2. Edit the *mytheme.yml* file to make just one change — replace the first line `extends : default' with `extends : default-for-print-theme.yml' and save.
3. Now use AsciiDoctor-PDF to render this file issuing the following command from the terminal :
   `$ asciidoctor-pdf --theme mytheme.yml master.adoc`

20.7. Page Numbering for Front Matter and Body Text

You might have observed that in most books, page numbering on front matter pages is in *roman numerals* while page numbering starts in *Arabic numerals* from 1 in the main body of text. By front matter, we mean all pages like preface, TOC etc. that appear before the main body of text i.e. the first page of chapter 1. To implement this in AsciiDoctor, we need to include the *page → numbering → start-at* category key sequence in our *mytheme.yml* file. For example, if we assume that the running text or main body of your book starts from page 20, we can include the following *start-at* key in our *mytheme.yml* file:

```
page:
  numbering:
    start-at: 20
```

❗ 👉 *Do not* duplicate the *page* category in the yml file. If you already have the page category for margins as shown in Example 197, just add *numbering:* and *start-at: 20* under it as shown in Example 200.

Example 200. Offset Arabic numeral page numbering

```
page:
  margin: [1in, 1in, 1in, 1in]
  margin-inner: 0.75in
  margin-outer:
  numbering:
    start-at: 20
```

This will start *Arabic* page numbering from physical page 20 (it can be any page) and assign it page number 1 and continue from there. For all pages before page 20 (i.e. pages 1-19), AsciiDoctor automatically inserts *roman* numbering. If you have set `:media: prepress`, you might get some blank page inserts as part of the *automatic facing pages* feature and would need to count them in the front matter pages. The `start_at` key, can also be to set to start numbering from the first page of toc (start-at: toc), after-toc (start-at: after-toc), and from the title page (start-at: title).

20.8. Prefixing Level 1 Headings With 'Chapter'

If the *doctype* attribute in the AsciiDoc document header is set to *book* i.e.+ `:doctype: book`+ and the attribute `:sectnums:` is also present in the header, every level 1 heading (headings starting with `== Heading`) automatically gets prefixed with the word 'Chapter' followed by the chapter number (automatically generated in sequence) as shown in Figure 152 by the arrow callout.

Chapter 1. Introduction

"Simplicity is the ultimate sophistication." ~ Clare Boothe Luce, Stuffed Shirts,1931

In this chapter we will see how AsciiDoc presents an entirely new paradigm for creation of documents which is quite different from regular word processing software that most people are accustomed to. The documents created using

Figure 152. Automatic Prefixing of chapter titles with the word 'Chapter'

If you wish to prefix the chapter title with a word other than the default 'Chapter', you will need to invoke the `:chapter-signifier:` attribute and set its value to the word you would like to prefix. For example in French, the word you might prefer could be "Chapitre" which can be specified in the *chapter signifier* attribute as shown below:

```
:chapter-signifier: Chapitre
```

The *chapter signifier* attribute has to be placed in the AsciiDoc document header. Once set, you will see the word "Chapitre" prefixed to every chapter title in your book as can be seen in Figure 153.

Chapitre 1. Introduction

"Simplicity is the ultimate sophistication." ~ Clare Boothe Luce, Stuffed Shirts,1931

In this chapter we will see how AsciiDoc presents an entirely new paradigm for creation of documents which is quite different from regular word processing

Figure 153. Chapter prefix changed by the chapter-signifier attribute

Please note that the `chapter prefix` described above, at the time of writing, does not appear in the TOC. For example, **Chapter 1. Introduction** would appear as **1.Introduction** in the TOC.

20.9. Adding Front Cover and Back Cover Images

You can create a front and back cover for your book using some graphic designing software or using book cover templates available at sites like Canva [https://www.canva.com/] and save them as PDF files. The covers can then be included in your book by placing the following attributes in the header of your AsciiDoc document:

```
:front-cover-image: front-cover.pdf
:back-cover-image: back-cover.pdf
```

The front and back cover can also be included in the extended theme file (our *mytheme.yml* file mentioned in previous sections). You can refer to the AsciiDoctor PDF cover category key page [https://docs.asciidoctor.org/pdf-converter/latest/theme/cover/] for more details on how to do this.

If you do not wish to have a title page automatically generated by AsciiDoctor (as you already have a front cover), you can place the following attribute in the header of your AsciiDoc document:

```
:notitle:
```

Please note that the above covers are useful for PDF versions of your book that will be viewed on a computer screen. For a printed paper book however, the above covers will not hold good and you will need to design a single book cover having both front and back cover and a spine of appropriate width (thickness) as discussed later in Section 20.16 — point 3.

20.10. Changing the Color of Headings for Full Color Printing or On-Screen Reading

So far we have discussed how to create a *print-ready* PDF specifically targeting books that will be printed in black and white. What if you wanted to generate a print-ready copy of your book (or other documents like lecture notes, concept briefs, articles, technical reports etc.) suited for *full color* printing ? While the PDFs that we have created so far can surely be used for creating color prints (all figures are in color), all levels of headings however appear in black color. This is something that you might want to change to utilize *color printing* to the fullest and pep up the document further with a dash of color. You can change the color of all levels of headings (i.e one color for all headings) by adding the *heading* category and *font-color* key to your *mythme.yml* file as shown in Example 201.

Example 201. The font-color key under Heading category

```
heading:
  font-color: #0288D1
```

You can replace `#0288D1` with any hex color of your choice. An expansive list of HTML colors and their hex values are available on the W3 schools website [https://www.w3schools.com/colors/colors_names.asp]. The website also provides access to handy color mixer and color picker tools that permit you to choose from hundreds of color shades.

If you want to change the colors of specific levels of headings (H1 to H6) rather than have all headings in one color, you can use a heading specific *font-color* key in *mytheme.yml* as shown in Example 202 .

Example 202. Different colors for different heading levels

```
heading:
  h1-font-color: #0288d1
  h2-font-color: #b71c1c
  h3-font-color: #009688
```

To see these changes, you will need to generate your PDF using the extended theme file — *mythme.yml*. Figure 154(a) shows the results of applying a single color to all headings while Figure 154(b) shows H1 (Level 0 or =), H2 (level 1 or ==) and H3 (level 2 or ===) in three different colors — blue, red and green respectively.

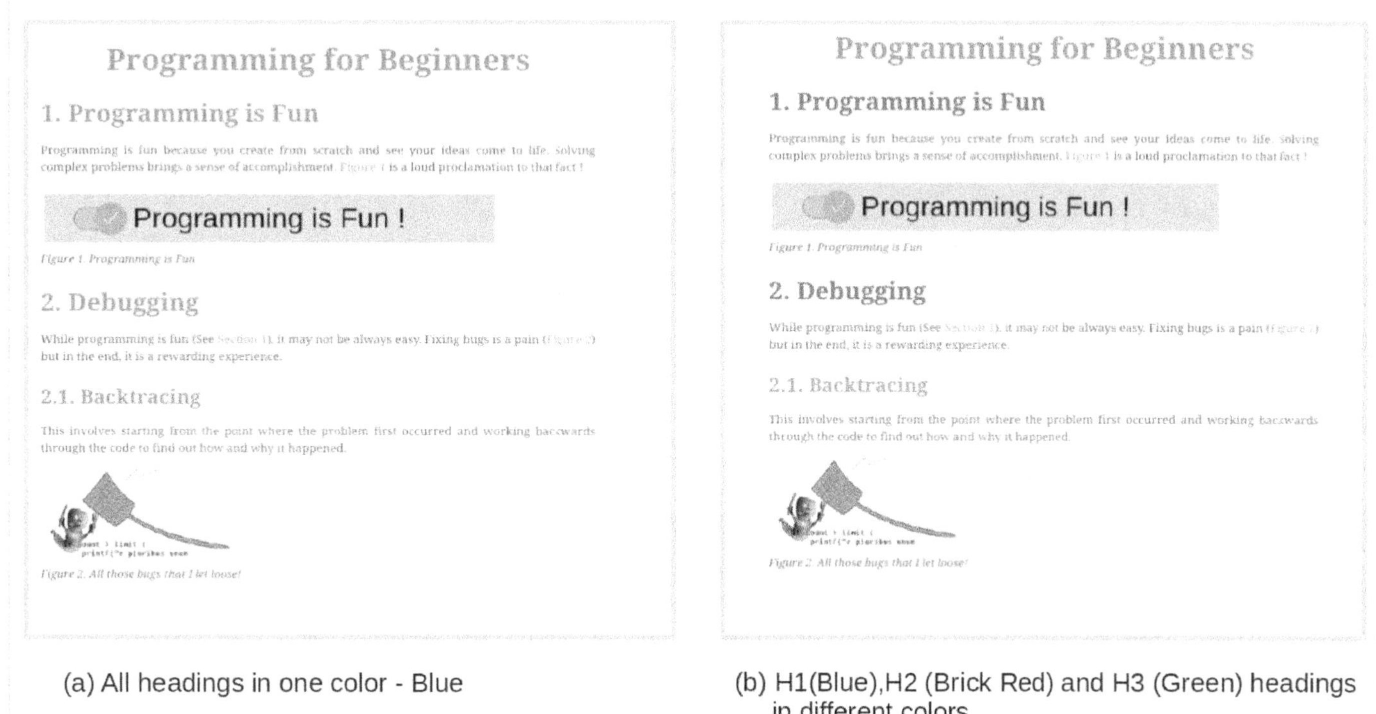

Figure 154. Headings in Color in rendered PDF output with extended theme

You can add colors for other heading levels (H4,H5,H6) as demonstrated in Example 202. If you are reading the printed version of this book, you will not see these colors but you can try this yourself on your computer.

The incorporation of vibrant colors into digital PDF headings can significantly improve the on-screen readability and overall aesthetic appeal of a document. By strategically utilizing a diverse range of colors, you can create a visually engaging and immersive experience for readers.

Apart from the hex format, colors can also be specified in the RGB format — font-color: [255, 0, 0] — or the CYMK format — font-color:[0,45%, 70%, 15%]. You can also set the background and border colors to transparent (no color). Please visit https://docs.asciidoctor.org/pdf-converter/latest/theme/color/ for more details.

20.11. Including Front Matter in the Book

Books usually start with some front matter pages like colophon, dedication, preface and acknowledgements. This is in addition to the table of contents. There is nothing special about these front matter pages in AsciiDoc i.e. they are created as any regular AsciiDoc page or file. However, AsciiDoc provides special *section styles* for these pages as detailed in the AsciiDoc documentation on Section Styles [https://docs.asciidoctor.org/asciidoc/latest/sections/section-ref/#section-styles]. Example 203 shows how you can create these pages (saved as independent AsciiDoc files) and start each one of them with their respective section styles.

Example 203. Book front matter page styling

```
// Preface page saved as - preface.adoc
[preface]
== Preface
preface text comes here

// Acknowledgements page saved as - ack.adoc
[acknowledgements]
== Acknowledgements
Acknowledgements text comes here

// Dedication page saved as - dedication.adoc
[dedication%notitle]      ①
== Dedication
dedication text comes here

//Colophon page saved as - colophon.adoc
[colophon%non-facing]     ②
colophon text comes here
```

① Dedication page should not show a title — the `%notitle` option suppresses the title.

② Colophon is usually printed on the verso side of the Title page. The `%non-facing` option permits this when the `media` attribute is set to *prepress*.

20.12. Creating an Appendix

Books usually also carry multiple appendix pages that provide supplementary information on a topic that is helpful but might not be directly needed in the running text. Appendix files are regular AsciiDoc files but carry the `[appendix]` section styling on the top as shown in Example 204.

Example 204. Appendix styling

```
[appendix]      ①
== Data Sources  ②
appendix text comes here
```

① Appendix page starts with this directive

② Appendix title

Appendices are *sequentially labelled* by AsciiDoctor if they appear in one AsciiDoc file and also when they are included via a master document as independent AsciiDoc files.

Let's see this with a small example. Example 205 shows two appendices one after the other in the same Asciidoc file (all appendices in one file scenario). Figure 155 shows how this file is rendered displaying sequentially labelled appendices by AsciiDoctor and AsciiDoctor-PDF.

Example 205. Two appendices in one AsciiDoc file

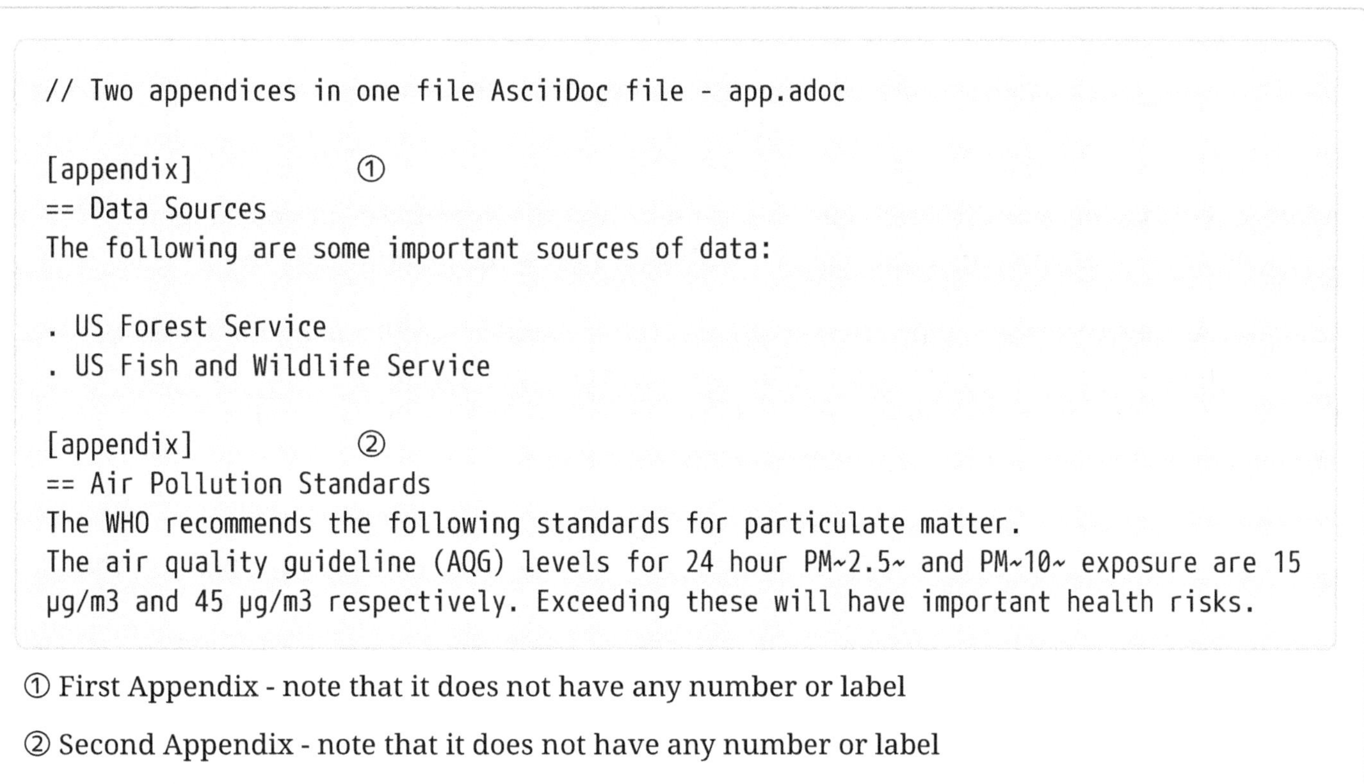

```
// Two appendices in one file AsciiDoc file - app.adoc

[appendix]          ①
== Data Sources
The following are some important sources of data:

. US Forest Service
. US Fish and Wildlife Service

[appendix]          ②
== Air Pollution Standards
The WHO recommends the following standards for particulate matter.
The air quality guideline (AQG) levels for 24 hour PM~2.5~ and PM~10~ exposure are 15
µg/m3 and 45 µg/m3 respectively. Exceeding these will have important health risks.
```

① First Appendix - note that it does not have any number or label

② Second Appendix - note that it does not have any number or label

Will be rendered as...

Appendix A: Data Sources

The following are some important sources of data:

1. US Forest Service
2. US Fish and Wildlife Service

Appendix B: Air Pollution Standards

The WHO recommends the following standards for particulate matter. The air quality guideline (AQG) levels for 24 hour $PM_{2.5}$ and PM_{10} exposure are 15 µg/m3 and 45 µg/m3 respectively. Exceeding these will have important health risks.

Figure 155. Sequential labeling of appendix

Notice that while the rendered output shows each appendix sequentially labelled, the markup in Example 205 does not have any number or label hardwired into them. It is AsciiDoctor that labels them dynamically as A, B, C, D and so on in sequence of their appearance in the document at the time of rendering. This means you can easily move and reposition the appendices in your appendix file and the appendices will be correctly relabeled by AsciiDoctor following the new sequence.

By default, AsciiDoctor labels appendices as `Appendix A-B-C` and so on prefixing the word `Appendix` to the incrementing alphabet sequence. If for some reason you want to replace the word *Appendix* by any other word like *supplement* or *note* or *exhibit*, you can do so by adding the :appendix-caption: attribute to the header of the document as shown in Example 206.

Example 206. Changing the appendix caption term

```
= My Book
:appendix-caption: Supplement
```

Referring to Figure 155 again, the *appendix-caption* attribute as shown in Example 206 will change the caption word from Appendix-A and Appendix-B to Supplement-A and Supplement-B. You can also use `:figure-caption:` , `:example-caption:` and `:table-caption:` in a similar way to change default captions for figures, examples and tables. See https://docs.asciidoctor.org/asciidoc/latest/attributes/document-attributes-ref/#builtin-attributes-i18n for more details.

20.13. Creating a Glossary of Key terms

Glossary files typically consist of a series *term-definition* pairs. In AsciiDoc, we use the `Term::` macro to define these pairs to first display a term and then follow it up with its definition. You can create a nicely styled glossary for your book using the AsciiDoc markup shown in Example 207.

AsciiDoc Markup

Example 207. Creating a glossary of terms

```
// Asciidoc file - glossary.adoc

 [glossary]
 == Glossary of Key Terms

 Term:: A ①
 Definition of term  A ②

 Term:: B
 Definition of term B

 Term:: C
 Definition of term C
```

① Replace A (and B, C) with the actual term that you wish to define — example: Python

② Replace the *definition line* for term A (and B, C) by a definition or description of that term — example: An object oriented computer programming language.

20.14. Book Parts

Many times, book chapters are organized into parts. This is particularly useful when covering large or comprehensive topics, or when there is a clear thematic organization in the text. It can also be helpful when dealing with complex or technical topics, or when presenting different perspectives or approaches. AsciiDoc permits you to easily organize your book into book parts. You can introduce parts in your book by introducing *level 1 headings* for *each part* as shown in Example 208. Results after rendering with AsciiDoctor or AsciiDoctor-PDF are shown in Figure 156.

AsciiDoc Markup

Example 208. Organizing chapters in book parts

```
= Climate Change                ①
:doctype: book
:sectnums:
:partnums:
:part-signifier: Part           ②
:chapter-signifier: Chapter     ③


= How Did We get Here ?         ④

== Pre-Industrial Revolution    ⑤
Chapter 1 Text

== Post-Industrial Revolution ⑥
Chapter 2 Text

= Solutions                     ⑦

== Eliminating Fossil Fuels     ⑧
Chapter 3 Text

== Preventing Deforestation     ⑨
Chapter 4 Text
```

① Book title — this is a Level 0 heading.

② You need this attribute to prefix part headings with the word. *Part* if you render to HTML. Don't need this if you render to PDF.

③ Prefixes *Chapter* to every chapter heading if you render to HTML. Don't need this if you render to PDF.

④ Part 1 heading - This is a level 0 heading.

⑤ Chapter 1 heading under part 1 - level 1 heading.

⑥ Chapter 2 heading under part 1 - level 1 heading.

⑦ Part 2 heading - again a level 0 heading.

⑧ Chapter 3 heading under part 2 - level 1 heading.

⑨ Chapter 4 heading under part 2 - level 1 heading.

Will be rendered as...

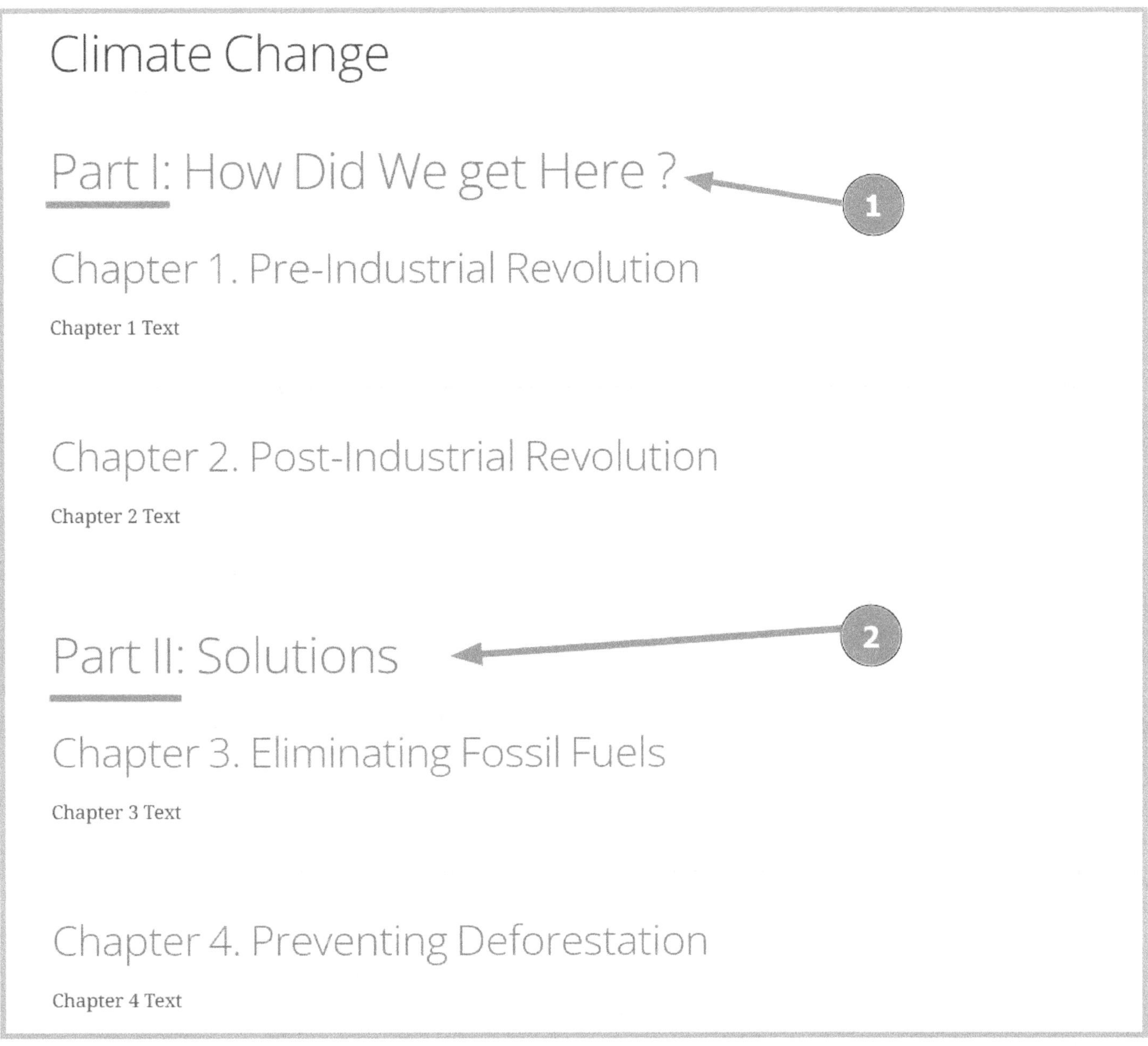

Figure 156. Rendered display showing book parts at callouts 1 and 2 and chapters under them

20.15. How to Include PDFs in Your AsciiDoc Documents

Sometimes you may need to include a few pages from a PDF file in your book. Typical scenarios include inner cover page, the colophon page or some complex diagram saved as a PDF which you would like to incorporate in your AsciiDoc file. You can do this quite easily using the markup shown in Example 209.

Example 209. Inserting PDF pages in your Asciidoc document

```
// V1- Inserts only the first page of the PDF
image::cover-page.pdf[]
```

```
// V2-Inserts the requested pages from the PDF
image::diagrams.pdf[pages=1..4]
```

```
 // V3-Inserts non-contiguous pages from the PDF
 image::diagrams.pdf[pages=3;5..7]
---
```

In Example 209, you can see three versions or options of the *image* macro for inserting pages from a PDF. V1 inserts only the first page of the PDF, V2 inserts selected contiguous pages from the PDF and V3 — non-contiguous pages from the PDF. You can use any one of these as per your need.

20.16. Helpful Tips for Creating and Editing Book Content

In the concluding section of this final chapter, I share some pointers that might be of help when you embark on a book writing project in AsciiDoc.

1. When you change the page size for your book, the content that fits on the default A4 page size will require adjustment for the new page size. If you have lots of figures in your book, you might find that figures are pushed to the next page leaving a large blank or empty area on a page. There is no easy fix for this but you can try either reducing the size of the figure, or moving some text from the next page to fill in the blank area. You can also consider creating a meaningful information box (*note admonition*) to fill the gap or use a relevant image. If you knew the page size of your book, setting it upfront before writing content can be of help. Even so, if you have figures, table or large code blocks, you might have to, live with blank areas on some pages which is quite okay. You can look at some existing printed books to see how such issues were resolved in that book.
2. If you plan to have an index in your printed book, it might be a good idea to keep marking terms that you would like to include in the book's index (see Chapter 13). It is a good idea to keep noting (in a notebook or in a file) terms that you have marked for indexing in your text. This can be very useful if these terms appear on subsequent pages where you can mark them for indexing using the spelling or hierarchical structure used before. This practice might save a lot of work later as you don't have to build the entire index from scratch after you have finished writing your book. As you

complete a chapter, it might also be a good idea to render a PDF and generate an index for that chapter to get a preview of the indexed words as they would appear in the final consolidated index. This will help spot indexing errors and correct them instantly.

3. For a book to be printed, you require a single cover with an appropriate bleed [https://packoi.com/blog/bleed-and-margin-in-printing/] that has:
   - The front cover
   - A spine with thickness proportionate to the page count in your book and text on the spine. You can refer to the Project Gutenberg spine width calculator [https://www.gutenberg.com.mt/spine-width-calculator], the AskPrint website [https://www.askprint.co.uk/howto/Hardback-book-cover-specifications.php] or the KDP cover guidelines page [https://kdp.amazon.com/en_US/help/topic/G201953020] for help on calculating spine width.
   - A back cover
4. If you are aiming to print your book on paper as a black and white impression, take care to ensure that your figures do not have elements that rely solely on color to illustrate whatever the figure is illustrating. For every figure you include, ask yourself how it would look when printed in black & white and make necessary changes if required. Whenever that is not possible, create a black & white friendly version of that figure and use it (replacing the color version of the figure) in the PDF version that will be used for printing.
5. For books that will be printed on paper, be careful not to use language like *refer to this section* or *this figure* or *can be found here*. While such a practice of hyperlnking words like *this resource* or *can be read here* might be common for an on-screen or online version of the document, in a printed book, this might frustrate the reader as they cannot tap the hyperlinked text to go anywhere. Make sure therefore to cite sections, figures, tables , examples with their numbers as discussed in Section 20.1. That way, your text will always refer to a numbered section, figure, example or table which works with both on-screen and printed versions of your book.
6. There might be a situation where you may want the header to show up with a border line but the footer border to not show up. Achieving this can be a bit frustrating because using the `:nofooter:` attribute does not do away with the *footer border*. I have used this scheme in this book where there is a header but no footer. However getting rid of the footer (or header) border can be done easily by adding the following *border-color* and / or *border-width* keys in your *mythme.yml* file under the footer category as shown in Example 210.

Example 210. Making the footer border invisible

```
footer:
 border-color: transparent
 border-width: ~  ①
```

① the tilde character ~ means no border

In conclusion, it should be apparent that AsciiDoc is very well suited for writing books due to its simplicity and flexibility. Its ability to maintain consistent numbering of figures, examples, sections and tables takes a lot of pain out of book writing. It allows authors to create beautiful blocks, highlight code, create index, bibliography, glossary and appendices with minimal effort. The flexibility that AsciiDoc provides to organize, re-organize and assemble individual chapters into a well structured book is truly remarkable. Above all, the ability to render your document in various output formats, including PDF, HTML, and EPUB, makes AsciiDoc an ideal choice for publishing books both in print and digital formats. Its lightweight syntax also makes it an excellent choice for collaborative writing and editing.

At the end of the day, all you need is a plain text editor!

20.17. Chapter Summary

Key learnings in this chapter are:

- Generating a print ready PDF i.e. a PDF version that will be used to create a printed book, requires special settings to facilitate book production. Knowing about these before you start your book writing project in AsciiDoc can save a lot of time and frustration later.
- It is a good idea to cite sections, figures, tables and examples in running matter after setting the *xrefstyle* attribute such that the text includes accurate references to section numbers, figure numbers, table numbers and example numbers when the book is collated. This practice also guides readers of the printed version of your book to cited items in the document. Please refer to Section 20.1 for a quick recap.
- The default page size is A4 but printed books rarely use that size. For printed versions of your AsciiDoc book, you need to set a standard trim size or page size like 6 inches by 9 inches or any other standard trim size. Please see Section 20.2 for a recap on how to set a custom trim size.
- You need to set up top, right , bottom and left margins carefully for books to be printed. As printed books are bound, sufficient gutter margin needs to be set such that readers do not face any difficulty reading content located close to the spine of the book. Please see Section 20.3 for a discussion on how to set these margins correctly by extending the default AsciiDoctor PDF theme.
- Headers and footers can be added to display page numbers , chapter and book titles alternating on recto and verso pages. Please re-visit Example 199 for more details on how to do this in AsciiDoc.
- By adding `:sectnums:` and `:chapter-signifier:` attributes to the AsciiDoc file header, a word like 'Chapter' can be prefixed to every level 1 heading. Section 20.8 provides details on how to achieve this.

- For books that will be printed in black & white, the *default AsciiDoctor-PDF theme* might not offer the best contrast. We can extend the default theme using elements from a different theme that ensures a darker and sharper print. Section 20.6 describes how to download and use a theme that is more suited for printing.
- Roman page numbers for front matter pages and Arabic numbers for pages in the main body of the book text can be easily implemented using the *start at* key under the page category in the extended theme file. Please see Section 20.7 for a recap.
- If you wish to print your book in full color or wish to circulate a PDF for on-screen reading, you can change the color of different heading levels to make the document appear more attractive and reader friendly. Please see Section 20.10 for a recap on how to do this.

20.18. Try it Yourself

The *mytheme.yml* and other documents used in the following exercises can be found in the chapter exercise folder. Please remember that all changes in tasks given below will only be visible when you render your AsciiDoc document to PDF using *mytheme.yml* as shown below:

```
$ asciidoctor-pdf --theme mytheme.yml mybook.adoc
```

1. Open the *mytheme.yml* file and examine it to see how headers, footers and margins can be set.
2. Change the four margins to a value of 0.5 inches and see the difference by rendering an AsciiDoc file as shown below. Do the margins move?

   ```
   $ asciidcotor-pdf --theme mytheme.yml myasciidocfile.adoc
   ```

3. Can you alter the inner and outer margins so as to leave a gutter margin of 0.5 inches on either side of the book spine? Hint: See Example 197.
4. Set alternate chapter and book titles and page numbers in the header for recto and verso pages of any AsciiDoc file that you have as discussed in Example 199.
5. Can you switch off page numbers in the headers and instead print centered page numbers in the footer ? Hint: Uncomment and use the footer statements in Example 199.
6. Following discussions in this chapter, try to create header borders (see Section 20.4.2), prefix the word 'Chapter' to chapter titles (see Section 20.8) and try out the *default-for-print-theme.yml* (see

Section 20.6) for printing PDFs by adding its contents to *mytheme.yml*. (Download *default-for-print-theme.yml* from https://github.com/asciidoctor/asciidoctor-pdf/blob/main/data/themes/default-for-print-theme.yml)

7. Introduce a front cover in your AsciiDoc file (See Section 20.9).
8. Following the discussion in Section 20.10, change (a) the color of all headings of the *demoxref.adoc* document to a single color and (b) assign different colors to different heading levels. You will see this change only after you render your AsciiDoc file to PDF.
9. Create an appendix file with two appendecies as shown in Section 20.12.
10. Open the *glossary.txt* file in the chapter exercise folder. You will find 5 climate change terms and their definitions. Following the discussion in Section 20.13, create a well styled glossary in a new or existing AsciiDoc file.
11. Can you replicate the book parts example shown in Example 208 ?
12. Read and reflect on the tips presented in Section 20.16.

Epilogue

While we have covered a lot of ground in this book, there are many features of AsciiDoc that we could not discuss in this beginners text. As is the case with any academic quest, after you get started, you invariably realize that there is a lot more to learn. So a good question is — *where do I go from here ?* and the answer is — *forward !*

In Appendix F, I have compiled a list of some great resources that you can consult to take your AsciiDoc journey forward from here. The list has websites that you can browse, documentation links that you can consult and cheat sheets that you can refer to. And in case you still have questions, the list also has details of a very vibrant and dedicated AsciiDoc forum in which the developers of AsciiDoctor and the AsciiDoc user community are always willing to help.

There is no better way to learn than to take up a small and meaningful project and start using AsciiDoc. This could be creating the next lecture note for your students, the next assignment that you need to submit to your professor, a note documenting a new skill that you have learned, creating documentation for your code, compiling a collection of your poems, an article, a novel or even a book! Just throw yourself into the deep end and you will be surprised how quickly you can master AsciiDoc. Aristotle sums this up beautifully — *"For the things we have to learn before we can do them, we learn by doing them."*

Felix sit tua via — May your path be joyful !

—

Epilogue

[illegible]

[illegible]

[illegible]

[illegible]

Appendix A: Explanation of Commands Used in Command Line Install of AsciiDoctor

If you are new to Linux and need a more detailed step-by-step guide of the above installation, please read on for detailed explanation. Also included in the discussion below are some additional commands that can be used to verify that the installation has been successful and also to know which versions of the software has been installed.

A.1. Installing Ruby

As AsciiDoctor has been written in the Ruby programming language, it needs the Ruby environment to run. It is super easy to install Ruby by issuing one single command from the terminal. Before doing that however, it is prudent to first check if Ruby is already installed using the following command:

```
$ ruby -v
```

If Ruby is NOT Installed, you will see a response like the one shown in Figure 157 otherwise you will get a response showing the installed version of Ruby, in which case you do not need to install Ruby.

```
mint@mint:~$ ruby -v
Command 'ruby' not found, but can be installed with:
sudo apt install ruby
```

Figure 157. Response of Ruby Version Command when Ruby is not Installed

Assuming that we get a response as shown in Figure 157 indicating that Ruby is not installed on our computer, we can issue the following command to install it.

```
$ sudo apt install ruby-full
```

This will install Ruby and you can repeat the `$ ruby -v` command in the terminal and get the response as seen in Figure 158 (maybe with another version number) if Ruby has been installed correctly.

```
mint@mint:~$ ruby -v
ruby 3.2.3 (2024-01-18 revision 52bb2ac0a6) [x86_64-linux-gnu]
```

Figure 158. Response of Ruby Version Command after Successful Installation (version number can be different)

Now with Ruby installed, we can quickly install AsciiDoctor tools.

A.2. Installing AsciiDoctor

AsciiDoctor gives us the capability to render an asciidoc file to HTML. To install *AsciiDoctor*, we need to issue the following command from the terminal:

Terminal Command

```
$ sudo gem install asciidoctor
```

This will install AsciiDoctor on your computer. We can now type the following command to see if the installation was successful and also see the installed version of AsciiDoctor:

Terminal Command

```
$ asciidoctor --version
```

A successful install should throw up a response shown in Figure 159 (may be with a different version number):

```
mint@mint:~$ asciidoctor --version
Asciidoctor 2.0.23 [https://asciidoctor.org]
Runtime Environment (ruby 3.2.3 (2024-01-18 revision 52bb2ac0a6) [x86_64-linux-gnu]) (lc:U
TF-8 fs:UTF-8 in:UTF-8 ex:UTF-8)
```

Figure 159. Response of AsciiDoctor Version Command

Installing AsciiDoctor-PDF

Likewise we will also install *asciidoctor-pdf*. The AsciiDoctor-PDF tools gives us the capability to render an asciidoc file to PDF. To install AsciiDoctor-PDF, we need to issue the following command from the terminal:

Terminal Command

$ sudo gem install asciidoctor-pdf

And after the installation, we can check for successful installation and installed version of asciidoctor-pdf using the following command:

Terminal Command

```
$ asciidoctor --version
```

A successful install should throw up a response shown in Figure 160 (may be with a different version number):

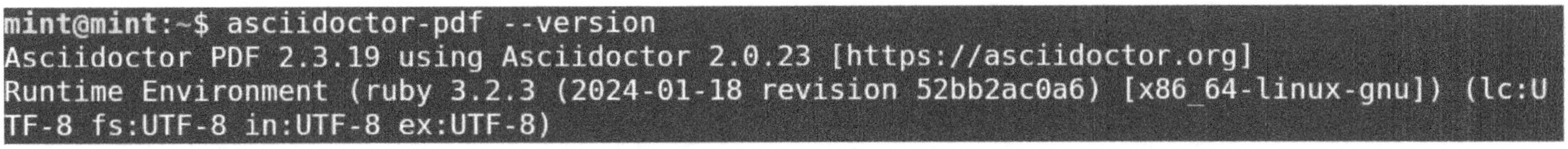

```
mint@mint:~$ asciidoctor-pdf --version
Asciidoctor PDF 2.3.19 using Asciidoctor 2.0.23 [https://asciidoctor.org]
Runtime Environment (ruby 3.2.3 (2024-01-18 revision 52bb2ac0a6) [x86_64-linux-gnu]) (lc:U
TF-8 fs:UTF-8 in:UTF-8 ex:UTF-8)
```

Figure 160. Response of asciidoctor-pdf Version Command

For more information on packages for non-debian linuxes, please see this AsciiDoctor Documentation Page [https://docs.asciidoctor.org/asciidoctor/latest/install/linux-packaging/]

Appendix B: Create a Shell Script to Start AsciiDoctor Docker Container

As mentioned above, the AsciiDoctor Docker container image can be started by first moving to he directory or folder that has your asciidoc files and then issuing the following command from the terminal:

```
$ podman run -it -v $(pwd):/documents/ docker.io/asciidoctor/docker-asciidoctor
```

If you do not wish to remember the the above podman command to invoke the AsciiDoctor Docker container, you can create a shell script and run that script from any folder to start the AsciiDoctor Docker image. The steps to create a shell script and run it are described below. Folder names, file names and the location of the folder in which the script resides can be anything:

1. Create a folder — *myscripts* — in you Home directory. If you wish this folder to be hidden (such that the script is not accidentally tampered or deleted), the name of the folder will have to be *.myscripts* (a . preceding the folder name).
2. Move inside the folder, open a text editor and type or paste in the following two lines (on two separate lines):

   ```
   #!/bin/bash
   podman run -it -v $(pwd):/documents/ docker.io/asciidoctor/docker-asciidoctor
   ```

3. Save the files as *runad.sh*
4. Make this file executable for all by either menu:[Right Click on File > Properties > Permissions > Advanced Permissions > check all boxes under X] or open a terminal in this folder (Menu:[Right Click > Open Terminal Here]) and type in the following command :

   ```
   $ chmod 755 runad.sh   (or your filename)
   ```

5. Copy the path to this folder (like type pwd in the terminal or click on the address bar of your file manager as seen in Figure 161)

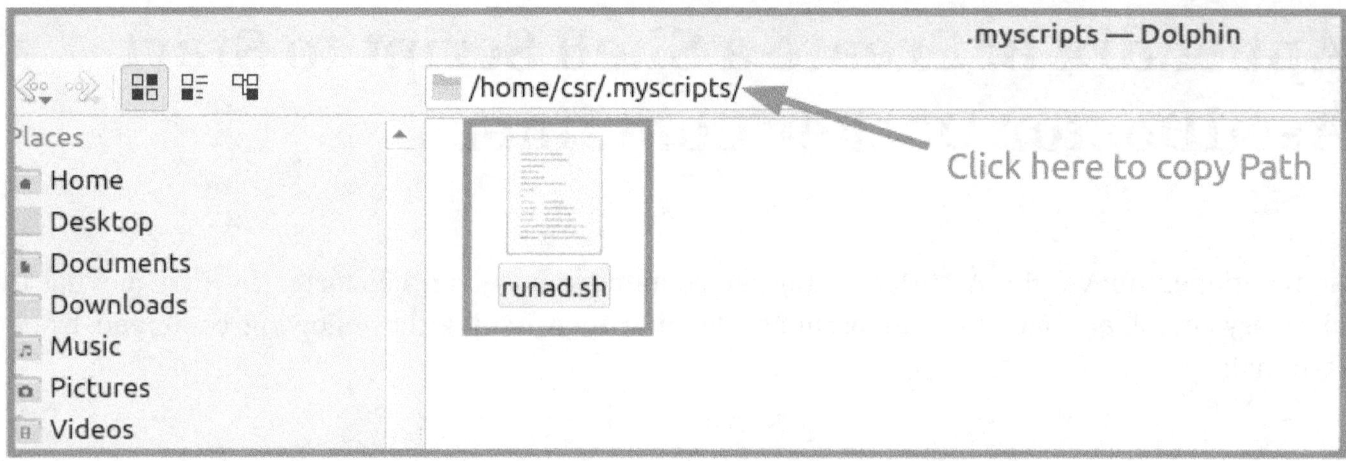

Figure 161. Script file seen inside the Dolphin file manager in Linux

6. Navigate out of this folder and back into your home directory and use your file manager to see hidden files (usually right click > Show Hidden File or `CTRL` + `H`)

7. This step has to be carefully executed. Find and open a file called *.profile* (or .bashrc) and on the last line of this file, carefully paste the following line replacing the folder name part (pointed by arrow in Figure 162) with the path that you copied in the above step and *save* this file. You must replace <paste-your-path> with your own path!

```
export PATH=$PATH:<paste-your-path>
```

```
# set PATH so it includes user's private bin if it exists
if [ -d "$HOME/.local/bin" ] ; then
    PATH="$HOME/.local/bin:$PATH"
fi

export PATH=$PATH:/home/csr/.myscripts
```

Figure 162. Adding the path to your myscripts folder to the PATH Variable in the .profile file

☞ Remember — if you mess up anything, you can always exit without saving and come back again.

8. Now logout and login again and you can now start the AsciiDoctor Docker Image by typing the following command from any folder (replace *runad* part with your filename if different):

```
$ runad.sh
```

In the above examples, I have used *myscripts* or *.myscripts* as folder name and *runad.sh* for the script file name. You can choose your own names but if you do, please change them in the commands above at appropriate places. If you choose to use the same names that I have chosen, you can use these commands verbatim. Please also note that your file manager might be different and so you might have to find equivalent menu options to complete tasks where menu sequences have been mentioned above.

Appendix C: Installing Podman and AsciiDoctor Docker Image on Windows

The installation of Podman and then running the AsciiDoctor container on Windows 11 involves a few steps but is still quite easy. If you have a fast internet connection, it should take around 5 minutes or so to complete. I recommend this install as you get access to the entire AsciiDoctor toolchain via the container image. You need to install nothing after this.

As I have mentioned in Chapter 2, containers are a Linux thing so they do not natively run on Windows. To make them run on Windows, we need to install the Windows Subsystem for Linux (WSL). WSL is a essentially a compatibility layer developed by Microsoft that allows users to run a Linux environment directly on Windows 10 and later versions. Essentially, WSL enables users to run a Linux distribution, such as Ubuntu, Debian, or Kali Linux, alongside their Windows operating system, *without the need for a separate virtual machine or dual-boot setup*. So, the general idea here is that we install WSL and get a Linux distro on it (Ubuntu) and then podman can happily run in that environment forever after. Terrifying as this may sound to some Windows users, there are'nt very many steps to accomplish this. We will use an install sequence involving issuing just a few commands from the terminal and Windows will do the rest for us.

If you have a computer with good resources like a fast processor and around 8 GB RAM, I highly recommend a Podman install of AsciiDoctor, which in a manner of speaking, gives you the key to all doors in the AsciiDoctor paradise. One other big advantage is that you also get full access to *AsciiDoctor-Mathematical* on your Windows machine which is,otherwise available only for Linux. But hey, as we will be running Ubuntu in WSL and that's Linux, we get access to AsciiDoctor Mathematical right inside Windows! So if you are a Windows AsciiDoc user and need to frequently include equations in your writing, the AsciiDoctor container image is your only way to include beautifully formatted equations as demonstrated in Chapter 14.

With this small background out of the way, let's dive straight into installing Podman and running the AsciiDoctor Docker container image. And don't you worry about all the commands — we got this!

C.1. Installing Podman CLI

Before we move ahead, I am assuming that you have a recent and reasonably fast computer with at least 8 GB RAM running Windows 11. This is because containers need their share of resources to run optimally and a fast processor and some extra RAM is of considerable help.

Now follow these steps carefully and sequentially and you will have the full AsciiDoctor install in the next 5 minutes.

1. Visit the https://podman.io/ and download the *Podman CLI* for Windows (around 29 MB) as pointed by the arrow in Figure 163.

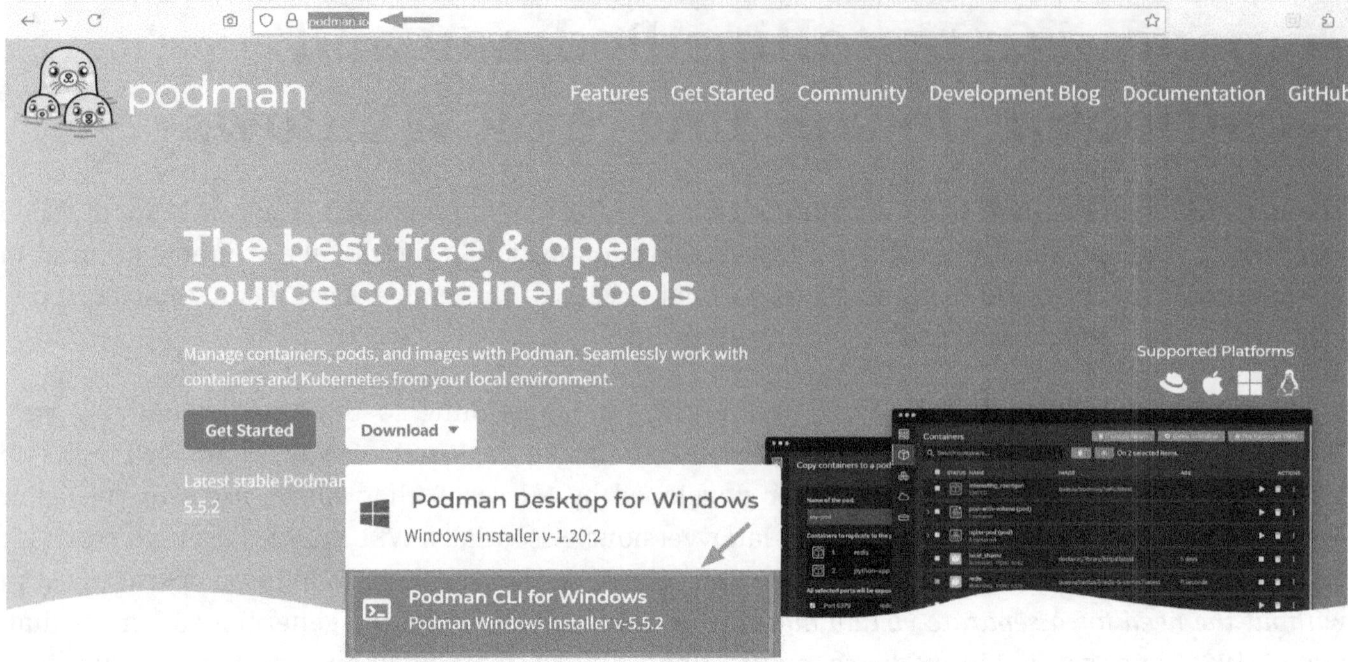

Figure 163. Download Podman CLI for Windows

2. Click on the downloaded *setup.exe* file and follow the screen instructions to install. You will see the installation screen shown in Figure 164 mentioning that Podman will need WSLv2 and if not already installed, it will have to be *done manually* (Highlighted rectangle). No problem. We will do it later.

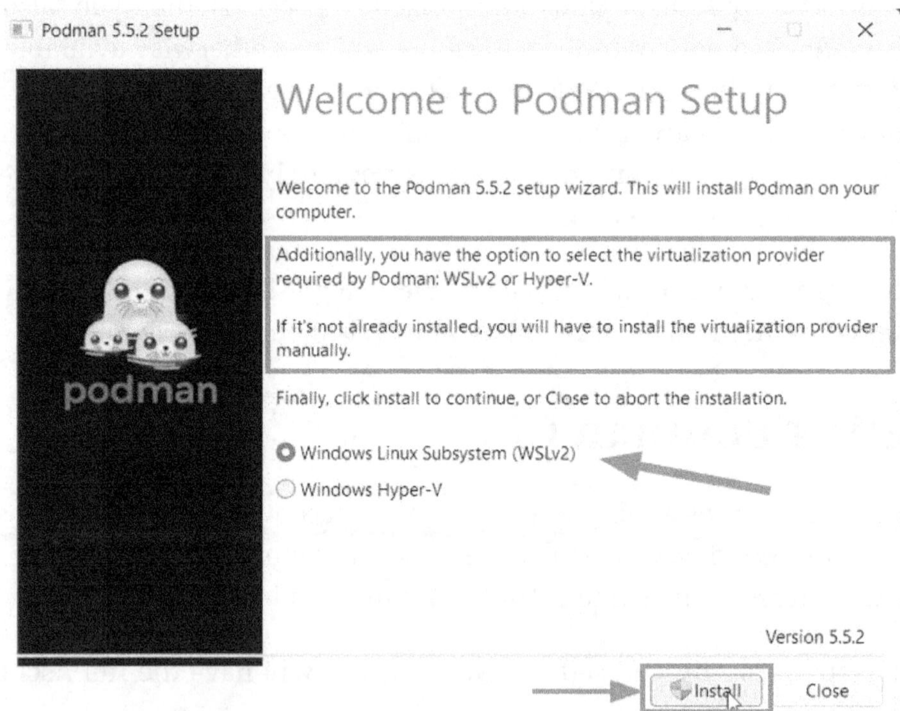

Figure 164. Installing Podman CLI

3. For now, press `install` and within a few seconds you will get a *installation successfully completed* message. But we are not out of the woods yet as the CLI installer informed us upfront that we need to install WSL manually. So let's do that in the next step and get it out of the way.

4. Open a Windows terminal (preferably admin terminal but a normal terminal should also do) and enter the following command to install WSL:

```
wsl.exe --install
```

This sets into motion a series of downloads and installs as shown in Figure 165.

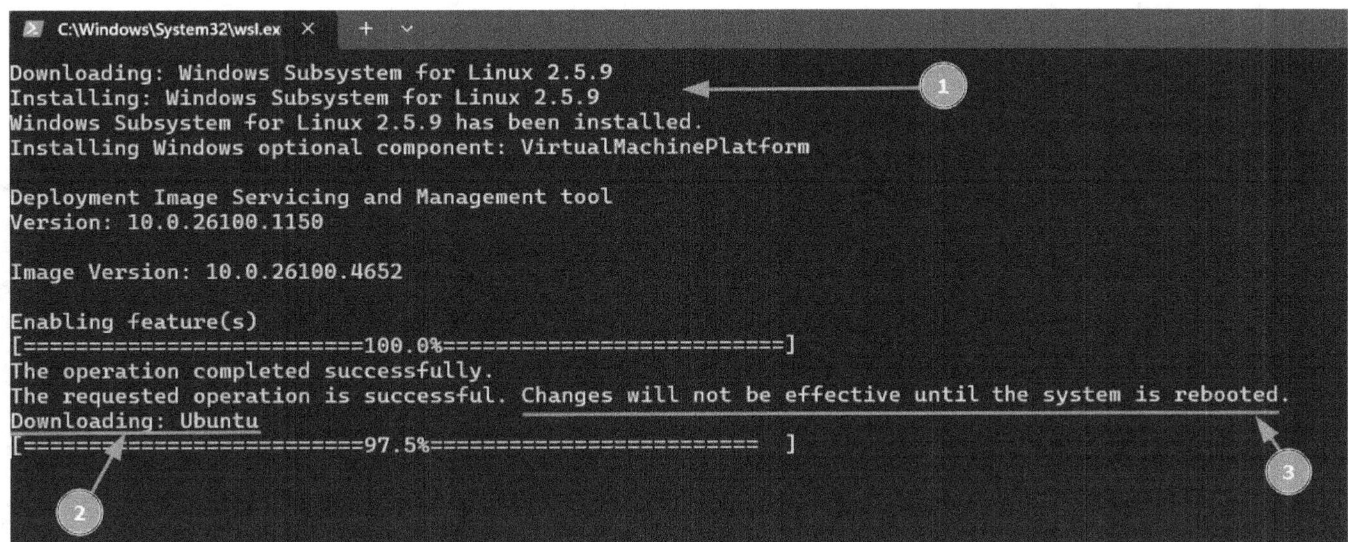

Figure 165. Installing WSL and Linux distro

In the above figure, first WSL is downloaded and installed (callout 1). This is immediately and automatically (without user intervention) followed by downloading and installing Ubuntu, a popular Debian based Linux distribution (callout 2). The user is also informed that when all this is finished, a reboot is required for changes to take effect (callout 3).

5. Wait for the downloads and installs to finish and after completion, *reboot or restart* your computer. Don't worry about any *error code message* that you may get when the command concludes. Just ignore them.

6. When your computer reboots, open a terminal and type the following command to verify that Podman CLI, which we had installed initially in steps 1-3 above, is now working:

```
podman --version
```

You should now get a response from Podman which would be something like — `podman version 5.5.2`, informing you about the installed version of Podman on your system. And that's good news!

7. With Podman alive and responding, we now need to issue the following two commands:

```
podman machine init
```

The Podman machine *init* command initializes a new Podman virtual machine, establishing the requisite environment for executing containers on platforms that do not natively support Podman, such as Windows or macOS. You will see stuff getting downloaded and installed. Give it some time to finish. While this happens, you are kept entertained by a variety of old school progress bars!

8. The above command concludes with the *operation completed successfully* and *machine init complete* messages as shown is figure Figure 166 (callout 1).

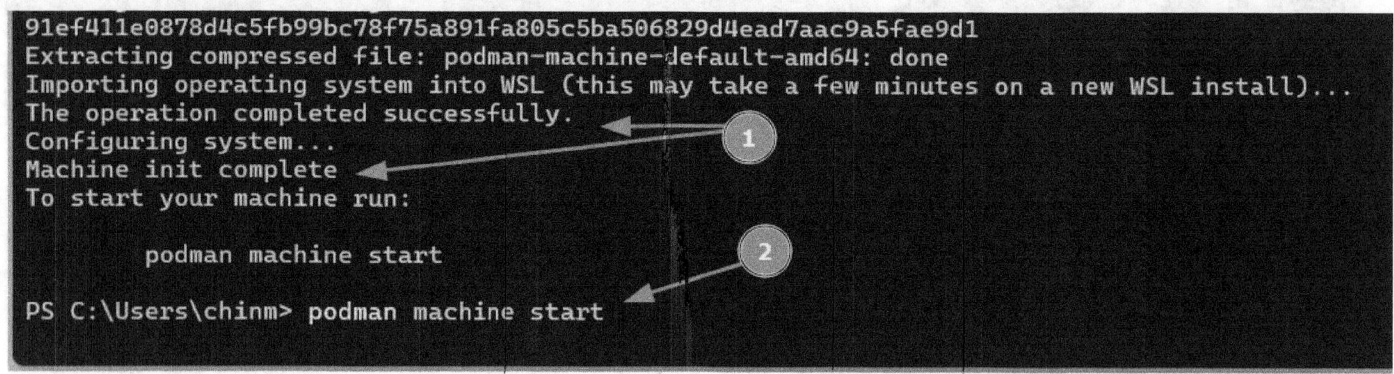

Figure 166. Podman machine initialization (1) successful completion messages (2) starting the podman machine

9. Finally, issue the following command from the terminal to start the Podman machine.

```
podman machine start
```

This command concludes quickly informing you that Podman is now running in a rootless mode (any user can access it) but if you have any issues you can run it in the rootful (available only to admin level users i.e. privileged access) mode by typing the command : `podman machine set --rootful` — this is just an advisory to be noted. We will let Podman run in its default *rootless* mode. If you see a Penguin icon in the status bar, don't be alarmed. Penguins are cute. Just click it and you will see the WSL screen. You can eyeball it and then close it.

10. Now that's Podman is all done and ready, we can now install the AsciiDoctor container image.

11. Now *move to the folder that has your Asciidoc Project files*. Make sure that no folders in the path have spaces in their names like — `C:/documents/book project`. If they do, remove the space and make it like — `C:/documents/book-project`. Podman does not like spaces in folder names.

12. Once inside your project folder, issue the following command to download and install the *latest* AsciiDoctor Docker container image and we are finally done! Remember, this command has to download a lot of stuff the first time — so please let it do its work in peace till it comes back with a # prompt! It will show you things that it is downloading and give you enough time to grab a coffee!

```
podman run -it -v "$(pwd):/documents/" podman run -it -v "$(pwd):/documents/"
docker.io/asciidoctor/docker-asciidoctor
```

☞ The difference from the Linux command is that `"$(pwd):/documents/"`, for Windows, is in quotes.

13. You will now see the AsciiDoctor container # prompt and you can issue AsciiDoctor commands — like `asciidoctor mybook.adoc` or `asciidoctor-pdf --theme mytheme.yml mybook.adoc` or even `asciidoctor-pdf --theme mytheme.yml -r asciidoctor-mathematical -a mathematical-format=svg mybook.adoc`, described in various chapters of this book.

14. To exit the container, type `exit` at the # prompt. Do *not* leave without *exiting* the container.

15. Step 12 above can also be done via Podman Desktop by directly pulling the AsciiDoctor container image from the Docker hub (see Section C.3).

16. Every time you need to start the the AsciiDoctor Podman container, just navigate to your project folder, *right click* in a blank area in the file explorer and choose *open in terminal*. This will open a terminal in your project folder. Just copy and paste the same Podman run command (reproduced below) from step 4 above and press enter to get your # prompt.

```
podman run -it -v "$(pwd):/documents/" podman run -it -v "$(pwd):/documents/"
docker.io/asciidoctor/docker-asciidoctor
```

Hail ye, the command line lovers — we are all set to use the AsciiDoctor toolchain on Windows!

C.2. Installing and Running the Podman Desktop

While the installation is complete, and you can use the Podman AsciiDoctor container image from the command line as we use on Linux, the last step above — Step 16, requiring to paste and run the Podman run command every time you want to use AsciiDoctor may be a deal breaker for many Windows users, who rarely ever encounter the command line. So, to make the regular use of the AsciiDoctor container image super easy i.e. without having the need to repeatedly type the Podman run command, we can go one step further and install the *Podman Desktop* from the Podman website.

Podman Desktop is free, open source and has a menu driven interface to work with containers. As everything that Podman Desktop needs to run has already been installed during the CLI installation, installing Podman Desktop takes just a few seconds using the steps outlined below:

1. Go to https://podman.io/ and download the *Podman Desktop for Windows* Installer.
2. Double click on the installer file and follow screen instructions to install using default options presented by the installer. It takes just a few seconds for the install to finish.
3. When you launch Podman Desktop after installation for the first time, you will be asked — *Do you want to allow public and private networks to access this app ?*. My choice is *allow*.
4. The Podman Desktop *dashboard* will now be up and running as seen in Figure 167.
5. All the items that you see listed on the *dashboard* here are default test containers — all of them can be deleted if you want later on. You should also see an AsciiDoctor container here as we created it during the CLI install. Even that container can be deleted later on as we will be creating fresh containers for our AsciiDoc projects.
6. Recall that we need to start AsciiDoctor in the folder where you have your AsciiDoc project files. To demonstrate how you can do that in Podman Desktop, I take the example of someone writing a book and all AsciiDoc files pertaining to the book project being placed in the `D:\documents\mybook` folder.

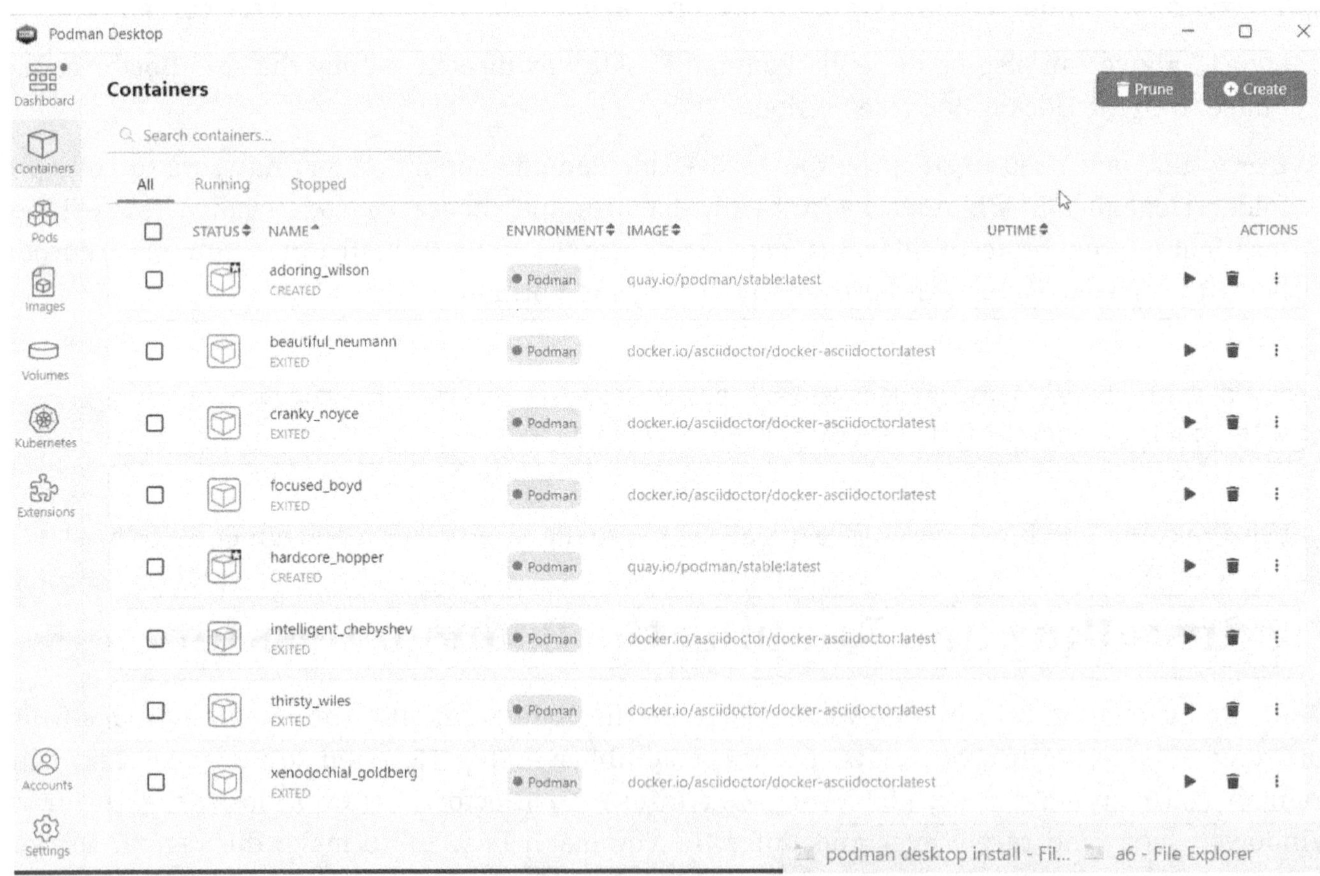

Figure 167. Podman Desktop opening screen

7. So to create an AsciiDoctor container that starts in this folder we do the following:

    a. Click on *images* in the left panel (callout 1) of the dashboard.

    b. Choose the AsciiDoctor image (shown enclosed in a rectangle) and press the ▶ run button (callout 2) as seen in Figure 168.

Figure 168. Creating an AsciiDoctor container for our Book Project

    c. Then on the resulting screen, paste the path (D:\Documents\MyBook in my example) where your AsciiDoc project files are located on your computer, in the Volume Section — *path on the host* field (callout1), `/documents` in the *path inside the container* field (callout 2) and give your container a name (without any spaces) like Mybook (callout 3) and press *start container* (callout 4) as shown in Figure 169.

Figure 169. Setting up the AsciiDoctor container to start in a folder

8. This starts the container in the designated folder. Click on the `Terminal Tab` and from here you can issue *all* AsciiDoctor commands as shown in Figure 170.
9. You can run any AsciiDoctor, AsciiDoctor-PDF and AsciiDoctor-EPUB 3 commands from here as described in the book. This includes AsciiDoctor-Mathematical, code highlighters and extensions that would otherwise need to be individually installed.
10. Press the ■ (stop button) to exit the container (equivalent of typing the `exit` command from the container # prompt). However, in Podman Desktop, *use the stop button* to exit. Containers take a few seconds to exit so please wait for them to stop.
11. The font size in the terminal is by default, very small and barely visible. We can however easily rectify this by increasing the size of the font in the settings. To increase the font size in the terminal, execute the following steps:
    a. Click on *Settings* — the ⚙ (gear icon) — located at the bottom left of the screen.
    b. Choose *Preferences* to expand it and click on *Terminal* (might have to scroll down a bit to see it).
    c. You can now increase the font size according to your preference. For me, a font size of say 18-20 and a line height to 2 does the trick. There is no option to choose a different font. You don't need to save the settings. They are automatically saved once you change them.
12. To exit, first make sure that no containers are running. Click on the `Containers` button in the left panel which shows all containers including MyBook. Just make sure no container says "Running" under it as shown in Figure 171.
13. If you find any running containers , press the ■ icon in front of them to stop. Containers take a few seconds to stop, so please wait till the running containers exit (stop icon turns to play icon).
14. Finally, click on X on the top right of the Podman Desktop dashboard window to exit.

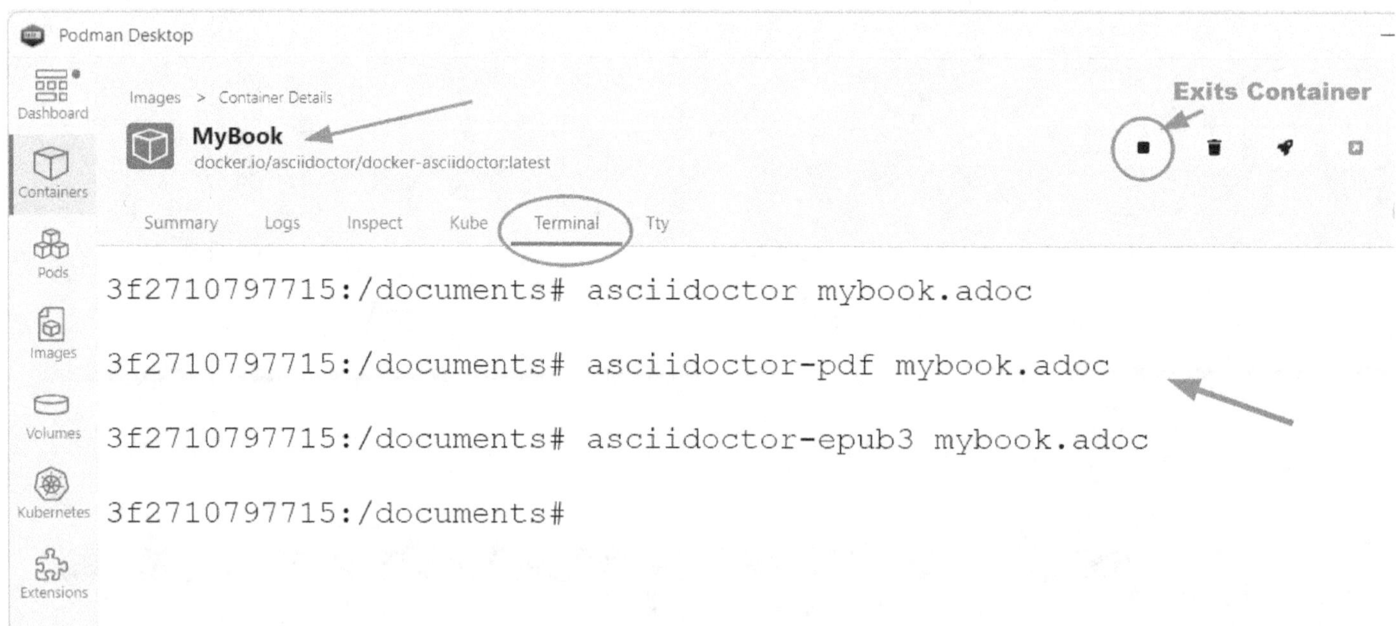

Figure 170. Running AsciiDoctor commands from the podman desktop terminal

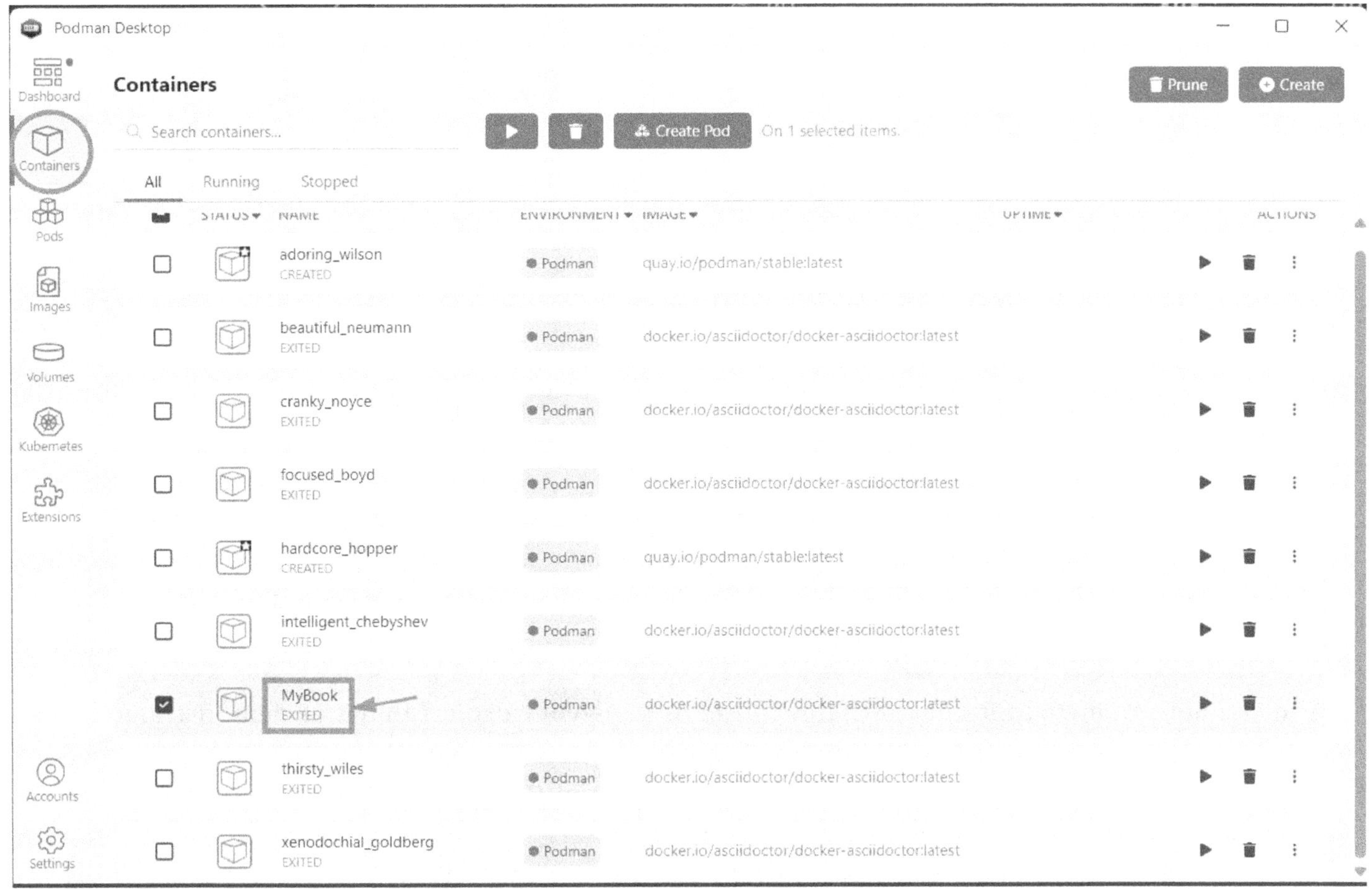

Figure 171. Exiting or Restarting Podman Desktop

15. To get access to your AsciiDoc container again after exiting, just start Podman Desktop from your start menu (or search for it) and you will see the dashboard seen in Figure 171. Click on `Containers` in the left panel, then click on *MyBook* (shown inside the rectangle) then click on the terminal tab and then click on the ▶ (play button) (top right) to start the AsciiDoctor container. You can now continue to work on your book project as before.

⚠ If you exit the Podman Desktop dashboard and some containers are still running, you can just start Podman Desktop again and stop those containers from the containers section by pressing the ■ `stop` button.

C.3. Pulling Docker Images Using Podman Desktop

One additional benefit of running Podman Desktop is that you can directly *pull* other container images from container image registries easily and run them from Podman Desktop. This opens up a new world of possibilities as you can run a huge number of applications (apart from AsciiDoctor) in Windows for which containerized images are available. To illustrate this capability, we will pull the Pandoc container image, a software that we use in Chapter 19. To pull a container image directly from Podman Desktop, you need to do the following:

1. Click on images in the left panel and click on Pull on the top right as shown in Figure 172.

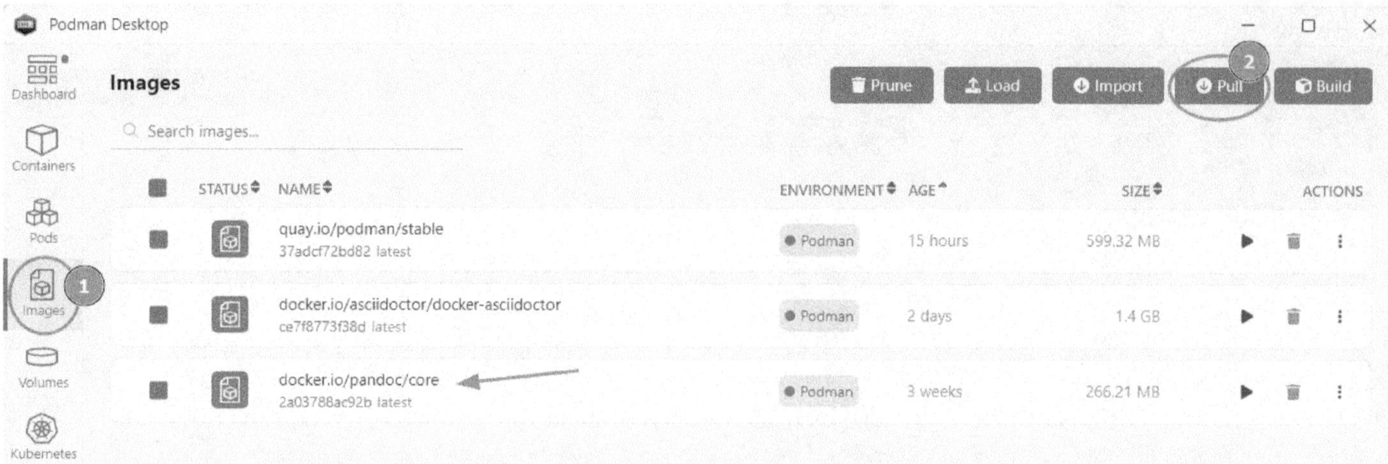

Figure 172. Pulling the Pandoc-core docker image (already done here) as pointed by the arrow

2. Now just search for the name of the image in the 'Image to Pull' box (for example type *pandoc*), choose an image (Pandoc core) and press `enter`. The image will start downloading (Figure 173).
3. Once done you can see it in the images section as pointed by the arrow in Figure 172.
4. You can now create a container with this image binding your project folder as demonstrated in step 7 (a-b-c). Once done, you can issue Pandoc commands in the container terminal to convert DocBook to MS Word or convert MS Word to AsciiDoc as shown in Chapter 19. The Podman Desktop opens up a new world of containers on your computer. In fact, if you delete your AsciiDoctor Docker image by mistake or if you wish to reinstall, you can just *pull* the latest image by searching for AsciiDoctor (in place of Pandoc) and you will get your AsciiDoctor image back in a few seconds!

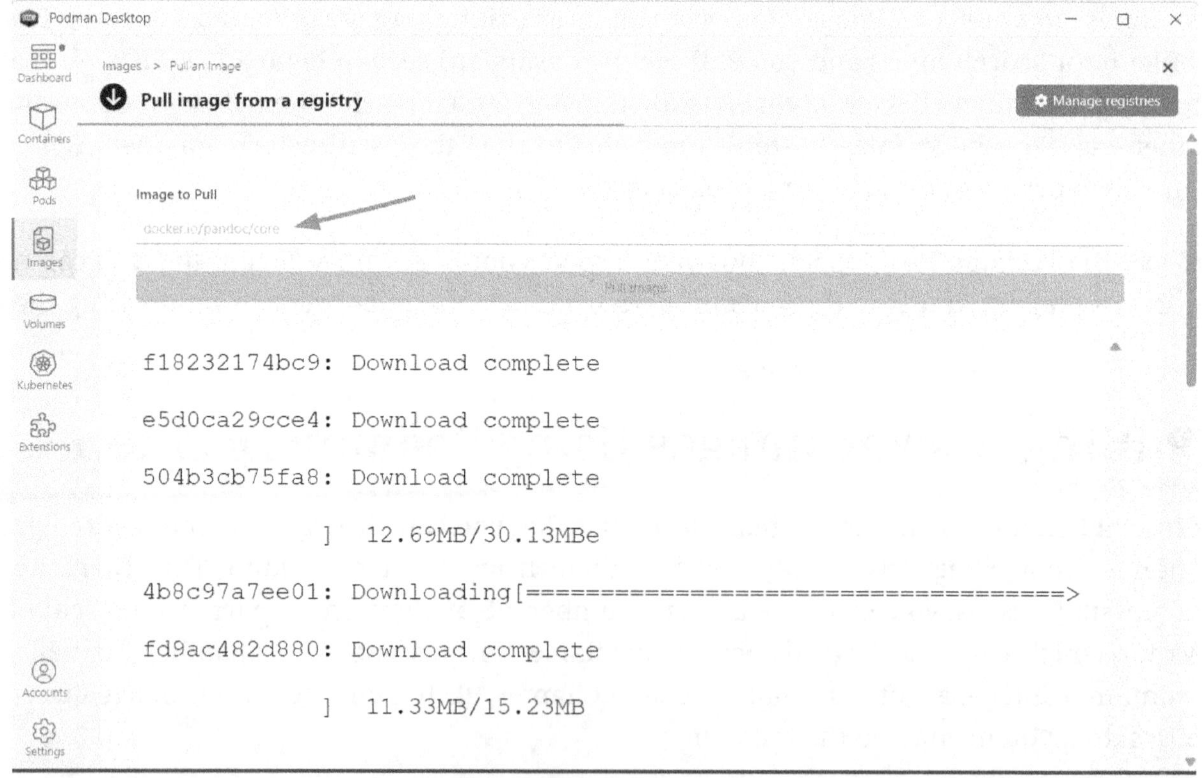

Figure 173. Downloading Pandoc docker image

C.4. Starting and Stopping the Podman Machine

If you have installed Podman Desktop, it is usually set up to start and remain ready for use with the Podman machine running in the background. You can see this if you click on the 'show hidden icons' button on the windows task bar. Figure 174 shows the hidden icons button (callout 1) pressing which you will see the Podman Desktop icon (encircled).

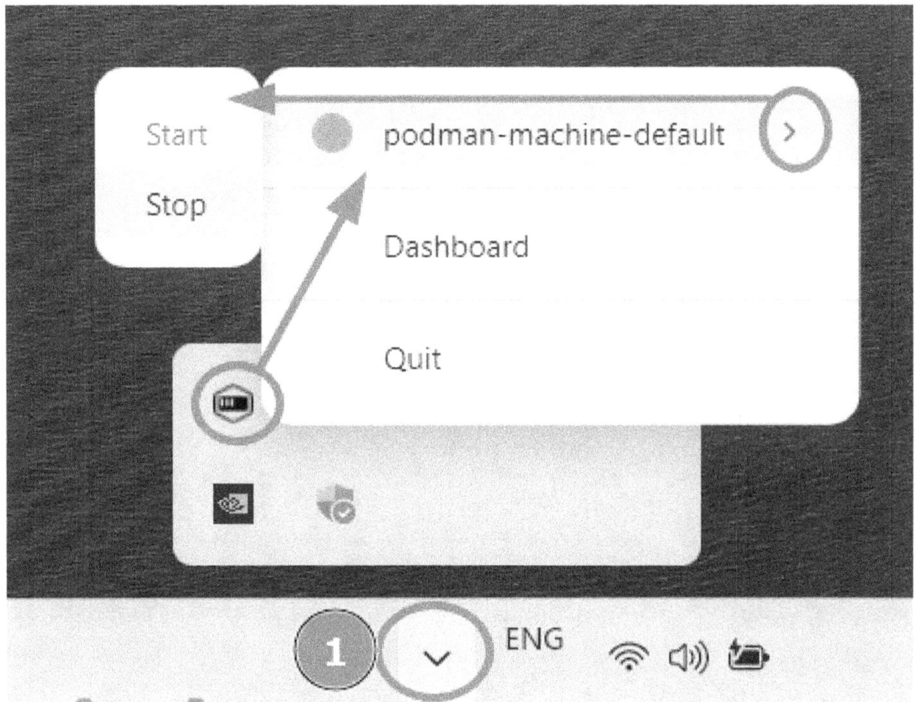

Figure 174. Podman Desktop running as seen in system tray

As can be seen in the figure above, clicking on the Podman Desktop icon shows the following three options:

1. Podman machine default — using which you can start or stop the Podman machine. If you are not using Podman, stopping frees some resources. You can re-start whenever you need to.
2. The Podman Desktop dashboard — from where you can run and manage containers and images.
3. Quit — to end Podman Desktop running in the background altogether. You can always restart Podman Desktop from the start menu.

Some Important Points to Remember while Running Containers

Please remember that Docker containers and virtual machines can consume significant CPU and memory resources. So try not to run many containers simultaneously. This can lead to your system becoming unresponsive. Also, it is important to gracefully close down your running containers after use to avoid data loss or corruption. Always use the stop button ■ when exiting Docker containers.

C.5. Troubleshooting Podman Desktop

While this is not a detailed troubleshooting guide, there is one issue that some people might confront infrequently. It is possible that on some day, you might not see the list of your containers in the containers section on your dashboard ☹. If you ever encounter this situation, click on *settings* (⚙) and in the resources section, restart the Podman Machine by pressing the restart icon (↻) as shown in Figure 175.

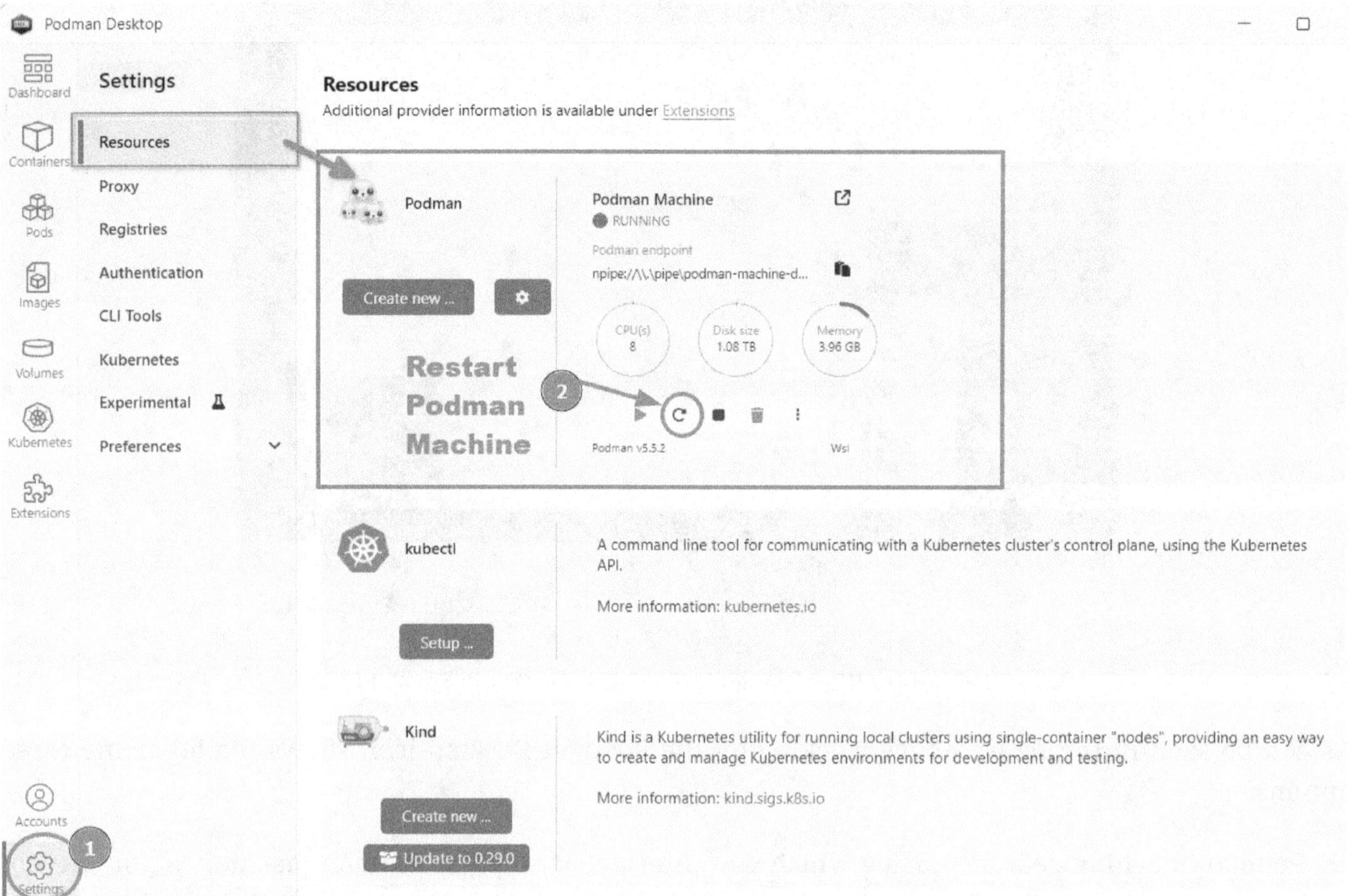

Figure 175. Restarting the Podman machine

You should now be able to see all your containers restored ☺.

Running the AsciiDoctor toolchain via a container in Windows is highly recommended. As your writing work will happen in a text editor or VS Code, you infrequently need AsciiDoctor via the container to render your AsciiDoc file to HTML, PDF and EPUB3. Having the full toolchain available in one install is a very comforting feeling!

☞ Some helpful information about installing Podman on Windows is available on the Podman website at https://podman.io/docs/installation#windows.

Appendix D: Some Useful Podman Commands

While this is not intended to be a Podman tutorial, it might be very helpful to get acquainted with a minimalist set of Podman commands that might be needed at times to manage the AsciiDoctor and Pandoc containers. Containers take up resources so it might be prudent from time to time to know the status of containers. If you start a container and exit it when you are done by issuing the *exit* command, you are in good stead. However it might me possible that you might have started multiple instances of the AsciiDoctor docker image in different terminal windows by accident or by design (yes it is possible!). When this happens, you might exit one container image while others might still be running. If you find yourself in such a situation, the following commands can help you gracefully shut all running images and exit cleanly. The following sections present a limited set of Podman commands to hep you deal with such issues.

Podman 'images' Command

```
$ podman images
```

Will display all images that you have on your local storage.

```
csr@faros:~/Documents/asciidoc_book/chapters/ch2$ podman images
REPOSITORY                              TAG       IMAGE ID      CREATED      SIZE
docker.io/pandoc/core                   latest    9352bb996a1a  3 weeks ago  266 MB
docker.io/asciidoctor/docker-asciidoctor  latest  81b99a5a5f2e  4 weeks ago  1.4 GB
csr@faros:~/Documents/asciidoc_book/chapters/ch2$
```

As you can see, I have a pandoc docker image which is 266 MB in size and the docker AsciiDocker image which is 1.4 GB in Size. Notice that each image also has a alphanumeric image id that uniquely identifies that image.

Podman 'ps' Command

```
$ podman ps
```

Will display all running container images

```
csr@faros:~/Documents/asciidoc_book/chapters/ch2$ podman ps
CONTAINER ID  IMAGE                                          COMMAND     CREATED      STATUS      PORTS   NAMES
c13eef7ff5bf  docker.io/asciidoctor/docker-asciidoctor:latest  /bin/bash  6 hours ago  Up 6 hours          brave_faraday
f153b8b1d1e5  docker.io/asciidoctor/docker-asciidoctor:latest  /bin/bash  6 hours ago  Up 6 hours          elastic_rubin
46adf82dae50  docker.io/asciidoctor/docker-asciidoctor:latest  /bin/bash  4 hours ago  Up 4 hours          nifty_kirch
csr@faros:~/Documents/asciidoc_book/chapters/ch2$ podman stop brave_faraday
WARN[0010] StopSignal SIGTERM failed to stop container brave_faraday in 10 seconds, resorting to SIGKILL
brave_faraday
csr@faros:~/Documents/asciidoc_book/chapters/ch2$
```

The response of the `podman ps`command (1) shows all currently running images. The *STATUS* column in the command output shows the duration of uptime for a particular image. the *NAMES* column (2) shows names of each image. These names are randomly generated by Podman and are very useful when you want to stop a particular image as seen in the next command.

The above command with the following additional flag shows *all* containers both *running* or *exited*:

```
$podman ps -a
```

Podman 'stop' Command

```
$ podman stop <image name>
```

The above command will stop a given container image.

Referring to the image in the previous example at (3), we have issued the podman stop command to stop the asciidoctor image named *brave_faraday* as follows:

```
$ podman stop brave_faraday
```

Podman responds back and shuts down the brave_faraday image. If you were to repeat the `podman ps` command once again, you will not see *the brave faraday* in the list of running image.

If you wish to stop all running images with one command rather than stop a particular image by name, you can use the following command:

```
$ podman stop -a
```

This will stop all running images.If you were to issue the `podman ps` command once again, you will not see any running images and a response that is shown below:

```
csr@faros:~$ podman ps
CONTAINER ID  IMAGE       COMMAND     CREATED     STATUS      PORTS       NAMES
csr@faros:~$
```

No running images are now listed—you see only column titles but nothing under them. This command however does not stop any containers that have been paused.

I would like to reiterate once again that this appendix is not meant to be a tutorial on Podman or Docker. The reason for sharing the above commands is that since we are running the Docker-asciidoctor container, there is an outside chance that on some occasion, there might arise a need to stop them properly. In such situations, the above commands will help you know the status of running containers and stop them if required.

Appendix E: The VS Code Cheatsheet and Some Helpful Hacks

E.1. Some Useful VS Code Keyboard (and Mouse) Shortcuts

Shortcut	Purpose	Extension
`CTRL` + `Home`	Go to Start of Document	None
`CTRL` + `End`	Go to End of Document	None
`CTRL` + `S`	Save Document	None
`CTRL` + `Q`	Quit VS Code	None
`CTRL` + `G`	Go to a Line Number	None
`CTRL` + `F`	Find a Term	None
`CTRL` + `H`	Find & Replace a Term	None
`CTRL` + `Z`	Undo	None
`CTRL` + `Y`	Redo	None
`CTRL` + `←`	Collapse Explorer Folders	None
`CTRL` + `.`	Correct Spelling	Code Spell Checker
`CTRL` + `ALT` + `K`	Place Bookmark at Current Location	Bookmarks
`CTRL` + `ALT` + `J`	Jump to Next Bookmark	Bookmarks
`CTRL` + `ALT` + `-`	Go Back(Navigate Back)	Bookmarks
`CTRL` + `SHIFT` + `P`	Open Command Pallette	None
Text ⇒ Drag & Drop	Move Selected Text Within the Document	None
`CTRL` + Text ⇒ Drag & Drop	Duplicate Selected Text Within the Document — a green symbol is seen as you drag	None

⇒ *Use Mouse to Select*

`CTRL` ⇒ Press `CTRL` key and then *Use Mouse to Select*

E.2. Spell Checking the Entire Document

While the code spell checker extension does not offer a direct full document spell check option, it shows all misspelled words in a document on the VS Code *problems tab* in the editor window. You can scroll through the list one by one and correct them. This is in fact such a convenient option that it completely bypasses the need to especially run a full spell check on your AsciiDoc document.

To see the list of all wrongly spelt words in your document, open the problems tab by using the Keyboard short cut — `CTRL` + `SHIFT` + `M` or from the menu by choosing View ⇒ Problems or by clicking on the ⚠ icon on the status bar on the bottom left of the screen (toggle to open or close tab) as seen in Figure 176(a).

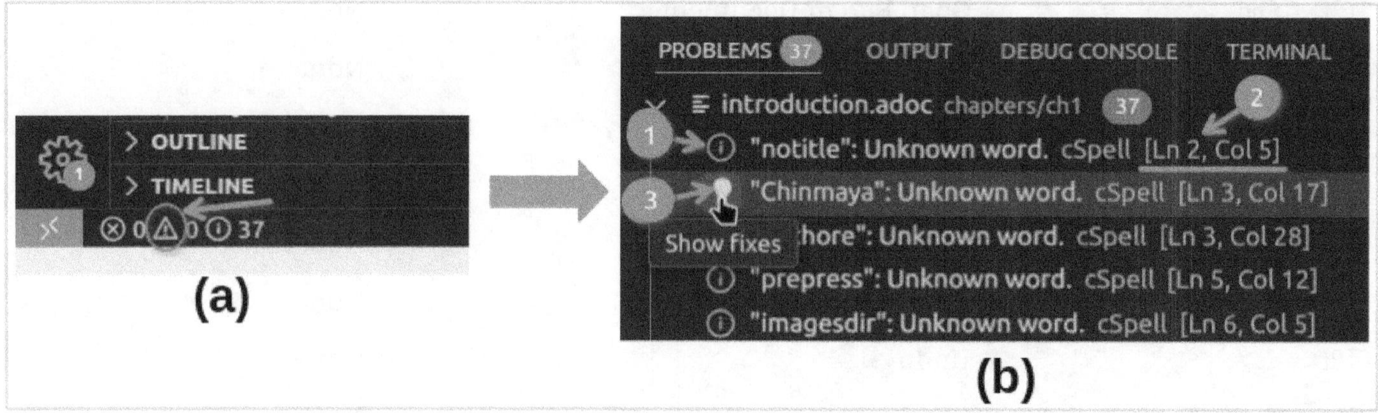

Figure 176. (a) The triangle-exclamation icon on the status bar opens the problems tab in the editor window (b) problems tab showing spelling errors (callout 1), location of the error (callout 2) and correction suggestions via light bulb (callout 3)

You will now see a list of *all misspelt words* — or what code spell checker thinks is misspelt — in front of a circled blue exclamation icon as seen in Figure 176(b) — callout 1. You can correct the spelling by clicking on the light bulb icon (callout 3) and choosing either a suggested spelling choice or directly typing the correct spelling in the running text if there is no satisfactory suggestion offered. You can click on any spelling error in the problems tab using your mouse to make the window active and then use the up and down arrow keys to move to the next or previous misspelt word which is also simultaneously shown highlighted in the running text. Please remember, *not all flagged words are spelling mistakes*. Code spell checker routinely flags technical terms, attribute names, people names, anchor ids or URLs etc. as spelling errors because these words are not part of code spell checker standard language dictionary. You just need to ignore such instances and move on to the next flagged words.

This is really a very cool feature and helps you do a deep spell check both during and after you have written your text. Some people prefer to keep the problems tab open as they type such that any spelling issues that might escape immediate attention in the flow of writing get listed in the box and can be corrected instantly.

E.3. Dealing with Heading Level Mismatch Errors

Apart from spelling errors, the problems page also tells you — using yellow triangle error signs — that there is a mismatch in your AsciiDoc heading levels. What this error essentially means is that at some location in the document, you have jumped a heading level — like after using == or level 1 heading, the next heading is ==== level 3 where it should have been === or level 2. This error usually triggers a series of cascading errors down the line with more yellow triangles popping up following the first one. The yellow triangle errors are shown in Figure 177.

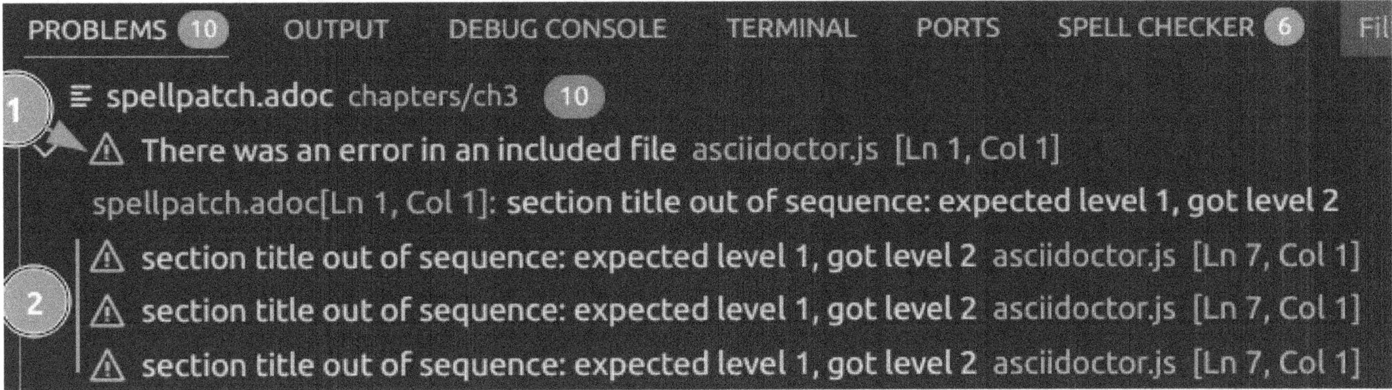

Figure 177. Heading level mismatch error

To resolve this problem, just click on the first error and make sure that the heading level is in sequential progression to the heading level before it i.e. if the previous heading level is ==, the heading level of the line in error should be === and not ====. This usually not only clears the first error, but in most cases, also subsequent errors (Figure 177, callout 2). If you still have yellow triangle errors left after correcting the first error for some reason, repeat the above heading level check on that line and bring it in incremental progression to the previous heading.

The problems page is a great tool that flags potential issues with you AsciiDoc files and another good reason to use VS Code as your primary AsciiDoc editor.

E.4. The Bookmark Extension Panel

The bookmark extension stores bookmarks until they are deleted and gives access to them even when a file is currently not open. If say, you stored a bookmark in file A and you are currently working on file B, you can open up the bookmark panel in your current document and it will show stored bookmarks in file A and all other files where bookmarks have been previously placed . If you click on any listed bookmark, that file will open at the bookmark location within the file. Figure 178 shows how you can see all stored bookmarks by clicking on the bookmark icon (callout 1) in the left panel of VS Code and see and access all stored bookmarks in all files (callouts 2,3).

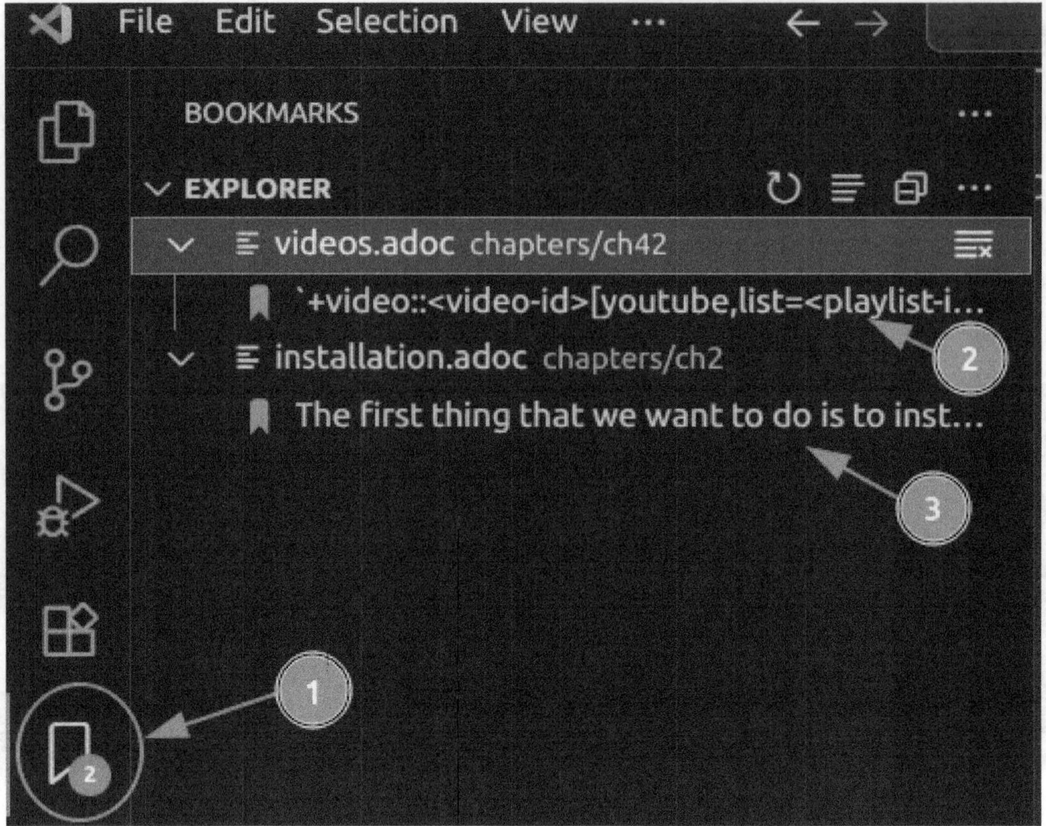

Figure 178. The bookmark extension panel showing all bookmarks

This is a great facility which permits you to quickly reach a bookmark not only in your current document but also in any other document even if that file is not currently open. In Figure 178, both displayed bookmarks are from files that are not in my currently open document and clicking on any of them will take me directly to that bookmark in *installation.adoc* (1) or *videos.adoc* (2). This is the fastest way to refer to something of interest in another document.

The number 2 displayed next to the bookmark extension icon (callout 1) shows the total number of stored bookmarks. You can delete any bookmark displayed in the bookmarks panel by right clicking on that bookmark and choosing *delete*.

If you are working on a multi-user Linux system and have installed VS Code extensions as a superuser, please be aware that while non-admin or standard users can access VS Code, they might not have access to extensions installed by the superuser. It might be easiest if standard users are advised to quickly install AsciiDoctor, Code Spell Checker and Bookmark extensions after they start VS Code from their account.

Appendix F: AsciiDoctor Online Resources

There are many good and detailed resources that are available to add more to your AsciiDoc knowledge and vocabulary. Readers are encouraged to consult these online resources to learn more about AsciiDoc Syntax and AsciiDoctor features.

F.1. AsciiDoc Language Home

🧭 Official AsciiDoc Language Home https://asciidoc.org/

The AsciiDoc Language home page --hosts information about the latest developments in the AsciiDoc Language specification. It has an online AsciiDoc Editor where people can try using AsciiDoc Markup and see the results instantly.

F.2. AsciiDoctor Writers Guide

🧭 AsciiDoc Writers Guide https://asciidoctor.org/docs/asciidoc-writers-guide/

A useful and comprehensive resource and a gentle introduction to AsciiDoc.

F.3. Important AsciiDoctor Documentation Pages

🧭 Official Asciidoctor Documentation https://docs.asciidoctor.org/

The official Asciidoctor documentation provides an exhaustive guide to the syntax and features of AsciiDoctor. This is the documentation landing page which leads you to other AsciiDoc and AsciiDoctor resources. Some direct links from this documentation landing page have been provided below for convenience.

🧭 AsciiDoc Language Documentation https://docs.asciidoctor.org/asciidoc/latest/

Complete documentation of the latest syntax for the AsciiDoc Language. This extends learnings in chapter [chap4-adsyntax] of this book.

🧭 AsciiDoc Syntax Quick Reference https://docs.asciidoctor.org/asciidoc/latest/syntax-quick-reference/

A great resource that recaps most commonly used AsciiDoc markup tags featuring many examples. A great learning resource.

🧭 AsciiDoctor-PDF Documentation https://docs.asciidoctor.org/pdf-converter/latest/

This page is a complete resource on the use of the *latest* AsciiDoc native PDF convertor — *AsciiDoctor-*

PDF. The *whats new* summarizes new features in the latest version of *AsciiDoctor-PDF*.

🧭 AsciiDoctor-PDF Theming Guide https://docs.asciidoctor.org/pdf-converter/latest/theme/

This is a complete resource on AsciiDoc PDF theme extension and the categories and keys that can be used to extend the default theme. An invaluable resource for those who wish to customize PDF output.This extends learnings in chapter Chapter 15 and Chapter 20 of this book.

🧭 AsciiDoctor-EPUB3 https://docs.asciidoctor.org/epub3-converter/latest/

The complete resource for the AsciiDoctor-EPUB3 convertor. This extends learnings in chapter [chap-epub3] of this book.

F.4. Cheat Sheets

https://powerman.name/doc/asciidoc

This is a great resource to bookmark in your browser and refer to whenever you get stuck trying to recall AsciiDoc commonly used markup syntax. Although this cheatsheet is for AsciiDoctor version 2.2.2, it holds good and has some great markup examples and how they appear after rendering in the HTML output.

🧭 AsciiDoc PDF Quick Reference by Dan Allen and Sarah White

https://asciidoctor.org/docs/asciidoc-syntax-quick-reference.pdf

This is a great and valuable resource by Dan Allen and Sarah White — AsciiDoctor Project Leads. Don't let the 2014 version date fool you. Everything included here just works ! You can download it as a PDF file.

F.5. Forums

🧭 AsciiDoctor Main User Group Chat Forum https://asciidoctor.zulipchat.com/

A very helpful and welcoming community where users can ask questions seeking solutions. Dan Allen — AsciiDoctor's project lead — has been personally answering questions on this and on the earlier forum chat [https://discuss.asciidoctor.org/] for over a decade ! You can get many solutions to your questions just browsing through the earlier forum posts.

🧭 A Dedicated AsciiDoctor Tag on Stack Overflow https://stackoverflow.com/questions/tagged/asciidoctor

Users can ask questions related to AsciiDoctor facilitating knowledge exchange and peer support.

F.6. On GitHub

AsciiDoctor GitHub Page https://github.com/asciidoctor

This is the landing page for AsciiDoctor on GitHub from where you can checkout all AsciiDoctor projects including AsciiDoctor, AsciiDoctor-PDF and AsciiDoctor-EPUB3 among others.

These links were operational and accessible in June 2025 at the time of writing this book.

Sample AsciiDoctor-PDF Themes on GitHub

https://gist.github.com/misuo/5b2af22ca78d5d87c522a817a7a8569d

Some very interesting AsciiDoctor-PDF sample themes that are readily usable and a great learning resource for readers who wish to dive deeper into AsciiDoctor-PDF theme customizations. Click on any theme to view and download the *YML* file.

Glossary of Key Terms

AsciiDoc

A lightweight markup language used for writing documentation, articles, and books in plain text format. It allows for easy conversion to various output formats such as HTML, PDF, and EPUB.

AsciiDoctor

An open-source toolchain for processing AsciiDoc content. It converts AsciiDoc files into various formats, including HTML5, PDF, and EPUB, and is widely used for documentation and publishing.

AsciiDoctor Toolchain

A collection of tools and libraries that facilitate the processing of AsciiDoc files. This includes the AsciiDoctor processor itself, along with extensions and plugins that enhance its functionality.

Atom Processor

An Atom processor is a type of low-power, low-voltage microprocessor designed by Intel for use in small, portable devices such as netbooks, smartphones, and tablets. Atom processors are known for their energy efficiency and are often used in devices where battery life is a priority.

BibTeX

A bibliographic reference management format used in academic writing to organize and cite sources, enabling automatic bibliography generation in LaTeX documents.

Cascading Style Sheet (CSS)

A stylesheet language used for describing the presentation of a document written in HTML or XML. CSS controls the layout, colors, fonts, and overall visual appearance of web pages, allowing for separation of content and design.

CodeRay

A syntax highlighting library for Ruby that is known for its speed and flexibility. CodeRay supports many programming languages and can be used to highlight code in web applications, documentation, and other contexts where code readability is important.

Comma-Separated Values (CSV)

A simple, plain-text file format used for storing tabular data, where each line represents a row and values within a row are separated by commas. CSV files are widely used for data exchange between different applications, spreadsheets, and databases. Each row typically contains the same number of fields, with the first row often serving as a header that describes the column names. CSV files can be easily opened and edited in spreadsheet software like Microsoft Excel, Google Sheets, or text editors, making them a universal and lightweight method for data storage and transfer.

DocBook

A semantic markup language for technical documentation, primarily used for writing books, articles, and other complex documents. DocBook is based on XML and provides a standardized way to represent structured content, making it easier to convert to various output formats such as HTML, PDF, and more.

Docker

A platform that enables developers to automate the deployment of applications inside lightweight, portable containers. Docker containers encapsulate an application and its dependencies, ensuring consistent environments across different systems.

Docker Image

Docker Image: A read-only template that contains a set of instructions for creating a Docker container. It includes the base operating system, application code, libraries, dependencies, and configuration. Images serve as blueprints for containers and can be stored in registries, versioned, and shared across different environments.

Docker Container

A runnable instance of a Docker image - a lightweight, isolated environment that can execute applications. Containers are executable packages that include everything needed to run an application, providing consistency across different computing environments. They can be started, stopped, moved, and deleted, and multiple containers can be created from a single image.

EPUB3

An electronic publication format that is widely used for eBooks. EPUB3 supports rich media, interactivity, and accessibility features, making it suitable for a variety of digital content, including text, images, audio, and video.

HTML Chunking

A technique used in web development and content management where large HTML documents are divided into smaller, manageable pieces or "chunks." This approach can improve loading times, enhance user experience, and facilitate easier updates and maintenance of web content.

LaTeX

A typesetting system commonly used for producing scientific and mathematical documents due to its powerful handling of formulas and bibliographies. LaTeX allows authors to focus on content while it manages the formatting.

LaTeX Math

A feature of LaTeX that allows users to typeset complex mathematical expressions and symbols with precision. LaTeX Math uses a specific syntax to represent mathematical notation, enabling the creation of equations, matrices, and other mathematical structures in a visually appealing format. It is widely used in scientific documents to present mathematical content clearly and professionally.

Markup Language

A markup language is a type of programming language used to add formatting and structure to plain text documents. Markup languages use a set of predefined tags or codes to indicate the formatting and layout of the text. Examples of markup languages include HTML (Hypertext Markup Language), XML (Extensible Markup Language), and Markdown.

MX-Linux Libretto

A lightweight version of the MX Linux operating system, designed to provide a fast and efficient computing experience on older or less powerful hardware. MX-Linux Libretto features a user-friendly interface and includes essential applications while maintaining a low resource footprint, making it suitable for users who require a functional yet minimalistic environment.Available in 32 bit and 64 bit versions.

Pandoc

A universal document converter that allows users to convert files between various markup formats, including Markdown, LaTeX, HTML, and more. Pandoc is widely used for its flexibility in handling different document types and its ability to produce high-quality output.

Podman

An open-source container management tool that allows users to create, manage, and run containers without requiring a daemon. Podman is compatible with Docker commands and is often used as a daemonless alternative to Docker.

Pygments

A popular syntax highlighting library written in Python. Pygments supports a wide range of programming languages and markup formats, allowing users to generate highlighted code snippets for use in web pages, documentation, and other applications.

Responsive Screen

A responsive screen is a type of display that can adapt its layout and content to fit different screen sizes and devices. Responsive screens use a combination of flexible grids, images, and media queries to adjust the layout and content of a website or application to fit different screen sizes, orientations, and devices.

Rouge

A pure Ruby syntax highlighter that is designed to be fast and easy to use. Rouge supports a variety of programming languages and is often used in conjunction with static site generators and documentation tools to provide syntax highlighting for code blocks.

Ruby

A dynamic, open-source programming language known for its simplicity and productivity. Ruby is often used for web development, particularly with the Ruby on Rails framework.

Ruby Gem

A package manager for Ruby that allows developers to easily share and distribute Ruby libraries and applications. Gems can be installed, updated, and managed using the command-line tool `gem`.

Syntax

Syntax refers to the rules and structure of a programming language or markup language. It defines how the language is written, including the use of keywords, symbols, and formatting. Syntax is used to convey meaning and structure in a language, and is essential for writing code that is correct and functional.

Syntax Highlighter

A feature in text editors and integrated development environments (IDEs) that displays code with different colors and fonts based on the category of terms. This enhances readability and helps programmers quickly identify different elements such as keywords, variables, and strings, making code easier to understand and debug.

Visual Studio Code

A free, open-source code editor developed by Microsoft. It supports various programming languages and features extensions, debugging capabilities, and integrated Git control, making it a popular choice among developers.

VS Codium

An open-source version of Visual Studio Code that is built from the same source code but does not include Microsoft's proprietary branding and telemetry. It aims to provide a fully open-source alternative for users who prefer not to use the official version.

Word Processor

A word processor is a type of software application used to create, edit, and print documents. Word processors provide a range of features and tools for formatting and editing text, including font styles, paragraph formatting, and spell checking. Examples of word processors include Microsoft Word, Google Docs, and LibreOffice.

Windows Subsystem for Linux (WSL)

A compatibility layer developed by Microsoft that allows running Linux binary executables natively on Windows 10 and Windows 11. WSL provides a lightweight virtual environment that enables users to run a Linux distribution directly on Windows without the need for a traditional virtual machine or dual-boot setup. It integrates Linux command-line tools, utilities, and applications seamlessly with the Windows operating system, offering developers and users a unified development and computing experience.

XML (eXtensible Markup Language)

A markup language that defines a set of rules for encoding documents in a format that is both human-readable and machine-readable. XML is used to store and transport data, and it allows users to create custom tags to structure information.

Zotero

A free, open-source reference management software that helps users collect, organize, cite, and share research materials. Zotero can automatically sense content in web browsers and allows users to create bibliographies in various citation styles.

ZoteroBib

ZoteroBib is a free, web-based tool for quickly creating bibliographies and in-text citations, developed by the team behind the popular reference management software, Zotero. It allows users to generate references from various sources (like URLs, ISBNs, DOIs, etc.) and format them in over 10,000 different citation styles. It permits export in BibTeX, RIS and other formats.

Index

W

X

Y

Z

www.ingramcontent.com/pod-product-compliance
Lightning Source LLC
Chambersburg PA
CBHW080242170726
48282CB00031B/1166

* 9 7 8 9 3 6 9 2 6 2 4 0 3 *